THE ULTIMATE DAILY SHOW AND PHILOSOPHY

The Blackwell Philosophy and PopCulture Series
Series Editor: William Irwin

A spoonful of sugar helps the medicine go down, and a healthy helping of popular culture clears the cobwebs from Kant. Philosophy has had a public relations problem for a few centuries now. This series aims to change that, showing that philosophy is relevant to your life—and not just for answering the big questions like "To be or not to be?" but for answering the little questions: "To watch or not to watch *South Park?*" Thinking deeply about TV, movies, and music doesn't make you a "complete idiot." In fact it might make you a philosopher, someone who believes the unexamined life is not worth living and the unexamined cartoon is not worth watching.

Already published in the series:

24 and Philosophy: The World According to Jack
Edited by Jennifer Hart Weed, Richard Brian Davis, and Ronald Weed

30 Rock and Philosophy: We Want to Go to There
Edited by J. Jeremy Wisnewski

Alice in Wonderland and Philosophy: Curiouser and Curiouser
Edited by Richard Brian Davis

Arrested Development and Philosophy: They've Made a Huge Mistake
Edited by Kristopher Phillips and J. Jeremy Wisnewski

The Avengers and Philosophy: Earth's Mightiest Thinkers
Edited by Mark D. White

Batman and Philosophy: The Dark Knight of the Soul
Edited by Mark D. White and Robert Arp

Battlestar Galactica and Philosophy: Knowledge Here Begins Out There
Edited by Jason T. Eberl

The Big Bang Theory and Philosophy: Rock, Paper, Scissors, Aristotle, Locke
Edited by Dean Kowalski

The Big Lebowski and Philosophy: Keeping Your Mind Limber with Abiding Wisdom
Edited by Peter S. Fosl

Black Sabbath and Philosophy: Mastering Reality
Edited by William Irwin

The Daily Show and Philosophy: Moments of Zen in the Art of Fake News
Edited by Jason Holt

Downton Abbey and Philosophy: The Truth Is Neither Here Nor There
Edited by Mark D. White

Ender's Game and Philosophy
Edited by Kevin S. Decker

Family Guy and Philosophy: A Cure for the Petarded
Edited by J. Jeremy Wisnewski

Final Fantasy and Philosophy: The Ultimate Walkthrough
Edited by Jason P. Blahuta and Michel S. Beaulieu

Game of Thrones and Philosophy: Logic Cuts Deeper Than Swords
Edited by Henry Jacoby

The Girl With the Dragon Tattoo and Philosophy: Everything is Fire
Edited by Eric Bronson

Green Lantern and Philosophy: No Evil Shall Escape this Book
Edited by Jane Dryden and Mark D. White

Heroes and Philosophy: Buy the Book, Save the World
Edited by David Kyle Johnson

The Hobbit and Philosophy: For When You've Lost Your Dwarves, Your Wizard, and Your Way
Edited by Gregory Bassham and Eric Bronson

House and Philosophy: Everybody Lies
Edited by Henry Jacoby

The Hunger Games and Philosophy: A Critique of Pure Treason
Edited by George Dunn and Nicolas Michaud

Inception and Philosophy: Because It's Never Just a Dream
Edited by David Johnson

Iron Man and Philosophy: Facing the Stark Reality
Edited by Mark D. White

Lost and Philosophy: The Island Has Its Reasons
Edited by Sharon M. Kaye

Mad Men and Philosophy: Nothing Is as It Seems
Edited by James South and Rod Carveth

Metallica and Philosophy: A Crash Course in Brain Surgery
Edited by William Irwin

The Office and Philosophy: Scenes from the Unfinished Life
Edited by J. Jeremy Wisnewski

South Park and Philosophy: You Know, I Learned Something Today
Edited by Robert Arp

Spider-Man and Philosophy: The Web of Inquiry
Edited by Jonathan Sanford

Superman and Philosophy: What Would the Man of Steel Do?
Edited by Mark D. White

Terminator and Philosophy: I'll Be Back, Therefore I Am
Edited by Richard Brown and Kevin S. Decker

True Blood and Philosophy: We Wanna Think Bad Things with You
Edited by George Dunn and Rebecca Housel

Twilight and Philosophy: Vampires, Vegetarians, and the Pursuit of Immortality
Edited by Rebecca Housel and J. Jeremy Wisnewski

The Ultimate Daily Show and Philosophy: More Moments of Zen, More Indecision Theory
Edited by Jason Holt

The Ultimate Harry Potter and Philosophy: Hogwarts for Muggles
Edited by Gregory Bassham

The Ultimate Lost and Philosophy: Think Together, Die Alone
Edited by Sharon Kaye

The Ultimate South Park and Philosophy: Respect My Philosophah!
Edited by Robert Arp and Kevin S. Decker

The Walking Dead and Philosophy: Shotgun. Machete. Reason.
Edited by Christopher Robichaud

Watchmen and Philosophy: A Rorschach Test
Edited by Mark D. White

X-Men and Philosophy: Astonishing Insight and Uncanny Argument in the Mutant X-Verse
Edited by Rebecca Housel and J. Jeremy Wisnewski

Forthcoming:

Sons of Anarchy and Philosophy
Edited by George Dunn and Jason Eberl

Supernatural and Philosophy
Edited by Galen A. Foresman

THE ULTIMATE DAILY SHOW AND PHILOSOPHY

MORE MOMENTS OF ZEN, MORE INDECISION THEORY

Edited by Jason Holt

WILEY Blackwell

This edition first published 2013
© 2013 John Wiley & Sons, Inc

Wiley-Blackwell is an imprint of John Wiley & Sons, formed by the merger of Wiley's
global Scientific, Technical and Medical business with Blackwell Publishing.

Registered Office
John Wiley & Sons, Ltd, The Atrium, Southern Gate, Chichester, West Sussex, PO19 8SQ, UK

Editorial Offices
350 Main Street, Malden, MA 02148-5020, USA
9600 Garsington Road, Oxford, OX4 2DQ, UK
The Atrium, Southern Gate, Chichester, West Sussex, PO19 8SQ, UK

For details of our global editorial offices, for customer services, and for information about
how to apply for permission to reuse the copyright material in this book please see our
website at www.wiley.com/wiley-blackwell.

The right of Jason Holt to be identified as the author of the editorial material in this work
has been asserted in accordance with the UK Copyright, Designs and Patents Act 1988.

Library of Congress Cataloging-in-Publication Data

The Ultimate Daily Show and Philosophy : More Moments of Zen, More Indecision
Theory / edited by Jason Holt.
    pages cm. – (The Blackwell Philosophy and PopCulture Series)
    Includes bibliographical references and index.
    ISBN 978-1-118-39768-8 (pbk. : alk. paper)
1. Daily show (Television program)   I. Holt, Jason, 1971– editor of compilation.
    PN1992.77.D28D35 2014
    791.45′72–dc23

                                                        2013006643

A catalogue record for this book is available from the British Library.

Cover image: Jon Stewart © Kristin Callahan/Rex Features; Socrates © thegreekphotoholic/
iStockphoto; Jean-Paul-Sartre © Bettmann/CORBIS
Cover design by www.simonlevy.co.uk

Set in 10.5/13pt Sabon by SPi Publisher Services, Pondicherry, India
Printed in Singapore by Ho Printing Singapore Pte Ltd

1   2013

To Megan

Contents

Acknowledgments   xi

Introduction: From Wiley-Blackwell's World Philosophy
Headquarters in Malden   1

Segment 1   Headlines: Faux News Is Good News   5

1   Rallying Against the Conflictinator: Jon Stewart,
Neil Postman, and Entertainment Bias   7
Gerald J. Erion

2   The Fake, the False, and the Fictional: *The Daily Show*
as News Source   23
Michael Gettings

3   *The Daily Show*: An Ethos for the Fifth Estate   38
Rachael Sotos

4   Seriously Funny: Mockery as a Political Weapon   56
Greg Littmann

5   Keeping It (Hyper) Real: Anchoring in the
Age of Fake News   69
Kellie Bean

**Segment 2   Live Report: Jon Stewart (Not Mill) as
Philosopher, Sort of   83**

6   Jon Stewart: The New *and Improved* Public Intellectual   85
Terrance MacMullan

7   Stewart and Socrates: Speaking Truth to Power   102
    Judith Barad

8   Jon the Cynic: Dog Philosophy 101   114
    Alejandro Bárcenas

9   "Jews! Camera 3": How Jon Stewart Echoes
    Martin Buber   125
    Joseph A. Edelheit

**Segment 3   Field Report: Politics and
                Critical Thinking**   **137**

10 More Bullshit: Political Spin and
    the PR-ization of Media   139
    Kimberly Blessing and Joseph Marren

11 The Senior Black Correspondent: Saying What Needs
    to Be Said   155
    John Scott Gray

12 *The Daily Show*'s Exposé of Political Rhetoric   167
    Liam P. Dempsey

13 The *Daily Show* Way: Critical Thinking, Civic Discourse,
    and Postmodern Consciousness   181
    Roben Torosyan

Segment 4   Interview: Religion and Culture   **197**

14 GOP Almighty: When God Tells Me (and My Opponents)
    to Run for President   199
    Roberto Sirvent and Neil Baker

15 Profaning the Sacred: The Challenge of Religious
    Diversity in "This Week in God"   211
    Matthew S. LoPresti

16 Jon Stewart and the Fictional War on Christmas   231
    David Kyle Johnson

17 Evolution, Schmevolution: Jon Stewart and
    the Culture Wars   247
    Massimo Pigliucci

Segment 5   Your Moment of Zen: Beyond
                 The Daily Show   **265**

18   *America (The Book)*: Textbook Parody and
     Democratic Theory   267
     Steve Vanderheiden

19   A Tea Party for *Me the People*: The Living
     Revolution Meets the Originalists   281
     Rachael Sotos

20   Neologization à la Stewart and Colbert   298
     Jason Holt

21   Irrationality and "Gut" Reasoning:
     Two Kinds of Truthiness   309
     Amber L. Griffioen

22   Thank God It's Stephen Colbert! The Rally to
     Restore Irony on *The Colbert Report*   326
     Kevin S. Decker

Senior Philosophical Correspondents   341

Index   348

Acknowledgments

Thanks to everyone at Wiley-Blackwell, especially Series Editor Bill Irwin, for making this book possible. Thanks also to the contributors, whose patient hard work made it actual. Thanks to *The Daily Show* (and *The Colbert Report*) for continuing to give so much to write about, and to those of you fan enough to buy this book.

Introduction

From Wiley-Blackwell's World Philosophy Headquarters in Malden

Welcome to *The Ultimate Daily Show and Philosophy*. I'm your editor, Jason Holt, and let me just say first off, thanks for not being deterred by the title. How brash to dub this the "ultimate" with the show still in production, popular as ever. Ultimate indeed! Other modifiers—"more," "2.0," "TNG," and such were considered, but here we are at "ultimate." If you thought the first edition was amazing, or pretty good, or just adequate, brace yourself. This one's, well, better.

I think we're okay with the subtitle: *More Moments of Zen, More Indecision Theory*. Everyone who's seen *The Daily Show* knows its practice of ending each show with a clip, the so-called moment of Zen. What could be more philosophical than a moment of Zen? When putting together the original volume in 2006, I supposed one of the contributors would explain moments of Zen, perhaps even devoting a chapter to the subject. Didn't happen. But, when the call came to put together this "ultimate" edition you now hold in your hand, or "on" your digital thingamabob, or listen to as an audiobook, it didn't happen either. So, I guess I'll have to say *something* about it here. It's a matter of conscience. So what are moments of Zen? Short video clips, usually of politicians or other public figures, which encapsulate an implicit yet evident point: be it the hypocrisy of the speaker, an obvious truth that's gone unsaid, criticism that's been marginalized, and so on. What do such often-poignant clips have to do with Zen? Well, not

The Ultimate Daily Show and Philosophy: More Moments of Zen, More Indecision Theory, First Edition. Edited by Jason Holt.

much, really. At most there might be a kind of loose acknowledgment by *The Daily Show* of the importance of simplicity, and of not trying to explicitly utter what perhaps can only, or best, be gestured at. Seems a bit "Zennish," even if it's not Zen.

As for "indecision theory," fans of *The Daily Show* are familiar with their longstanding election coverage tag: "Indecision 20__" (there having been Indecisions 2000, 2004, 2008, and 2012, plus midterm Indecisions 2002, 2006, and 2010—although "Democalypse 2012" seems to have proved a more popular label, at least up until Stewart and Colbert's joint election-night coverage). There's a branch of philosophy that studies how principles of rationality apply to decision-making: decision theory. As this book is—yes—philosophy, it only makes sense to combine the two, especially as one of *The Daily Show*'s ongoing concerns is how to critically evaluate information sources in making rational political choices.

It has been gratifying that in the years since the original edition was published there has been a palpable increase in scholarly interest in *The Daily Show* and its increasingly significant role in contemporary culture—whether this is seen through the lens of the alleged "*Daily Show* effect" or, more optimistically, that of acknowledging what is truly special—even profound—about the particular humor of the show. You know that *The Daily Show* is funny, really funny, and that the performers and writers are pretty sharp. You also know that it's much more than run-of-the-mill late night entertainment. In its over fifteen-year run *The Daily Show* has remained topical, and has achieved an undeniable cultural significance, as fit for ranting blogs as for academic treatises.

Why philosophy? Not only does *The Daily Show* tackle issues that interest philosophers and that matter in many people's daily lives, it does so in instructive ways that deserve and are well-served by philosophical treatment. Contemporary philosophers have even appeared as guests on the show. Each chapter in this book shows why and how *The Daily Show* is philosophically engaging and significant. If you're hoping that *The Colbert Report* also gets a going-over, you won't be disappointed.

Like the show itself, this book is divided into five "segments." We start by focusing on fake news: what's distinctive about it, what it does, how it works ("headlines"). Then we segue into discussions of Jon Stewart as a (kind of) philosopher figure, reflecting deep concerns some of which have existed for—literally—millennia ("live report"). Next comes politics and critical thinking ("field report"), followed by religion and culture ("interview"), and finally topics like *The Colbert Report* that are "*Daily Show* adjacent" ("moment of Zen").

On behalf of all the Senior Philosophical Correspondents here—and it's a cliché, I know, but it's also true—we hope you enjoy reading the book as much as we did writing it.

Segment 1

HEADLINES
FAUX NEWS IS GOOD NEWS

Chapter 1

Rallying Against the Conflictinator

Jon Stewart, Neil Postman, and Entertainment Bias

Gerald J. Erion

While *The Daily Show with Jon Stewart* is certainly entertaining, it can also deliver a deeper analysis of our contemporary media environment. Indeed, hidden within many of host Jon Stewart's funniest jokes are implicit critiques of the way television tends to conduct its public discussions of important issues. For instance, Stewart's opening rundown of the news as covered by the 24-hour cable networks doesn't merely ridicule the day's major players and events; often, it goes even further, making fun of television's most basic reporting and presentation techniques. In this way, over-the-top visual and audio elements, attractive but superficial "Senior Correspondents," and all the other trappings of TV newscasts become fodder for *The Daily Show*'s writing staff. Not simply a "fake news" program, then, *The Daily Show* offers a rare brand of humor that requires its audience to recognize a more serious and philosophical criticism of contemporary television journalism.

From time to time, Stewart takes these implicit criticisms of contemporary media and makes them explicit. Such was the case during his October 2004 appearance on CNN's *Crossfire*, during which he begged his hosts to "stop hurting America" with their substitution

The Ultimate Daily Show and Philosophy: More Moments of Zen, More Indecision Theory, First Edition. Edited by Jason Holt.
© 2013 John Wiley & Sons, Inc. Published 2013 by John Wiley & Sons, Inc.

of entertaining pseudo-journalism for serious reporting and debate. Through this bold, format-breaking effort, Stewart highlighted the difference between thoughtful discussion and the theater of today's vapid television punditry. Subsequent exchanges with CNBC's Jim Cramer and Fox's Chris Wallace allowed Stewart to further advance his argument. And as we will see, Stewart's analysis echoes that of the celebrated New York University media theorist Neil Postman, whose discerning insights seem to ground some of *The Daily Show*'s sharpest comic bits.

Amusing Ourselves to Death

Postman's *Amusing Ourselves to Death* is a book that aims to show how the media we use to communicate with one another can influence the content of our conversations. Postman acknowledges a significant intellectual debt to Marshall McLuhan, and sees his own thesis as something of a revised version of McLuhan's famous pronouncement that "the medium is the message."[1] However, Postman extends McLuhan's ideas in ways that are both distinctive and significant.

For example, consider Postman's discussion of smoke signals. While the medium of smoke might be an effective way to communicate relatively simple messages over intermediate distances, many other types of messages can't be carried this way. Philosophical arguments, for instance, would be especially difficult to conduct with smoke signals because, as Postman puts it,

> Puffs of smoke are insufficiently complex to express ideas on the nature of existence [or other philosophical concepts], and even if they were not, a Cherokee philosopher would run short of either wood or blankets long before he reached his second axiom. You cannot use smoke to do philosophy. Its form excludes the content.[2]

So, the medium of smoke has a significant influence on the kinds of content it can convey. At a minimum, smoke signaling restricts both the complexity and the duration of the messages it carries. Likewise, we shall see that television influences its content, and that *The Daily Show*'s jokes often poke fun at these effects.

The Huxleyan Warning

Now, as Postman sees it, *all* media shape their content, and in a multitude of different ways. He writes: "[Mine] is an argument that fixes its attention on the forms of human conversation, and postulates that how we are obliged to conduct such conversations will have the strongest possible influence on what ideas we can conveniently express."[3] This goes not only for smoke signals, but also for speech and written language, and even for the electronic media that are so important in our lives today.

Of particular interest is the ubiquitous medium of television, which Postman sees as a historic extension of such earlier media as the telegraph, photography, radio, and film.[4] How does television influence its content, according to Postman? His theory is complex, but in essence it maintains that television's inherent "bias" implies a tendency to render its content—even its most important news reporting, political and religious discussion, and educational instruction—more *entertaining* than it would be otherwise, and consequently less serious, less rational, less relevant, and less coherent as well.[5]

The fact that television provides entertainment isn't, in and of itself, a problem for Postman. However, he warns that dire consequences can result for cultures in which the most important public discourse, conducted via television, becomes little more than irrational, irrelevant, and incoherent entertainment. Again, we shall see that this is a point often suggested by *The Daily Show*'s biting satire. In a healthy democracy, the open discussion of important issues should be serious, rational, and coherent. But such discussion is often difficult and time-consuming, and thus incompatible with television's drive to entertain. So, it's hardly surprising to see television serving up important news analyses in short sound bites surrounded by irrelevant graphics and video footage, or substituting half-minute ad spots for substantial political debates. On television, thoughtful conversations about serious issues are reserved for only the lowest-rated niche programs. Just as ventriloquism and mime don't play well on radio, "thinking does not play well on television."[6] Instead, television serves as a hospitable home for the sort of "gut"-based discourse satirically championed by *Daily Show* alum Stephen Colbert.[7]

When we grow comfortable with the substitution of televised entertainment for serious public discourse, we begin the process of (to use Postman's words) "amusing ourselves to death." As Postman explains, this form of cultural corrosion is like that described in Aldous Huxley's classic novel *Brave New World*, in which the citizenry is comfortably and willingly distracted by the pleasures of *soma*, Centrifugal Bumble-puppy, and the feelies.[8]

Postman and Television News

To exemplify these points, Postman details some of the many ways in which television tends to degrade the presentation of its news content. Consider his explanation of the ironic title of his chapter on television news, "Now ... This": "There is no murder so brutal, no earthquake so devastating, no political blunder so costly—for that matter, no ball score so tantalizing or weather report so threatening—that it cannot be erased from our minds by a newscaster saying 'Now ... this'."[9] As Postman sees it, then, the use of "Now ... this" is a tacit admission of the incoherence of television news, and "a compact metaphor for the discontinuities in so much that passes for public discourse in present-day America."[10]

Of course, Postman believes that television does more to the news than disrupt its coherence. Revisiting his general thesis about how television influences its content, Postman also claims that televised news is irrational, irrelevant, and trivial. As he explains, television presents us "not only with fragmented news but news without context, without consequences, without value, and therefore without essential seriousness; that is to say, news as pure entertainment."[11] So, even weighty news subjects are driven to become entertaining under the influence of television, as the typical American newscast showcases a company of attractive reporters skipping from spectacular (if insignificant) local stories to spectacular (if insignificant) international stories, to celebrity gossip, to weather forecasts, to sports scores, to a closing story about babies or puppies or kittens. Commercials are scattered throughout. Music, graphics, and captivating video footage add touches of theater to the program. Quick transitions from one segment to the next ensure that audience members don't become bored—or troubled—for long.[12] Instead of useful and important information, then, viewers are treated to the impotent but entertaining trivia that Postman calls "disinformation," which isn't necessarily false but *misleading*, creating the *illusion of knowing* and undermining one's motivation to learn more.[13] Consequently, Postman writes, "Americans are the best entertained and quite likely the least well-informed people in the Western world."[14]

The Daily Show and Television News

Now, as far as we can tell, the writing staff of *The Daily Show* doesn't publicly acknowledge Postman's intellectual influence.[15] Nonetheless, it's clear that these general ideas about television news, whatever their sources, can help us to see the significance of some of the program's wittiest and most inspired jokes. *The Daily Show* is often described as a "fake news" program, but in fact, it's more than that. Much of its humor rests on Postman-like insights that highlight the peculiar ways in which the medium of television inevitably influences the news that it conveys.

For example, many episodes of *The Daily Show* begin with Stewart's selected rundown of the day's headlines as reported by the major television news networks. A comedy show that only does "fake news" could simply build jokes around the content of such headlines, or perhaps report fictional news stories in a humorous manner. On *The Daily Show*, though, the way in which television seems destined to render its news as entertainment frequently serves as the basis for these opening segments. Stewart and company often joke about the major networks' coverage of natural disasters, for instance. In many of these cases they simply replay absurd clips of television reporters standing outside during hurricanes and snowstorms, sitting in cars with giant thermometers during heat waves, or paddling canoes through inch-deep "flooded" city streets. Other pieces mock the way hordes of television reporters cover celebrity weddings, arrests, and criminal trials. Segments like "The Less You Know" and "International Pamphlet" poke fun at the shallowness of typical television news coverage. Exchanges between Stewart and his Senior Correspondents—"The Best F#@king News Team Ever"— parody their good-looking but sometimes ill-informed journalistic counterparts.[16] Clever graphics packages ("Indecision 2012," "Clusterf#@k to the Poor House," "Baracknophobia," "Mess O' Potamia," "Crises in Israfghyianonanaq," and so on) offer mocking imitations of the logos, diagrams, and pictorial illustrations so essential to today's television newscasts. With these segments and graphics, *The Daily Show* is clearly doing more than just "fake news." It is offering deep satire that relies on its audience's appreciation of the substance of Postman's thesis, that television has a significant and sometimes adverse influence on the news content it reports.

At this point, one might be tempted to suggest that *The Daily Show* simply furthers the unfortunate transformation of reporting into entertainment, as if *The Daily Show* were itself a source of news to its audience members. For instance, Bill O'Reilly (host of the Fox News program *The O'Reilly Factor*) once famously dubbed viewers of *The Daily Show* "stoned slackers" who "get their news from Jon Stewart."[17] However, at least one prominent study from the Annenberg Public Policy Center found that viewers of *The Daily Show* were better informed about the positions and backgrounds of candidates in the 2004 US Presidential Campaign than most others. More recent surveys by the Pew Research Center and Farleigh Dickinson University's PublicMind project have also found relatively high levels of current affairs knowledge in *The Daily Show*'s audience.[18] Indeed, it's difficult to see how the deepest *Daily Show* jokes could be appreciated by an audience unaware of the relevant social, political, and other newsworthy issues. As Annenberg analyst Dannagal Goldthwaite Young put it in a press release announcing the Center's Election Survey results, "*The Daily Show* assumes a fairly high level of political knowledge on the part of its audience."[19]

Conversation and *Crossfire*

Postman's ideas about television also illuminate Stewart's legendary October 2004 appearance on CNN's *Crossfire*. First aired in 1982, *Crossfire* was a long-running staple of CNN's lineup that featured curt discussion by hosts and guests supposedly representing both left- and right-wing positions on controversial political issues. Co-hosting for Stewart's visit were the unsuspecting Paul Begala and Tucker Carlson, neither of whom seemed prepared for what would become an extraordinary exchange. Instead of simply participating in a typical *Crossfire*-style debate (described by more than one observer as a "shoutfest"), Stewart quickly launched into a Postman-like criticism of the shallow and partisan punditry that passes for serious discussion on such programs.

In fact, this theme is one that Stewart had explored before his *Crossfire* appearance. An earlier *Daily Show* segment called "Great Moments in Punditry as Read by Children" drew laughs simply by having children read from transcripts of shows like *Crossfire*. Moreover, during a 2003 interview with Bill Moyers, Stewart claimed that both *Crossfire* and its MSNBC counterpart *Hardball* were "equally dispiriting" in the way their formats degrade political discourse.[20] And in a 2002 interview with CNN's Howard Kurtz, Stewart foreshadowed his *Crossfire* appearance by chiding the news network for offering entertainers instead of "real journalists" and pleaded, "You're the news .... People need you. Help us. Help us."[21]

On the *Crossfire* set, Stewart offered a sustained attack against the superficial conversational style of television. Before either Begala or Carlson could catch his balance, Stewart was already begging them to "stop, stop, stop, stop hurting America" with their "partisan hackery," which he claimed serves only politicians and corporations and does nothing to help ordinary citizens make informed decisions.[22] "We need help from the media," Stewart said, "and they're hurting us." Carlson tried to counter Stewart's charges with the allegation that Stewart himself had been too lenient during the *Daily Show* appearance of 2004 presidential candidate John Kerry. Stewart replied that there was a fundamental difference between journalism and comedy, snapping back, "I didn't realize that ... the news organizations look to [*The Daily Show*'s home network] Comedy Central for their cues on integrity." And when Begala tried to defend the *Crossfire* format by claiming that it was a "debate show," Stewart pointed to Carlson's trademark bow tie and charged, "you're doing theater, when you should be doing debate." Finally, Stewart charged, "You have a responsibility to the public discourse, and you fail miserably." Because of such remarks, Stewart's *Crossfire* appearance produced a rare opportunity for reflecting about the effects of television on public discourse. Indeed, the incident sparked a great deal of follow-up conversation in *The New York Times*, *Newsweek*, and countless other outlets.

We can see, once again, that these are the sorts of criticisms developed by Postman in *Amusing Ourselves to Death*. His deepest discussion of such issues concerns ABC's controversial 1983 broadcast of the film *The Day After*, which depicted the bleak effects of a nuclear strike on the American Midwest. Given the film's grave subject matter, ABC decided to follow it with a roundtable session moderated by Ted

Koppel and featuring such notable figures as Henry Kissinger, Elie Wiesel, Carl Sagan, and William F. Buckley.[23] With a serious theme and a guest list of unquestionable distinction, Koppel proceeded to march his cast through a fragmented 80 minutes of "conversation" in which the participants rarely engaged one another on points of substance. Instead, they used their camera time to push whatever points they had decided to make beforehand, without regard to the contributions of their fellow participants. Postman writes:

> Each of the six men was given approximately five minutes to say something about the subject. There was, however, no agreement on exactly what the subject was, and no one felt obliged to respond to anything anyone else had said. In fact, it would have been difficult to do so, since the participants were called upon seriatim, as if they were finalists in a beauty contest.[24]

To put it another way, this wasn't a genuine discussion, but a *pseudo-discussion* warped by television's drive to entertain. "There were no arguments or counterarguments, no scrutiny of assumptions, no explanations, no elaborations, no definitions,"[25] and yet each of these elements is essential to genuine and thoughtful dialogue.

So, how did ABC go wrong? According to Postman, the root problem remains that thoughtful conversation just isn't entertaining, and thus plays poorly on television. As a result, televised discussions about even the most serious of subjects tend to be rendered in forms that are more amusing or dramatic than reflective. On this, both Postman and the writing staff of *The Daily Show* seem to agree.[26] Moreover, CNN President Jonathan Klein cited Stewart's critique when he announced the cancellation of *Crossfire* in January 2005. In an interview with *The Washington Post*, Klein said, "I think [Stewart] made a good point about the noise level of these types of shows, which does nothing to illuminate the issues of the day."[27]

Business News, CNBC, and Jim Cramer

Stewart's *Crossfire* appearance is noteworthy because it offers an unusually direct expression of his deeper media critique. Here we can find a relatively clear and sharp indictment of television news, rather than a more ambiguous presentation filtered through assorted bits of comic material. And as if to make his critique even more forceful, Stewart followed up the *Crossfire* exchange with several additional instances of straightforward media criticism.

For example, Jim Cramer's March 2009 appearance on *The Daily Show*, tagged "Brawl Street," followed an extended buildup in which Stewart made repeated jokes at the expense of Cramer's employer, the business news network CNBC.[28] According to Stewart, CNBC and other such outlets had failed to adequately foresee (and perhaps forestall) the global financial crisis of 2008.[29] Of course, this line of attack is a specific version of Stewart's now familiar, Postman-like critique of television news; by focusing on popular entertainment-driven shows like *Fast Money*, *Squawk Box*, and Cramer's own *Mad Money*, CNBC was (in Stewart's view) neglecting its journalistic duties. Thus, CNBC and the other business news networks were in part responsible for a financial disaster that ultimately produced trillions of dollars worth of losses.

As he settled in for his *Daily Show* interview, Cramer offered a tepid defense of CNBC's work. "We've made some mistakes," he admitted. But when he claimed that "the regulators" needed to do a better job of policing short sales and other such "shenanigans," Stewart pounced:

> When you talk about the regulators, why not *the financial news network*? That's the whole point of this. CNBC could be an incredibly powerful tool of illumination.

Once again, then, we see Stewart's call for a more robust and vigilant form of television journalism. With the network's significant talent and resources, CNBC might help to educate its viewers, thereby protecting them from nefarious CEOs, traders, hedge fund managers, and financial advisors. But as Stewart sees it (perhaps following Postman's line), shows like *Mad Money* do little to further this sort of "illumination." And to the suggestion that business news networks might provide the kind of serious journalistic inquiry that could have helped to lessen the destructive effects of the 2008 collapse, Cramer offered this sobering reply:

> I'm not [legendary CBS journalist] Eric Severeid. I'm not [legendary CBS journalist] Edward R. Murrow. I'm a guy trying to do an entertainment show about business for people to watch.

In the end, under the heat of Stewart's repeated calls for journalistic reform in financial news reporting, Cramer relented: "How about if I try it?" The two men ended the interview with a handshake, and Stewart has offered few criticisms of Cramer in the years since.[30] Nonetheless, the exchange became a sensation, with many commentators applauding Stewart's performance.[31]

Fox News Sunday and TV's Entertainment Bias

Stewart's roving critique of 24-hour cable TV news has included a June 2011 exchange on *Fox News Sunday*,[32] an hour-long public affairs show that typically features extended newsmaker interviews followed by roundtable discussions with a rotating team of pundits. Stewart's appearance on *Fox News Sunday* was particularly noteworthy given his steady criticism, over many years, of the entire Fox News network. Indeed, after a bit of banter, host Chris Wallace opened the conversation with a selection of quotes in which Stewart charged that Fox's ideological conservatism undermined its journalistic integrity. To Stewart, Fox News was "a biased organization, relentlessly promoting an ideological agenda under the rubric of being a news organization." Instead of a genuine news source, he maintained, Fox was "a relentless agenda-driven 24-hour news opinion propaganda delivery system."

To counter such sweeping claims, Wallace suggested that mainstream news outlets promoted liberal causes and viewpoints; Fox News, then, could serve as an ideological counterweight to the left-leaning news divisions of networks like ABC, CBS, and NBC. Stewart's response to Wallace largely bypassed the question of *political* bias to focus on the more fundamental issue of how *the medium of television itself* subtly shapes the content of television journalism. As he explained, the principal biases of television news are not political at all. Rather, "The bias of the mainstream media is toward sensationalism, conflict, and laziness." To attract and maintain audiences, television news needs to follow the familiar formulas that make TV amusing, dramatic, or otherwise compelling. For example, zealous pundits who are quick to disagree and who are outrageous in their attacks on the opposition are especially welcome on the news networks.[33] Meanwhile, careful and thoughtful discussion is marginalized, or edited out entirely. The resulting content may be more entertaining for audiences, and more profitable for networks. But it is hardly informative or enlightening; from a journalistic standpoint, there is little to recommend it.

This concern about television's need to entertain, its tendency to render even its journalism as amusement, is of special interest to Postman, too. As he puts it in *Amusing Ourselves to Death*, "The problem is not that television presents us with entertaining subject matter but that all subject matter is presented as entertaining."[34] In particular, news reporting must pursue a mission that goes beyond mere entertainment if it is to be truly instructive. But of course, for so many reasons we now see, television news has a very difficult time overcoming its entertainment bias. The unfortunate result is that we are well entertained but poorly informed.

The Rally to Restore Sanity and/or Fear

Finally, we have the October 30, 2010 Rally to Restore Sanity and/or Fear in Washington, D.C., a curious co-production of *The Daily Show* and its Comedy Central spinoff, Stephen Colbert's *The Colbert Report*.[35] Part variety show, part political assembly, it brought some 200,000 people to the National Mall for an afternoon consisting largely of music and comedy performances. But given its timing just a few days before the 2010 midterm elections, the Rally had deeper aims as well.[36]

Indeed, the highlight of the day may have come as Stewart moved to close with "a moment, however brief, for some sincerity—if that's OK." Countering his Rally critics, Stewart stated emphatically that the event was not intended "to ridicule people of faith, or people of activism, or to look down our noses at the heartland, or passionate argument, or to suggest that times are not difficult and that we have nothing to fear." Rather, his principal target was once again television's detrimental influence on our public discourse.

On TV, Stewart argued, reporting and debate are run through a "24-hour politico pundit perpetual panic conflictinator" that exaggerates our political disagreements. This makes it difficult to reach the kinds of compromises that are essential in a democracy. So while this so-called "conflictinator" may produce dramatic and entertaining results, it cannot provide the critical exchange of ideas that our democratic system requires. As Stewart put it,

The image of Americans that is reflected back to us by our political and media process is false. It is us through a fun-house mirror; and not the good kind that makes you look slim in the waist, and maybe taller, but the kind where you have a giant forehead and an ass shaped like a month-old pumpkin and one eyeball. So why would we work together? Why would you reach across the aisle to a pumpkin-assed forehead eyeball monster?

But in the end, there is still hope. Stewart continued:

We hear every damn day about how fragile our country is, on the brink of catastrophe, torn by polarizing hate, and how it's a shame that we can't work together to get things done. But the truth is, *we do* ... impossible things, every day, that are only made possible through the little, reasonable compromises we all make.

In Stewart's view, then, television can complicate the democratic process, giving us another kind of "disinformation" that exaggerates our differences. But if we remember how the content of television news and commentary is shaped by the medium of television itself, we may be able to forge ahead with a more productive public discourse.

A Huxleyan Moment of Zen?

So, it appears that much of *The Daily Show*'s sharpest comedy requires its audience to grasp a Postman-like criticism of television news. In addition, Stewart himself seems to offer a more general critique of today's televised public discourse that is reminiscent of Postman's in several significant ways. This isn't to say, however, that Postman and Stewart are in perfect agreement. For one thing, Postman argues that the transformation of serious discussion into entertainment is all but inevitable when this discussion takes place on television. Stewart, on the other hand, seems to believe that television can do better. He's told *Rolling Stone* that "the [24-hour news] mechanism could be used to clarify rather than obfuscate," and that "CNN feels like an opportunity squandered."[37] And as we've seen, he has even appeared on the 24-hour cable news networks and used their own programs to issue his call for reform.

Postman and Stewart might also disagree about the suitability of television as a vehicle for sophisticated media criticism. Postman writes, for example, that any televised critique of television would likely be "co-opted" by the medium, and thus rendered in the typical fashion as mere entertainment.[38] In his eyes, television is simply incapable of carrying serious public discourse, including serious public discourse about mass communication itself. That Stewart uses television in his various attempts to address this issue suggests that he believes otherwise. No doubt this is a question worthy of further consideration, and through any medium capable of carrying thoughtful discussion.

Notes

1. Marshall McLuhan, *Understanding Media: The Extensions of Man* (New York: McGraw-Hill, 1964); see especially 7–21.
2. Neil Postman, *Amusing Ourselves to Death: Public Discourse in the Age of Show Business* (New York: Penguin, 1985), 7.
3. Ibid., 6.
4. Postman develops his sweeping history of American media in Chapter 5, "The Peek-a-Boo World," 64–80.
5. Ibid., 67–80, 85–98.
6. Ibid., 90. Postman acknowledges that, in other parts of the world (85–86) or in non-commercial contexts (105–106), television may serve different purposes. However, as he sees it, this does nothing to change the way that television most typically functions in contemporary American society.
7. Colbert mocked the use of one's gut in the search for truth during the debut episode of *The Colbert Report* (October 17, 2005) with this absurd bit of "insight":

> That's where the truth comes from, ladies and gentlemen: the gut. Do you know you have more nerve endings in your stomach than in your head? Look it up. Now, somebody's going to say, "I did look that up, and it's wrong." Well, mister, that's because you looked it up in a book. Next time, try looking it up in your gut. I did. And my gut tells me that's how our nervous system works.

For more on Colbert's thoughts about truth, see Amber L. Griffioen, "Irrationality and 'Gut' Reasoning: Two Kinds of Truthiness," in this volume.
8. Postman, *Amusing Ourselves to Death*, vii–viii, 155–156.
9. Ibid., 99.

10. Ibid.

11. Ibid., 100.

12. As Postman writes, "While brevity does not always suggest triviality, in this case it surely does. It is simply not possible to convey a sense of seriousness about any event if its implications are exhausted in less than one minute's time" (*Amusing Ourselves to Death*, 103).

13. Ibid., 107.

14. Ibid., 106.

15. However, Postman did appear on the show's July 14, 2003 episode to discuss his book *Technopoly: The Surrender of Culture to Technology* (New York: Knopf, 1992). In a segment titled "Lies of the Machines," correspondent Rob Corddry applied Postman's ideas in a rather ridiculous warning about the dangers of smart bagel toasters.

16. See also "Stephen Colbert's Guide to Dressing and Expressing Like a TV Journalist" in Jon Stewart, Ben Karlin, and David Javerbaum, *America (The Book): A Citizen's Guide to Democracy Inaction* (New York: Warner Books, 2004), 142–143.

17. *The O'Reilly Factor*, Fox News (September 17, 2004).

18. For the Pew studies, see "What Americans Know: 1989–2007" (April 15, 2007), 13–14, "Audience Segments in a Changing News Environment" (August 17, 2008), 42–44, and "Ideological News Sources: Who Watches and Why" (September 12, 2010), 69–70. The PublicMind results appear in "What You Know Depends on What You Watch" (May 3, 2012).

19. "National Annenberg Election Survey" (Press Release), *Annenberg Public Policy Center* (September 21, 2004), 2.

20. *Now*, PBS (July 11, 2003).

21. *Reliable Sources*, CNN (November 2, 2002).

22. *Crossfire*, CNN (October 15, 2004). All quotes below are from CNN's rush transcript of this episode.

23. Postman actually cites Buckley's own legendary program *Firing Line* as a rare example of television as a "carrier of coherent language and thought in process" that "occasionally shows people in the act of thinking but who also happen to have television cameras pointed at them" (*Amusing Ourselves to Death*, 91). *Firing Line* never received high ratings, though, and spent most of its 33 years on public television.

24. Ibid., 89.

25. Ibid., 90.

26. Postman's son Andrew sums up all of this nicely in his "Introduction" to the Twentieth Anniversary Edition of *Amusing Ourselves to Death*, writing: "When Jon Stewart, host of Comedy Central's *The Daily Show*, went on CNN's *Crossfire* to make this very point—that serious news and

show business ought to be distinguishable, for the sake of public discourse and the republic—the hosts seemed incapable of even understanding the words coming out of his mouth" (xiii–xiv).

27. Howard Kurtz, "Carlson & 'Crossfire': Exit Stage Left & Right," *Washington Post* (January 6, 2005), C1.

28. *The Daily Show*, Comedy Central (March 12, 2009).

29. See, especially, the March 4, 2009 episode of *The Daily Show*, which included a brutal segment titled "CNBC Financial Advice." Quipped Stewart: "If I'd only followed CNBC's advice, I'd have $1 million today. Provided I'd started with $100 million."

30. Indeed, Stewart even mocked his own work during the Cramer interview in a March 17, 2009 segment titled "IndigNation! Populist Uprising '09—The Enragening." But for some later jokes directed at Cramer, see for example "Lenny Dykstra's Financial Career" (July 14, 2009), "Indecision 2010—The Re-Changening" (January 20, 2010), and "These F@#king Guys—Goldman Sachs" (April 19, 2010).

31. For a brief survey of such commentary, see Eric Etheridge's "Fight Night: Cramer vs. Stewart," http://opinionator.blogs.nytimes.com/2009/03/13/fight-night-cramer-vs-stewart, accessed January 30, 2013.

32. *Fox News Sunday*, Fox News (June 19, 2011).

33. In a moment that was unfortunately cut from the final broadcast, Stewart elaborated:

> In the absence of [truly major news events like the September 11 terrorist attacks], they're not just going to say, "There's not that much that's urgent or important or conflicted happening today. So we are going to gin up, we are going to bring forth more conflict and more sensationalism because we want you to continue watching us 24 hours a day 7 days a week, even when the news doesn't necessarily warrant that type of behavior."

34. Postman, *Amusing Ourselves to Death*, 87.

35. The Rally's comically awkward name was a result of the fact that it was originally conceived as two distinct and opposing events: Stewart's Rally to Restore Sanity and Colbert's March to Keep Fear Alive.

36. As Stewart explained on MSNBC's *The Rachel Maddow Show* (November 11, 2010), "I felt like, in 12 years, I'd earned a moment to tell people who I was. And that's what I did."

37. See Eric Bates, "Jon Stewart: The *Rolling Stone* Interview," *Rolling Stone* (September 29, 2011), 44–52.

38. Postman, *Amusing Ourselves to Death*, 161. In the final chapter of *Amusing Ourselves to Death*, Postman describes a then-hypothetical but subversive anti-television television program that's eerily similar to

The Daily Show. According to Postman, this program would serve an important educational purpose by demonstrating how television recreates and degrades news, political debate, religious thought, and so on. He writes: "I imagine such demonstrations would of necessity take the form of parodies, along the lines of *Saturday Night Live* and *Monty Python*, the idea being to induce a national horse laugh over television's control of the public discourse" (161–162). In the end, Postman rejects the idea of such a show as "nonsense," since he thinks that serious and intelligent televised discussion could never attract an audience large enough to make a difference.

Chapter 2

The Fake, the False, and the Fictional
The Daily Show as News Source

Michael Gettings

Someone kidnapped the Lindbergh baby? … Oh, I'm sorry, I get all my news from The Daily Show.

Jon Stewart (November 2, 2011)

We might assume naively that the purpose of serious journalism in a democratic society is to inform the citizenry, and that this requires delivering real news that is widely distributed. But according to a survey conducted by the Pew Research Institute, regular *Daily Show* viewers seem to learn about current events from the self-billed "fake news" program. The survey polled regular viewers, readers, or listeners of various news and entertainment media, and 30% of regular *Daily Show* viewers scored in the "high knowledge" category. While this wasn't as high a percentage as those who regularly read *The Atlantic Monthly* or listen to NPR, it was higher than the results for daily newspaper readers and MSNBC, CNN, and CBS, NBC, ABC and Fox News viewers.[1] This raises the question of how it is possible that viewers might learn real news from a fake news show, possibly even more than they learn from so-called "real" news media.

The question of how fake news can inform people about real news touches on a question posed by philosophers: How do we learn truth from a work of fiction, something typically full of falsehoods? After all, a typical work of fiction is about pretend characters in pretend situations

The Ultimate Daily Show and Philosophy: More Moments of Zen, More Indecision Theory, First Edition. Edited by Jason Holt.

doing pretend things. Where's the truth in such a story, where's the reality? If fake news is classified as fiction, and if we can understand how fiction conveys truth, then we can understand how *The Daily Show* conveys real news to its viewers. Along the way, we'll look at many examples to see just how *The Daily Show* pulls this off.

Is *The Daily Show* Fiction?

Our first question should be this: What is a work of fiction? Our rough understanding may be that fictions simply aren't true, they're false, fake instead of real. But this can't be the whole story, since a fake Rolex isn't a work of fiction, nor is a fib a child tells her mother, at least not in the sense that Melville's novel *Billy Budd*, for example, is a work of fiction. The rather obvious problem with calling the fake Rolex a fiction is that it's not a story, it's a watch. So when we're talking about fiction, we should restrict ourselves to stories, or narratives. *Daily Show* news reports are narratives in this sense— they tell stories. Real news reports tell stories as well, it's just that those stories are purportedly true. A child's fib is a kind of narrative too. The reason we don't classify fibs, or lies in general, as fictions in the relevant sense is that fibs and lies are intended to deceive the audience. Most fictions aren't intended to deceive, and this is true of *The Daily Show* just as it is of *The Last Picture Show*. We might think then that the distinction between fiction and non-fiction is that fictions are false and not intended to deceive while non-fictions are simply true.

This is closer, but it's still not a complete account of fiction. A poorly researched work of non-fiction isn't intended to deceive and may contain many falsehoods, but that doesn't make it fictional. A simple work of fiction might accidentally contain many truths, but that doesn't make it non-fictional. So the ratio of falsehoods to truths doesn't account for the distinction between fiction and non-fiction. For example, in the television coverage of the 2000 US Presidential Election, Fox News, CNN, NBC, CBS, and ABC incorrectly reported that Al Gore was the winner and our next President. While false and not intended to deceive, these reports weren't works of fiction. Compare this to Stephen Colbert's statement on *The Daily Show* on May 5, 2003, roughly 18 months before the election:

> At 11:09 Eastern Standard Time, *The Daily Show* is projecting that George Walker Bush has won reelection and will remain in office until 2008.

While what Colbert said turned out to be true, this doesn't make his report non-fictional. It's still fake news. As Stewart replied:

> There's 18 months to go in this campaign, and I think it's a little ridiculous to say that George W. Bush has won anything at this point.

One difference between Stephen Colbert and a network news anchor such as Brian Williams is that Williams has a staff that carefully researches the stories he reads on air. Colbert has a staff of writers who carefully research certain *parts* of his commentary, and then make the rest up. Thorough research, however, is neither necessary nor sufficient to make a work non-fiction. A personal memoir might demand little research, yet it's non-fiction, while some historical fiction demands a great deal of research. A better place to look for the distinction between fiction and non-fiction is in the authors' intentions in writing such narratives.

Hilarious Make-'Em-Ups

In a July 12, 2006 story on Senator Rick Santorum's campaign struggles, Jon Stewart reported that Santorum's campaign had issued a flyer entitled "50 Things You May Not Know About Rick Santorum." Stewart presented the audience with a quiz, asking them to identify which items on a list were included in the flyer and which were not. Some of the items, such as "Rick has been leading the fight against AIDS and world poverty, working closely with U2's Bono" came straight from the campaign literature. Others, including "Rick once compared Democrats fighting to preserve the filibuster to Nazis," which Stewart identified as true, "didn't really make it into the pamphlet." The rest of the quiz, for example, "Rick's S&M safe word is 'applesauce,'" was, in Stewart's words, "what we in the business call 'hilarious make-'em-ups.'"

It's this last category that puts *Daily Show* reports into the category of fiction. The writers make up parts of the narrative knowingly and intentionally. Though usually this results in stories that are at least partially false, this isn't essential to the narratives being fictional. If Rick Santorum had a safe word, and if it really were "applesauce," it would turn out that the writers, to their and our surprise, accidentally reported something true. The report would still be a work of fiction, however.

Notice that to make something up in this way, one does so deliberately, but without any intention to deceive the audience. As we saw, this is what distinguishes typical fictions from lies. Writers of fiction don't intend to deceive the audience, and the same goes for the writers of *The Daily Show*.

So what makes a narrative fictional is that it consists, in part at least, of non-deceptive pretense (i.e., it is intentionally made-up), but not in a manner to deceive the audience into believing it. Part of the fiction can be literally true, but part of it must be make-believe. The question of learning truth from fiction is one of distinguishing what is make-believe in the narrative from what is to be believed. The key to unlocking truth from *The Daily Show* is an understanding of what is true in the show and what is make-believe.

So the question to answer here is how does the audience learn from *The Daily Show* if the news stories are works of fiction? The problem is complicated by the fact that what distinguishes non-fiction from make-'em-ups depends on the intentions of the writers. Sometimes the intentions are clear. In describing Texas Governor and then-Presidential candidate Rick Perry, Jon Stewart let the audience know which part of his description was make-believe: "James Richard Perry, 'Rick'. The tough-talkin', God-fearin', boot-wearin', prisoner-killin', Pez dispenser-collectin' (that last one's probably not right), Texan" (November 12, 2011). But the writers' intentions aren't always obvious to viewers. In fact, it's part of the show's design that the same deadpan delivery is used when relating both real news and fictional jokes.

Sheer Outrageousness and Surprising Truth

In 1729 Jonathan Swift published his controversial pamphlet "A Modest Proposal," in which he apparently advocated breeding human babies as a food source in order to combat famine. That essay is now regarded as a paradigm of satire, though at the time it was met with great outrage and indignation. How was the audience to know that Swift wasn't serious? Swift's earnest tone fooled many readers into thinking he *was* serious, but the content of the essay, namely its promotion of the patently ridiculous measure of cannibalistic infanticide, was a telling clue that he wasn't.

Jon Stewart and his correspondents regularly use an earnest tone when delivering their reports. It's the content of what they say that often tips off viewers that parts of the reports are made up. Sheer outrageousness or hyperbole is one of the clearest indicators that part of a fictional narrative is false or made up. *The Daily Show* uses this technique regularly to indicate to its audience what's true and what's false. For example, on November 29, 2010, *The Daily Show* reported rising military tensions between North and South Korea, and showed a clip of North Korean soldiers marching in precision lockstep. Correspondent "Kim" Sam Bee commented on the military exercises:

BEE: All these people do is militarily exercise. It's a nation of military Jack LaLannes. Everyone in that video can swim across a lake towing an ICBM chained to his testicles. They can. Yes.

STEWART: Are those skills remotely useful in combat?

BEE: If you need to get a missile across a lake by your balls it is.

The audience understands that the soldiers cannot really do this, but the point is made—North Korea is gearing up for battle with South Korea.

Outrageousness or hyperbole is not a foolproof test of the fake, however. As the saying goes, sometimes the truth is stranger than fiction. And when a story is true, but outrageous, Stewart sometimes has to use more direct means to make clear what's real and what's fake. In an August 2, 2006 story on an Arabic-language translator discharged from the Army, Stewart reported as follows:

This week, Bleu Copas became the fifty-fifth Arabic translator discharged under the Army's "Don't Ask, Don't Tell" policy. How did they know Copas was gay? After being tipped off by anonymous emails, investigators asked him if he had any gay friends, and—this is true—if he was involved in community theater.

The onscreen graphic contained the quotation "if he was involved in community theater," taken straight from a CNN.com story, and backing up Stewart's assertion "This is true." Without Stewart's assurance of its truth and the graphic displaying the quotation, viewers might easily assume that the community theater question was made up by *The Daily Show* writers, which otherwise would be an understandable mistake, given the writers' sense of humor.

The Role of "Senior" Correspondents

Examples such as the North Korea story above illustrate a second feature of *The Daily Show* that helps the audience distinguish the fake from the real. When Stewart talks with his correspondents and commentators, he almost always plays the straight man, stating the truth about the topic under discussion, while the correspondent or commentator often makes the jokes, albeit with a straight face. The details Samantha Bee shared about the North Korean soldiers' abilities were fake, but the questions Stewart asked about the military exercises touched on real issues concerning North Korea's intentions towards South Korea.

In another exchange (June 19, 2012) Stewart reported that both Barack Obama and Mitt Romney were pandering to the electorate, in an effort to curry favor with voters ("The Democalypse: Pander Express Edition"). Representing the Democrats and Republicans, respectively, John Oliver and Wyatt Cenac discussed their candidates' next moves in their campaigns. This included the following exchange between Stewart and Oliver:

OLIVER: Tomorrow, the President will be announcing that all children of Jewish mothers are now doctors.
STEWART: Can the President do that?
OLIVER: Of course the President can do that, Dr. Stewart, and congratulations, by the way. It's been done before. In 1951, President Truman turned all of America's Filipinos into podiatrists. It's a fact. That's history.

Now despite Oliver's claim to relate facts, we know that his report is false, about both Obama and Truman. What is true is that Obama issued an executive order to suspend deportation of illegal immigrants who pose no risk to public safety or national security, which is what Stewart reported. But as with so many *Daily Show* reports, Stewart speaks the truth and the correspondents make up stories. Not only is the joke on the politicians, but also on the news media, in this case reporters who make claims with little evidence, but assert them as facts.

The audience quickly understands the roles of Stewart and his correspondents. After you've seen *The Daily Show* a few times, it's clear that he's more likely to speak the truth while they're more likely to make things up. Genre fiction often works in a similar way. For example, take typical first-person detective fiction. When one reads a detective story told in the first person, the narrator tends to be reliable. What we know as fact, at least within the story, is what the detective/narrator relates to us. But other characters in the story, particularly those who are potential suspects, aren't reliable; what another character says might be false, and as readers we understand this because of our familiarity with the genre. One way *The Daily Show* helps us distinguish the real from the fake comes from the implicit conventions of complementary anchor/correspondent roles to which we quickly become accustomed.

Playing Dumb

Regular viewers are also familiar with another common practice, that of correspondents being surprisingly ignorant of the stories they cover, often discussing some topic other than the story they're supposed to be covering. This allows Stewart to ask leading questions or make comments about the real story, while the seeming ineptitude of the correspondents provides laughs. On July 20, 2005, Stewart and Ed Helms discussed President Bush's nomination of John Roberts to the Supreme Court:

HELMS: The left wishes the President picked someone they wanted, not someone he wanted. I mean, who gave him the authority? It's an abuse of power.
STEWART: I think it's in the Constitution.

Any eighth-grade civics student knows that the Constitution grants the President the power to make Supreme Court nominations, but

Helms's apparent ignorance gives Stewart the opportunity to remind the audience, in case they've forgotten. Works of fiction frequently use this device. Insert an ignorant character into a situation so that relevant information has to be explained to that character, and you thereby inform the audience.

So in Stewart's interaction with correspondents we see that correspondents are often the ones who make things up, and they play ignorant, leaving Stewart as the reliable source of real news. Of course, when Stewart delivers news stories on his own, not everything he says is reliable. For one thing, *The Daily Show* is comedy, and viewers understand that every fake news story has a punch line, if not several. Since *The Daily Show* makes fun of real news, usually the structure of a fake news story is to begin with facts and end in farce. This means that the beginning of Stewart's report is mostly real, while the ending tends to be fake. Visual cues, such as photographs and graphics, help indicate to the viewer when the story has turned fake, a device used frequently by both Stewart and the correspondents. On May 10, 2012, Jason Jones reported on a fundraiser for Barack Obama held by George Clooney. Jones claimed to have taken a photo of the event from inside Clooney's house, and it was displayed on screen. It consisted of a large ballroom full of people, including a line in front of a photo booth repurposed as an "Abortion Booth," Sean Penn doing a keg stand next to Fidel Castro, and Martin Scorsese and Leonardo DiCaprio with someone who looks like Michael Jackson. Jon Stewart asks Jason Jones "Is that Osama Bin Laden?" Jones replies, searching for a plausible answer "No, no, of course not … that's … that's not … Obama killed him, we all know that … that's just … Christian Bale … preparing for a role … that guy is method." The photo is obviously a fabrication, but even those viewers who somehow failed to notice this when they saw Sean Penn doing a keg stand won't fail to notice it's fake when a dead man appears in it. The photo also conveys a sense of what conservatives are supposed to fear about liberals—in addition to being friendly to terrorists and communists and having low moral values, they promote easy access to abortions.

So we have seen that there are at least three general means for the audience to determine what is real and what is fake when they watch *The Daily Show*: hyperbole or outrageousness, the complementary host/correspondent roles, and the use of graphics and photos. In our examples so far the truths conveyed by the show have been particular facts, such as "The Constitution grants the President the power to make Supreme Court nominations" and "North Korea's increased military activity might be a sign that they are planning for succession as their leader's health declines." But the scope of truths conveyed by the show isn't limited to particular facts.

The Daily Show, Our Government, and Other News Outlets

Philosophers distinguish at least two kinds of truths expressed in fiction. The first kind consists of particular truths, as we've seen in examples from the show. But the second category of truths—general truths—is no less, and perhaps more, important. For example, Jane Austen's *Pride and Prejudice* begins with the general observation "It is a truth universally acknowledged, that a single man in possession of a good fortune must be in want of a wife."[2] Such general claims in fiction often serve as commentaries on the human condition or the state of the world, and help explain the action to follow. *The Daily Show* tends to focus its general commentaries on two topics: the government and the news media, particularly the cable TV news channels.

The Daily Show repeatedly touches on certain themes concerning the President, Congress, and politicians in general. These themes can amount to running jokes, but unlike the "hilarious make-'em-ups", they express what Stewart and the writers apparently consider general truths. One theme is the willingness of politicians to say anything to get their way. For example, during congressional budget disputes in April 2011, Senator John Kyl (R-Arizona) argued that the budget for Planned Parenthood should be cut because "well over 90%" of what Planned Parenthood does is perform abortions. Jon Stewart expressed surprise at this high number, and then ran a CNN clip of Bill Adair, editor of Politifact.com, who stated that the number is closer to 3%. In another clip, CNN read a statement from Senator Kyl's office saying that "his remark was not intended to be a factual statement, but rather to illustrate that Planned Parenthood, an organization that receives millions in taxpayer dollars, does subsidize abortions." After this, Stewart brings in Senior Political Strategist Wyatt Cenac to explain Senator Kyl's lie. Stewart asks Cenac: "Why did he lie?"

CENAC: (*a bit dumbfounded that Stewart doesn't see the obvious answer*) Because he thought it would help his argument.

STEWART: But you can't just lie. Why not make a compelling and honest argument?

CENAC: Because he doesn't want Planned Parenthood to get money, and the true facts in the case don't favor him. But the lie-facts stack up very strongly in Kyl's favor.

Here we have an example of *The Daily Show* exposing a politician's willingness to lie, or in this case, make up falsehoods, in an attempt to support his position. Note that Kyl's statement is not a "hilarious make-'em up" or work of fiction, since the intent was to deceive, or at least to lead the audience to believe the statement. Cenac and Stewart use Kyl's remarks to illustrate a broader trend among politicians— they act in ways that ordinary people would find inappropriate, if not unethical.[3]

The second topic of general commentary is the news media itself, particularly 24-hour television news such as CNN, MSNBC, and Fox News. *The Daily Show* considers these news outlets sensationalistic, inclined to copy each other, prone to overexposing news stories, and desperate to manufacture news in order to fill airtime. When the Supreme Court heard a case that challenged the constitutionality of the Patient Protection and Affordable Care Act, often dubbed "Obamacare," CNN and Fox News raced to be the first to cover the Court's decision. In their haste to be first, however, it appeared CNN and Fox failed to read the Court document carefully. On June 28, 2012, Stewart ran a clip that had aired on CNN at 10:07 a.m.:

CNN REPORTER: I want to bring the breaking news that according to producer Bill Mears the individual mandate is not a valid ... is not a valid exercise of the commerce clause. So it appears as if the Supreme Court justices have struck down the individual mandate, the centerpiece of the health care legislation.

Eight seconds later, Fox News reported the same thing. Wolf Blitzer remarked "Wow, that's a dramatic moment." Jon Stewart agreed that it was a moment of great drama, but pointed out that the problem with the report was that "like many of our greatest dramas, [it's] a work of complete fiction." The real story, as Stewart clarified, was that the Court ruled that the individual mandate was unconstitutional under the commerce clause, but that the mandate was constitutional under Congress's power to levy taxes. As he put it, "very confusing ... unless you read up to page four."

Here we have an excellent example of how *The Daily Show* not only critiques 24-hour cable news, but can better inform its viewers. Because of CNN and Fox News's haste to break the story, both initially gave incorrect reports about the Court's decision. *Daily Show* viewers, however, can better understand the Court's decision because they not only get the correct report, but they see the false story as shared by CNN and Fox.

Sometimes *The Daily Show* critiques both politicians and the media in the same story. On January 20, 2011, Jon Stewart reported remarks made by Rep. Steve Cohen (D-Tennessee) on the House floor. Cohen called for a return to civil discourse in politics, entreating his colleagues to avoid name-calling and personal attacks. One week after this speech, Cohen himself compared Republicans to Nazis, saying that Republicans were lying about the President's proposed healthcare plan like Goebbels lied to the German people. Stewart pointed out Cohen's hypocrisy, of course, but he went farther. He explained how sharing one trait in common with Nazis does not make one a Nazi, illustrating this by showing photos of decisively non-Nazi individuals: a school marching band (in precision formation, like Nazis), a UPS man (wearing a brown shirt, naturally), and a baby with his hand in the air, his hair parted on the side and food on his upper lip (resembling Hitler in these respects). More generally, Stewart revealed the common tactic of so many politicians and pundits—making unfair comparisons to some reviled person or group on only the most tenuous similarity. Stewart showed that Cohen's tactic was a kind of fear-inducing hyperbole designed to undermine his opponents, quite inconsistent with civil discourse.

The following week, Stewart returned to the story, after various news outlets, including Fox News, reacted to Cohen's remarks. Many Fox News hosts and pundits, including Bill O'Reilly, Greta Van Susteren, Sean Hannity, and Karl Rove, were incensed, claiming that the media would have made a much bigger deal out of this had it been a Republican who made such comments. Fox News's Megyn Kelly went so far as to say that Fox News never engaged in the same tactics as Cohen had. Stewart then proceeded to humorously challenge his team of writers to find Fox News personalities making exactly the same comparison Cohen did. They found clips of Bill O'Reilly, Glenn Beck, and others comparing liberals and progressives to Nazis; in addition, Bernie Goldberg made the comparison, as he was being interviewed by Megyn Kelly on *her* show. So not only does *The Daily Show* illustrate hypocrisy in politics, but also the irresponsibility of the news media, especially the 24-hour cable news.

The Daily Show v. The Onion

If one is looking for fake news, *The Daily Show* is not the only option. Though it bills itself as "America's Finest News Source," *The Onion* has been a source of fake news since 1988. The differences between *The Daily Show* and *The Onion* illustrate how the former can inform us about the news, whereas the latter rarely does.

The Daily Show draws its stories from the day's events, what is currently happening in the world and in politics. *The Onion*, on the other hand, depends heavily on the humor of its headlines, and rarely pulls from actual news events. Instead, it relies on broad characterizations of individuals and groups, cultural references, and stereotypes in its humor. Here are sample headlines from the June 21, 2012 issue of *The Onion*:

> Woman, Gay Best Friend Go Off On Another One Of Their Little Crazy Adventures
> Herman Cain Endorses Who Gives A Fuck
> Americans Enjoying 3 Months Of Vegging Out Before Responsibilities Of Fall Programming Resume
> Donald Trump Stares Forlornly At Tiny, Aged Penis In Mirror Before Putting On Clothes, Beginning Day
> New Commercials For Old Milwaukee Beer Feature Group Of Friends Contemplating Suicide

Note that only one of these mentions a political figure, Herman Cain, who was really more of a former political figure at the time of the headline, having dropped out of the contest for the Republican Presidential nomination more than six months earlier. The headline even pokes fun at Cain's fall from prominence in the political landscape. The other headlines (and the stories that accompany them) rely on the woman/gay best friend stereotype, the Americans-as-couch-potatoes stereotype, Donald Trump's public persona, and the nearly universal party atmosphere of the beer commercial. To get the humor, one needs to grasp certain American cultural attitudes, but little else. Very little understanding of politics and current events is found here, and the stories are almost entirely made of whole cloth.

Flipping to the Politics page of *The Onion* doesn't change things significantly. The June 2012 edition included 11 headlines, seven of which made fun of one of the two main Presidential candidates, Barack Obama and Mitt Romney. Some of these, such as "Obama's Approval Rating Down After Photos Surface Of Him Eating Big Sandwich All Alone," contained almost no specific information about the candidate. Others, such as "Ann Romney Says Husband Has Deeply Principled Side No One Ever Sees In Public," mentioned the common impression that Romney's positions on issues change over time, but nothing specific about events concerning Romney. The four remaining headlines consisted of a completely fabricated story about Vice President Joe Biden ("Biden To Honor Fallen Soldiers By Jumping Motorcycle Over Vietnam Memorial"), and three general stories about the Tea Party, Republicans, and an unnamed Governor ("Tea Party Quiet ... Too Quiet," "Republicans Stalling Obama's Agenda By Speaking, Moving In Slow Motion," and "Governor Too Embarrassed To Say Which State He Leads"). None of these shared specific information about current events in politics. What these examples show is that *The Onion* begins with only the barest facts, but moves quickly into the realm of make-believe. As fake news goes, *The Onion* makes up its stories from almost the very beginning.

Contrast this with *The Daily Show*, which generally begins with real information before launching into jokes. For example, in August, 2011, *The Daily Show* aired a CNN report that Joe Biden rents a cottage behind his Greenville, DE mansion to his secret service agents for $2,200 a month. So far, so factual. Stewart used this story to make several jokes about Biden as a landlord (STEWART: "How come he's such a good negotiator on rent?") and ended with a fake photo of Biden showing plumber's crack as he bends down to look at the pipes under a kitchen sink (STEWART: "I don't care how clogged your sink is, no one needs to see this"). So while *The Onion* finds humor in making stories up almost entirely from scratch, *The Daily Show* uses the day's news as a launching point for its jokes, and thus it communicates real information as it makes us laugh. The lack of real information content doesn't detract from the humor of *The Onion*, it only shows that the fake news of *The Daily Show* contains a great deal more real information about current events than the fake news of *The Onion*.

Fake News, Real Messages

Works of fiction convey truth to the attentive reader. Sometimes these truths are mundane, such as the true descriptions of nineteenth-century whaling vessels found in *Moby Dick*. Sometimes they are more general truths about human affairs, nature and the world at large, which are also found in *Moby Dick*. *Daily Show* reports are works of fiction, and similarly convey truths both mundane and more general. The mundane truths tend to be about the day's events in politics, and domestic and world events. The more general truths concern American government and the media. What the *Daily Show* explores more seriously is the role of our elected officials, their responsibilities to the country, and the role of the media in a democracy. Like any good work of fiction, *The Daily Show* can both convey truth and entertain at the same time. And if you can learn while laughing, why not get your news this way?

Notes

1. Pew Research Center for People and the Press, "Audience Segments in a Changing News Environment," 2008, www.people-press.org/reports/pdf/444.pdf, accessed January 30, 2013. *Daily Show* fans may delight in the fact that Fox News was at the very bottom of the "high knowledge" rankings. To be fair, though, *the Daily Show* scored well below some of the cable shows ridiculed regularly on the program, including *Hannity & Colmes*, *Hardball*, and Rush Limbaugh's radio show. It also bears mentioning that the results of the Pew study have been met with some skepticism. See Jody Baumgartner and Jonathan S. Morris, "Stoned Slackers or Super Citizens?: The *Daily Show* Viewing and Political Engagement of Young Adults," in *The Stewart/Colbert Effect: Essays on the Real Impacts of Fake News*, eds. A. Amarasingam and R. W. McChesney (Jefferson, NC: McFarland & Co., 2011), 63–78. For the purposes here, however, the question does not concern how much viewers learn from *The Daily Show*, but how such learning is even possible.

2. Jane Austen, *Pride and Prejudice* (New York: Bantam Books, 1981), 1. We might debate whether Austen's statement is actually true. Rather than worry about the actual truth of what Austen, or *The Daily Show* for that matter, says, for convenience I will continue to call these "general truths." More accurately, they're general assertions the writer or speaker makes, that is, they're asserted as truths believed by the speaker or writer.

3. Note that Kyl's assertion might also or otherwise count as bullshit. See Kimberly Blessing and Joseph Marren, "More Bullshit: Political Spin and the PR-ization of Media," in this volume.

Chapter 3

The Daily Show
An Ethos for the Fifth Estate

Rachael Sotos

As the mainstream news media has fallen on hard times (lacking revenue, falling prey to corporate influence, failing to fulfill its function), a new institution, similar to the press, but distinct from it, has emerged: *a watcher for the watchdogs*, a voice of the people when the news (the Fourth Estate) isn't doing its job. This so-called Fifth Estate is an institution "of the people" insofar as they express themselves as media critics, activists, artists, and "comedian pundit talker guys" like Jon Stewart and Stephen Colbert.[1] Who exactly inhabits the Fifth Estate, and what precisely they do, remains uncertain. But there is a general consensus that in North America the Fifth Estate has a symbiotic relationship with the crisis-ridden "free press."

Some theorists, such as Ian Reilly, locate satirical fake news like *The Daily Show* at the very core of the Fifth Estate. Satirical fake news not only monitors the failures of the press, it "speaks truth to power," reframes the representation of issues, and encourages resistance, protest, and positive change.[2] This viewpoint embraces the quasi-institutional features of the networked world (enhanced citizen communication and new forms of advocacy) yet also relegates blogocentrism to a secondary role relative to satirical fake news.

Although *The Daily Show* exemplifies the Fifth Estate for Reilly, his ideal vision of satirical fake news as linking theory and practice, critique and action, is better reflected by media hoaxsters the Yes

The Ultimate Daily Show and Philosophy: More Moments of Zen, More Indecision Theory, First Edition. Edited by Jason Holt.
© 2013 John Wiley & Sons, Inc. Published 2013 by John Wiley & Sons, Inc.

Men. Here we are on different terrain, for the culture jamming Yes Men, whose spectacular feats of corporate impersonation strive to elicit citizen action more than to entertain, are up to something different than *The Daily Show*.[3] Reilly quotes Stewart on the question of activism in an interview with Bill Moyers. Stewart explains that he has, "great respect for people who are in the front lines and the trenches of trying to enact social change." He understands himself rather as, "a comedian who has the pleasure of writing jokes about things [he] really care[s] about."[4] In the end, Reilly cannot abide what he sees as Stewart's own resistance to activism, or his allegiance to the comedic vocation, and he interprets Stewart's remark as a confession of corporate whoredom.

Without foolishly denying the reality of corporate power, or its many annoyances (commercials, product placement, and so on), we have good cause to take Stewart at his word. To be sure, viewing Stewart first and foremost *as a comedian* and *The Daily Show* primarily *as a comedy show* won't provide us a substitute for social mobilization or direct action; Jon Stewart will not appear as Che Guevara. It just might, however, indicate the fake news' actual function within the interlinking networks of the nascent Fifth Estate. As political theorist Hannah Arendt (1906–1975) explains, there is much to be said for the distinction between "the actor" and "the spectator." Whether the spectator is a judge, journalist, historian, critic, poet, pundit, writer, *or comedian*, traditionally speaking, it is by virtue of withdrawal from the exigencies of action that he or she has a kind of authority in the public conversation. The spectator, *not the actor*, gives meaning to the events in the world, and functions as a voice of conscience, proving the "moral character" of mankind.[5]

Reilly, for his part, touches on this question of the spectator when he mentions, albeit in passing, "that some scholars have turned to political pundits as important figures in the elaboration of a fifth estate ethos."[6] The text Reilly references here, one of the earliest on the so-called Fifth Estate (from 1992, Nimmo and Combs' *The Political Pundits*), obviously has nothing to say about either *The Daily Show* or the blogosphere.[7] Nimmo and Combs' distinction between "priestly pundits" and "the bards" makes it pretty easy to locate *The Daily Show*, however. The priests are typically an elite group of serious experts, closely tied to the powers that be, pundits who "pontificate via serious, abstract and conceptual analysis." By contrast, "the bard is a storyteller, a weaver of humorous narratives that give humane and empathetic force to unfolding events and processes."[8] The humorous storytelling bard has appeared as a kind of a pundit at many points in American history. Notably, we already see a critique of the mainstream media in historical figures like Ben Franklin, Mark Twain, Will Rogers, and Paul Harvey. As the populist elaborator of the cultural ethos, the bard is fundamentally optimistic about the common sense and capacity of the collective to effect change in the world. He appeals to "the American collective voice" and, as if speaking with us and through us, "reminds us of our identity as a people." With seemingly magical powers of charismatic speech, "the bard makes 'We the People' exist, and reminds us that 'We the People' is sovereign."[9]

To appreciate the function of the fake news elaborating the ethos of the Fifth Estate, it is instructive to consider places outside of North America where Fifth Estate actors are clearly doing something more than journalism critique. It is noteworthy that the Arab Spring and *The Daily Show* have, perhaps surprisingly, developed in tandem. In addition to the half-hour per week *Global Edition* that had been broadcast on CNN International since 2002, the regular version of *The Daily Show* (edited according to local laws and sensibilities) has been broadcast on Showtime Arabia in North Africa and the Middle East since 2008. And however we understand the sparks of the "youthquake" that began at the end of 2010 (economic, political, spiritual, technological), when the video of Mohammed Bouazizi's self-immolation went viral, one fact is uncontestable: a fake news publication inspired by *The Onion*, *El Koshary Today*, had been online since 2009.[10] And today, in post-Mubarak Egypt, Bassem Yousef, "Egypt's Jon Stewart," broadcasts *Al Bernameg* (*The Show*). Of course some may believe that *Al Bernameg* and *El Koshary* have sold out, that they are the stooges of the American-Zionist empire, or whatever. On the other hand, it seems that these fake news institutions do articulate an ethos for "We, the Egyptian, People:" "Aiming to both inform and entertain," *Al Bernameg* mocks the military *and* politicians.[11] El Koshy spoofs "political and religious issues—pushing boundaries but not breaking them … to engage people not enrage them."

For my part, I am among the ordinary people Jon Stewart addressed at the "first official gathering of the Fifth Estate," the 2010 Rally to Restore Sanity. I recognize myself in the ethos articulated that sunny

October day, "We live in hard times, not end times." And I definitely see myself as one of the many "just a little bit late for something [I] have to do." Yet, in my "armchair revolutionary" way, I'd like to think that I've been doing my part. Way back in 2007, in the earlier version of this essay you're now reading, entitled, "The Fake News and the Fifth Estate," I argued that *The Daily Show* is pretty gosh darn patriotic, the very embodiment of the revolutionary spirit, *a television show with a constitutional function*. Although I didn't explicitly thematize the ethos of the Fifth Estate in that essay, implicitly at least, I think I made a good start. I'll return to the revolutionary terrain of colonial America later, but not because the Founding Fathers are the ethically flawless, nor is Jon Stewart going to appear as George Washington (though Colbert does a pretty good Ben Franklin). The early Americans can teach us the ABC's of a fake news ethos because they themselves were fake news aficionados, and because in large measure Americans owe their freedom and independence to the fake news. For these reasons alone meditating on the comparable fake news landscapes of the present and past is no frivolous enterprise. We discover rather the rightful place of *The Daily Show* in American political culture, its venerable literary lineage, and how obviously well-qualified Comedy Central style fake news is to elaborate an ethos for the Fifth Estate.

All the Fake News Fit to Print

It might seem odd for the denizens of the Fifth Estate, many of whom are motivated by the failings of the Fourth, to entrust their ethos to the fake news. But in fact, our worry is not necessarily with the fake news itself. Historically speaking, the fake news precedes the straight news by several hundred years. As Harvard historian Jill Lepore reminds us, "the elusive pursuit of journalistic objectivity only began in the nineteenth century."[12] Previously newspapers, "paper bullets," were unabashedly propaganda, polemics, opinions; no one considered rigidly distinguishing between entertainment and information. Even the most highly independent and vigilantly accurate newspapers printed a mishmash of gossip, satire, and entertainment. *The New England Courant*, the short-lived paper begun by Ben Franklin's's older brother James, is an excellent case in point. This rebel paper, the first in the colonies printed "without authority," that is, without a license granting prior approval from Church and State, is rightly seen as the beginning of the independent colonial press. Making a space for the voice of the people, it was the first paper to report on legislative vote counts, and the first to strive for something like "impartiality," soliciting opinions from "all Men, who have Leisure, Inclination and Ability, to speak their Minds with Freedom."[13] In James Franklin's paper, decades before the American Revolution, we recognize the revolutionary spirit, and a public ethos. For what Voltaire exemplified in France, and what journalism professors today recognize as "the stock and trade" of *The Daily Show*, "exposing hypocrisy," was the highest badge of honor to both Franklins, both being in conflict with Puritan authority in New England.[14] James Franklin, in fact, was jailed for his parody of the witch-burner Cotton Mather, "Essay Against Hypocrites."[15]

People in the eighteenth century were regular fake news aficionados. Like many young people today, they preferred their news entertaining, playfulness to direct speech, pseudonymously expressed opinion to dogmatic assertion. Eran Shalev explains that the fake news was felt to accord with the dignity of "republican" autonomy.[16] It was often preferred that public discussions be initiated, not from the top down, *not*, that is, by specially authorized persons speaking *ex cathedra*, but more indirectly, from the bottom up, in the literary performances of pseudonymous persona. It wasn't accidental that "Publius" quilled the *Federalist Papers*, or that young Ben Franklin had his first literary success posing as the frisky middle-aged widow Silence Dogood.

Like Jon Stewart, Ben Franklin's Polly Baker did not speak from a position of authority. Polly Baker didn't offer *an abstract indictment* of the Puritanical legal code that deemed unwed mothers *criminals*. The "poor unhappy Woman" spoke in her own vernacular, boasting that her fifth bastard should earn, not a whipping, but "instead of a Whipping, to have a Statue erected to my Memory."[17] Like the traditional bard or storyteller, the fake news cares enough about the world to take sides, yet retains a playful respect for its audience. It satirizes the hypocrites without infringing on individual autonomy with fixed dogmas, elitist discourses, or uncontestable ideologies.

Separated by two centuries and many technological "advances," it is surprising how the news landscape of colonial America mirrors the fake news of today's Comedy Central. As *The Daily Show* is populated by a small team of "Senior Correspondents"—Larry Wilmore, "Senior Black Correspondent," Aasif Mandivi, "Senior Muslim Correspondent," and so on, so the colonial newspapers proliferated all manner of pseudonymous pundits. In New Jersey's *Constitutional Courant*, Freedom-lover Philoleutheros and Country-lover Philopatriae raged *pseudonymously* against the Stamp Act.[18] On the other side of the pond, while serving as colonial representative, Benjamin Franklin struck the pose of an aggressively patriotic Brit in the British papers. Under the pseudonym Vindex Patriae, "Defender of the Country," he presents the pro-Stamp Tax argument with obviously incompetent imperial hubris. Franklin then responded to his own fake news pieces in the pseudonymous voices of other more reasonable "Englishmen" who critiqued Vindex Patriae's "flimsey arguments" and "insolence, contempt and abuse."[19] Likewise Franklin's last satirical peacemaking effort before the war, "Rules by Which a Great Empire May be Reduced to a Small One," purported to be a "leaked" British document.[20] Franklin's reactionary posing for ulterior purposes cannot help but bring Colbert to mind. In fact, the affinities between Ben and Stephen are many, and profound. In just ten years Colbert will have played his beloved high-status idiot for as long as Franklin kept the Poor Richard Saunders shtick going. Two irrepressible Americans, equal parts goofiness and decency, each brash enough to claim, in his way, "I Am America (And So Can You!)"

The surprising similarities we find between the fake news of today and the pseudonymous creations of early Americans does not imply that all the fake news in the American colonies was fit to print, or that every Founding Father had a playful relation to reality worth emulating. As Fox News reporter and historian Eric Burns has it, in the colonial era there was a range of more and less reputable characters, more and less upstanding journalistic practices, fake news and *fake* fake news, if you will.[21] At one end of the spectrum was Sam Adams. Not just a "brewer and a patriot," but a muckraker so committed to the Revolution that he turned yellow fighting for the red, white, and blue. Adams notoriously fabricated stories to turn the tide of public opinion, falsely accusing British soldiers of "beating children, forcing their attention on young ladies, stealing merchandise from shopkeepers, and violating the Sabbath by getting drunk and racing horses through the streets of Boston."[22] On the other side of the ethical spectrum was the media mogul Franklin, who had his plump fingers in a whole network of colonial newspapers. Franklin stands out, even though "he deceived on occasion," because he did so *artistically*." He thought it "a better way to tell a story"; and because, "he believed his readers were sophisticated enough to know the ruse and understand that it served a deeper purpose."[23] Fake news aficionados take note: America's "first humorist," Ben Franklin, was, "as ethical a journalist as America produced in the eighteenth century" *because he was a fake news satirist* and didn't *seriously* deny being an artist, that is, a practitioner of the fake ne*ws* (although he did have much fun over the years in his faux disavowals of Poor Richard).[24] And we ourselves may judge his fake news from the principles elaborated in his "Apology for the Printers." Franklin explains that his tribe of newspapermen, "the printers," should be forgiven their fake news transgressions insofar as they have been "educated in the Belief, that when Men differ in Opinion, both Sides ought equally to have the Advantage of being heard by the Publick; and that when Truth and Error have fair Play, the former is always an overmatch for the latter."[25]

To one in search of an ethos for the contemporary Fifth Estate, comparisons with Franklin and Adams are irresistible. For we too have dodgy newspaper men, the like of Sam Adams, "journalists" who present *fake* fake news, straight propaganda expressed in imperatives and claiming all the exigencies of an absolute emergency. In an uncharacteristic moment of self-disclosure, the histrionic Glenn Beck, master of constitutional emergencies, "scholar" of the Founding Fathers, tells Brian Stelter and Bill Carter of *The New York Times* what he does *not* tell his audience, obviously not deeming them "sophisticated enough to know the ruse." Beck knows that he is a *fake* fake newsman; with the outward expression of sincerity, in fact, a "rodeo clown" with "great skill."[26] Rush Limbaugh, aptly pegged as "part vaudeville showman and part ward leader," likewise fits the bill.[27] Limbaugh clearly does *not* consider his listeners (the self-dubbed Dittoheads) "sophisticated enough to know the ruse." Or perhaps the fact that they call themselves "Dittoheads" implies that they have no desire to confront thought-provoking ruses. It's only when Limbaugh's diatribes cross the line and he finds himself under pressure (from his sponsors no doubt) that he makes a fuss about being an "entertainer ... [with] great song-and-dance routines."[28]

No doubt millions of people find Limbaugh entertaining, and apparently "edifying," as he is the 2009 recipient of CPAC's "Defender of the Constitution" award, a free-speech prize perversely inspired by Ben Franklin. "Perversely," one must insist, because Limbaugh's meteoric rise and billion-dollar mega-empire are the result of the very policies that have brought the Fourth Estate to the point of crisis. Limbaugh found himself at the right place at the right time, with a shtick well-suited to the Reagan Administration's *repeal* of the Fairness Doctrine, the FCC regulation that, since 1949, had required radio stations to provide free airtime to discuss the different sides of controversial opinions.[29] If only the folks at CPAC knew their history, they would have named the award for Sam Adams. The repeal of the Fairness Doctrine *is precisely the opposite* of the ethos expressed by James Franklin soliciting opinions from "all Men, who have Leisure, Inclination and Ability, to speak their Minds with Freedom." The repeal of the Fairness Doctrine is exactly counter to the ethos of Franklin's printers, "both Sides ought equally to have the Advantage of being heard by the Publick."

The Voice of the People

In the first version of this essay I discussed *The Daily Show* as a Fifth Estate agent in a few different respects, though it didn't occur to me to pose the question of an ethos. In the subsequent years I have discovered a whole phalanx of like-minded thinkers, and it has been most interesting to discover my essay cited by both satire skeptics and fake news aficionados. Because I cooked up my notion of the Fifth Estate by digging up insights from undergraduate days—Poli Sci 101—at the time I didn't fancy myself *original*. But I had *no idea* at all how *unoriginal* I was! I had no idea, that is, how many comrades I would discover similarly applying the lessons of Poli Sci 101. And credit where credit is due. Years before I put fingers to keyboard, Robert J. Thompson, Professor of Television and Radio at Syracuse University, was praising *The Daily Show* for asking questions in the lead-up to the second Iraq War. Here's Professor Thompson in 2004: "I'd go so far to say that … in some ways the fifth estate of comedy is able to keep the fourth estate of journalism in line."[30]

Professor Thompson, like many commentators, and many sympathetic to *The Daily Show*, can't quite reconcile himself to the seemingly lowly stature of the comedy genre. If there is an ethos of the Fifth Estate, it is apparently to be elaborated by "the public intellectual," not the comic qua comic. In a 2008 interview Thompson notes that Stewart is "tough"; he explains that, "Colbert and Stewart are public intellectuals and *they just happen* to be working in the idiom of comedy as opposed to in the industry of journalism" (my emphasis).[31] Two years later, in *The New York Times*, Thompson promoted Stewart to "advocate journalist." Thanks to his support for the 9/11 First Responders Bill stalled in Congress, Stewart left the lower rungs and joined the ranks of Edward R. Murrow and Walter Cronkite.[32]

Of course there is something right in the kudos Thompson extends to Stewart and company. In the first version of this essay I highlighted two epic moments when the fake news affected history, taking the Fourth Estate to the woodshed, as my grandfather would say. Is there anyone who was politically conscious in 2004 who can forget Stewart's charging Tucker Carlson and Paul Begala with "political hackery" on CNN's soon-to-be-cancelled *Crossfire*? Did not Colbert's tour de force hosting of the White House Correspondents' Association Dinner make for a night that will never be forgotten (May 3, 2006)? And yet there is a danger in ignoring Stewart's continual refusal to accept any such "promotion" to journalist. There is a risk in substituting "public intellectual" or "pundit" for "comedian." If we are to appreciate the ethos of the Fifth Estate, we must keep firmly in mind that the bard is not an authoritative expert. By contrast, Edward R. Murrow, "the conscience of CBS," who veritably reeked of gravitas and condescension, is one of the "priestly pundits," the "organized intelligence" envisioned by Walter Lippman:

> a professional press corps knowledgeable of social science that could interpret, not reduce, information so that citizens could understand and be persuaded to proper courses of action ... The journalist would join a technocratic elite which was possessed of skills to probe the nature of things and to communicate special knowledge to the mass public. Journalism would become not only an art but also a science. News would provide not stereotypes but a "picture of reality" on which citizens could act.[33]

Now, if, hypothetically speaking, the Fifth Estate were an actual institution, and it were necessary to apply for the position of "ethos elaborator," I wouldn't advise *The Daily Show* to list Professor Thompson as a reference. With all due respect, Stewart and Colbert aren't "public intellectuals," who just happen to be practicing in the field of comedy instead of the field of journalism.[34] It is not as latter-day Cronkites and Murrows, but as fake news satirists that they have ensured their place in a venerable lineage stretching at least as far back as Benjamin Franklin, lover of "pseudonyms, satires, and shams of every sort."[35] After Franklin (and other funny, pseudonymously inclined Framers), we find Mark Twain, Orson Wells, Charlie Chaplin, Alfred E. Newman, *Saturday Night Live*, and *The Onion*, among others. In fact, the American fake news Hall of Fame stretches pretty gosh darn far out, especially when one includes experimental theater, mockumentaries, culture jamming, and the style of gonzo journalism made famous by the late great Hunter S. Thompson.

And if any question regarding the origin of *The Daily Show*'s satirically inclined ethos should arise, rather than appealing to a rarified notion of pure journalism, one would be better served revisiting the eighteenth century and the habits and modes of expression known then. *The Daily Show* carries on the satirical tradition of the Enlightened American forebears, and one can recognize this literary legacy even in those epic historical moments that first appear to be straight journalism critique. To begin, Ben Franklin and his fellow colonists came by their satirical wits honestly: it was their inheritance as Englishmen after all. The Glorious Revolution of 1688 had established the supremacy of Parliament, religious tolerance, and the right of free speech, ushering in the Golden Age of British satire. Whether Whig or Tory, Loyalist or rebel, the men who enjoyed "the rights of Englishmen" knew their Pope and Swift, their Juvenal and Horace. Without question, satire was "the most popular and politically important literary form in early American political life."[36] Years before that first shot was heard around the world, the colonies were the scene of a "literary and ideological war," and when the Revolution came, "quills were wielded just as adeptly as muskets."[37] "Paper bullets" came hot off the constantly sizzling colonial presses. In quirky rebus puzzles, cartoons, epic ballads, folksongs, jokes, and jingles, King George and the Loyalists were caricatured, licketysplit. Satire wasn't just common or popular, it was *the* revolutionary medium. Even more fascinatingly, as Colin Wells explains, the American revolutionaries had a pronounced predilection for fake news:

American satirists were especially drawn, for instance, to writing verse parodies of other printed texts such as newspaper articles or official

> government documents. During the war broadsides proclaiming
> martial law or demanding the arrest of rebels were frequently answered
> by anonymous verse parodies ... ridiculing not only the colonial
> official who issued the proclamation but the language of political
> authority itself.[38]

Two hundred and fifty years have passed and the media have changed;
a fake news activist today requires the ability to blog, rather than,
say, any facility with iambic pentameter. Yet the same sorts of hijinks
are perpetrated: parody of official discourse, and mockery of the
language of political authority itself. Put another way, as once the
rebellious colonists, so today the folks from *The Daily Show* make it
their business to appropriate, mediate, and communicate fake news in
the dominant media modes of the powers that be.

Stewart's self-explanation to Bill Moyers as "a comedian who has
the pleasure of writing jokes about things that I actually care about,"
invites comparison to the great Roman satirist Juvenal's famous
phrase *insanible cacaethos scribendi*, "that incurable habit of writing."
One poet's pleasure is another man's addiction. For present purposes
the point is that Stewart, like Lewis Black, Jonathan Swift, and
the Roman original, Juvenal, has truck with righteous indignation
(*indignatio*), an emotion that we never see expressed with immediacy
by either Colbert or the gentle Horace.[39] But it is in this way that
Juvenalian satire pays back the world with words, which also seems to
reflect Stewart's self-description. And as we think back over the times
when Stewart has intervened directly in the world, taking the failing
Fourth Estate to task, for instance, as he did on CNN in 2004, or on
behalf of the First Responders in 2010, we shouldn't assume that the
comedian pundit talker guy has completely removed his mask. The
fact of the matter is that the expression of *indignatio*, a genuine feeling,
often essential in an ethos concerned with justice, is part of the
Juvenalian satirist's shtick.

Lee Roussof allows us to revisit another epic moment that offers
insight into just this question.[40] As Roussof revisits the Clusterf#@k to
the Poorhouse, he focuses on Stewart's vocational identity: journalist
or comedian? First it seems obvious: Stewart "actually functions
as something much more powerful and important than a simple
funnyman." But, in the end, Roussof concludes, it is *because* he is a
comedian, and therefore not bound by a journalist's standards of
"objectivity and detachment" that he actually is able to express the

gravitas that he does.[41] Exemplifying this point, at the end of his thesis Roussof reviews the drama of March 4, 2008. On that night *The Daily Show* broadcast a damning eight-minute video of CNBC pundits making ill-fated bank stock recommendations: Bear Stearns, AIG, and Merrill Lynch. The video is uncharacteristically somber, the denouement unexpected: Stewart looks into the camera and directly addresses CNBC: "Fuck you."

Roussof explains that in this moment Stewart, "becomes spokesman for his audience and for all the victims of the economic crisis ... [saying] what most Americans only wished they could say to the people who caused the financial crisis."[42] Juvenal likewise spoke for the everyman who felt disgust at the corruption and depravity of first-century Rome. In the famous first lines of Satire I, with so much demanding to be paid back, "it is hard *not* to write satire."[43] This is not the only side of Stewart of course, but a Juvenalian, Swiftian side is definitely present. Flirting with the force of *indignatio* that inspired Swift's "A Modest Proposal," there is a biting edge in *Earth (The Book)*, *posthumously* addressed, after we have "sucked her dry."

If Juvenal "punishes" with his satire, metaphorically "paying back" the world with his words, Horace self-consciously refuses to judge. Even when operating in poetic modes devoted to "blaming," Horace demands a more refined mode of discourse from himself, and invariably chooses expression in lighter modes of expression, "a laugh will cut the matter short."[44] Parallel to Colbert it appears, and Ben Franklin, he viewed vice as folly rather than evil and met it with playfully moralizing critiques and parodies, often made at his own expense: "it is a pleasure to play the fool." Consider for a moment the Super PAC saga that Stewart and Colbert elaborately unfolded in the wake of the Citizens United decision. Horror, resentment, and despair would be normal reactions in any citizen concerned with unlimited and anonymous corporate money at work in politics. Heroically steadfast in the face of inimical forces threatening disenfranchisement and demoralization, Colbert never fails in his Horatian ethos, "telling truths as he laughs."[45]

If anyone ever should need reminding that education can be fun, even when it concerns seemingly arcane legalese, they would do well to reacquaint themselves with Stephen Colbert's persona, pontificating neither "propaganda" nor "ideology," but rather "a playful way of addressing reality, one which necessarily assumes that there is more than one way of interpreting things."[46] Colbert, the master of Horatian sublation, never for a moment loses this plasticity, but always retains a playful relation to reality, and thus always preserves the possibility of his audience achieving more elevated potentials.

The Fifth Estate as a State of Mind

In the first version of the essay you are reading now I considered the Fifth Estate primarily as a corrective to the failing Fourth. In highlighting some of the virtual hijinks perpetrated by the Colbert Nation in the name of "truthiness" back in 2006, I *hinted* at the interlinked networks of the Fifth Estate. Reading generously one might discern an implicit ethos of critical reflection and media resistance in the piece. Ian Reilly, discussed above, has found useful my account of the *philosophical function The Daily Show* performs via its synthetic presentations of the news from multiple sources, the "metaview" we receive watching *The Daily Show* "covering the news media covering the news." From here Reilly immediately takes off with the idea that the satirical fake news helps us to "reframe" the issues at hand and embarks on his ambitious activist agenda. Flattering to me, and I did mean to indicate the fake news "metaview" providing a wedge against ideological manipulations.[47] But here there is something that speaks to the question of the ethos too; the Fifth Estate is somehow also a *state of mind*. Along these lines, in 2007 I suggested that the absurdist, critical tidbit of our "moment of Zen" takes us, if but momentarily, to a transcendent sphere, as if inoculating us against the "cynical onslaught of pandering infotainment."

About the same time as I was cooking up these observations for "The Fake News and the Fifth Estate," but unbeknownst to me, Ronald Jay Magill was also reckoning with the *philosophical* function of *The Daily Show* and the "Fifth Estate."[48] Magill too emphasizes the importance of media literacy, the function of the fake news in revealing the "operational strategies, false sentiments, and techno-aesthetics" of other programs.[49] But much more interesting and pertinent to our present quest for the ethos of the Fifth Estate, Magill hypothesizes that *The Daily Show* bespeaks a potential community of ironically-inclined *Romantic spectators* (yes! in the nineteenth-century sense of "Romantic irony"):

> Importantly, the Romantic of today finds a real connection, a sense of groundedness, with others through irony, with those who understand what is meant without having to say it, with those who also question the saccharine quality of contemporary commercial culture, with those who are certain that all diatribes of virtue-lament will turn out to have been made by some gambling, lying, hypocritical talk-show host/senator overly fond of interns/pages.[50]

Perhaps this potential community of Romantic ironists speaks to the as yet indeterminate content of the Fifth Estate? Does irony unify the denizens of the Fifth Estate, the disparate bloggers, activists, artists, and so on? Perhaps it is a moment of Romantic "groundedness" which Stewart experiences at the Rally to Restore Sanity, reporting to the crowd that he feels "good—strangely, calmly, good"?[51] His sanity is restored, not simply by media critique, however important this is (the media is "our immune system" and we become ill when "it overreacts to everything"). Stewart tells us himself, reflecting immediately after the Rally in noticeably specific terms: "We had some really incredible music performances here today. I hope you enjoyed them. We've had what some would *classify* as comedy as well."[52]

"Classify" indeed! While it might be coincidence, there's no mistaking the fact that the fake news' Rally to Restore Sanity brought together the fundamental elements of the comedy of Aristophanes, the most famous and profound of ancient Greek comic poets.[53] Stewart's closing remarks at the Rally, "A Moment of Sincerity," looks an awful like the *parabasis* in Old Comedy, the stepping out (transgression) in which the poet (or the chorus leader for the poet) directly addresses the audience. Stewart says he knows, "there are boundaries for a comedian pundit talker guy," but he need not worry as, knowingly or unknowingly, step by step, scene by scene, he has been following the ancient playbook. Don't be fooled by the low-key rhetoric, when, for instance, in the official announcement Stewart says that the Rally will be "less of a sausage fest" than the Million Man March. For even if Stewart and Colbert are not donning the four-foot dangling *phalloi* that were de rigueur in Old Comedy, with their ridiculous star-spangled, red, white, and blue pantsuits, they let us know they're wearing the twenty-first century American equivalents. Taking pages from the ancient playbook, Stewart and company take us (1) to the festival, "Woodstock, but with the nudity and drugs replaced by respectful disagreement"; (2) the contest (*agon*), Stewart versus Colbert, but also as Cat Stevens' (now Yusuf Islam's) "Peace Train" versus Ozzy's "Crazy Train"; (3) the transformation of the hero and chorus from belligerents to lovers (the O'Jays' "Love Train" trumps all); (4) finally, and most importantly, the inevitable happy ending, which for the ancients typically culminates in *hieros gamos*, a "sacred marriage" that connotes restoration, reconciliation, rejuvenation. In Aristophanes, this was a rally on every level, bringing peace, festivity, love, and often wisdom. In his Woodstock to restore respectful disagreement, Stewart speaks to the first official gathering of the Fifth Estate: "Sanity will always be and has always been in the eye of the beholder. To see you here today and the kind of people that you are has restored mine."

Notes

1. "Comedian pundit talker guy" is Jon Stewart's self-characterization in his concluding remarks at the October 30, 2010 Rally to Restore Sanity, "A Moment of Sincerity."
2. Ian Reilly, "The Satirical Fake News and the Politics of the Fifth Estate" (Unpublished dissertation, Literary Studies, University of Guelph), 106.
3. As Reilly rightly has it, when the Yes Men perpetrate a spectacular media hoax that raises the possibility that Dow *is* ready to pay compensation to the victims of the Bhopal chemical disaster, or that the Chamber of Commerce has reversed its position on climate change, they show "political satirists a way of regaining access to dominant channels of communication." Ibid., 216–217.
4. Ibid, 224.
5. Hannah Arendt, *Lectures on Kant's Political Philosophy* (Chicago: University of Chicago Press, 1982), 46.
6. Reilly, "The Satirical Fake News," 104.
7. Dan Nimmo and James E. Combs, *The Political Pundits* (New York: Praeger, 1992).
8. Ibid., 29.
9. Ibid., 51–52.
10. Pakinam Amer, "El Koshary: Egypt's Online 'Fake News' Paper," in *Egypt Independent* (November 18, 2009), www.egyptindependent.com/news/el-koshary-today-egypts-online-fake-news-paper, accessed January 30, 2013.

11. Willem Marx, "Bassem Youssef: Egypt's Jon Stewart," *Bloomberg Businessweek Lifestyle* (March 29, 2012), www.businessweek.com/articles/ 2012-03-29/bassem-youssef-egypts-jon-stewart, accessed February 7, 2013.
12. Jill Lepore, *The Whites of Their Eyes: The Tea Party's Revolution and the Battle over American History* (Princeton: Princeton University Press, 2012), 40.
13. Ibid., 31.
14. Rachel Smolkin, "What the Mainstream Media Can Learn from Jon Stewart," *American Journalism Review* (June/July 2012), www.ajr.org/ article.asp?id=4329, accessed January 30, 2013.
15. Jim Willis, *100 Media Moments that Changed America* (Santa Barbara, CA: Greenwood Press [ABC-CLIO], 2010), p. 3.
16. Eran Shalev, "Ancient Masks, American Fathers: Classical Pseudonyms during the American Revolution and Early Republic," *Journal of the Early Republic* 23 (2) (2003), 156.
17. Benjamin Franklin, "The Speech of Miss Polly Baker," originally published in *The General Advertiser* (April 15, 1747), *The Papers of Benjamin Franklin* 3 (1745–1750) (New Haven, CT: Yale University Press, 1961), 120.
18. Ralph Frasca, "Benjamin Franklin's Printing Network," *Pennsylvania History* 71 (4) (2004), 412–413.
19. Todd Thompson, "'Invectives … Against the Americans': Benjamin Franklin's Satiric Nationalism in the Stamp Act Crisis," *Journal of the Midwest Modern Language Association* 40 (1) (2007), 27.
20. Benjamin Franklin, "Rules by Which a Great Empire May be Reduced to a Small One," originally published in *The Public Advertiser* (September 11, 1773), www.franklinpapers.org, accessed January 30, 2013.
21. Eric Burns, *Infamous Scribblers: the Founding Fathers and the Rowdy Beginnings of American Journalism* (New York: Public Affairs, 2006).
22. Ibid., 148.
23. Ibid., 91.
24. Ibid.
25. Benjamin Franklin, "Apology for Printers," originally published in *The Pennsylvania Gazette* (June 10, 1731), *The Papers of Benjamin Franklin* 1 (1706–1734) (New Haven, CT: Yale University Press, 1959), 194.
26. Brian Stelter and Bill Carter, "Fox News's Mad, Apocalyptic, Tearful Rising Star," *New York Times* (March 29, 2009), www.nytimes.com/2009/ 03/30/business/media/30beck.html?_r=1&partner=rss&emc=rss, accessed January 30, 2013.
27. Jesse Walker, "The Age of Limbaugh," *Reason Foundation Magazine* (July 16, 2010), www.reason.org/news/show/age-of-limbaugh, accessed January 30, 2013.

28. "A Few Words for Michael Steele," *The Rush Limbaugh Show* (March 2, 2009), www.rushlimbaugh.com/daily/2009/03/02/a_few_words_for_michael_steele, accessed January 30, 2013.

29. For more on the Fairness Doctrine and its possible reinstatement, see *NOW*, PBS (December 17, 2004), www.pbs.org/now/politics/fairness.html, accessed January 30, 2013.

30. Robert J. Thomas cited by Mark de la Viña, "Political Humor Takes on a Nastier Tone," *San Jose Mercury News* (August 16, 2004), 1C, www.mercurynews.com, accessed January 30, 2013. (Note: this article is only accessible with a paid subscription at www.nl.newsbank.com/nl-search/we/archives?p_action=print&p_docid=104870749508A76A.)

31. Interview with Joe Windish, "Stephen Colbert: A Media Maestro Plays Philly" (April 14, 2008), http://themoderatevoice.com/18944/stephen-colbert-a-media-maestro-plays-philly-guest-voice, accessed January 30, 2013.

32. Bill Carter and Brian Stelter, "In 'Daily Show' Role on 9/11 Bill, Echoes of Murrow," *New York Times* (December 26, 2010), www.nytimes.com/2010/12/27/business/media/27stewart.html?pagewanted=all, accessed January 30, 2013.

33. Nimmo and Combs, *The Political Pundits*, 31, quoting from Walter Lippman, *Public Opinion* (New York: Macmillan, 1922), 233.

34. For a somewhat different perspective, see Terrance MacMullan, "Jon Stewart: The New *and Improved* Public Intellectual," in this volume.

35. Lepore, *The Whites of Their Eyes*, 64.

36. Colin Wells, "Satire," *Encyclopedia of the New American Nation*, ed. Paul Finkelman (New York: Charles Scribners' Sons, 2006), 158.

37. Ibid., 159.

38. Ibid.

39. For more on Juvenal, see Greg Littman, "Seriously Funny: Mockery as a Political Weapon," in this volume. For more on Swift, see John Scott Gray, "The Senior Black Correspondent: Saying What Needs to Be Said," also in this volume.

40. Lee Roussof, "Deconstructing Press Coverage of the Economic Meltdown: The Daily Show as the 5th Estate," *Brooklyn College Undergraduate Research Journal* 2, (2010), www.brooklyn.cuny.edu/pub/departments/bcurj/vol2.htm, accessed January 30, 2013.

41. Ibid., 15–16.

42. Ibid., 35–36.

43. *Juvenal and Perseus*, ed. and trans. Susanna Morton Braund (Cambridge, MA: Harvard University Press, 2004), 133 (Satire I, line 33).

44. Horace, *Satires, Epistles and Ars Poetica*, trans. H. Rushton Fairclough (Cambridge, MA: Harvard University Press, 2005 [1929]), 133 (Satires Book II, Satire I, line 86).

45. Ibid., 7 (Satires Book I, Satire I, line 24).

46. Ibid., 4.

47. Reilly, "The Satirical Fake News," 118 (in original version of my essay, 36).

48. Ronald Jay Magill, *Chic Ironic Bitterness* (Ann Arbor: University of Michigan Press, 2007).

49. Ibid., 46.

50. Ibid., 251.

51. Liz Brown, "Rally to Restore Sanity: Jon Stewart's Closing Speech" (full text), *examiner.com* www.examiner.com/article/rally-to-restore-sanity-jon-stewart-s-closing-speech-full-text, accessed January 30, 2013.

52. Ibid. (my emphasis).

53. The *locus classicus* remains Francis MacDonald Cornford's *The Origin of Attic Comedy* (Cambridge: Cambridge University Press, 1934). In the present context the virulently agitated protests that Cornford's work garnered, on the grounds that the comic festivals of reconciliation and restoration that he described were not particular to Greece but endemic to ancient fertility religions generally, seems rather a point in the theory's favor. Ancient Greek comedy is interesting insofar as it speaks to human possibility generally, not just a few dead white men. For more on the academic kerfuffle among pointy-headed classicists, see Erich Segal, *The Death of Comedy* (Cambridge, MA: Harvard University Press, 2001), 5–9.

Chapter 4

Seriously Funny
Mockery as a Political Weapon

Greg Littmann

The Daily Show is simultaneously one of the funniest television programs ever made and one of the most earnest voices calling for political change in the United States. On the surface, such a combination of the frivolous and the deeply serious is peculiar. The demand for political change rests on an insistence on facing the truth, yet comedy by its very nature relies on absurdity and distortion. On *The Daily Show*, Jon Stewart and the correspondents make false and outrageous claims.[1] Stewart informs the viewer, for instance, that he celebrated Thanksgiving the old-fashioned way, by feasting his neighbors and then killing them and taking their land; and that Fox News Chief Roger Ailes once admitted to him in a bar that the original slogan for Fox News was to be "A Fanatically Micro-Managed Media Fiefdom Where My Own Far-Right Agenda and Personal Sense of Victimhood Drive Every Aspect of the Operation ... and Balanced." Similarly, correspondent Wyatt Cenac assures us that Sarah Palin thinks that billboards are postcards from giants, while correspondent Samantha Bee announces that George W. Bush once molested her grandmother while John Kerry held her down with bags of money provided by gay French Jews. How can a program that trades in mockery, like *The Daily Show*, be an appropriate vehicle for political thought?

The Ultimate Daily Show and Philosophy: More Moments of Zen, More Indecision Theory,
First Edition. Edited by Jason Holt.
© 2013 John Wiley & Sons, Inc. Published 2013 by John Wiley & Sons, Inc.

The puzzle is an ancient one, and what we say about the role of *The Daily Show* will have implications for much of our cultural heritage. *The Daily Show* relies on up-to-the-minute commentary on breaking news, but the very act of providing comic commentary on the latest news is one of the oldest artistic traditions humanity has, and lies at the heart of our intellectual history. In the West, the first known political comedies appeared at about the same time as the first known works of political philosophy, around two and a half thousand years ago, in ancient Greece. The comic playwright Aristophanes (446–386 BCE), for example, mercilessly sends up the popular Athenian politician Cleon, implying that he is a thoughtless demagogue with a thirst for war. Aristophanes savages the conduct of the Peloponnesian War against Sparta with no less passion than *The Daily Show* would the American military involvement in Iraq and Afghanistan two and a half thousand years later.

No doubt, political mockery is much older than written comedy. After all, laughing at power, whether it consists in the mockery of enemies who threaten you or the leaders who push you around, seems to be a fundamental human instinct, one that children naturally develop very early. Likewise, political caricature per se was nothing new even back in Aristophanes' day—exaggeration is an intrinsic element of almost every image a ruler has ever commissioned of themselves. When the Egyptian pharaoh Ramses II (1279–1212 BCE) had himself carved as a giant, slaughtering his Hittite enemies on the battlefield, he was exaggerating his role and achievements to improve his political image—like American President Bush II landing on an aircraft carrier in a military flight suit to stand beneath a huge sign reading "MISSION ACCOMPLISHED."[2] However, Aristophanes and other Greek playwrights were doing something new to the historical record in that instead of exaggerating the positive to flatter a ruler's ego, they were exaggerating the negative in order to couch political criticism in the form of comedy. They were tempting audiences to the theater by offering them a few laughs and then feeding them messages about the state of Athens and the world.

Political mockery has been a mainstay of literature ever since. The Roman poet Juvenal (55–127) satirized the pomposity, corruption, and greed of his fellow Romans, while the Arabic poet al-Jahiz (776–869) leveled the same charges at his contemporaries in medieval Baghdad. For literature written in English, political mockery lies at the heart of the canon. The bitter criticism of church corruption implicit in the work of Geoffrey Chaucer (1343–1400) still offends conservative sensibilities today, while the depiction of the French as pretentious, foolish and effeminate in the plays of William Shakespeare (1564–1616) would surely offend liberal sensibilities if it appeared in the work of a modern writer. Furthermore, political mockery is as American as apple pie, the flag, and homicide by firearm. Benjamin Franklin (1706–1790) used satire to attack England's exploitation of the colonists, Mark Twain (1835–1910) used it to attack the practice of slavery, and Joseph Heller (1923–1999) used it to attack militarism and military bureaucracy. Clearly, to examine the role of *The Daily Show* is not just to consider the significance of one television program, however influential, but to examine the role of an artistic tradition that is a fundamental part of our culture.

The Politics of Laughter

Why engage in political mockery like that seen on *The Daily Show*? Obviously, we like to be entertained, and *The Daily Show* is very funny; but like the work of other political satirists throughout history, *The Daily Show* also serves to promote a political agenda. While *The Daily Show* is willing to target individuals from across the political spectrum, the program is hardly neutral on issues such as whether Americans should receive universal healthcare, whether the wars in the Middle East were a good idea, and whether America should torture its prisoners. One traditional justification for political mockery is that the shame of being satirized would cause wicked people to change their ways. Juvenal said of the satirist that "his hearers go red; their conscience freezes with their crimes, their innards swear in awareness of unacknowledged guilt."[3]

This is a beautiful idea in theory. Who wouldn't want to see media mogul Rupert Murdoch respond to being lampooned by *The Daily Show* by reforming his character, perhaps after the recent segment on Murdoch's phone-hacking scandal, the one labeled "Citizen Shame" that ends with Jon Stewart's appeal "C'mon, Rupert Murdoch! Don't shit on my chest and tell me it's Vegemite!" Imagine Murdoch appearing tearfully on the show to apologize for his past behavior and to thank Stewart for showing him where he went wrong! However,

I don't think that Juvenal's hope of reforming people through laughing at them is realistic. In fact, mocking someone is a *particularly* bad tool for making a point to them. People who are mocked feel disrespected and people tend not to listen to those they think are disrespecting them.

A more likely benefit of political mockery is that it keeps important political issues on people's minds. It may well be that no hateful racist ever reformed their character out of shame as a result of reading Mark Twain's *Huckleberry Finn* or *Pudd'nhead Wilson*. However, novels like these help to keep racism in the public consciousness, making such works useful political tools. It is in this way that *The Daily Show* has an important positive social effect. We can't expect Glenn Beck to stop saying crazy stuff just because Jon Stewart called him "a guy who says what people who aren't thinking are thinking." But jokes about Beck and other venomous political entertainers can help to remind the viewer about what dangerous nonsense many people listen to and take seriously. Similarly, it's unlikely that any warmongering politicians will reexamine their lives because correspondent Stephen Colbert satirized their attitudes with the advice, "We won. Rebuilding is for losers. Time to party. And then it's off to Syria for the next invasion." Yet jokes like these can help remind a public with a short attention span about the ongoing American commitments in the Middle East and the dangers of applying simplistic military solutions to complex political and economic problems.

Besides, Juvenal's justification of political mockery on the grounds that it shames its targets into reform offers no defense for all of that political mockery, on *The Daily Show* and throughout history, that doesn't take the form of fair criticism. Satire is exaggeration based on observation. The satirist presents a distorted image of the truth in order to highlight certain features of it, holding them up for public condemnation. Much of the *Daily Show* takes this form. Stewart explained to Bill Moyers on *NOW*: "I think we don't make things up. We just distill it to, hopefully, its most humorous nugget. And in that sense it seems faked and skewed just because we don't have to be objective or pretend to be objective. We can just put it out there."

However, a lot of political satire, including satire on *The Daily Show*, is unrelated to any justified political complaint. For example, pointing out the uncanny resemblance between one-time Republican

National Committee Chairman Michael Steele and a certain disgruntled muppet on *Sesame Street* who can't get good service in Grover's restaurant is not to point out any flaw in Michael Steele's behavior or platform. It *is* observational humor: Michael Steele *does* look like a muppet. But the observation is not politically relevant—George Washington had the face of an elderly lady eternally on the verge of throwing up, but he served well as president.

Likewise, *The Daily Show* was quick to notice that a double-meaning could be read into claims by members of the Tea Party movement that they would be "tea-bagging" Washington politicians, providing fuel for what Jon Stewart described as "hours of scrotum-based humor." (I had to look up what "tea-bagging" was when *The Daily Show* first started making these jokes. I don't think we have this in Illinois.) The gags are funny, but suggesting that members of the Tea Party movement would like to put their balls where they don't belong isn't to make an observation about any genuine flaws the Tea Party might have. It's just to mock the way that some of its members speak.

Again, *The Daily Show* is following an ancient tradition by peppering its political comedy with jabs that have no political justification. The Athenian Molon was famous enough in his day to be swiped at by Aristophanes in his play *The Frogs*, but Molon's sole legacy to posterity is that Aristophanes thought he was hilariously short. Similarly, when Juvenal himself tells us in his fourth satire that the consul Montanus was so fat that his stomach dragged on the ground, or that Montanus' compatriot Crispinus wore so much perfume that he was "more aromatic than two funerals put together,"[4] his satire of these politicians offers no politically relevant criticism.[5] If we dismiss *The Daily Show* for indulging in political satire that makes no relevant political point, we must do the same to a great deal of our cultural heritage.

Furthermore, some political mockery doesn't involve satire at all, because it isn't based on observation but sheer invention. For example, when *The Daily Show* popularized the definition of the word "santorum" as "the frothy mixture of lube and fecal matter that is sometimes the byproduct of anal sex," the show wasn't making a satirical observation about the policies or personality of candidate for the 2012 Republican Party presidential nomination, Rick Santorum. They were just making a rude word out of his name. The name-calling may be specifically intended to remind us about Santorum's intolerance towards homosexuals, but no observation is offered beyond the insinuation that Rick Santorum is smelly.

Such non-satirical mockery is, yet again, an ancient and persistent element of our culture. In Aristophanes' play *The Clouds*, the philosopher Socrates travels from place to place in a flying basket, not because Socrates ever invented anything, but just because Aristophanes thought it was a suitably ridiculous way to travel. Similarly, in Juvenal's second satire, he describes in creative detail the horror that the souls of Romans from previous generations would feel upon meeting the souls of corrupt modern Romans in the afterlife, even though Juvenal also notes that the existence of an afterlife is a fable that only a child would believe. If we dismiss *The Daily Show* for indulging in political mockery that is not even satirical but simply absurd, we shall again have to dismiss much of our cultural heritage.

The Dark Side of Mockery

One legitimate concern we might have about the use of mockery as a political tool is that mockery can discourage people from listening to others and taking what they have to say seriously. We notice this effect most easily when the mockery is coming from someone we disagree with. When Rush Limbaugh calls feminists "feminazis," he's dismissing what they have to say without *addressing* what they have to say, or presenting any evidence that they are wrong. We can expect a significant proportion of Rush's audience to follow his lead, dismissing political viewpoints, not because they have considered them and found them lacking, but because Rush mocked them on the show. Most of us accept that the censoring of political opinions is always or almost always wrong. Yet the damage often done by political mockery is of much the same kind as that done by censorship. That is, political mockery often leads to ideas not being heard.

Obviously, political mockery differs importantly from censorship in that political mockery does not restrict anyone's freedoms. Rush Limbaugh may insist that women who march in protest against sexual harassment in the workplace are doing so because they are upset that *they* aren't the ones being sexually harassed, but nobody twists the listener's arm to force them to be dismissive about sexual harassment.

All the same, enough people are willing to use mockery as a substitute for reasoned thought that Limbaugh and similar entertainers do considerable damage to the political discourse in the United States. The political rhetoric in the United States has grown increasingly angry and combative, with paranoid vilification of people one disagrees with taking the place of reasoned debate. For many Americans, the closest they get to hearing the political opinions of those they disagree with is hearing them mocked and distorted by entertainers. Programs like *The Rush Limbaugh Show*, *The Sean Hannity Show*, and *The O'Reilly Factor* rely on mockery to push their agendas just as heavily as *The Daily Show* does, even though the mockery is intended less to make the viewer laugh than to convince the viewer on political points without engaging their faculties of reason.

Of course—unlike such programs as *The Rush Limbaugh Show*, *TheSean Hannity Show*, and *The O'Reilly Factor*—*The Daily Show*'s political agendas tend to be sane and constructive. You may or may not agree, depending on where you stand on the political spectrum, but I'm sure that I'm not alone among fans of *The Daily Show* in thinking that more often than not, the writers are on the correct side of the fence. It might be argued that the use of political mockery by *The Daily Show* is justified on these grounds alone. If the political views that people might pick up from watching *The Daily Show* are the correct political views, then doesn't that make *The Daily Show* a positive political force, even if viewers were to rely on mockery rather than informed reason when forming their political opinions? We need to be careful about drawing that conclusion because it is based on the same rationale that Limbaugh's listeners could give for basing their views on Rush's mockery.

It can be tempting to view the battle for the public's political support in terms of making sure that enough people express the right political views, rather than making sure that they understand *why* those are the right political views. After all, ultimate power in a democracy lies at the ballot box, and at the ballot box, a voter's impact is restricted to a few simple multiple-choice decisions. If the American people do well enough on these "exams," we get freedom and compassionate government. If they do badly enough, we get poverty, war, and cruelty. It's thus easy to think that drilling the public in the right answers is all that matters, regardless of whether people are persuaded by reasoned arguments or just dismiss the alternatives because they were roundly mocked on television.

However, as enticing as this view might be for someone desperate to see an electoral victory, exchanging mockery for reasoned analysis is ultimately dangerous to society, even when directed by good intentions. Once again, a comparison between political mockery and political censorship can help demonstrate the problem. The aim of a political censor may well be to make sure that good political ideas are spread while bad political ideas are not. Yet it doesn't follow that the censor is a force for political good, even if the censor supports the right political policies. There is value in the spread of ideas even in the case of ideas that seem bad to us.

Mockery, Censorship, and the Free Spread of Ideas

The two best arguments I know against censorship were presented by the nineteenth-century English philosopher John Stuart Mill (1806–1873, no relation to Jon Stewart) in his political treatise *On Liberty*. Firstly, we can never know with complete certainty that the opinion we are suppressing is wrong. Mill wrote, "All silencing of discussion is an assumption of infallibility."[6] Secondly, it is good for people to hear false opinions because it will allow them to gain a better understanding of *why* those opinions are false. Mill wrote that the spread of false opinion allows people to have "the clearer perception and livelier impression of truth, produced by its collision with error."[7]

How does this relate to *The Daily Show* and the issue of political mockery? If a viewer of *The Daily Show* were to be politically swayed by mockery rather than by reason, if they were to fail to fairly consider the ideas held by targets of *The Daily Show*'s jokes, then the effect would be the same as if the state had prevented them from hearing those ideas in the first place. Free public discussion is essential for just the reasons Mill gave, but such discussion is only of benefit if we actually *listen* to the people we disagree with and give their ideas fair consideration. We must consider them for two important reasons: firstly, because we are capable of making mistakes, we might find out that the people we've been disagreeing with were right all along; secondly, we must consider them because by refuting them, we gain a firmer understanding of why they are false, and so a firmer grasp on the truth.

Of course, in the case of some of *The Daily Show*'s targets, the chance that the views being attacked are *correct* seems extremely small. For example, *The Daily Show* loves to make fun of Rush Limbaugh, with Jon Stewart telling us, among other things, that Limbaugh understands so little about the need for contraception because he has only ever had sex by drugging women into unconsciousness. Can we take seriously the suggestion that we must give the ideas of *Rush Limbaugh* a hearing on the grounds that for all we can know, he might be right?

Keep in mind, if Rush Limbaugh is right, then (among other things) president Obama intends to lead a war on conventional marriage, liberals should have their speech controlled to prevent the spread of liberal ideas, and the abuse of prisoners at Abu Ghraib, so graphically captured in unauthorized photographs, was nothing but a little harmless blowing off of steam. Even the idea that Rush is right on one or two significant points amidst all the nonsense seems rather farfetched. Still, even if the probability that a given view is right seems extremely small to us, Mill is correct that giving all views a hearing provides the best environment for truth to come to light. Limbaugh may have no useful insights to bring to the table, but by having a policy of not dismissing what anyone has to say without considering it first, we are less likely to miss hearing someone who *does* have useful insights that simply clash with our preexisting beliefs.

Further, Mill is surely also right that by listening carefully to incorrect opinions, we are in a better position to appreciate what is *wrong* with them, and exactly where false reasoning has led the speaker astray. We might, for example, agree with the writers of *The Daily Show* that the mainstream media is usually biased against the Palestinians in discussing the Israeli–Palestinian conflict: "It's the Möbius strip of issues, it only has one side!" announces Jon Stewart. Yet it's still useful to listen to those who argue that Israel has acted entirely, or almost entirely, appropriately, and that all significant blame lies on the Palestinian side. If we are to reject this view of events in the Middle East, then we must understand why it doesn't match up to reality. By analyzing exactly what is *wrong* with what is being said, we can strengthen our own grasp of history.

A public who voted in accordance with which TV shows make them laugh would be a disaster waiting to happen. All that it would take to shift their views is a successful new comedy. It's true that politically extreme comedians (along with conservative comedians in general for some reason), are rarely particularly funny (your tastes may differ—some people find Ben Stein hilarious). However, we can't take it as a given that comedic talent will always be distributed in roughly the same proportion as political sense, nor that the public perception of what's humorous will remain as it is now. Seventy years ago, the American people thought that *The Three Stooges* were pretty damn funny. Who knows what people will think is funny seventy years from now?

The ancient Greek philosopher Plato (429–347 BCE) pointed out in his dialogue *Meno* that people who are simply taught *what* to believe, without understanding *how* we know these things to be true, are unreliable. He reasoned that people who are convinced on some point just because they were told it's true might become convinced of the opposite just because someone tells them that *that's* true. On the other hand, those who understand how we know the truth won't change their minds just because someone else insists on a falsehood. Plato wrote, "True opinions, as long as they stay put, are a fine thing and do us a whole lot of good. Only they tend not to stay put for very long. They're always scampering away from a person's soul. So they're not very valuable until you shackle them by figuring out what makes them true"[8]

So, for instance, if the only reason that someone believes that there are two sides to the Israeli–Palestinian conflict is that Jon Stewart said so on *The Daily Show*, then they might change their opinion when they hear someone else on television state that Israel has done nothing wrong. On the other hand, if someone has a firm enough grasp on history to understand *why* it's true that there are two sides to the conflict, then they aren't going to change their mind just because they hear someone claim that the conflict is a clash between the forces of good and evil.

The Place of Mockery in Politics

Of course, there are enormous differences between political mockery as we see it on *The Daily Show* and political mockery as we see it on shows like *The Rush Limbaugh Show*, *The Sean Hannity Show*, and *The O'Reilly Factor*. The most important of these is that Stewart and the team bill themselves as comedians and *The Daily Show* runs on Comedy Central. As Stewart explained to Tucker Carlson on *Crossfire*, "You're on CNN. The show that leads into me is puppets making crank phone calls." The greatest problem with Rush Limbaugh is not that he holds terrible political views nor that he mocks the people he disagrees with politically; the greatest problem with Rush Limbaugh is that he tells his audience to take him seriously as a source of political wisdom, while using mockery, wild exaggeration, and sheer invention in place of well-reasoned arguments. Mockery, wild exaggeration, and sheer invention are also *The Daily Show*'s stock in trade, but *The Daily Show* never suggests that we should treat its comedy as a substitute for educating ourselves about politics and the world. Nor does *The Daily Show* ever indicate to its viewers that they shouldn't listen to the political figures who are mocked on the show. When Jon Stewart announced that the tax plan introduced by the second president Bush would lead to a future of "subsistence farming and roving motorcycle gangs," he was clearly making a joke. When Rush Limbaugh announced that president Obama "hates this country," and that his philosophy appeals to "people with miserable, meaningless lives," he treated it as serious political commentary. Rush's mockery thus serves to discourage people from listening to the political views of those he disagrees with, and to rely on Rush for their opinions rather than reasoning things through for themselves. Like a censor, Rush functions to shield the public from considering different ideas. If misused, *The Daily Show* could have a similar effect. Frighteningly, studies by Pew Research Center for the People and the Press consistently show that many people under 30 rely on *The Daily Show* for their political information. Mill, on the other hand, believed that "the only way in which a human being can make some approach to knowing the whole of a subject, is by hearing what can be said about it by persons of every variety of opinion, and studying all modes in which it can be looked at by every character of mind."[9]

Political mockery has always carried with it the danger of mockery being used as a substitute for reasoned thought. Aristophanes' play *The Clouds* paints an outrageously inaccurate image of Socrates, presenting the poor philosopher as an affluent con man, using slippery reasoning to trick people out of their money. Unfortunately, this depiction influenced the public perception of Socrates in Athens and was one of the factors leading to his unjust trial and execution (two and a half thousand years later, philosophers are still bitter about this). As for Juvenal, while he attacked greed, corruption, and cruelty in Rome, he reserved his greatest contempt for foreigners and low-born upstarts who were getting ahead in Rome through clever-ness and industry, while Romans of good breeding like himself had to choose between poverty and working for a living. His contempt for homosexuals was enormous, though like many moral commentators today, he combined his passionate disgust with a morbid fascination with the awful things he imagined homosexuals getting up to. Even philosophers weren't beyond Juvenal's condemnation, his main complaint being that as soon as the philosophy meetings are over, we have the most incredible wild gay transvestite sex parties (I've *never* witnessed this, but perhaps I'm not invited). Clearly, if people blindly took Juvenal's advice, the effects would be socially harmful. The same applies for very many others who've traded in political mockery, historically, and in the present day.

As citizens in a democracy, we must consume media in a respon-sible manner. If we are passive recipients of opinions, or if we rely on mockery rather than reason when deciding on, defending, or promoting our political beliefs, then we do social harm in the long term. Political mockery has done a lot of damage in the United States, and while most of this harm has come from the political right, people from anywhere in the political spectrum are capable of relying on mockery instead of argument when thinking about or discussing politics. Jon Stewart explained to *Rolling Stone*:

> We are not warriors in anyone's army. And that is not trying to be self-deprecating. I'm proud of what we do. I really like these two shows. I like making 'em. I like watching them. I'm really proud of them. But I understand their place. I don't view us as people who lead social movements.[10]

Stewart is wise not to regard himself as the leader of a social movement or to see *The Daily Show* as an appropriate source of news or information. All the same, *The Daily Show* is a powerful tool for political reform because it has a capacity to keep important political issues in the public consciousness. Of course, the appeal of the show is not that it's politically important, but that it's hilarious. I don't love *The Daily Show* because it's politically useful; I love *The Daily Show* because it makes me laugh. Yet it's precisely *The Daily Show*'s ability to make us laugh that makes it politically useful—people are reminded about important political issues as a side effect. Jon Stewart and the team behind *The Daily Show* may not be warriors in anybody's army, but signing up to take and give orders in the regular army isn't the only way to contribute to a war effort. Sometimes, the best way to help the cause may be to kick back and make some jokes about where other people put their balls.

Notes

1. For more on the relationship between fiction and truth, see Michael Gettings, "The Fake, the False, and the Fictional: *The Daily Show* as News Source," in this volume.
2. For other historical examples, see Alejandro Bárcenas, "Jon the Cynic: Dog Philosophy 101," in this volume.
3. Juvenal, *Sixteen Satires*, trans. Peter Green (London: Penguin, 1999), 7.
4. Ibid., 27.
5. It might be argued that all mockery of political figures is politically relevant in that it serves to remind people that political figures are mere human beings, not to be idolized. Certainly, politicians have always been eager to assume superhuman authority. In Juvenal's Rome, it had been customary to declare the emperor's gods after their deaths. In the modern USA, it is merely customary for political figures to speak on *behalf* of God.
6. John Stuart Mill, "On Liberty," in *On Liberty and The Subjection of Women* (London: Penguin, 2007), 19.
7. Ibid., 18.
8. Plato, *Meno*, trans. Lesley Brown (London: Penguin, 2006), 130.
9. Mill, "On Liberty," 27.
10. Maureen Dowd, "America's Anchors," *Rolling Stone* (October 2006).

Chapter 5

Keeping It (Hyper) Real
Anchoring in the Age of Fake News

Kellie Bean

Stephen Colbert and Jon Stewart are *not* the *only* purveyors of fake news, but they are among the few media figures willing to admit it. For its part, *The Colbert Report* reminds us of political pundits who seem like fakers (yet call themselves "real") with Colbert's over-the-top lampooning of Fox News' Bill O'Reilly. And *The Daily Show* exposes fake news with Stewart's dogged examination of actual news stories and reportage. Both men enact the typical, self-consciously performative, anchor role (in a broad sense, since Stewart performs a more traditional anchor role than Colbert, who more closely resembles an op-ed political pundit). Following the standards of the day, both offer up a surplus of (mock) outrage and indignation when reporting carefully selected bits of "news." On any given day, the performances of these fake anchors are no more outrageous, no more theatrical or self-conscious, than those anchors hosting actual news programs.

Fake news looks a lot like actual news (think here of *The Onion*). But the content of fake news deliberately calls attention to the failure of conventional mainstream "news" to reliably deliver a verifiable truth, or accurately report world events.[1] Both *The Colbert Report* and *The Daily Show* do precisely this, and both shows comment frankly on this failure as culturally significant. Fake news is arguably an invention of the Left, and this identifiable ideological bent suggests

The Ultimate Daily Show and Philosophy: More Moments of Zen, More Indecision Theory, First Edition. Edited by Jason Holt.
© 2013 John Wiley & Sons, Inc. Published 2013 by John Wiley & Sons, Inc.

that fake news is satiric: political critique and commentary designed to call out folly, vice, and mischief. As we'll see, both *The Colbert Report* and *The Daily Show* push fake news beyond satire. Rather than scrutinizing the target of their critique, they embody it instead. As a result, they enact the postmodern condition described in the philosophical works of Jean Baudrillard (1929–2007). In Baudrillard's terms, these shows are only possible in an age when news has become a simulacrum of "news," an image of "news" radically unmoored from verifiable reality. The simulacrum functions to (1) reiterate itself (since it can't *mean* anything else, it is its own reason for being), and (2) distract from its lack of meaning. Images are shiny things, and we can't help but look for meaning in them, until finally images stand in for the meaning lost and we (as consumers of massive mass media) lose track of the fact that images have taken on a life of their own apart from meaning. Simulated news now stands in for what once actually was the news.

Baudrillard's World[2]

Certain philosophers of postmodernity, including Jean Baudrillard, take as their starting point that contemporary culture is defined by technology/media. Cultural institutions, mores, and even interpersonal experience must be seen as at the very least influenced by, if not entirely defined by, media. Media stands between us and the real, where "the real" represents actual experience, verifiable data, and "the media" represents the technology through which we observe and understand those things. In postmodern philosophy, this configuration permanently alters our manner of perceiving, and eliminates the possibility of directly experiencing information. In fact, *The Colbert Report* and *The Daily Show* so perfectly enact Baudrillard's theories of media, they seem at times designed specifically to prove his notions correct. For example, after his opening monologue Jon Stewart will often call on a "Senior Correspondent" to comment on the topic at hand. Correspondents join Stewart at the desk or appear "on location" in front of a green screen showing stock, sometimes meaningless, footage. On one night Stewart welcomes Aasif Mandvi as "Senior Muslim Correspondent" and on another he introduces Mandvi as "Senior Middle East Correspondent." On the evening John

McCain announced Sarah Palin as his running mate, "Senior Female and Women's Issues Correspondent" Samantha Bee appeared at the desk across from Stewart "with more on this [important event]" (August 29, 2008). Stewart asked how she felt about the extraordinary achievement for women, since Bee had been so keen on Hilary Clinton's run for President. Bee responded, "It's amazing, Jon, and as a proud vagina-American myself, I can tell you I'll be voting for McCain in November." Stewart then asked, "That's it? You just vote for whoever has a … [*trails off*]?" He then pointed out, with apparent growing confusion, "but in many ways Governor Palin is the ideological opposite of Senator Clinton." "Oh, yes," Bee answered, as if talking to a small child, "but she's her gynecological twin." Mocking the single-minded, ideologically self-reflexive posture that character-izes news analysis on the Left and Right, Bee clings to a single issue and refuses to renounce it or consider alternatives. She likes Sarah Palin for Vice President for the same reason that she liked Hilary Clinton for President. It's the only standard for winning her vote. "The thing is," she explains, "they both have vaginas."

Baudrillard begins his famous discussion of simulation and media this way: "We live in a world where there is more and more information and less and less meaning."[3] The "vagina-American" bit illustrates this claim: Bee offers nothing meaningful, but looks earnestly into the camera, makes her empty argument with seriousness and, finally, conveys no new information. With one exception—and this is the Baudrillardian point—Bee's circular argument reinforces her momen-tary identity as "Senior Female and Women's Issues Correspondent"—and nothing else. Ours is a media-saturated world. Hardware stands between us and reality in the form of screens, particularly computer and television screens. Consider the enormous digital signage in places like Times Square, or the Jumbotron, where we watch digitized versions of ourselves watching digitized versions of ourselves visiting Times Square; where we can watch the projected images of a band whose performance we are attending rather than looking directly at the musicians themselves; where we confirm close plays in a sporting event, the virtual image carrying more authority than the witnessed event. Such virtual experiences have come to dominate our daily lives, to mediate our interaction with the larger world. Delivered to us as, and converted to, images—flat, virtual, unreal—that world is no longer real, but imaginary, a product of an invention, an invention that bears no organic, no necessary, relationship to us and our world, but which we have embraced. What is lost, according to this philosophy, is the familiar system of communication. Simply put, we tend to think of communication this way: us—[sign]—meaning. Or, apropos of news, us—[anchor/show]—news. Think of signification in this case as a vector running from us (audience/reader) through language (sign) to clear comprehension of meaning. We assume the news in particular to be a generally reliable transmitter of accurate data/information: our window on the world.

This assumption is no longer tenable, because today's media conveys meaning—or signifies—through images, and images have subsumed both ends of the system described above. In the wake of postmodernity, images have evolved from standing as "the reflection of a profound reality" to having "no relation to any reality whatsoever," and finally, to being their "own pure simulacrum."[4] In other words, images signify *themselves*, assuring their continued existence. They are now in and of themselves their own reason for being. We live captivated and enslaved by images, a condition Baudrillard describes as our "brute fascination for images."[5] His philosophy concerns the lure of media images, which *seem* to mean, when in fact they have replaced meaning with its simulacrum: images that resemble the signs we once used to gain genuine access to lived experience, or to acquire knowledge. The implications? Images are inherently not the thing they signify/point to; they are unmoored from the real. Therefore, if they now constitute what was once real, we no longer have access to the real through them. Yet—and here's the Baudrillardian rub—we have grown increasingly dependent upon images to gather information, create knowledge, see, feel, and understand the world around us.

Key terms to help clarify Baudrillard's work and how it illuminates postmodern features of *The Colbert Report* and *The Daily Show* include the following:

- "The real": That which can be experienced directly, unmediated. In order to make this term a noun, theorists add the definite article "the."
- "Sign": An image/piece of language that "exchanges for" meaning, indeed guarantees this exchange. In Baudrillardian terms, media images preempt this exchange, leaving images to signify only a lack of meaning.

- "Simulation": Modern media images devour/destroy meaning and instead replace lived experience, authentic feeling with a virtual copy. Signs "dissimulate that there is nothing";[6] this is the postmodern condition of signs.
- "Simulacrum": Image that is an indicator of no meaning existing beyond itself, a sign that is always exchanged only for itself.
- "Hyperreal": The condition of being "more real" than the real, describes simulacra.

In these terms, fake news takes as its subject the "simulated" news—or mainstream news. However, according to Baudrillard, modern media images cannot be properly said to fake meaning, because the term "fake" suggests a kind of mistake, a misunderstanding, signification just missing the mark. Baudrillard argues that in this age images pretend that there is meaning to signify where there is none. It's not that news images are mistakes, that we've misunderstood them, that they've missed the target. There *is* no target. There's nothing to fake.

The Walking Talking Hyperreal

The Colbert Report and *The Daily Show* work as both entertainment and, significantly, as useful sources of the actual news of the day. However, Stewart and Colbert don't serve up fake news in precisely the same manner. Whereas Colbert maintains a seamless hyper-performativity, Stewart offers his viewers the opportunity to identify with the disjunction between reported news and lived experience. "Stephen Colbert" is a walking talking simulacrum. For example, *The Colbert Report* routinely features a segment, called "The Wørd," in which Colbert parses the language of a recent event or controversy, ostensibly to buttress his faux conservative argument. This bit mocks the habit of some anchors and pundits (mostly "Papa Bear" Bill O'Reilly) to appear to step outside their newsman role, become a concerned citizen, and deliver a rant against what can only be described as an offense to all things good (or to the show's political bent). The segment features a split screen, with Colbert on the left and graphics on the right displaying the word whose meaning he is dissecting. The projected word changes into informed response, elaboration, and interpretation to his rant and consistently undermines (even mocks) his ostensible argument.

In a piece on abstinence education, for example, Colbert introduces the controversy by explaining, "I am a big proponent of abstinence education, which is proven effective with only one exception: it doesn't work" (April 18, 2012). He moves onto the evening's Wørd, "Gateway Hug." He explains that the problem with abstinence education is that it doesn't teach students to abstain from enough activities; for example, the activities that lead to activities that lead to sex, like "first base, second base." As he speaks, the "Wørd" changes from "Gateway Hug" to "Charging the Mound," rendering his claims mildly vulgar and patently offensive (and pretty funny.) When he insists that "kissing and hugging are just the last stop before the train pulls into 'Groin Central Station,'" the graphic flashes "Balls Aboard!" Finally, when he asks, "You know what really leads to leading to sex?" up comes "Joining Secret Service." The show makes an argument against political sexual hypocrisy by appearing not to. Colbert mocks abstinence education as a bad idea, by appearing to endorse it, then allowing the medium itself to undermine that stand and make his case.

As a walking, talking model of the hyperreal, Stephen Colbert can seem more like Bill O'Reilly than even Bill O'Reilly does. In this case, Colbert enacts Baudrillard's notion of the hyperreal, which argues that "signs are dedicated exclusively to their recurrence as signs."[7] In other words, the media personality O'Reilly can only be experienced by us as an indicator of an image, not an irreducible reality. So the anchor "Bill O'Reilly" is an image of an anchor we know as "Bill O'Reilly" and if we were to meet the flesh and bone O'Reilly we could not comprehend his identity outside of the mediated system that transmits him into our homes and lives. That is, even the flesh and bone anchor can only signify the media image; can only refer back to the media image that is now permanently imposed between us and the thing itself. This is the reverse of watching an anchor like Walter Cronkite and being impressed that the picture we see confirms the existence of an actual human being. Now, anchors are also celebrities of the highest order, and we are confronted with images of Bill O'Reilly, Katie Couric, Keith Olbermann, or Anderson Cooper, for example, on billboards, late night talk shows, in the supermarket checkout lane, on programs like *Entertainment Tonight*, keeping their image(s) in an endless feedback loop guaranteeing their status as signs of signs. This process is highlighted in Colbert's famous portrait. Hanging over the fireplace of his set, the original portrait featured Colbert standing before the same mantle with his portrait hanging above it. This painting has been through no fewer than five iterations and now features images of Colbert five-deep, receding into the background, each "Colbert" striking a different, though equally august, pose in front of the same fireplace. These portraits-in-a-portrait use one simulacrum—a painting of a man posing as "Stephen Colbert," a fictional character—as the "meaning" behind each subsequent portrait. Since "Stephen Colbert" doesn't exist in reality, there is no meaning behind these images, a perfect display of Baudrillard's notion of the simulacrum.[8]

Like the "real" news show it spoofs, *The Colbert Report* opens with the anchor sitting at an imposing desk, placed in a garish studio ablaze in red, white, and blue graphics. He previews the night's stories and guests to swooping crane shots and startling cuts from one side of the desk to the other. Each shot brings a serious, glowering Colbert catechizing into the camera, addressing us directly, "Nation ...." How can Colbert seem more like O'Reilly than O'Reilly himself? In the wake of *The Colbert Report*, one can't watch *The O'Reilly Factor* without being reminded of the *Report*. And, having learned to identify empty images through Colbert, we now see more clearly the simulated nature of O'Reilly. For example, O'Reilly features a bit that Colbert lampoons in "The Wørd." Fox News' bit is called "Talking Points Memo" and features graphics almost identical to those used in "The Wørd"; the anchor appears on the left-hand side of the screen and text appears on the right. The text is meant to underscore the meaning of his spoken commentary. In a September 28, 2012 broadcast, "Talking Points" concerns the "Dangers of a Nuclear Iran." O'Reilly begins his commentary saying that Ahmadinejad is "in New York threatening Jews and demeaning gay people." These words appear to the right, as he continues: "That's what the man does." O'Reilly delivers this line with exaggerated seriousness, giving each word weight, as if it were its own sentence: "That's. What. The man. Does. [*pregnant pause*]." Next he adds, "Ahmadinejad is also presiding over the building of a nuclear weapon." This assertion is mirrored in the text onscreen. The non-sequitur, the overheated rhetoric, and the juxtaposition between the gossipy commentary and the danger of nuclear war mirror

Colbert's style of reportage. Watching these broadcasts side by side, it isn't always clear who's mocking whom.

If the image of O'Reilly confirms the "lost possibility" of a *real* O'Reilly, then the performance of that image further distances the meaning of the anchor image from the reality of the anchor. So, in his performance, Colbert performs simulation, a deliberate simulation with no lost meaning, no reality to which he fails to refer. There is no *real* Colbert; he is a character, a fiction. Indeed, he is the medium— a fake news anchor, on a fake news show, in a fake news studio—and therefore more authentically represents simulated news than "real" (simulated) news. Paradoxically, this opens up the possibility for authentic commentary and exchange of information. In segments like "The Wørd," Colbert succeeds in inserting meaning into his simulation, as we see in the above example. As he stages a fake news show, he creates meaning.

Organize a Fake News Broadcast

Baudrillard suggests organizing a fake holdup in order to "test the reaction of the apparatus to a perfect simulacrum," and concludes: "You won't be able to do it."[9] The system of staged signs will invariably fall into the real, as "artificial signs will become inextricably mixed up with real elements." Someone will call the real police, a guard will panic and fire real bullets. Now, organize a fake news show. Verify that your setting is authentic—anchor desk, conservative suit, understated tie, small sheaf of papers in hand, earpiece—and invite compelling guests, be sure to cover the actual events of the day. Be sure the "operation" approximates real news as much as possible. Use fetching graphics, express outrage, raise eyebrows in exasperation, invite correspondent reports, ask for clarification, hold your earpiece, ask for further explanation, feign outrage and a little surprise, and issue a personal comment as if pressed by the momentum of events. In the case of fake news, the "fall into real elements" might include a guest expressing a sincere opinion, an audience member learning something new, the facts of a political story being accurately reported. Even if the real surfaces momentarily, Baudrillard's point isn't that simulation fails in performance, but that the performance of simulation is impossible because "the real is no longer possible."[10]

Unlike Baudrillard's fake holdup, the fake news of *The Daily Show* and *The Colbert Report* isn't a matter of staged simulations, for that is a guaranteed retreat into the real. They are rather examples of simulacra, of the hyperreal, news shows modeled on American mainstream news, which no longer reliably mediates between "one reality and another."[11] No longer (a phrase that reveals our nostalgia for signification) are media and their "message" two parts of a larger system. Baudrillard describes the collapse of this system, à la McLuhan's slogan "the medium is the message," as an "implosion" in which the real and the medium collapse into a hyperreal "nebula."[12] With this catastrophe, the actions of media and message are no longer distinct: "the medium is the message—the sender the receiver ..." Finally, the logic of the argument suggests "There are no more media in the literal sense of the word ... that is, of a mediating power between one reality and another," or between sign and meaning. And the efficacy of those actions is immediate, generating, in a simultaneous expression: message, medium, and the real. To claim that Colbert is more O'Reilly than O'Reilly is to confirm Baudrillard's anxious prediction; in the age of hyperreality, images become "[m]ore real than real" and that's "how the real is abolished."[13]

The "Best F#@king News Team Ever"

The Daily Show and *The Colbert Report* openly exploit the divergence between the real and the mediated for comedic effect. But their larger projects are ideological: both stage withering cases against contemporary media's embrace of the hyperreal and the cynicism that produces. Whereas Stephen Colbert is a walking talking simulacrum, Jon Stewart broadcasts from a simulacrum of a simulacrum—a television news studio—and his reporting routinely punctures the skin of the hyperreal to expose the flesh of the real. Stewart pointedly and directly addresses the simulated quality of mainstream news. This is why I do not say *The Daily Show* engages in satire.[14] Where Colbert is an ironist par excellence, Stewart's point of view is emphatically not ironic, although he exposes and denounces folly and vice, he generally, unlike Colbert, says what he means.

For example, in reporting on Obama's acceptance of the nomination at the 2012 Democratic National convention (September 7, 2012),

Stewart parses the language of Obama's speech. Regarding his plans for the economy, Obama admits in a clip, "I won't pretend the path I'm offering is quick or easy." Cut to Stewart explaining with a touch of dismay that the President sought "to replace the audacity of hope with the more reasonable calibration of expectations." Stewart might as well have qualified his analysis with, "What the ambassador meant to say," for he simply restated what the political rhetoric actually meant. He exploded the myth that Obama's ideas could rightly be appraised as completely new, or that Americans haven't been misled by certain statements by him. Although it appears in a virtual medium, Stewart's fake news creates knowledge in the viewer, in that he cracks open simulation passing as news to expose a reality behind it, and he refuses to "dissimulate there is nothing," choosing instead to reject the cynicism that such dissimulation has produced.

On the same evening he reported on Obama's acceptance speech, Stewart ran a clip of Laura Ingraham arguing with a guest over the significance of the Republican Party's platform to Mitt Romney's campaign. She argued, "Mitt Romney doesn't write the platform … and he actually doesn't have to abide by the platform. It's written by other people." Stewart then delivers his commentary in the vocal fry of a Valley Girl: "Yeah. I mean, the platform is just the statement of the party's core beliefs. I mean, whateverrrr. I mean Mitt Romney, Mitt Romney can wipe his ass with it for all we care." Isn't that pretty much what Ingraham was getting at? Stewart seems to say, puncturing any pretense that Ingraham offers serious analysis, any hope that her appearance has anything to do with creating knowledge. "Laura Ingraham" points back to "Laura Ingraham" as a consumable image, one that guarantees, if anything, only its own return, and its own ideological position. This is the nightmare conclusion of Baudrillard's anxieties about the consumption of mass media images. Media personalities stand for a position (extreme Left, extreme Right, Pro-one thing, Anti-another) and have finally succeeded in destroying the possibility of genuine exchange of actual ideas in virtual media—once the center of its utopian democratizing dream. In response to this nightmare, *The Daily Show*, in calling themselves the "Best F#@king News Team Ever," says what other programs/stations want you to believe when they trumpet their own alleged virtues. The *Daily Show* slogan is in effect no less hyperbolic than Fox News' claim to being "Fair and Balanced," no less cloying than

MSNBC's avuncular "Lean Forward." The *Daily Show* slogan expresses the hollow heart of claims like "First. Fast. Accurate." and "The Name You Know. The News You Need." Consider that ABC's "See the Whole Picture" claims to provide viewers with all the news they need and, in fact, all the information available. Consider my local news team slogan, "First at Five." This team gets there first, reports first. Simply put, this team is better than all the others. By what measure can this distinction be made among news teams? This is hardly even a sensible question in the postmodern, media-saturated world. We have become acclimated to the unverifiable quality of information. The title of Jon Stewart's show rejects the hyperbole of other news show slogans by asserting what cannot be disputed: the show appears on a daily basis (or at least four times a week). Broadcast news is and always has been a "daily show."

The Larger Argument

The Daily Show and *The Colbert Report* seem to be exceptions to Baudrillard's notion of the hyperreal. Both shows avoid the loss of signification, the emptying of signs symptomatic of postmodern culture. But can this be? *The Daily Show* has all the trappings of a television newscast, deploys many of the same strategies as mainstream media news, and at least some of the time offers the same result: reporting selected bits of the news of the day. Further, the show appears on television—in a virtual medium. Doesn't Baudrillard's theory insist that there can be no escape from the dark postmodern truth of the image, the dark truth that "information devours its own content ... Rather than producing meaning, [it] exhausts itself in the staging of meaning."[15] The critical difference is that Stewart and Colbert take media and reportage as their subject. While both shows deal in fake news, they aren't fake in Baudrillard's sense. In that sense, Stewart reports *on* fake news and Colbert *stages* a fake news show. They address the postmodern status of images directly. Following the logic of Baudrillard's fake holdup, *The Daily Show* falls into the real precisely because it does not traffic in fake news but rather performs and comments upon the simulation of news.

Jon Stewart plays two roles at once. He is the stupefied anchor, tasked with bringing us the news of the day, such as it is, registering what must surely be our own dismay. He also acts as our surrogate. Make no mistake, *Daily Show* audiences are meant and expected to see him, this anchor, as our spokesman, the one who reflects for us our own ideological position as the correct one, the wisest, hippest position. Stewart is the Walter Cronkite, the Edward R. Murrow, of our day. If these men were transparent indicators of our better selves, of who and what we might like to believe we were as citizens of a country whose anchors could reflect such seamless rectitude, then Stewart indicates that we can no longer see what we believe. For the news anchor function has devolved from deliverer of the once-verifiable, real, edifying news of the day, to simulation peddler. Stewart occupies an always already empty seat: a simulacrum of a simulacrum, the news anchor's chair. This shift in the anchor role came as the apparatus of media technology and technique increasingly imposed itself between anchor and audience. Think here of sweeping crane shots, the camera pinballing from one enormous touchscreen to another, or CNN's use of holograms on election night 2008: effects that render news programs less like practical modes of conveying information and more like Michael Bay films.

If the virtual image is the site of the "disappearance of meaning and representation," why do Jon Stewart and Stephen Colbert signify—or seem to—so heavily, with such cultural and ideological weight? Because it is in the *loss* of meaning that their performances reside; they occupy the very seat of loss, which is to say, they recognize the emptiness of mainstream media images. Baudrillard fears that mass media images dissimulate "an absence of an absence," and audiences are therefore convinced that the empty space of the image is actually the real. Stewart and Colbert roll back this dissimulation, exposing and therefore filling the absence with meaning.

The Daily Show and *The Colbert Report* take seriously the status of news in American life. These shows address the elements of broadcast news that we have all come to recognize and worry about. More than that, these shows remind us that we have failed to fight for the real, failed to struggle for signification, failed to resist our fall into media saturation adequately. If we are passive in the face of increasingly cynical and propagandistic shows telling us "We Report. You Decide," it is perhaps because we no longer seek sense in images. Perhaps audiences have grown neutral before meaninglessness, seeking out shiny, soothing things, rather than knowledge, verifiable facts, news.

But in the face of such complacency, Stewart and Colbert ask, "How can you believe this stuff?" These anchors lay out the fake news, and in their own ways ask how on earth we have come to believe any of it. Why have we allowed ourselves to be pulled in by it? Where's the response? The uprising? If media neutralize both meaning and response, then the postmodern outlook is truly bleak. Baudrillard has characterized "media as the institution ... of communication without a response" where this lack of response implicates the audience in the "violence perpetrated on meaning."[16] But neither *The Daily Show* nor *The Colbert Report* allows their audiences to remain neutral; through humor they trigger audience engagement. *The Daily Show* in particular encourages our engagement with the news by situating Stewart as our surrogate. Both shows force a confrontation with simulated news, turning it against itself, and refusing to let us viewers off the hook. In a postmodern culture that tempts us to deny that there even is a hook, Stewart and Colbert, as anchors, anchor us to the real.

Notes

1. For more on this, see Rachael Sotos, "*The Daily Show*: An Ethos for the Fifth Estate," in this volume.
2. For the purposes of this essay, I will select from Baudrillard's work on simulacra and simulation and will necessarily gloss over many details of what is a complex body of work and philosophical career.
3. Jean Baudrillard, *Simulacra and Simulation* (Ann Arbor: University of Michigan Press, 1994), 79.
4. Ibid., 6.
5. Jean Baudrillard, "The Evil Demon of Images and the Precession of Simulacra," in Thomas Docherty, ed., *The Postmodern Reader* (New York: Columbia University Press, 1993), 194.
6. Baudrillard, *Simulacra and Simulation*, 6.
7. Ibid., 21.
8. Fittingly, on his tour of the Smithsonian's "Treasures of American History" exhibit, Colbert mistakes an authentic historical artifact for a television prop. When Marc Pachter, director of the American History Museum, shows him George Washington's military uniform, Colbert asks, "So, this is Seinfeld's puffy shirt?" *The Colbert Report* (February 11, 2008).
9. Baudrillard, "Evil Demon of Images," 196.
10. Baudrillard, *Simulacra and Simulation*, 19.

11. Ibid., 82.
12. Ibid., 83.
13. Ibid., 81.
14. Compare, by contrast, Greg Littmann, "Seriously Funny: Mockery as a Political Weapon," in this volume.
15. Baudrillard, *Simulacra and Simulation*, 80.
16. Ibid., 84.

Segment 2

LIVE REPORT
JON STEWART (NOT MILL) AS PHILOSOPHER, SORT OF

Chapter 6

Jon Stewart
The New *and Improved* Public Intellectual

Terrance MacMullan

No one ever went broke underestimating the intelligence of the American people.

H.L. Mencken

I think it's clear: I'm going to be the nominee.

Newt Gingrich

I do.

Kim Kardashian

Six years ago, I wrote a book chapter about why intellectuals, especially philosophers, should study and emulate Jon Stewart if they want to return to being relevant public intellectuals. I reluctantly take full credit for the fact that because of my writing an increasing number of serious intellectuals have finally taken notice of Jon Stewart. A few of them have done something even better: they've taken notice of me.

For example, in "Race and Beyond: Dumbing it Down on Fox News" the Pulitzer Prize-eligible journalist Sam Fulwood III uses, you guessed it, the earlier version of the chapter you are now reading to prove that "[o]ur nation, which once valued education as the great social equalizer, finds itself with a slate of conservative presidential candidates forced to the far-right fringe to pander to a dumbed-down public."[1] We find an even more encouraging sign in the work of

The Ultimate Daily Show and Philosophy: More Moments of Zen, More Indecision Theory, First Edition. Edited by Jason Holt.
© 2013 John Wiley & Sons, Inc. Published 2013 by John Wiley & Sons, Inc.

another brilliant academic who can really spot excellent scholarship named Kahyan Parsi. Dr. Parsi quoted my trailblazing work on the civic relevance of Jon Stewart to support the argument that "Stewart has emerged as our voice of sanity in a sea of insanity in a new media age with its ephemeral nature and lack of substance."[2] I really hope that you read the footnote at the end of the previous sentence, because it will show you that I was cited as a source in the *American Journal of Bioethics*, a publication so legit that it normally would not give me a subscription, let alone publish me.

Now, to use a technical philosophical term, the media went absolutely ape-poopy over these publications.[3] Perhaps they went ape because by mentioning me these stories reminded the media that philosophy professors still live, breathe, and indoctrinate among regular, hardworking Americans. It's more likely that they messed themselves because they were surprised to read that a couple of bona fide smarty-pantses thought that Jon Stewart was not just a very lucky stand-up comedian who had landed a sweet gig, but the most influential smarty-pants in America.

Stewart's considerable intellectual clout surely *is* a bit odd, especially considering that his Tuesday lead-in on Comedy Central is the show *Workaholics*, which is basically an American version of *Downton Abbey*, except with slightly more drug use, stripper penis-grabbing, and urination.[4] Stewart isn't even an academic, but is rather host of the fake news program *The Daily Show* and the lead author of *America (The Book)* and *Earth (The Book)*. However, anyone who's watched his show without first getting high[5] knows that he's more than just funny: he's our most effective public intellectual and satirist. Stewart, along with his brilliant writers and co-stars, draws hilarious comedy from the hypocrisy, banality, and just plain stupidity of powerful figures in the media, government, and industry. In so doing, he fosters critical thinking across an enormous audience and defends democratic principles from erosion by partisan punditry and our culture's disregard for genuine debate.

Stewart is a living testament to the obvious yet easily forgotten truth that in order to be a public intellectual, the public first needs to hear you. He illustrates how a well-crafted presentation style is essential for cutting through the din of proliferating media voices to reach an audience. Stewart doesn't expect people to listen to him simply because he offers a cogent critique of the government and the media. Instead, he uses a wide range of tools, especially irony, to make his audience think while they laugh. Stewart certainly sacrifices a lot of intellectual street-cred for dressing up as a "sexy" French maid, nearly eviscerating himself while trying to talk and drink a margarita at the same time, or dedicating *an entire week* to they-write-themselves Anthony Wiener jokes, but such bits allow him to educate an audience many times larger than that of any conventional intellectual.

America needs his brand of popular intellectual criticism even more than we did six years ago, as our civic and political discourse has been almost entirely eclipsed by nasty invective and political spin. Indeed, Stewart's fake news is actually one of our last examples of real, engaged political philosophy that was originally cultivated by some of America's best philosophers. But before we look more closely at Stewart, let's consider why Americans hate intellectuals.

Why Americans Hate Intellectuals

We Americans distrust smart people.[6] Decent Americans know, deep in their guts, that in order to be tricky, you must first be smart. For example, we all love to trick our dogs with that fake throw-the-ball thing. We say to our pet, "You are *so* stupid, you stupid dog! I only *pretended* to throw the ball, but I really held it in my hand, stupid!" While we trick our dogs, our dogs never trick us. They might chew our shoes or poop on our couches, but those aren't tricks; those are just gross, stupid things our dogs do while we're out doing things that they couldn't even *comprehend*, like googling our names at work. Americans don't like smart people because we suspect they might trick us like we trick our dogs.

Being a philosopher, I will use a very old tool of philosophy, called a syllogism, to examine the sort of reasoning that leads many Americans to distrust smart people.

(1)   All tricky people are smart.
(2)   No tricky people should be trusted.

Therefore,
(3)   No smart people should be trusted.

As a philosopher, I have to point out that this is actually an example of a fallacy, an error in reasoning. Even if all tricky people are both smart and untrustworthy, it doesn't follow that all smart people are tricky. Someone might be smart *and* honest (like Yoda or Jesus).

But there I go, trying to be smart! "*Ooh*, look at how smart I am," I'm saying. "I studied Aristotle, so I know what a syllogism is, while you went to business school for three years just to learn 'Buy low, sell high.'" Now you hate me. Worse yet, I'm a *long-winded* elitist smarty who's gone on for nearly a page without mentioning *The Daily Show* or Jon Stewart, which is what this chapter is about. Sorry.

In addition to making the mistake of thinking that smart people are tricky, Americans also make the opposite mistake of thinking that dumb people are honest. That's why George W. Bush won the presidency—*twice*. Or tied once, won once. Whatever. We elected him because he was a regular guy and not some elitist egghead from New England (even though he was born a millionaire in New Haven, Connecticut and had two Ivy League degrees). Whatever. Eggheads poked fun at him for saying stuff like, "You teach a child to read, and he or her will be able to pass a literacy test," or "We need an energy bill that encourages consumption," and of course, "My answer is: Bring them on."[7] But eggheads still don't understand that these statements *proved* his honesty for many Americans! They showed us that he was the opposite of Bill Clinton, who's very smart and therefore very tricky, so tricky, in fact, that he tried to trick us about simple words like "is" and "sex."

Apparently, Americans still really like dumb people. How else can we explain the popularity of *Jersey Shore* or the existence of *The Ed Show?* Or the success of Tea Party politicians? Their argument is *literally* "Elect us to run the government because we think government is inherently evil, and we will shrink government at all costs." The fact that most Americans think that smart people are tricky and that dumb people are honest makes it difficult to be a public intellectual in America. Luckily, Americans also enjoy a good laugh, which is why people who want to be public intellectuals should learn from Jon Stewart.

You Know It's Hard out Here for a Public Intellectual[8]

It's hard to say exactly what a public intellectual is. Perhaps they're a bit like what Justice Potter Stewart said about pornography: you can't define them, but you know them when you see them. Prominent legal scholar Richard Posner wrote a book titled *Public Intellectuals: A Study of Decline*, which gives a pretty straightforward analysis of how the once proud office of public intellectual has degenerated into schlocky punditry. Posner describes a public intellectual as "a person who, drawing on his intellectual resources, addresses a broad though educated public on issues with political or ideological dimensions."[9] Despite his frequent protestations to the contrary, this description fits Jon Stewart to a T.

As a wannabe intellectual myself, I've read many books, some of which indicate that Americans didn't always hate intellectuals. Apparently at one time we actually respected them for dedicating their lives to the cultivation of an informed democratic citizenry.[10] Americans used to listen to them, and even weirder, *read* their work! Another big difference between then and now is that intellectuals used to speak to the entire public, instead of just to each other, which is what they mostly do these days. Public intellectuals of yore—people like Ralph Waldo Emerson (1803–1882), William James (1842–1910), Jane Addams (1860–1935), John Dewey (1859–1952), and W.E.B. Du Bois (1868–1963)—knew how to connect with a very broad audience without dumbing down their message.

Furthermore, public intellectuals played a special role in the unique philosophical tradition of the United States. Cornel West—public intellectual, superstar academic, rapper, Council Elder in the *Matrix* trilogy, turtleneck sweater aficionado, and all around cool guy—argued in his classic book, *The American Evasion of Philosophy*, that the only school of philosophy indigenous to the United States—pragmatism—distinguishes itself from other philosophical traditions by urging philosophers to be less "academic" and more publicly engaged.

> [Pragmatism is] a form of cultural criticism in which the meaning of America is put forward by intellectuals in response to distinct social and cultural crises. In this sense, American pragmatism is less a philosophical tradition putting forward solutions to perennial problems in the Western philosophical conversation initiated by Plato and more a continuous cultural commentary or set of interpretations that attempt to explain America to itself at a particular historical moment.[11]

This ideal of the articulate thinker who spurs informed debate and fosters democracy is still cherished by many philosophers who think that philosophy should matter to all people.[12] They try to make philosophy relevant by recovering it in each new age. As John Dewey, the most renowned American public philosopher, wrote: "Philosophy recovers itself when it ceases to be a device for dealing with the problems of philosophers and becomes a method, cultivated by philosophers, for dealing with the problems of men."[13]

Unfortunately, this connection between philosophy and the public has largely broken down and public intellectuals command only a tiny fraction of the influence wielded by celebrities like Donald Trump and Kim Kardashian.

One reason for this is that we have shorter attention spans than we used to.[14] Another reason that the public doesn't pay much attention to intellectuals is that intellectuals as a whole simply don't bother engaging the public. This isolation started in large part with the radicalization of American universities in the 1960s, which led many intellectuals to write off non-intellectuals as dupes, and many non-intellectuals to dismiss academics as leftist propagandists. This disdain for university intellectuals was perhaps best expressed by the lion of American conservatism, William F. Buckley, when he famously said in the 1960s, "I would rather be governed by the first 2000 names in the Boston phone book than by the faculty of Harvard University."[15] The isolation of intellectuals got worse when they started emulating certain European theorists, such as Jacques Derrida (1930–2004), whose writing was extremely dense and jargon-laden. Perhaps academics speak mostly to each other because they think other academics are the only people who can keep up with them intellectually. However, I think this isolation is largely self-imposed for the sake of convenience, since it's easier and more comfortable to speak to someone who shares your assumptions and uses your terms than someone who might challenge your assumptions in unexpected ways or ask you to explain what you mean. Richard Rorty (1931–2007), perhaps the most influential American philosopher in recent decades, argued that this isolation from the public has caused the intellectual left to become "extraordinarily self-obsessed and ingrown."[16]

The sad result of these two factors—the public's short attention span and intellectuals' failure to address a public audience—is that the mantle of the public intellectual has fallen to media pundits who are rarely wise or observant and are generally more interested in advancing a particular partisan narrative than in illuminating our current situation. Most intellectuals would be horrified at the idea of calling people like Ed Shultz or Sean Hannity intellectuals, since such figures play on the fears and prejudices of their audiences, substituting rhetoric for reason and corroding genuine debate. However, if intellectuals are ever going to connect with the public again and improve the quality of crucial public debates, they need to accept responsibility for their share of the problem by stepping down from the Ivory Tower and communicating with the general public.

Stewart's Ironic Blah, Blah, Blah

Jon Stewart offers valuable insights for how to make intellectuals more public and the public more intellectual. Stewart's brand of public intellectualism involves extensive use of irony, a very hot topic nowadays.[17] Much ink has been spilt about this word, but irony in this sense is when there is a gap between what is *literally said* and what is *actually meant* or understood. Just about every aspect of *The Daily Show* mines irony for laughter: the graphics that look just like the ones from real news shows, the catchy headline segments (like their long-running series on the Middle East, "Mess O' Potamia") and the field reports from their staff of all "senior correspondents," including Samantha Bee, Senior South American Security Correspondent and Jessica Williams, Senior Youth Correspondent.

The Daily Show isn't *just* funny and ironic, however. If that were all it had to offer, *The Daily Show* wouldn't have won two Peabody Awards and sixteen Emmys while averaging two million viewers. *The Daily Show* satisfies a desire among Americans (who might not be that daft after all)[18] for critical commentary. The greatest irony of the show is that even though Stewart isn't a news anchor and his writers couldn't even get jobs on *Family Guy*, they're still able to exceed, in many respects and for a fraction of the cost, the quality of news shows produced by real journalists. As fake reporters, the staff of *The Daily Show* is able to one-up the real journalists by speaking the truth about our society, government, and media that conventional news usually either can't or won't. The program actually fits West's definition of pragmatist philosophy, by "explaining America to itself at a particular historical moment."[19] Along with making us laugh, *The Daily Show* encourages us to be skeptical about the media and the government, both of which can seem dangerously disconnected from reality.

The *Daily Show* came into its own during the Bush Administration, which many Americans (and most Canadians) suspected had raised the bar on lying, spin, and bullshit.[20] One particularly chilling indicator of its cynical relationship to reality was the now famous story in the *New York Times* by Ron Suskind called "Without a Doubt," in which he presented a portrait of the last superpower nominally headed by a man with no intellectual curiosity and who steered the ship of state with his gut. Suskind describes the most disturbing element of this fact-free presidency: "open dialogue, based on facts, is not seen as something of inherent value."[21] Even more disturbing was the conversation with an unnamed senior advisor who chided Suskind for failing to understand how the world now works:

> The aide said that guys like me were "in what we call the reality-based community," which he defined as people who "believe that solutions emerge from your judicious study of discernible reality." I nodded and murmured something about enlightenment principles and empiricism. He cut me off. "That's not the way the world really works anymore," he continued. "We're an empire now, and when we act, we create our own reality. And while you're studying that reality … we'll act again, creating other new realities, which you can study too, and that's how things will sort out."[22]

This really scared a lot of people across the political spectrum. People who base their beliefs on experiences of discernible reality and open debate used to be called "sane," while people who create private realities in this way were deemed "crazy." Now we're just two different "communities," like cat-owners and dog-owners. What's even scarier is that after this piece Bush *won re-election*! There was clear evidence that world-changing decisions were being made by someone who didn't know the difference between Switzerland and Sweden, while television news outlets were more interested in John Kerry's Vietnam War record. It was only in August 2005, when the grotesque devastation of Hurricane Katrina served as the backdrop for Bush's "Heckuva job!" congratulation of FEMA Director Mike Brown, that the mainstream media finally caught on that the emperor had no clothes (or emergency-preparedness plans).

The *Daily Show* explains our political landscape to us by poking fun at both the government's casual disregard for facts and the media's apparent willingness to play along. Take, for example, this exchange from July 12, 2005 between Stewart and his "Senior Journalistologist" Stephen Colbert (back when he was just Stephen Colbert, "*Daily Show* stooge," and not "Stephen Colbert of *The Colbert Report*") about reports that Karl Rove, despite his denials, was involved in leaking former CIA agent Valerie Plame's identity:

STEWART: What are the ramifications of this now that Rove's involvement is known?

COLBERT: Well, Bush has a real problem on his hands here, Jon. What honor should he bestow on Karl Rove?

STEWART: Did you say "what honor"?

COLBERT: Yes Jon. George "Slam-dunk" Tenent got us into Iraq on mistaken intel. He got the Medal of Freedom. Condi Rice sees a memo warning "Bin-Laden Determined to strike the United States," ignores it. Boom! Gets kicked upstairs to the Secretary of State. For a bungle this bad, I think we might be looking at Chief Justice Karl Rove.

This exchange is a perfect example of pragmatist philosophy à la Cornel West, showing Americans that their government's disregard for reality is a serious political crisis. By lampooning the way government tries to spin every mistake as a triumph, *The Daily Show* spurs the sort of debate and critical thinking that are central to healthy democracies and yet are under assault in an "either you're with us or you're with the terrorists" political climate.

The Daily Show also plays an important public intellectual function by serving as a kind of critical cultural memory that helps us understand the present in the light of historical events. In a culture obsessed with being the first or the fastest, these acts of cultural memory are crucial for curing our frequent bouts of political amnesia. One of the funniest examples of *The Daily Show* as way-back-when machine was the segment titled "Victory Lapse" (May 1, 2012). It starts by airing clips of Republicans being absolutely indignant at an Obama election ad that used the killing of Osama Bin Laden as evidence of the President's leadership. They are shocked, *shocked*, that Obama would dare use his wartime leadership to his own political advantage. Stewart sees their indignation, and raises it to incredulity:

So let me get this straight. Republicans, you are annoyed by the arrogance and braggadocio of a wartime president's political add. You think he's divisively and unfairly belittling his opponents. I see. I have

a question. ARE YOU ON CRACK?! Were you alive lo these past
10 years? It seems unseemly for the president to spike the football?!
Bush landed on a f#%king aircraft carrier with a football-stuffed
codpiece! He spiked the football before the game even started! Yes, your
Republican caterwauling and outrage is the subject of our new segment:
"You are aware that the frontal lobe of the cerebral cortex gives us the
ability to store and recall past events as they occurred, right?"

The segment is hilarious, in no small part because it is one of the
frequent instances where Stewart is not so much doing a bit, but is
genuinely flabbergasted at just how stupid they must think we are.
This sort of historically grounded argument by counterexample is an
important tool of political criticism that is generally off limits for
conventional news reporters but is thankfully fair game for Stewart
and Colbert.

As Democrats gained a measure of power in the last few years, they
did not hesitate to do the very same things they pitched a fit over
when Republicans had done them only a few years earlier. Their
conditional moral outrage and highly selective memory also begets
great comedy as cultural memory. For example, the June 21, 2012
segment "Glock and Spiels—Obama's Executive Privilege" contrasts
the Democrats' rage at Republicans in 2012 for implying nefarious
intentions behind Obama's assertions of executive privilege regarding
documents related to the botched Fast and Furious program with
Democrats implying that nefarious intentions drove Bush era assertions of executive privilege. The juxtaposition is just so perfect—with
present-day Democrats defending Obama's use of executive privilege
with the very same arguments they scoffed at when made by Bush-era
Republicans—that all Stewart can do is channel his inner Bob Barker
and lead us in a round of "Differentiate Your Party's Assertion of
Executive Privilege from the Previous Administration's." This game
shines an especially harsh light on one Democrat in particular: a
"handsome high-school senior" who in 2007 chastised President Bush
for hiding behind executive privilege and urged him to come clean.
His name was Senator Barack Obama.

This brings us to the topic of Stewart's relationship to Obama,
which is both complex and evolving. From the 2008 presidential
campaign through the early days of the Obama presidency Stewart
was a sympathetic defender of the presidency. He openly wept with
joy when Obama was elected and he frequently defended the President

against conservative attacks. Stewart's early man-crush on the president was so strong that on January 3, 2011 he aired a segment titled "Barack Obama is Luke Skywalker"! However, Stewart's treatment of the President has grown steadily less sympathetic and more critical as we've had time to compare Obama's actual performance as President against the promises he made during his campaign and his image as a transformational and progressive politician. A recurring bit that is particularly damning of Obama is the bizarre series on "Gitmo's World," where a bearded Elmo puppet named Gitmo, controlled by Stewart (who proves to be a hilariously inept puppeteer), reports on his detention within the very much still-functioning Guantanamo Prison that Obama promised to close. The visual comedy of this bit is silly in the extreme, but the subject matter—human beings detained indefinitely in a windowless, legal Limbo—is as grave and disturbing as could be. Lest we try to comfort ourselves by thinking that these kinds of facilities are not meant for us, Little Gitmo reminds us in "Lockup Everyone" (January 3, 2012) that we might soon be joining him since Obama signed a bill in 2011 that eliminated due process for any American citizen suspected of being a terrorist.

No segment better encapsulates Stewart's (and all Obama supporters') conflicted feelings towards the new President than "Meet the Depressed" (September 21, 2010) which dissects a CNBC town-hall meeting at which Obama answers questions and complaints from citizens. In it we hear a cutting and lucid critique of Obama's failure to live up to his campaign promises from "Obama's kryptonite": an African American woman who is a Democrat, a financial analyst, a military veteran, and a beleaguered Obama supporter who confesses to Obama, "Quite frankly, I'm exhausted. I'm exhausted of defending you, defending your administration, defending the mantle of change that I voted for, and deeply disappointed with where we are right now." Stewart tries to explain her frustration to the President at Camera 3, where he contrasts clips of Obama's rousing speeches where he promises to reform immigration, close Guantanamo, clean up the banking industry, and get America back to work, with more recent clips of a markedly less optimistic Obama weakly explaining that he is trying but that change is hard. Comparing Obama to a Magic Bullet blender that looked great in the 2 a.m. infomercial but turns out to be a huge disappointment,

Stewart ends by saying, "I don't know who is to blame: you for making this s#%t look so good, or us for believing it."

"Help Us Hebrew One! You're Our Only Hope!"

Stewart's greatest quality as a public intellectual is his faith in America and his commitment to democracy as an evolving, experimental process that needs debate to survive. Note Thomas Jefferson's fake foreword to *America (The Book)*, where Stewart lampoons American idolatry of the Constitution:

> I was ... looking forward to this opportunity to dispel some of the mythology surrounding myself and my fellow Founders—particularly the myth of our infallibility. You moderns have a tendency to worship at the altar of the Fathers. "The First Amendment is sacrosanct!" "We will die to protect the Second Amendment!" So dramatic. Do you know why we called them amendments? Because they *amend*! They fix mistakes or correct omissions and they themselves can be changed. If we had meant for the Constitution to be written in stone we would have written it in stone. Most things were written in stone back then, you know. I'm not trying to be difficult but it's bothersome when you blame your own inflexibility and extremism on us.[23]

Stewart's critique in clown-paint reflects Dewey's statement that democracy should be understood as "a way of life ... controlled by personal faith in personal day-by-day working together with others."[24]

Sometimes we see Stewart's commitment to democracy in his humble and sincere efforts to praise Americans who serve others, like his many segments highlighting the sacrifices made by veterans of the wars in Iraq and Afghanistan, such as Sgt. 1st Class Leroy Petry who appeared on the *Daily Show* (July 14, 2011) to talk about the leadership and personal bravery that earned him the Congressional Medal of Honor. Stewart's personal faith in working with others was also behind his October 30, 2010 "Rally to Restore Sanity," which was a peaceful gathering of "people who think shouting is annoying, counterproductive, and terrible for your throat; who feel that the loudest voices shouldn't be the only ones that get heard."[25]

Stewart also shows us how to be a good "little-d" democrat when he invites conservatives onto his show, like the author David Barton or Senator Marco Rubio, for honest and pointed debate. These conversations are fantastic not just because they involve eloquent interlocutors with opposing views: they are some of the best, most widely viewed examples of what a *real debate* should look like! These conversations are nothing like the discussion on cable or network news shows where a panel of "experts" spout pre-fab talking points at each other like competitors a political battle royal. Instead, Stewart shows genuine respect for his guests and curiosity about their beliefs while still pointedly and honestly voicing his own opposing position. Stewart's willingness to engage in vigorous but amicable debate is one of his greatest contributions to our democracy because it models for us the sort of dialogue we need to be having with each other if we are ever going to address the challenges that affect us all.

However Stewart has recently shown us a very different side to his commitment to democracy as a working faith in people. It reveals a different Stewart from the funny and ironic man who cordially sips Gatorade with Pervez Musharraf while politely asking him why Osama Bin Laden was found in Pakistan when Musharraf said he did not know where he was. This other Stewart is just plain ol' f#@king pissed. He's like an American version of a Biblical prophet. I don't just mean he's cranky, old, and Jewish. He's a man whose heart is broken when he sees his people failing and betraying each other. In these moments, Stewart steps away from comedy almost entirely to serve as our collective conscience, forcing us to feel angry or sad or just simply hurt by injustices that we might otherwise gloss over and forget.

We see this rage in the long-running series on the economic crisis called "Clusterf#@k to the Poor House" where he hammers politicians, the media, and corporations for either precipitating the Great Recession that fell in 2008 or for sitting idly by as it wrecked countless lives. During the March 2009 interviews of Jim Cramer, Stewart barely concealed his anger at Cramer and CNBC for portraying themselves as tenacious financial reporters while in actuality defending Wall Street as they "burned the f#@king house down with our money and walked away rich as hell, and you guys knew that that was going on." Stewart was not only angry at the thought of bankers and traders making millions off other people's misery: it was the fact that by gambling with our homes, savings, and retirements without risking anything of theirs they betrayed the trust that is the bedrock of not only our financial system but our nation as a whole.

As considerable as these acts of public intellectualism were—both friendly and indignant—they are meager when compared with his greatest moment, when he made us all confront an unfathomable travesty. In "Worst Responders" (December 16, 2010) Stewart wrapped up an excruciating week of focusing our attention on how all Americans—but especially our Congress and the media—failed the 9/11 first responders. In particular, he trains his attention on the Republican filibuster of the Zadroga Bill, which was designed to provide financial support to the first responders to help them cover the cost of the extremely expensive medical treatment they needed because of their exposure to toxins during the terrorist attack. The "win–win–win" of helping the people who got fatally sick because they bravely risked their lives *saving strangers from a terrorist attack* was apparently too much to ask of our Congress, even though on the very same week they were able to come together to cut taxes, especially for the wealthy. Stewart proudly announces that this "is astoundingly good news ... for firefighters who make more than $200,000 a year." To make matters worse, he points out that none of the three major news networks had talked about the Zadroga bill for two and a half months, perhaps because they were too focused on the huge story that Beatles songs were now available on iTunes. Stewart then turns in vain to Fox News, "America's source for 9/11-based outrage," for some appropriate anger at Republicans for blocking healthcare for the 9/11 responders. Sadly, he finds none. He is not kidding when he pleads with us to see that "[t]his is an outrageous abdication of our responsibility to those who were most heroic on 9/11."

In the subsequent segment he invited four 9/11 responders to remind us about not only the horror of the attack, but also the agony of their medical trials and how insulted and hurt they are by the fact that they have to go bankrupt paying the medical bills they've incurred because of their bravery. Stewart shows them a recent clip of Mitch McConnell *crying on the floor of the Senate over the retirement of a Congress colleague* but unable to care enough to help heroes dying of the worst diseases imaginable. John Devlin, an engineer who worked for weeks clearing away rubble to help find the remains of the innocent and who contracted stage four inoperable throat cancer for his courage, told Stewart early in the interview, "We went down there for the love of this country and of the love of our city. We didn't turn our back on anybody." This is the very love of fellow citizens that Dewey associates with democracy at its best, that is absent among the powerful in government and the media, that Stewart hopes we will show each other, and that these men and women exemplified, literally to their dying breaths. None of this is funny: it's agonizing, disgusting, and heartbreaking. Nonetheless, he was right to make us watch because it was a dose of strong and bitter medicine that we all needed.

If Stewart burns out and wastes the rest of his time on *The Daily Show* on dumb wiener jokes and bad puppetry he will still be one of our greatest public intellectuals, because what he and his staff and writers did in December of 2010 *worked*. They described America to itself, and made us mindful of a wrong that had to be righted. They made us listen to these four wounded responders who spoke for hundreds more, and either out of shame or a sane recollection of what should matter most, Congress did the right thing and passed the Zagroda Bill on December 22, 2010 that was then signed into law on January 2, 2011. It is hard to imagine a better example of how real change can come about because of a voice that clearly forces us to think about what we are and what we ought to be. Behind all the jokes, both witty and sophomoric, is an unalloyed faith in people and the hope that we can do right by each other, if we would just stop, think, and talk with each other.

Notes

1. Sam Fulwood III, "Race and Beyond: Dumbing It Down on Fox News," *Center for American Progress* (November 29, 2011), www. americanprogress.org/issues/2011/11/rab_112911.html, accessed January 30, 2013.
2. Kayhan Parsi, "The Political Satirist as Public Intellectual: The Case of Jon Stewart," *American Journal of Bioethics* 11 (12) (2011), 4.
3. After a quick google search I counted 40 stories in the media that picked up the Parsi story alone. After that I stopped counting because I was just so freaking pissed. I write a book chapter that gets mentioned twice in six years and then Mr. I-Publish-in-Tier-1-Journals piggy-backs on my work and all of a sudden *he's* the one who blows everyone's mind with the whole "Jon Stewart is a public intellectual" argument. It sickens me. Oh, and if he winds up sitting across from Jon Stewart before me, I will plotz! I will seriously and totally just f#@king plotz!

4. Little known fact: the pilot for *Downton Abbey* has a scene set in an opium den where the Dowager Countess does a *lot* of penis-grabbing and urinating.

5. Admittedly, this is a very small population group.

6. Smart people sometimes write smart books about why Americans don't like smart people. Since these books do not have sparkly vampires or sexually deviant housewives, few people read them. If you want to be hated by the members of your book club, have them read Charles Pierce, *Idiot America: How Stupidity Became a Virtue in the Land of the Free* (New York: Doubleday, 2009) and Susan Jacoby, *The Age of American Unreason* (New York: Pantheon Books, 2008).

7. http://politicalhumor.about.com/library/blbushdumbquotes2.htm, accessed January 30, 2013.

8. This title was heli-funny in 2006 when I first wrote it, because Hustle and Flow had just come out and that song "It's Hard out Here for a Pimp" had just won an Oscar, and it was funny to juxtapose pimps with public intellectuals.

9. Richard Posner, *Public Intellectuals: A Study of Decline* (Cambridge, MA: Harvard University Press, 2003), 170.

10. For a good history of intellectuals in America, see Russell Jacoby, *The Last Intellectuals: American Culture of Academe* (New York: Basic Books, 1987), and the classic by Richard Hofstadter, *Anti-Intellectualism in American Life* (New York: Knopf, 1963).

11. Cornel West, *The American Evasion of Philosophy* (Madison: University of Wisconsin Press, 1989), 5.

12. One group that I think is doing great work toward this end is the Society for the Advancement of American Philosophy.

13. John Dewey, "The Need for a Recovery of Philosophy" [1917], in *The Middle Works*, vol. 10, ed. Jo Ann Boydston. (Carbondale: Southern Illinois University Press, 1980), 46.

14. Oh! Remember we're talking about Jon Stewart and *The Daily Show*, and how he's the new public intellectual?

15. http://en.wikipedia.org/wiki/William_F._Buckley,_Jr.#Quotations, accessed January 30, 2013.

16. Richard Rorty, "The Humanistic Intellectual," in *Philosophy and Social Hope* (New York, Penguin Books, 1999), 129.

17. For more on irony, see Kevin Decker, "Thank God It's Stephen Colbert: The Rally to Restore Irony on *The Colbert Report*," in this volume.

18. For a great book defending the unlikely thesis that America, far from being an intellectual wasteland, is in fact the world's preeminent philosophical nation, read Carlin Romano, *America the Philosophical* (New York: Knopf, 2012).

19. West, *American Evasion*, 5.
20. For a great study of the Bush Administration's Orwellian manipulation of language, see Henry Giroux, "The Politics of Lying," *Tikkun* 21 (2) (2006), 36–40.
21. Ron Suskind, "Without a Doubt," *New York Times: Sunday Magazine* (October 17, 2004), 47.
22. Ibid., 51.
23. Jon Stewart, Ben Karlin, and David Javerbaum, *America (The Book): A Citizen's Guide to Democracy Inaction* (New York: Warner Books, 2004), x.
24. John Dewey, "Creative Democracy—The Task Before Us," in *The Later Works* (vol. 14), ed. Jo Ann Boydston (Carbondale: Southern Illinois University Press, 1988), 228.
25. "Rally to Restore Sanity," www.rallytorestoresanity.com/, accessed January 30, 2013.

Chapter 7

Stewart and Socrates
Speaking Truth to Power

Judith Barad

Consider this description of a society:

- People pride themselves on their democratic form of government and constitution.
- There are great differences in wealth and social status; many of the poor join the military.
- People are very materialistic and concerned with "getting ahead."
- The arts flourish and people love entertainment.
- There are two political factions, often at odds with each another.
- It's a great manufacturing power, supplying other nations with industrial products.
- It's a great military power, which belongs to a coalition of other nations.
- There is a problem with immigrants crossing its borders.
- The political climate is tense.
- Although in principle religion and state are separate, in practice they overlap.

Now the question: Which society is being described? Twenty-first-century America? Or fifth-century BCE Athens? Without any further details, the description could apply just as well to either. And the two societies have one other thing in common. They both have controversial

The Ultimate Daily Show and Philosophy: More Moments of Zen, More Indecision Theory, First Edition. Edited by Jason Holt.

reformers who use similar methods to urge people to *think*. However unlikely it may sound, Jon Stewart plays the role of reformer in America today much as Socrates (470–399 BCE) did in Athens long ago.

Here Come the Sophists!

As in America, so in Athens, citizens received a basic education that made them literate and gave them simple skills. But if Athenian families wanted their children to be successful, more was needed. This concern with success led to the birth of sophism in the second half of the fifth century BCE. Traveling from one city to another and charging *very* hefty fees, the sophists claimed that their students would become admired, competent, and, above all, rich. For those able to afford their teaching, the sophists emphasized rhetoric, the art of persuasion. More specifically, they taught their students to persuasively argue both sides of any case. And from teaching people how to make the weaker argument appear to be the stronger, it was just a short step to questioning whether there even *is* such a thing as true or false, right or wrong. Unfortunately, the sophists didn't care *what* their students were trying to persuade others to do or believe. And so, in effect, the sophists helped people to promote their own interests, even if it meant sacrificing the interests of their community.

Although the roots of sophistry lie in ancient Greece, the practice has never gone out of style. After all, isn't the primary goal of advertisers and salespeople to persuade a consumer to purchase a product regardless of whether the product is good for her or not? Don't public relations specialists manipulate the uninformed public? Don't defense attorneys try to persuade juries that their guilty-as-hell clients are innocent? Thankfully, *The Daily Show* commonly takes on such sophists in its satirical news segments. It's surprisingly easy to do. A reporter simply asks audacious questions of people so blinded by their pursuits that they don't even realize they're being mocked.

To Scoff at the Sophist in Office

Stewart's primary objects of derision, though, are sophists in politics and the mainstream media. Political sophists do their best to persuade their constituencies to vote for them, but their deceptive rhetoric wouldn't be so successful without the media sophists. So Stewart regularly attacks media sophists for their complicity with political sophists by delivering verbal jabs at both. During the 2004 presidential elections, Stewart asked then-"reporter" Ed Helms if he knew what was going to happen at the presidential debates the next day. Helms read him the report he was going to file. Stewart responded that Helms had written the report as if the debates had already happened. Helms admitted that he wrote the report the day before the event. Incredulous, Stewart asked him, "You write your stories in advance and then put it in the past tense?" Admitting "all the reporters do that," Helms explained, "we write stories in advance based on conventional wisdom and then whatever happens, we make it fit that storyline." When Stewart asked why they do that, Helms answered, "We're lazy? Lazy thinkers?"

Opposing the way the traditional media stayed clear of confrontations with the Bush administration since 9/11, *The Daily Show* is unrelenting in its ironic assaults, highlighting how media sophists sacrifice the investigation of newsworthy stories for ratings and access to the White House. Stewart called *Crossfire* hosts Tucker Carlson and Paul Begala "partisan hacks" and berated them for not raising the level of discourse on their show beyond sloganeering. At a time when the mainstream media was focused on Vice President Cheney's daughter, Stewart continued to hammer the media for its coverage of the presidential debates. He said, "The thing is, we need your help. Right now, you're helping the politicians and the corporations and we're left out there to mow our lawns." In contrast to such self-interested agendas, Stewart uses the following criteria in deciding to put something on *The Daily Show*: "Is that funny? Is that smart? Is that good?"[1] As a matter of moral principle, Stewart has said that there are some guests he simply wouldn't invite on his show, such as Mike Tyson and Bob Novak.[2] Indeed, Stewart has called Novak, who revealed the identity of a CIA agent, a "douchebag for liberty" and awarded him, in absentia, the "Congressional Medal of Douchebaggery."

The moral question is something sophists simply don't consider. Instead of asking whether an action is right or just, the sophist asks, "Will reporting this story or supporting this policy advance my career?"

Media sophists, like Ann Coulter, encourage conformity with the tacit message that what most people think is how everyone should think. When people buy this message, the sophists simply have to announce what most people think. The unfortunate outcome is that the general public become disinclined to think for themselves. Instead, they uncritically accept the ideas or values of a larger group, such as their church or their political party or Fox News host Bill O'Reilly's audience. Blindly conforming to majority opinion, they don't consider that most people once believed that the Earth is flat, that slavery is natural, and that women belong in the home.

Men with a Mission

Newsweek's description of Stewart as offering "fearless social satire" while "battling pomposity and misinformation,"[3] fits Socrates like a glove. And just as Stewart is now being taken seriously as a politico-societal force, Socrates was a politico-societal force in his day.

In ancient Athens, people wanted the same thing most contemporary Americans want—pleasure and material success. These desires, however, were in conflict with their traditional moral and religious values, including patriotism and regular temple (church) attendance. The Athenian government, desiring stability and cohesiveness, saw these values as a means to their end. Much like contemporary conservative politicians, ancient Athenian politicians tried to preserve the traditional religious beliefs and values as much as possible. If anyone questioned these beliefs and values, the government interpreted this as an attack on the state.

Enter Socrates, who encouraged people to raise questions about accepted customs in ethical and religious behavior. The philosopher who asked "Is something pious because the gods love it? Or do the gods love it because it is pious?" would certainly applaud "This Week in God." But in societies that are so absorbed with getting ahead and so preoccupied with being entertained, *how* can anyone motivate others to raise questions about traditional values and beliefs? It ain't easy, so our boys better have a method for their mission.

Socrates' mission was "to persuade each one of you not to think more of practical advantages than of his mental and moral well-being, or ... to think more of advantage than of well-being in the case of the state or of anything else."[4] He was sure that wisdom and virtue are far more important for individuals than money and power. So too, the good of the state lies first and foremost in its wisdom and virtue rather than in profit or political might.

Like Socrates, Stewart knows that the ethical and political well-being of any society depends of the ethical and political well-being of each of its citizens.[5] But people sometimes need prompting to put important issues in the right perspective. As Stewart put it, describing *The Daily Show* in *Newsweek*, "This is a show grounded in passion, not cynicism."[6] People sometimes experience the passion of Socrates and Stewart as unsettling since their questions raise serious doubts about some aspects of socially accepted values.

Ignorance often gets in the way of pursuing the truth. To fulfill their mission, Socrates and Stewart are driven to tear off the masks of arrogance and self-deception that allow ignorance to masquerade as wisdom and knowledge. For instance, to show that anyone can be called an "expert," correspondents on *The Daily Show* are always labeled as "Senior Correspondents" in whatever area they are reporting on, usually for the first time. The show has featured, among others, a "Senior Futlbologist," a "Senior Terrorist Analyst," and a "Chief International Finance Correspondent."

The process of unmasking "experts" and exposing ignorance has had an effect on *The Daily Show*'s audience. According to one study, viewers of *The Daily Show* had a more accurate understanding of the facts behind the 2004 presidential election than people who primarily read newspapers and watched major network newscasts.[7] Socrates and Stewart know that ignorance isn't dependent on one's formal education or status in society. To discover the truth all that's needed is the spirit of inquiry and an open mind.

Although viewing others as ignorant may seem arrogant, neither Socrates nor Stewart are elitist. Knowing they're fallible, they regularly confess their own ignorance. Frequently, they insist that they're exploring territory that's as uncharted to them as it is to the person each man talks with. Indeed, this insistence is part of their method.

A Method to Their Madness

Socrates' method of fulfilling his mission was so unique it became known as the "Socratic method." The method, which is now one of the classic question-and-answer techniques of education, is distinctive in its reliance on one-on-one encounters. Socrates was convinced that the only way to reach people is to treat them as individuals capable of independent judgment.

Here's how his method works. First, Socrates approaches someone who claims to know something about a subject like justice, courage, or politics. He flatters the guy and thanks his lucky stars that he's found someone who really knows something that he, Socrates, has been searching for all his life. He then humbly entreats the "expert" to impart his wisdom. The man, at this point, is confident he knows the answer and condescendingly "teaches" Socrates, who seems very impressed by the response. I imagine Socrates may even have made one of those awestruck faces Jon Stewart is famous for.

At this point, the expert gets a swelled head. Yet, in the expert's self-confident response, Socrates finds one or two little difficulties that provide material for another question, a deeper one. The man offers what he thinks is a quick fix, by providing some conventional "wisdom." After Socrates asks him to draw out the consequences of the quick fix, the man realizes that he's trapped in a position he can't reasonably hold, often a contradiction. Peeling away layer after layer of shallow beliefs, Socrates exposes not only the bruised fruit of false opinions, but also the ripe core of truth.

The method Stewart and *The Daily Show*'s correspondents use in questioning their guests has an uncanny resemblance to Socrates' method. Approaching someone who claims to know a lot about a subject, the correspondents proceed to flatter them. Then they entreat the expert to impart his or her wisdom. At first, the "expert" confidently proceeds to produce his case until the correspondent picks out one or two minor problems, which provide material for another question, a deeper one. The expert offers what he thinks is a quick fix, by providing some conventional "wisdom." After the correspondents ask him to draw out the consequences of the quick fix, the person realizes that he's trapped in a position he can't reasonably hold, often a contradiction. In these interactions, the correspondents follow the practice of Socrates, who, peeling away layer after layer of shallow beliefs, exposes not only the bruised fruit of false opinion, but the ripe core of truth.

Like Socrates, Stewart usually refrains from lengthy speeches that might simply overwhelm his listeners. He shares Socrates' appreciation of one-on-one encounters, and he resembles the ancient sage when he pretends to be confused and requests explanations that underscore how ridiculous someone else sounds. Neither Socrates nor Stewart merely present and dissect ideas, remaining detached from the focus of the discussion. Instead, they enter the stage and become the actors and the focal points of action, the watching audience and the watched performers. Neither wants people to agree with them for reasons they don't understand. So they ask questions. While asking these questions, Stewart, like Socrates, actually listens to the people he's conversing with, attempting to understand what they're saying.

Since many of us prefer to hear our own voices, we don't often really listen to other people. We often see disagreement as a competition where the object is simply to win. With this attitude, so very characteristic of sophists, people become angry with one another and raise their voices to drown out or continually interrupt other people. (For an abundance of examples, just tune in to *The O'Reilly Factor* any night of the week.) Listening indicates that you're secure enough in your position that you're not threatened by someone's differing viewpoint. When you calmly listen to someone else, you drop your defenses and it's more likely the other person will respond in kind.

The Audience: Questioning Youths or Stoned Slackers?

By exposing the ignorance of politicians and other know-it-alls, Socrates taught people to look at their cultural traditions and laws in a new light. His unsparing criticisms of the politicians' incompetence and narrow-minded patriotism fostered a critical attitude towards the government and its laws among the younger generation. Socrates showed them that people may have high positions and power, yet at the same time be irrational and deeply confused. He revealed politicians' irrationality and confusion by continually cross-examining them with questions they should have been able to answer, such as: Since you're a leader of the state, where exactly are you leading the state? Since you're in a position of authority, what are your credentials for that authority? What does justice really mean?

Although Socrates turned the conversation to intellectual subjects, he didn't put on intellectual airs. Like Stewart, he was a man of the people and spoke only the vernacular of his friends. Like Stewart, he saw himself as short, amusing, and unimportant. A group of appreciative young men began to follow Socrates. When they saw that the politicians couldn't support their answers to Socrates' questions, not only were the young men entertained, they learned a valuable lesson: don't simply assume those in authority possess knowledge and wisdom. They adored Socrates for his efforts, the ultimate in questioning authority. And having witnessed Socrates' cross-examinations, his followers started questioning authority themselves.

Like Socrates, Stewart is aware that democracy is only effective to the extent that the public are well-informed about issues and can think independently and critically about those issues. Stewart, too, has a large group of young people who follow him on a regular basis. The median age of *The Daily Show* audience is 33, which is relatively young compared to that of traditional news shows. Most viewers (73%) fall in the 18–49 age range, a demographic that sophists in the advertising industry and the political arena are eager to cultivate.

The Daily Show is particularly popular among college students. As Katherine Bullen, a University of Iowa sophomore, explained in *Newsweek*, "He's one of the few 'adults' that mocks the things we mock, and he can do that without talking down to us."[8] More specifically, the 2004 Class Day speaker of Yale University said that students don't have "a spectrum of critical analyses represented in the mainstream media" and this is why *The Daily Show* has substituted for the traditional news. "Stewart's combination of irony and satire, of facts and jokes, his willingness to lay bare the process of 'news' fabrication, has endeared his brand of humor to so many of us, and won him the kind of critical acclaim that indicates just how influential his show is."[9]

Not everyone, however, sees the attraction of youth to *The Daily Show* as something positive. Bill O'Reilly, for instance, disparages Stewart's hold on what he calls the "stoned slacker" crowd,[10] claiming that "dopey college kids" like Bullen must be "stoned" to watch *The Daily Show*.[11] Had he been there, O'Reilly might well have made similar comments about the youthful crowd that gathered around Socrates. But of course this crowd would have included one very famous slacker—Plato! Time will tell who will emerge from Stewart's crowd.

The Irony of It All

As the Yale student observed, the way that Stewart accomplishes his mission relies heavily on ironic humor. Socrates was also well known for using ironic humor to achieve his mission. "Socratic irony," as it came to be called, involves pretending to be ignorant, to know less than you really know. Not simply a verbal disclaimer of knowledge, Socratic irony involves a way of behaving. As Socrates' reputation grew, it became difficult to convince other people to converse with him. So he behaved as a humble inquirer claiming to need instruction from an expert. Stewart, of course, adopts a similar pose on *The Daily Show*.[12]

Disarming as the unassuming façade of both men may be, lurking beneath it lies a sharp-witted intelligence, which quickly perceives the paradoxical and the ironic. But what is irony? Irony can take many shapes, such as understating or overstating the point. Stewart used understatement to emphasize the audacity of then-Defense Secretary Rumsfeld's comment (issued during the Senate hearings on the torture of Iraqi prisoners at Abu Ghraib), "They are human beings." Stewart quipped, "It may not seem like much, but for this administration it's a huge policy shift." Irony can also take the form of saying the exact opposite of what you mean or using an ambiguous expression deliberately. Generally, irony is a method of communication in which someone intends to get across one meaning while saying something that seems to have another meaning. The real meaning, which isn't obvious, is detected by certain hints, such as the context in which the words are used or the tone of voice expressing the words. Think, for instance, of billing *The Daily Show* as "The most mistrusted name in fake news!"

Another kind of irony comes from the background knowledge shared by the ironist and the audience who appreciates the real meaning of the words. When irony depends on the mutual background, it's like a private joke between the ironist and the audience to whom the real meaning is directed. For instance, *Newsweek* reported that prior to taping one episode, Stewart announced excitedly, "We've got us a Democratic general!" Then he quipped, "That's like a gay black Republican. It's a rare beast."[13] Understanding the private joke, the audience cracked up.

Irony can also be similar to a riddle intended to amuse people who are sufficiently perceptive to recognize the difference between the real meaning and the sham one. During George W. Bush's time in office, Stewart would often show a brief clip of the President speaking and then, without a word, look quite confused, dumbfounded, or horrified. The camera just showed his facial expressions and mute astonishment, which said all that needed to be said. Of course, even if the irony is obvious, some people are such idiots they won't "get it." Yet if they do get it, the irony's effect can be thought-provoking. In suddenly perceiving the irony of a statement, a person can achieve a depth of insight into its truth that can't usually be matched by a more explicit, straightforward method.

Since Obama has become president, Stewart no longer spends much time using Socratic irony against the President. His barbs are rather sporadic as opposed to ongoing. However, he directs his ironic commentary frequently against Congress and Obama's rival, Mitt Romney, as the 2012 presidential campaign has unfolded.

"Monkey" Idol or Thoughtful Partisan Satirist?

Stewart's use of irony has raised some serious questions. Ken Tucker, writing in *New York* magazine, asks, "Is [Stewart] the Emmy-winning 'monkey,' idol to millions of young couch-skeptics, or the thoughtful partisan satirist who'd like to be a player in the national discourse?"[14] Tucker suggests that if Stewart were *really* a political critic, he would concentrate on getting results and downplay his use of irony. Is there a tension between Stewart the entertainer, who aims at provoking laughter, and Stewart the political critic, who has some responsibility to the truth?

The question Tucker raises was highlighted when Stewart appeared on CNN's *Crossfire* in October 2004. Stewart derided the two hosts for their dishonest "partisan hackery," rather than holding themselves to journalistic integrity. Tucker Carlson, a Republican commentator, said, "I thought you were going to be funny. Come on. Be funny." Stewart fired back, "No. No. I'm not going to be your monkey." Earnestly stating his purpose in attending the show, Stewart said, "I'm here to confront you, because we need help from the media and they're hurting us." Stewart was suggesting that the media is hurting Americans by keeping them ignorant of important information. So, he charged, although *The Daily Show* bills itself as doing fake news, it was actually *Crossfire* that was hurting the public through its incessant spin and fake debates. As a result of this confrontation, Stewart received wide public support, and in January 2005, *Crossfire* was taken off the air.

Given all the commonalities between Stewart and Socrates, we could also ask the same question of his ancient Greek counterpart: "Hey, Socrates! Are you merely trying to entertain people or are you a serious critic who is trying to bring out the truth?" Now the fact that Socrates aims at truth is hardly to be doubted. Looking back at Socrates, we get a broader perspective on him than we'd be able to get if he were around today. It's easy to see that he used irony as a *means* to getting at the truth. Can we say the same thing about Stewart? We can, since not only are laughter and truth compatible, the one can be a particularly useful means of arriving at the other. Messages about serious, important issues are more digestible if delivered with a smile, not a scream.

The ironic element in Socrates' and Stewart's method should not be denigrated or underestimated, for it's what helps both of them to attract such large audiences. By having more than a superficial meaning, irony keeps listeners on their toes. For Socrates and Stewart, the most important point of communicating with others is to engage them in an issue. Irony helps to keep their audiences alert, actively listening, and critically thinking. It also keeps people aware that things may not always be what they seem. For instance, when the Republicans kept referring to a Democrat-proposed Iraq exit strategy as "cut and run," Stewart asked us to reflect on whether exit strategies can be broken down to just two verbs and a conjunction. People appreciate the use of ironic humor to make such a point. Why? It's simply more enjoyable to use the mind in an active way rather than passively absorb information. Irony requires the mind to be active since it makes us "read between the lines." Enjoyment also makes the message more likely to stick. When people catch on, they're entertained. Yet, at the same time, irony helps people to establish a network of likeminded individuals. Based on a shared understanding of the deeper underlying meaning of an ironic exchange, people bond, and bond more closely. In their way, both Socrates and Stewart seek to create a dialogue among people who use their minds in an active way. Just as Socrates was the inspiration for a network of change in his time, Stewart may provide the same inspiration in ours. Socrates was, of course, ultimately convicted of impiety and corrupting the youth, and he was executed. Thankfully, no matter how much Stewart may rub some people the wrong way, he's safe from sharing Socrates' fate—I think.

Notes

1. Gary Younge, "Such a Tease," *The Guardian* (October 1, 2005), http://arts.guardian.co.uk/features/story/0,11710,1582009,00.html, accessed February 5, 2013.
2. "Speech for Newhouse School," *American Perspectives*, C-SPAN (October 14, 2004).
3. Marc Peyser, "Who's Next 2004: Red, White & Funny," *Newsweek* 143 (December 29, 2003), 71.
4. Plato, *Apology*, trans. Hugh Tredennick, in *The Collected Dialogues of Plato*, eds. Edith Hamilton and Huntington Cairns (Princeton, NJ: Princeton University, 1978), 21.
5. On *Larry King Live* (February 27, 2006), Stewart said that there's no such thing as "*the* American people .... I mean the whole thing is a melting pot, a collective of individuals."
6. Peyser, "Who's Next 2004," 71.
7. Annenberg Public Policy Center Report (Press Release) (September 21, 2004), www.annenbergpublicpolicycenter.org/Downloads/Political_Communication/naes/2004_03_late-night-knowledge-2_9-21_pr.pdf, accessed February 7, 2013. The survey was conducted at the University of Pennsylvania.
8. Peyser, "Who's Next 2004," 71.
9. "2004 Class Day Speaker Needs Irony, Wit," *Yale Daily News* (January 12, 2004).
10. *The O'Reilly Factor*, Fox News (September 17, 2004).
11. O'Reilly made this comment about college kids who watch *The Daily Show* on the June 14, 2006 edition of his nationally syndicated radio show.
12. For a discussion of irony and Stephen Colbert, see Kevin S. Decker, "Thank God It's Stephen Colbert! The Rally to Restore Irony on *The Colbert Report*," in this volume.
13. Peyser, "Who's Next 2004," 71.
14. Ken Tucker, "You Can't Be Serious!" *New York Magazine* 37 (November 1, 2004), 63.

Chapter 8

Jon the Cynic
Dog Philosophy 101

Alejandro Bárcenas

I am the "Highlander." You know, there has been a form of me around in—forever.

> Jon Stewart on *The Rachel Maddow Show*
> (November 19, 2010)

Jon Stewart, a cynic? Perhaps not, according to some die-hard fans. But it's not difficult to imagine that for many viewers of *The Daily Show*, even those who enjoy watching the host "speak truth to power," Stewart is no more than a neatly dressed cynic. Critical articles in newspapers, magazines, and scholarly journals reveal growing concern about how *The Daily Show* might be affecting its viewers, perhaps instilling disillusionment and apathy in young people. These concerns have been reinforced by a survey-based study published in 2006 on this so-called "*Daily Show* Effect." After exposing a group of college students to clips taken from *The Daily Show*'s coverage of the 2004 Presidential campaign, the researchers concluded that "increased exposure to TDS is significantly related to cynicism for young adults."[1] The same researchers affirmed their position in 2011 by stating that "it is a possibility that cannot be ruled out" that viewing *The Daily Show* leads to greater levels of cynicism among young adults.[2] Their conclusion seems to confirm what many had already suspected: lampooning politicians and other public figures might, despite the

The Ultimate Daily Show and Philosophy: More Moments of Zen, More Indecision Theory, First Edition. Edited by Jason Holt.
© 2013 John Wiley & Sons, Inc. Published 2013 by John Wiley & Sons, Inc.

humor, have a down side. Perhaps the laughs come at the high price of generating a jaded audience, decreased trust in politicians, the media, and even democracy itself.

Even if *The Daily Show* has this effect, of course, the key question is whether or not such cynicism is warranted. So before we start a campaign to cancel the show, let's consider some historical and philosophical facts concerning the word "cynic." Nowadays we generally think of a cynic as someone with a very low opinion of humanity. Stewart's popularity rests in part on his irreverent and amusing news reports, where no topic is sacred, no institution off limits, no person beyond criticism, and this seems to fit the mold of a modern cynic. But calling him a cynic in this sense might be, to a certain extent, misleading. Stewart seems much more negative about institutions, conventions, and *certain* people than he is about humanity as a whole, which means that he might be a cynic in a different, much older, and much richer sense.

Cynicism originated in ancient Greece, and it's important to realize that the label initially had very different connotations from what our current term would suggest. The ancient cynics were a ragtag bunch of philosophers who were seen—really—as dog-like (*kynikos* or "cynic" in Greek). Why dog-like? What do dogs have to do with philosophy? We tend to think of dogs as loyal, devoted, and obedient creatures, but the Greeks saw them very differently, as indecent, corrupt, and disobedient animals. Dogs symbolized shamelessness, audacity, and a kind of immoral independence, because even though they lived among people and shared their homes, they didn't follow human customs, but only their own true nature (*physis*). For those who wanted to bark at, or take a bite out of, the prevailing social norms, an association with the canine species wasn't at all inappropriate or displeasing. In turn, the cynics came to embrace this popular characterization of their actions, in particular the most notorious "dog philosopher" of all, Diogenes of Sinope (ca. 412–324 BCE)— later we'll see how Diogenes earned this notoriety.

Provoking outrage was the cynics' calling card. The cynics lived in the heart of ancient democracies, confronting accepted habits, unchallenged assumptions, and above all institutional corruption. They confronted those who abused their power in the manner they knew best: by being outrageous (*anaideia*). Their aim wasn't just to avoid what they considered to be harmful pursuits and practices, but to expose and ridicule those traditions that most people unreflectively considered moral and proper. If we look at Stewart in the context of this "dog philosophy," we'll shed light on the meaning of his role in contemporary culture. We might find that he not only bears similarities to, but also at heart is a modern version of, these ancient dog philosophers.

Rebel with a Cause

We have precious little from the early cynics themselves. For the most part, we must rely on a few scattered fragments and the biographies by third-century Greek historian Diogenes Laertius.[3] We have, however, a very accurate picture of the politics of ancient Greece, which bears surprising resemblance to ours. The cynics lived in Athens during turbulent times (fourth and third centuries BCE), when the political system of the city-state was the precarious first democracy the world had ever seen.

Ancient Athenian democracy didn't function the way ours does today.[4] Rather, it involved direct participation in government. Any free male citizen native to the city could potentially lead the administration if he was able to convince the assembly (*ekklesia*) to vote in favor of his proposals. But the most radical aspect of the Athenian practice of direct democracy was that holding some special offices, such as being a member of the *boule*—a 500-member council— was decided, believe it or not, by lottery. In contrast, modern democracies are representative; citizens aren't assembled to cast votes on every single issue. And, of course, no lottery system is in effect; rather, people are elected to represent various constituencies. The Founding Fathers, in fact, intentionally avoided, or to be more accurate, feared the Athenian model of "pure" democracy because of its tendency to move back and forth between tyranny and anarchy.

Putting aside some of the organizational differences between the two democracies, there are, owing to human frailty, many commonalities as well. One characteristic of all democracies deserves special attention, namely that becoming a leader depends on the abilities of the individual candidate. In contrast to other, non-democratic systems of government, individuals aren't born into positions of power, nor do they depend on a king or religious leader to entitle them to power.

They must rather obtain positions of power by winning the approval of ordinary citizens.

Citizens needed certain skills, rhetoric in particular, to participate effectively in politics. Consequently, public-speaking teachers, such as Gorgias, Prodicus, Hippias, and other Sophists, roamed the streets of the city-states seeking students who aspired to rule. One such student was the notorious Alcibiades, who came to represent the ugly side of the participatory system for being able to seduce crowds into voting for his own ultimately selfish schemes. Alcibiades, however, wasn't an isolated case; many of the initiatives brought up in the assembly were motivated by personal agendas. Eloquent speakers could persuade others to accept measures of benefit to the speakers and their families, without any concern for what would benefit society as a whole. Such trends in contemporary politics are, of course, common targets of *Daily Show* humor. A persuasive politician in Athens could convince the assembly to vote for an ill-considered war (the expedition to Syracuse in 415 BCE, for instance). Witnesses to turbulent times, the cynics—just like Stewart in airing regular installments of "Mess O' Potamia" and "Crises in Israfghyianonanaq"—decided that the best response wasn't to stay quiet, but to speak out against what they saw as bad policy. Their irreverent, non-conformist responses to self-destructive, unreasonable behavior continued the tradition, started by Socrates (470–399 BCE), of exposing and ridiculing those who were responsible for such social unrest and political debacles. In their time, they too "spoke truth to power."

The cynics were relentless in their denunciation of the moral corruption of those in power, despite the perils in which such opposition placed them. Even the Macedonian kings Philip II and Alexander the Great, who conquered Greece and temporarily suspended Athenian democracy, were confronted by the daring cynics. It's said that Diogenes, after being captured in Chaeronea (338 BCE), the key battle for the control of Greece, was violently brought to King Philip II. Fighting on the losing side of the Athenians, he was very likely to end up as a slave or even be executed right on the spot. But after Diogenes told the king that he was a longtime observer of the ruler's "insatiable greed," Philip set him free in admiration.[5] Diogenes knew that kings, and others enamored with their own status and power, tend to crave praise, and they often don't realize the dangerous consequences of their usually blind ambition. Since Diogenes was released, the point of the story might be that the king sought, but seldom got, honesty from people. Perhaps Philip realized the truth of the cynic's daring words, and so respected Diogenes for being something other than a timid "yes man," whose words are nothing but empty flattery, even in the face of death. Later on, we'll see what happened when Diogenes met Alexander the Great.

In less harsh circumstances, Stewart regularly voices his discontent with the current political climate, showing the harmful side of common practices, attitudes, and assumptions. He regularly exhibits his concerns about the way discussions take place in Congress, when, despite their apparent seriousness, in most cases important issues and debates are either diffused by irrelevant considerations, or reduced to a battle of slogans and superficial metaphors. Also, in the aftermath of the financial crisis of 2008 in the segments "Clusterf#@k to the Poor House" and "Wall Street Watch: These F@#king Guys," Stewart has exposed not only the hypocrisy of Wall Street but, most importantly, the incompetence of the lawmakers who are supposed to regulate fraudulent banking practices so that such economic meltdowns can't occur in the first place.

Stewart also uses the "fake news" format to express his profound disapproval of contemporary journalism. The media's general lack of depth and too-common appeal to what sells over what really matters is a recurring theme of *The Daily Show*. The defunct *Daily Show* segment "Even Stevphen," with alumni Steve Carell and Stephen Colbert, highlighted how what many media outlets present as legitimate debate, as two opposing sides defending their respective positions, is indeed what, on CNN's *Crossfire*, Stewart called "partisan hackery" (October 15, 2004). Only the day before the now infamous *Crossfire* appearance, Stewart had announced publicly, "I'm advocating that the media come back to work for us ... Their job can't be: 'What do you think Donna Brazile? OK. What do you think Bay Buchanan? We'll be right back.' That's not a job, that's nothing."[6] Returning to the case of the financial crisis, Stewart felt that the financial news industry was "not just guilty of the sin of omission but of commission," as he told Jim Cramer from CNBC during his appearance on the show (March 12, 2009), since they did not use their expertise to expose the shenanigans that were occurring behind closed doors on Wall Street. When Cramer complained that several CEOs lied to him when he had them on his program "Mad Money,"

Stewart responded by saying, "I'm under the assumption—and maybe this is purely ridiculous—that you don't take their word at face value, that you go around and try to figure it out."

The ancient cynics and the contemporary Jon Stewart share and express a pervasive sense of discontent with the dangerous, uncritically accepted aspects of their cultures. This discontent unfolds, deliberately or not, into a search for the truth that lies behind the façade of common practice and public perception.

Humor Leads to Truth

As we've seen, ancient cynicism emerged during a period of unrest and discontent in Athens, and it became the leading subversive response to the culture of the time. The rebellious manner of the cynics was intended to overcome ignorance and passive consent by denouncing, in unusual ways, the breakdown of society. Often this criticism took the form of odd behavior, in direct opposition to accepted customs, in extreme, ridiculous ways, with the intention of poking fun at things generally considered serious, important, and not inherently funny. Stewart's scribbling and doodling at the start of each episode ironically undermines the seriousness of taking crucial, last-minute notes on headline news segments. Similarly, but more extremely, Diogenes lived in a bathtub to show that the pursuit of wealth and comfort was taken much too seriously in his time, that it's not wealth or comfort that makes us human, or morally good, for that matter. Such actions characterize the rebellious side of philosophical cynicism. But their playfulness can be deceiving. Both Stewart's and the cynics' attitudes are well considered and their actions carefully orchestrated. The purpose of their comedic, often outrageous acts isn't simply entertainment; the means are entertaining, but the objective is very serious.

On the other hand, Stewart was criticized on *Crossfire* for not living up to the standards that he asks others, particularly journalists, to follow. However, his role as a comedian, as important as it might be, shouldn't be confused with journalism, as Stewart continually points out. For instance, it would be unreasonable to expect that *The Daily Show* should, or could, assume the same responsibility for reporting as is supposed to be assumed by news agencies. As Stewart told Paul Begala and Tucker Carlson, "I didn't realize that—and maybe this explains quite a bit—that the news organizations look to Comedy Central for their cues on integrity. After all," he continued, "you're on CNN. The show that leads into me is puppets making crank phone calls."[7] Stewart has trying to clarify that *The Daily Show*'s main mission is to entertain and not to inform. In contrast, news channels have sacrificed content and research for entertainment. Needless to say, nobody really believed that Stewart's credibility was somehow undermined by *Crank Yankers*, the preceding show on Comedy Central at the time. When he's sitting behind that desk, Stewart means serious business. What he says carries a lot of weight even if, and especially because, his methods are entertaining.

Stewart confronted the hosts of *Crossfire* face to face, with the gravitas of a cynic, but Begala and Carlson weren't the first ones to recognize the potentially powerful influence of the seemingly innocent comedy of the "dog philosophers." The cynics were a force to be reckoned with right from the start. The Roman Emperor Julian (332–363 CE) acknowledged them as his "most estimable rivals," and even Alexander the Great realized how formidable they really were in his famous encounter with Diogenes. Alexander supposedly told Diogenes to ask for anything that he wished, to which Diogenes replied, "Do not shade me; stand out of my light."[8] Obviously there's more to the story than Diogenes' desire to mock the great ruler. The cynic's intention was to show that Alexander's display of power was not only, in effect, insignificant but also ultimately irrelevant, a mere hindrance, to the search for wisdom. By blocking from Diogenes' view a traditional symbol of truth, the sun, the Macedonian ruler was seen to represent the corrupt nature of politics. As a philosopher, Diogenes, not Alexander, however great, is the one in direct contact with the truth, and his aim was to teach people the path to discovering and fulfilling their nature as rational beings. It was those who were true to their nature—to themselves—that Diogenes famously sought—but didn't find—when he walked about in broad daylight with his lamp.[9]

The cynics offered an unorthodox method, disguised in the comedic style, to get out of the "deception lane" created by the demagogues. Although counter-conventional, their methods weren't intended to deviate from, but rather to help in reaching, the highest and noblest philosophical end, namely wisdom. This alternative method of instilling or "awakening" knowledge, by example and through humor, is importantly distinct from more traditional methods of argumentation and debate. Since they were clearly among the best-educated people in Athens, the cynics weren't opposed to culture or education (*paideia*) generally, but only to culture that hindered the natural, rational development of human beings. In fact, another influential cynic, a student of Diogenes, Crates of Thebes (ca. 368–288 BCE), said, "One should study philosophy until seeing in generals nothing but donkey drivers,"[10] a statement that the *Daily Show* writers would no doubt happily approve.

The use of humor as a guide in the discovery of wisdom was aimed to generate in the public the kind of "awakening" described by Aristotle (384–322 BCE) in his *Poetics*, a transformation caused by the sudden recognition of truth (*anagnorisis*).[11] Comedy helps the observer to become aware of deception and to understand how common conceptions and opinions (*doxa*) that "look like" (*pseudos*) the real thing, pretend to stand in for truth and knowledge. Coming to a recognition (*anagnorisis*) of reality *as it truly is* is perhaps one of the best expressions of the ancient Greek idea of truth as arriving at the unhidden (*aletheia*).

Despite the many similarities between ancient cynicism and *The Daily Show*, the program has no explicit pretensions of having such a philosophical agenda. Still, it's not hard to see how Stewart's reporting, in particular during the opening headlines segment, doesn't indulge in merely provoking empty laughs, but presents issues from a delightful and instructive perspective, helping to reinforce an awareness of things *as they are*, in contrast to how they're often presented by politicians and the media at large.

A Healthy Dose of Cynicism

Although the early cynic movement originated in antiquity during a time of democratic crisis, it didn't disappear completely after the crisis. Some forms of philosophical cynicism survived beyond the Hellenistic era and into the Roman Republic. The cynic's attitude thrived wherever discussion and argumentation were valued in a culture. Philosophical cynicism flourished in its most refined form in this more open-minded historical context, and I'd like to think, and there's reason to suppose, that it's a key distinguishing feature of democracy. With our political system comparable, in many ways, to that of ancient Athens, it might be more useful than ever to reflect on the role played by cynicism in ancient Greece, particularly when today there are signs of comparable attitudes among influential people, like Stewart.

First, let's see how political influence is achieved in a democracy. Generally speaking, in ancient and modern democracies, those who receive the approval of the majority are rewarded with prestige and authority. High popular recognition (*eudoxia*) can be considered "virtuous" in a democratic system because it gives a person power. According to the cynics, though, pursuing this kind of success promotes mostly demagogy and deception, and so turns politics into a struggle for mere popularity and not for what's truly virtuous (*arete*). The cynic, intending to oppose and denounce the moral and ethical shortcomings of those who corrupt the system and abuse their power for mere personal gain, naturally becomes the target of the offended parties. Because of distorted public perceptions, the cynics actually considered unpopularity (*adoxia*) to be a good thing (*agathon*), a sign that they were getting at the truth, that their opposition was on track.[12] In Stewart's case, too, it's perfectly fitting, even necessary, for him to have, and to have *earned*, a "bad reputation" (*adoxia*), because his way of thinking diverges from that of the majority. In this respect Stewart, in true cynic fashion, understands and accepts his lot: "As someone who is held in contempt by much of the country," he said at the Newhouse School Press Breakfast, "it's really not that bad. You will get some stares at the mall, every now and again an email referring to your heritage ... but other than that, being held in contempt is quite comfortable."

The role that the "dog philosophers" took on, regardless of public perception, was to embrace certain essential elements of democracy to help turn the system away from its vicious and corrupt ways. For example, access to public spaces allowed the cynics to speak freely (*parrhesia*). Not surprisingly, Athenians often abused free speech, using rhetoric to placate crowds by appealing to the lowest common denominator, furthering their own interests in the process. The cynics, however, transformed *parrhesia* from a servant of decadence into an instrument of democratic shock therapy.

When Diogenes was asked "what's the most beautiful thing in the world?" his answer was *parrhesia*.[13] *Parrhesia* became the key instrument for "defacing the currency" of tradition, a cynic's metaphor for the conflict between philosophy (which does the defacing) and common opinion (the currency). Diogenes, like Socrates before him, thought that conventions needed to be confronted with knowledge of the true nature of things (*physis*), passion with reason (*logos*).[14] He intended to improve the lives of the citizenry by encouraging the development of reason. In this sense, the cynics continued the Socratic tradition in their appreciation of education and the belief that, through introspection, virtue can be taught. In addition, philosophy has the capacity to teach people how to recognize when language is being used in a deceitful way. It's very important for a citizen in a democracy to have that capacity, because it allows a person to exercise the right to vote in a responsible way. Only then can true citizens participate well in a democracy, instead of blindly accepting the opinion or the will of the majority. After all to be ignorant was, and to some extent still is, seen as a sign of *irresponsibility* in the democratic context.

Still, cynicism has been portrayed by some, then as now, as a destructive cultural force. So, if Stewart's attitude fits so well into the mold of the ancient cynics, what does this say about him? Is he also destructive? Were the original cynics? Maybe if Stewart's message were that politics is pointless. But that's not the message. *The Daily Show* presents a different, in some ways more complete view of politics than is usually aired on the networks. Cynicism certainly can be destructive, but only in the sense of highlighting and undermining reckless practices, unreflective understanding, which, left alone, become detrimental to society. The Socratic teaching of a cynic, like Diogenes or Stewart, is that we should develop self-sufficiency (*autarkeia*) in our judgment of things and a willingness to question authority, particularly if the authority has been found less than reliable. When humor is mixed in, the cynic becomes a Socratic "gadfly," irritating society by poking fun at its failings and foibles, until it, at last, wakes up to itself.

Stewart is no philosopher, nor does he intend to be one. *The Daily Show*, however, delivers the undeniably philosophical message of just how important earnestness, honesty, and integrity are in the political sphere. It seems that both Stewart and the ancient cynics share the belief that a better society can only be constructed by people who are open-minded and critical about destructive practices and dogmas. I have no doubt that Diogenes would recognize Stewart as a fellow "dog." Sadly, though, some people are still put off, even outraged, by the cynic's form of humor, sometimes condemning it as an enemy of democracy, instead of seeing dog philosophy for what it is, democracy's best friend.[15]

Notes

1. Jody Baumgartner and Jonathan S. Morris, "*The Daily Show* Effect: Candidate Evaluations, Efficacy, and American Youth," *American Politics Research* 34 (2006), 360.
2. Jody Baumgartner and Jonathan S. Morris, "Stoned Slackers or Super-citizens? 'The Daily Show' Viewing and the Political Engagement of Young Adults," in *The Stewart/Colbert Effect: Essays on the Real Impacts of Fake News*, ed. Amarnath Amarasingam (New York: McFarland, 2011), 77.
3. Diogenes Laertius, *Lives of Eminent Philosophers* (Cambridge, MA: Harvard University Press, 2005). All translations are mine.
4. See Jon Stewart, Ben Karlin, and David Javerbaum, *America (The Book): A Citizen's Guide to Democracy Inaction* (New York: Warner Books, 2004), chapter 1.
5. Diogenes Laertius, *Lives*, 44.
6. "Newhouse School Press Breakfast: Presidential Election Politics," *American Perspectives*, C-SPAN (New York: October 14, 2004).
7. "Jon Stewart's America," *Crossfire*, CNN (Washington: October 15, 2004).
8. Diogenes Laertius, *Lives*, 40.
9. Ibid., 42.
10. Ibid., 94.
11. In the *Poetics* (1452a) Aristotle spoke of this kind of transformation in the context of tragedies, in particular *Oedipus Rex*. But it's plausible to suppose such a phenomenon might also occur in comedy. The *Poetics* supposedly contained a second book dedicated exclusively to comedy, but there are no surviving manuscripts of that part of the text. Umberto Eco was in part inspired to write *The Name of the Rose* by speculating on the contents of Aristotle's second book and the conflict between Aristotle's defense of comedy and the doctrines of medieval Christianity.
12. Diogenes Laertius, *Lives*, 12.
13. Ibid., 70.
14. Ibid., 40.
15. Many thanks to Jason Holt and Robert J. Littman for comments on an earlier draft of this chapter.

Chapter 9

"Jews! Camera 3"
How Jon Stewart Echoes Martin Buber

Joseph A. Edelheit

At his 80th birthday party, Martin Buber (1878–1965), the great Jewish philosopher and author of *I and Thou*, said, "I am no philosopher, prophet, or theologian, but a man who has seen something and who goes to the window and points to what he has seen."[1] Buber's humility is striking and underscores his commitment to a life of action, not merely thinking about acting.

Similarly, Jon Stewart consistently denies that he is a journalist, always claiming only that he is a comedian mocking the ridiculousness of contemporary politics and media. Like Buber, though, he has seen something: men and women who claim the mantle of journalist or political leader. Having witnessed the abuses of news and politics, Stewart uses *The Daily Show*'s fake news format to ridicule politicians and the media.

Many pop culture pundits find characteristics of Jewish humor in their analysis of Stewart's Jewish identity. Though no one has ever suggested that Stewart's a "good Jew," Stewart still radiates a Jewish persona. As we'll see, this persona and Stewart's satiric treatment of Judaism echo Buber's philosophy. What links the great humanist and the contemporary television satirist is that both point to the outside world and then explain to others what they should have seen. Our pursuit of Buber begins with Stewart's life as a Jew.

The Ultimate Daily Show and Philosophy: More Moments of Zen, More Indecision Theory, First Edition. Edited by Jason Holt.
© 2013 John Wiley & Sons, Inc. Published 2013 by John Wiley & Sons, Inc.

Really? You're Jewish?

Stewart's role as *Daily Show* anchor has become a prism of contemporary American culture, and so to some extent has Stewart's Jewishness. In a 2008 *Moment* magazine review, "Meet Jonathan Stuart Leibowitz (aka) Jon Stewart: The Wildly Zeitgeisty *Daily Show* Host," Jeremy Gillick and Nonna Gorilovskaya rave about Stewart's use of his Jewish identity as an essential component of the show's appeal and popularity:

> It's impossible to watch *The Daily Show* without quickly divining that Stewart is Jewish ... Well-versed in Jewish affairs, he is the first to admit that his knowledge of the religion doesn't run deep. "I'm not a religious scholar ... Let's face facts: Very few people would confuse me with Maimonides." ... Stewart's lampooning of America's political and media elites also has Jewish roots ... Stewart himself counts Woody Allen (born Allan Stewart Konigsberg) and Lenny Bruce (born Leonard Alfred Schneider) among his influences.[2]

Mark Oppenheimer calls Stewart a "religion teacher extraordinaire," praising his depth and breadth of religious content, and most importantly, his role in raising many religious issues that others aren't as willing to engage:

> *The Daily Show* approaches American religion ... not with the wimpy, eager-to-please hand wringing that characterizes so much liberal dialogue in this country. Rather, religions are shown to be strange and possibly cringe inducing: our job is to take an honest look, then tolerate them anyway ... Stewart himself ... is clearly non-practicing by most any definition: he has gone to work, and recorded shows, on the High Holidays, for example ... Jon Stewart may not be a believer—he did boast that he had a bacon croissanwich for Passover—but he is one hell of a teacher.[3]

Whereas Oppenheimer observes Stewart's non-observance without judging it, Jacob Silverman, writing for a specifically Jewish website, criticizes Stewart for his lack of Jewish knowledge, especially given his position and the power he has gained:

> Like a seventh-grade class clown refusing to learn his Torah portion, he's ignorant of most things Jewish, and he sees no problem with that.

But that is a problem when Stewart is perhaps the most famous Jewish television personality working today. He is unavoidably the standard-bearer in the august tradition of Jewish comedy, and his flag is looking tattered.[4]

Stewart himself doesn't say much about his level of observance, knowledge, commitment, or his credentials for representing Jews, Jewish life, or Judaism; he simply makes it clear in his manner, content, and tone that he is a Jew and lives a Jewish life as he defines it. Stewart is open about his marriage to a Catholic and raising their two children in an interfaith family. Yet in the press conference immediately following his Rally for Sanity in Washington DC (October 30, 2010), when the Comedy Central spokesperson asked everyone to state their name and affiliation, Stewart yelled out, "Jon Stewart, Reform Jew."

Buber's educational philosophy offers us the description of an idealized teacher, which Stewart, in his way, reflects: "The core of his teaching is this: he lets his students participate in his life, and so he lets them grasp the secret of action."[5] Such teachers dare to use non-academic and individualized methods by which students may gain knowledge of "good and bad."[6] For such teachers:

> Education which deserves the name is essentially education of character. It has to do not only with the single functions of the pupils, but also with the pupil as a total human being, with his "present actuality" as well as with the fullness of his possibilities.[7]

Although Oppenheimer's claim that Jon Stewart is a "religion teacher extraordinaire" wasn't referencing Buber's philosophy, his insight, as we shall see, is illuminated by Buber's philosophical views.

Team Buber

While it's impossible to watch *The Daily Show* without Stewart's Jewish persona being obvious, hearing an echo of Martin Buber's philosophy of engagement requires that we carefully review how Stewart's Jewish persona represents the great humanist. Buber insisted on political involvement and the seamless convergence of religion, ethics, politics, education, and art:

> When Buber was asked in 1919 "what is to be done"—i.e., what political or unpolitical action or unaction was to be recommended in the confusion of post-war Europe—his answer was: "You shall not withhold yourself." ... Nor can [man] avoid being involved in political action unless he intentionally blinds himself against reality. Even if he is not able to exert his influence and to form life according to his ideas, he must try to take as many steps in the right direction as is humanly possible in a given situation.[8]

Stewart's unique satire can be heard as taking this call seriously, and as being what Buber calls a "prophetic" voice. Ethically, Judaism has a special relation to politics in that the prophetic impulse is directed to the nation: "What is essential in prophecy is that it be based on the reality of history as it is happening ..."[9] That is arguably the anchor of *The Daily Show*'s use of politics and fake news: to require that the viewer be a fully engaged citizen by critically examining the seemingly endless cycles of political and media exaggeration, hypocrisy, and polarization.

Stewart has confronted several actual journalists on their failures to be honest or provide their viewers with a reasonable interpretation of reality. Such criticism publicly challenges the media for politicizing what they claim is objective reportage. His famous confrontation in 2004 on CNN's *Crossfire* is a prime example.[10] Buber's dialogical philosophy of I and Thou (the shared experience of reality) was evident in Stewart's face-to-face challenge of political pundits Paul Begala and Tucker Carlson. Buber would have applauded this as an act of responsibility, one of responding to the "lived concrete." Such responsiveness requires understanding that the authentic human experience comes from full engagement and understanding of human existence as it is lived and not merely described. Buber is unequivocal: "Genuine responsibility exists only where there is real responding."[11] Stewart models this kind of responsibility and uses it as leverage for his well-honed deadpan incredulity when responding time and time again to the shallow and hypocritical abuse of media.

Stewart's demand that real journalists be honest about the biases that influence them requires that he too be transparent to his audience. Consider for example that Israel is constantly in the news and that it would be impossible for Stewart and *The Daily Show* to ignore it. No single topic gets Jews to argue among themselves more than Israel and, as a Jew living after Auschwitz, Stewart can't pretend that Israel can be judged in a straightforwardly objective way. When he reports on Israel, his own views are woven into the satire. He has said several times that he has been to Israel and is glad that the Jewish people have a country.

On December 8, 2011, Stewart used the gathering of Republican presidential candidates at the Republican Jewish Coalition to deliver a tour de force about political sycophancy and Jewish identity. The segment titled, "The Matzorian Candidate" follows an opening about "the war on Christmas," which permits Stewart to segue by asking the audience if they knew that there are Americans who don't celebrate Christmas? He answers his own question: "Many American Jews celebrate a holiday called, Ha—ow come we don't get to celebrate Christmas?" Then after a deadpan silence and whiny Yiddish accent "I kid!" he deftly moves on to a discussion of the Republican Jewish Coalition. In so doing, Stewart reminds the audience that Jews are the minority, emphasizing the sycophancy shown toward Israel in news footage of the presidential candidates. Stewart's running commentary on each candidate's promises and personal attempts to identify with Jews is hilarious. He puts up a graphic he calls the "Yarmulkometer" with various Jewish grades: "Such a Nice Boy," "Calls His Mother," "A Doctor (podiatrist)," "A Real Doctor," "Mensch," "A Real Mensch," "Super Star of David." As usual, Stewart doesn't translate or explain the categories, allowing the viewers to understand the humor literally or contextually. He has the most fun with Michele Bachmann who declares that the day after she graduated from high school she went to Israel to work on a kibbutz! "Holy *Shikze*, we have a winner! Michele Bachmann loves Israel so much that she was willing to work on a Socialist collective!" She attempts to end her speech with some Hebrew, which Stewart immediately references in a video of her mispronouncing "chutzpah." He concludes his deft deconstruction of each candidate by noting the absence of Ron Paul, who wasn't invited because he had said he would end all foreign aid, including aid to Israel. Stewart suggests that Paul's absence precludes actual debate, since only those who agreed with the Republican Jewish Coalition were invited. Then, in a self-mocking aside, Stewart suggests that the last thing Jews like to do is argue.

According to Hans Ur von Balthasar,

One central concern remains unchanged in the interpretations of Judaism which accompany Buber's long road: the unification of the

particularity and the universality of the essence of Judaism … Judaism
is original humanism and, *qua* such, is, whether openly or concealed,
the form and propelling force of world history.[12]

Maybe this is what Stewart continues to model—probably
unknowingly—in his many satiric lessons of Jews and Jewish life. He
uses Yiddish without translation, assuming his audience will understand either by context or because certain aspects of Jewish life have
been absorbed into American culture. Stewart's challenge to everyone,
sometimes particularly to Jews, isn't the utter failure of religion or
rituals, but rather the ridiculous misrepresentation of the values that
still motivate him.

Passover v. Easter

On April 9, 2012, *The Daily Show* aired "Faith/Off," a segment
Stewart begins by noting that both Passover and Easter have been
observed during the weekend prior to this Monday night show. He
uses a classic painting of the crucifixion to explain the sacred importance of Easter as a lead-in to news video of the 130th annual White
House Easter egg hunt, showing a collection of children's television
characters in costume. The juxtaposition of classic representation and
television characters is framed with Stewart's perfect silent deadpan
expression of disbelief. Then he moves to the observance of Passover
at the White House Seder and news footage of the President explaining
how they'll have a traditional Seder and that he's looking forward to
a good bowl of matzah ball soup!
    This gives Stewart a segue to the second segment, which compares
Passover and Easter from the children's point of view. Breaking character
and turning personal, Stewart explains that he's raising his children in
an interfaith home where they're exposed to both Jewish and Christian
observances. Turning away from the camera he says, "Jews! Camera 3."
The mock-journalist thumps his chest as a sign of familial intimacy and
warns that Christians have long understood that if you get the children
you've won, and that Jews have already had to concede the Christmas v.
Hanukkah competition and can't lose this one!
    Like Woody Allen, Stewart is a master of the sight gag.[13] In this
segment he brings out a very large Easter basket filled with candies

and plastic yellow grass, which he compares to an actual ritual Passover Plate on which he points to all of the traditional Seder meal symbols: roasted shank bone, parsley, horse-radish root, lettuce, *charosset*, and a hard-boiled egg. He compares a child's choice between a chocolate egg filled with chocolate left by a magical bunny to the hard-boiled egg filled with "egg," the simple meal of the slave, adding the reminder: don't forget to dip it in the salt water to remember the sadness of our ancestors. Stewart is brilliant in his use of props and his facial and vocal tones to emphasize the ridiculous nature of the choice. Stewart is also providing his audience with a satiric rebuke of commercialized misrepresentations of religious significance. The opening graphic represents Easter in a classic painting of the crucifixion of Jesus, an image mocked by the overflowing basket of Easter candy: salvation marketed through chocolate!

Stewart uses a common symbol and common experience of Christianity's most theologically sensitive observance. His satire focuses on both the simplest and most obviously consumer-related object. Yet he asks Jews to take seriously what he and his Catholic wife are asking themselves: how do you raise children in a community that offers the tragic choice between chocolate candy or matzah, roasted lamb bones, and hard-boiled eggs? The answer is found in the reality of shopping for Passover: There is now chocolate that is appropriate for eating during Passover that is even used to cover matzah. In living increasingly assimilated lives, American Jews have come to understand that actual religious competition means winning over the children.

Stewart's mocking rhetorical question about how religion has to be formulated for winning over the kids was illuminated when the Reverend Ed Young, pastor of Second Baptist Church in Houston, a megachurch of five campuses and 58,000 members, confirmed Stewart's insightful parody:

> "We discovered something very simple ... You may not like me, my church, what I say. But if your kids and grandkids have a super experience with what we do, I'll have a chance." ... The Rev. Ed Young has reapplied the principle of evangelical enticement as he has overseen the creation of Vacation Bible School for the 21st century— an over-the-top amalgam of Christian rock, humorous skits, Broadway-style musicals and, lest we forget, strobe lights and fog machines.[14]

The Daily Show's satire is not merely hilarious; it makes a significant statement of cultural and political importance when you consider the power of Evangelical enticement throughout America. Stewart completes the satire with silly suggestions for his "*mishpoocha*" (family) including a competing children's animal for Jews, "Pete the Pizza eating guitar-playing lion" in lieu of the Easter bunny! Stewart admits that you're not supposed to eat pizza during Passover, but suggests we could tell the truth when children reach age 13—the universally known age of Bar and Bat Mitzvah! Then he suggests using the Jewish story of freedom, crossing the Red Sea, for instance, as an amusement park water ride, or wandering in the desert as a video game.

Stewart's open and unapologetic announcements during his shows that were taped during Jewish holy days—first night of Passover, *Erev* (evening of) *Rosh Hashanah*, and *Yom Kippur*—were not belligerent, self-hating, or guilt-tinged. Rather, they were open declarations that he is a Jew working on a Jewish holy day—get over it!

The rate of interfaith marriages is one of the reasons that so many Jews share a universal set of values rather than the particularistic rites that define traditional Jewish life. President Clinton's daughter married a Jew and a rabbi co-officiated; Vice President Biden's daughter married the stereotypic Jewish doctor, and again a rabbi co-officiated with Christian clergy. Stewart's own interfaith family is not a public rebuke of Jewish culture, but rather the norm among non-Orthodox Jews.

Even as Jews have been so publicly assimilated during Stewart's tenure at *The Daily Show*, there was an Orthodox Jew nominated for Vice President, Senator Joseph Lieberman of Connecticut, one of Stewart's favorite political impressions. Other high-profile Jews spotlighted on the show include Michael Bloomberg, three-term Jewish billionaire mayor of New York City, Bernie Madoff, who stole billions from Jews, the Coen Brothers (some of whose movies offer biting cultural statements about Jewish life), New York Congressman and Stewart's personal friend Anthony Weiner (who resigned over lewd cell-phone photos), and Sheldon Adelson, the billionaire gaming politico supporting first Newt Gingrich and then Mitt Romney's Super PACs. In other words, the Jewish cultural world in which Stewart looks for political comedy is overflowing with the tragedy of ridiculous Jewish life ridiculing Jewish values. He doesn't have to stretch very far to the find ways to mock his own people as satiric foil for the community-at-large.

Earth (The Book)–Mocking the Sacred

Earth (The Book), chapter 7, offers us another example of how *The Daily Show* ridicules the ridiculous in all religions. This is not Bill Maher's angry rant in favor of atheism, but satire and sarcasm that's both very funny and at times actually profound. For instance, next to a photo of an unrolled Torah scroll in which the Hebrew words are actually upside-down is the following caption: "The Jewish *Torah* (German for 'kindling') was read aloud over a year's time in a language most Jews didn't understand."[15] The parenthetical reference to Nazi anti-Semitism, *Kristallnacht* (the November 9–10, 1938 pogrom which destroyed synagogues and Jewish businesses throughout Germany), and burning books is both a serious history lesson and tragic humor. Although he might not appreciate this himself, Stewart's reference to reading in a language that 90% of Jews today can't understand (Hebrew, of course), echoes the fact that Ezra (in 444 BCE) needed to create a translation from biblical Hebrew to Aramaic for the Israelites of his time to understand public readings of the scroll.

Stewart uses yellow highlighting of an actual photo of the Torah scroll to create a satiric translation Genesis 22, the Binding of Isaac:

> 10 And Abraham stretched forth his hand, and took the knife to slay his son. 11 and yea did he hear tittering from on high; for the LORD was richly amused; 12 And He came down in a cloud of thunder, saying, "Oh! Thou shouldst see the look on thy face!"; 13 And Abraham threw down his knife in great confusion, saying, "Wouldst thou truly hath had me extinguish my beloved son?" And he wept with anguish; 14 And the LORD said "Surely thou art awestruck, in the fullness of thy punking." 15 But Abraham would not be consoled.[16]

The horror of the biblical text, God commanding Abraham to sacrifice his son as a test of faith, is ripe for satire. Woody Allen's essay, "The Scrolls," is a similar attempt to rewrite the biblical text humorously: "And the Lord said, 'It proves that some men will follow any order no matter how asinine as long as it comes from a resonant, well-modulated voice.'"[17] Stewart, like most Jews today, finds this passage of Torah to be embarrassing if not offensive. So his intentional revision means that he wants to make sense of a truly nonsensical ancient text.

His refusal to ignore it means he is both aware of its significance and its glaring challenge to any contemporary Jewish parent.

Stewart's self-labeling as a Reform Jew doesn't imply that he is affiliated with a Reform synagogue or even knows how Reform Jews observe, but chapter 7 of *Earth (The Book)* mirrors several times his consistent self-identification. In a section on Prayer are eight different categories, each with a photo and graphics of different religions and their stereotypic prayers. For Judaism there is a photo of a man in a black suit wearing a traditional *Talit* (prayer shawl) and *Tifilin* (phylacteries) facing a Torah Scroll: "*Typical prayer*: 'Please protect me from violent pogroms/offensive stereotypes/negative reviews of my new Broadway show or novel/negligence lawsuits from podiatry practice.'"[18] On the far edge of the next page as a separate category is Reform Judaism, which shows a blurry photo of a man carrying a briefcase walking out of the frame: "*Typical Prayer*: 'If I leave now I can make it home in time for *Friday Night Lights*.'"[19] The satire of the stereotypes is perfect! Mocking prayer "from within," rather than mocking the act of prayer itself, makes the reader stop and consider the complexities of contemporary religious reality.

The New Jersey Connection

Even if Stewart's non-observance, self-mockery, and self-identification as a Reform Jew only imperfectly reflect the humble yet lofty remark of Martin Buber mentioned at the outset, maybe it's more reasonable to imagine the influence of Reform rabbi and German refugee, Rabbi Joachim Prinz, the spiritual leader of *Temple B'nai Abraham* of Newark, NJ (Stewart grew up in Lawrenceville, NJ). Prinz gave the sermon immediately before Dr. Martin Luther King delivered his "I Have a Dream" speech. In introducing Dr. King, Rabbi Prinz said,

> When I was the rabbi of the Jewish community in Berlin under the Hitler regime, I learned many things. The most important thing that I learned under those tragic circumstances was that bigotry and hatred are not the most urgent problem. The most urgent, the most disgraceful, the most shameful and the most tragic problem is silence.[20]

Rabbi Prinz's eloquent challenge is anchored in the teaching of Martin Buber, who taught in Berlin and, like Prinz, fled Nazi Germany. Silence, for both Prinz and Buber, is the evil opposite of dialogue. Similarly, Stewart's role on *The Daily Show* is one of vocal (and visual) mockery of the shallowness and polarizing nature of politics and the media. So he intentionally ridicules the tone and content of real news with fake news. Stewart and his writing staff use every tool of satire at their disposal. Religion is in the news so often that Stewart doesn't need to hunt opportunities, and his own religious experiences, questions, and identity are always transparent—the very thing he seeks but seldom finds in those he mocks. Through his robust and complex Jewish identity, Stewart models satire as a valid form of Buberian dialogue and engagement.

Notes

1. Martin Buber, *Meetings—Autobiographical Fragments*, ed. Maurice Friedman (London: Routledge, 2002), 8–9.
2. Jeremy Gillick and Nonna Gorilovskaya, "Meet Jonathan Stuart Leibowitz (aka) Jon Stewart: The Wildly Zeitgeisty *Daily Show* Host," *Moment Magazine*, (November/December 2008), www.oldsite.momentmag.net/moment/issues/2008/12/JonStewart.html, accessed February 7, 2012.
3. Mark Oppenheimer, "Jon Stewart, Religious Teacher Extraordinaire," *Religion & Politics: Fit for Polite Society* (May 1, 2012), http://religionandpolitics.org, accessed February 5, 2013.
4. Jacob Silverman, "Culture Kvetch: Jon Stewart's Happily Ignorant Jew Routine is Getting Stale," *Jewcy.com* (May 30, 2012), http://www.jewcy.com/arts-and-culture/culture-kvetch-jon-stewarts-happily-ignorant-jew-routine-is-getting-stale, accessed February 5, 2013.
5. Ernst Simon, "Martin Buber, the Educator," in *The Philosophy of Martin Buber*, eds. Paul Arthur Schilpp and Maurice Friedman (LaSalle, IL: Open Court, 1991), 556.
6. Ibid., 560.
7. Ibid., 563.
8. Robert Weltsch, "Buber's Political Philosophy," in *The Philosophy of Martin Buber*, eds. Paul Arthur Schilpp and Maurice Friedman (LaSalle, IL: Open Court, 1991), 446.
9. Maurice Friedman, "The Bases of Buber's Ethics," in *The Philosophy of Martin Buber*, eds. Paul Arthur Schilpp and Maurice Friedman (LaSalle, IL: Open Court, 1991), 247.
10. For more on Stewart's infamous *Crossfire* appearance, see Gerald J. Erion, "Rallying Against the Conflictinator: Jon Stewart, Neil Postman, and Entertainment Bias," in this volume.

11. Martin Buber, *Between Man and Man* (Boston, MA: Beacon, 1955), 16.

12. Hans Urs von Balthasar, "Martin Buber and Christianity," in *The Philosophy of Martin Buber*, eds. Paul Arthur Schilpp and Maurice Friedman (LaSalle, IL: Open Court, 1991), 352.

13. Woody Allen in a classic scene of Jewish self-deprecation in *Annie Hall* appears suddenly dressed as a Hassid (an ultra-Orthodox Jew) while eating ham at an Easter family dinner. Allen also uses the sight gag without any oral/aural explanation in *Hannah and Her Sisters* when Mickey (Allen's character), who is considering conversion to Catholicism, opens a brown paper bag and removes a crucifix, a portrait of Christ, a jar of Hellman's mayonnaise, and a loaf of Wonder Bread. The juxtaposition of two sacred objects and two mundane ones, especially dietary examples of blandness, is a classic visual of Jewish satire.

14. Samuel G. Freedman, "Giving Vacation Bible School an Update for the 21st Century," *New York Times* (July 27, 2012).

15. Jon Stewart, David Javerbaum, Rory Albanese, Steve Bodow, and Josh Lieb, *Earth (The Book)* (New York: Grand Central Publishing, 2010), 150.

16. Ibid.

17. Woody Allen, "The Scrolls," in *The Insanity Defense: The Complete Prose* (New York: Random House, 2007), 138.

18. Stewart et al., *Earth (The Book)*, 162.

19. Ibid., 163.

20. See www.joachimprinz.com/civilrights.htm, accessed February 5, 2013.

Segment 3

FIELD REPORT
POLITICS AND CRITICAL THINKING

Chapter 10

More Bullshit
Political Spin and the PR-ization of Media

Kimberly Blessing and Joseph Marren

Magician-comedians Penn and Teller have a show dedicated to it on Showtime. MIT (the Massachusetts Institute of Tauroscatology) publishes it as a weekly gazette. It can be played as a card game or a drinking game. Deflectors for it are available on the Web. It spent 27 weeks on the *New York Times* bestseller list. What is it? Bullshit. It was only a matter of time before Jon Stewart would wade in.

In an interview in *Rolling Stone* magazine, Stewart explained that the point of view of *The Daily Show* "is that we're passionately opposed to bullshit."[1] This might explain why Stewart invited Ivy League philosopher Harry Frankfurt to appear on *The Daily Show* (March 14, 2005) to discuss his bestseller *On Bullshit*.[2] Stewart proved himself an able student of philosophy as he guided the discussion on the distinction between lying and bullshit. For Frankfurt, bullshit is more corrosive to society than lies because bullshitters don't care about the truth. Even though the liar intentionally distorts or misrepresents the truth (think of finger-wagging Bill Clinton: "I did not have sexual relations with that woman"), at least the liar knows, and by implication cares about, what is true. Bullshitters don't.

Philosopher-comedian Stewart followed up the discussion of the lie/bullshit distinction with the following question, which he posed to Frankfurt but never quite let him answer: "What is the difference

The Ultimate Daily Show and Philosophy: More Moments of Zen, More Indecision Theory,
First Edition. Edited by Jason Holt.
© 2013 John Wiley & Sons, Inc. Published 2013 by John Wiley & Sons, Inc.

between bullshit and political spin?" We'll take up Stewart's question and consider how *The Daily Show* handles both bullshit and spin. We'll also briefly consider Frankfurt's second visit to *The Daily Show* (January 9, 2007) when he discussed a much less sensational topic than bullshit. In his second very little book entitled *On Truth*[3]—with its gold-foiled cover that made Stewart think it would contain chocolates—Frankfurt is not very concerned with the "boring" philosophical question about the nature, or definition, of truth. He accepts a common sense understanding of what it means to tell the truth (for example, your name, social security number, and so on) and give a false account (for example, the authors of this paper are Ivy League professors), and argues in support of the value and importance of truth. Before we get to truth, however, let's answer a less boring question, "What is bullshit?"

The Essence of Bullshit and the Truth about Lies

Stewart began his interview by asking how Frankfurt's book *On Bullshit* came about.

STEWART:	When did you write it?
FRANKFURT:	1980 ... 5.
STEWART:	Don't bullshit me.
FRANKFURT:	No, well, '85 and a half?
STEWART:	Now, tell us how it came to be released as a book, only recently, no?
FRANKFURT:	Yeah, in January. My editor at Princeton University Press got the idea of publishing it as a book. And when he brought it up I said, "What are you talking about? It's a 25-page essay. How can you bring it out as a book?" He said, "Well we can do lots of things with margins, and types of fonts, and page sizes," and that's what they did.
STEWART:	Really? That's lovely. [*Flips through book*] Boy, he's not kidding around here. They're like little affirmations. It's really interesting and very apropos for today.

It's too bad Stewart didn't pick up on the fact that the whole idea of playing around with font size on an already-published essay, in order to market it as a book, might strike some as another kind of bullshit. In other interviews, Frankfurt tells how he came to address the topic of bullshit in the first place, which he explains in terms of his training as an analytic philosopher. (Analytic philosophy is an Anglo-American movement that began in the twentieth century, focusing on the study of language and logical analysis of concepts.) Given what he viewed as the increasing volume of bullshit in the culture at the time, Frankfurt thought the concept worthy of analysis. In fact this delicious little book (as well as its sequel *On Truth*) is a great illustration of analytic philosophy doing what it does best—clarifying concepts and the meaning of words.

To polish that gem of clarification, Stewart cross-examined his guest in a manner that would have made Socrates proud:

STEWART: You say that bullshit is not lying.
FRANKFURT: No, it's not lying. Lying consists in believing that you know the truth, and saying something else.
STEWART: It's willful.
FRANKFURT: It's willful. And the bullshitter doesn't really care whether what he says is true or false.
              [*Audience laughter*]
STEWART: I should warn you that when they hear the word, it tickles them. They love the word.
FRANKFURT: I know, especially coming from an Ivy League professor. There's something special about that, I know.
STEWART: For me, it's really ... It almost glasses me up.
FRANKFURT: I'm glad I could help.

Frankfurt spells out this distinction in more detail in his books. Liars care about what's true, which means they have a respect for the truth, if not always for telling it. By contrast, the bullshitter shows a lack of concern for the distinction between truth and falsity. Bullshitters *appear* to be interested in simply conveying information. In reality, however, they are "fakers and phonies who are attempting by what they say to manipulate the opinions and attitudes of those to whom they speak."[4] With bullshitting, the aim is to serve some purpose other than stating what's true or false, for example self-promotion, or promotion of some other person, program, or product. Since bullshitters primarily care about being *effective* in their manipulation, they are indifferent to whether what they say is true or false. Liars, on the other hand, are deliberately trying to lead the listener away from the truth. Even though they are also concerned with being effective in their deception, liars cannot be indifferent to whether or not what they are saying is true:

It is impossible for someone to lie unless he thinks he knows the truth. Producing bullshit requires no such conviction. A person who lies is thereby responding to the truth, and he is to that extent respectful of it. When an honest man speaks, he says only what he believes to be true; and for the liar, it is correspondingly indispensable that he considers his statements to be false. For the bullshitter, however, all these bets are off: he is neither on the side of the true nor on the side of the false. His eye is not on the facts at all, as the eyes of the honest man and of the liar are, except insofar as they may be pertinent to his interest in getting away with what he says. He does not care whether the things he says describe reality correctly. He just picks them out, or makes them up, to suit his purpose.[5]

Thus the key differences between bullshit and lies are in the speakers' different *attitudes* toward the truth and *intentions* in making the statements in question. Bullshitters are lackadaisical about the truth. They might be intellectually lazy, or perhaps they simply see their interests as better served by paying attention to something they *do* care about, like self-promotion. Liars aren't so lazy. They try to figure out the truth (even if they end up being wrong about it), and speak with the express intention of misleading their listeners, or turning them away from the truth.

Liars, Liars, Pants on Fire

Real-life examples of liars abound. US Congressman and Presidential candidate John Edwards denied his extra-marital affair (which he had while his wife was undergoing treatment for breast cancer), as well as his child. Then there was Weinergate. Caught with his hand in the cookie jar, so to speak, US Congressman Anthony Weiner adamantly denied sexting a 21-year-old woman. At least US Congressman Chris Lee had the decency to admit to lying about his marital status when he was caught sending out shirtless photos of himself to a woman he connected with on the "Women Seeking Men" section of Craigslist. Finally, it was never proved whether or not French Presidential hopeful and former director of the International Monetary Fund, Dominique Strauss-Kahn, raped his hotel maid during a recent visit to the Big Apple. But this much is true, either the maid or the politician was lying. Liars, liars, pants on fire!

Frankfurt would certainly not condone any of these behaviors. He would point out, however, that these liars at least cared enough about the truth to know what it was and then state the opposite. In each of these cases of lying there is a truth of the matter, which means that it is possible to get to the bottom of it and proceed accordingly.

As for bullshit, it's harder to figure out what is true or false because bullshitters don't necessarily know which is which, because they don't care. Bullshit artists simply say whatever they need to say in order to achieve their end or purpose, which is not to tell the truth or provide accurate information about the world or reality. There is a difference between lying on a first date ("I own a vineyard in Tuscany") or on a job application ("I graduated from Princeton with a 4.0") on the one hand, and faking, or bullshitting, on the other. We can easily imagine the single person who fabricates a story about why his date can't visit the vineyard in the off-season, or the applicant who desperately needs employment and says whatever he thinks the interviewer wants to hear so he can land the job. Buzz words and phrases like "proactive," "synergy," "thinking outside the box," "I'm a people person," "self-starter," and so on come to mind.

We tend to see a lot of bullshit in advertising and sales, where the primary interest is in making a sale, not necessarily providing consumers with the information they need to make a sound decision. In 2007, the hotel chain Travelodge used a range of techniques to get its name out into the British information marketplace: it told reporters about a couple that had lived in a Travelodge for 22 years; it offered reporters data that suggested which cities in Britain had the worst snoring problems; it offered a study on the benefits tourists would bring when London would host the 2012 Summer Olympics; it publicized plans to hire more unemployed people in the hotels; and it also publicized hotel openings that involved celebrities. The hotel chain counted on the public being distracted by the glitz and manipulation of the news media by skilled practitioners. Bullshit. Ka-ching.

Even if cases like these might seem harmless, others may be less so. Consider, for example, the recent subprime mortgage mess. Happy to collect their bonuses for landing their loans, lenders, that is the banks, didn't really care about whether or not people applying for mortgages could actually afford the houses in question, whether modest dwellings or opulent McMansions. As a result, lots of well-meaning prospective homeowners found themselves in houses they simply could not afford. Those involved in the transactions made huge amounts of money and kindly passed the risk on to somebody else, namely, big banks and giant mortgage companies that originally underwrote the mortgages and then turned around to resell them back to big New York investment houses. A sows' ear turns into a silk purse. Ka-ching, ka-ching.

More Bullshit, Piled Higher and Deeper

Having distinguished lies from bullshit, Stewart asked Frankfurt about the relative harm of lying and bullshit.

STEWART: Which do you think is more corrosive to society, the lie or bullshit?

FRANKFURT: Well, I claim that bullshit is a more insidious threat to society, because it undermines respect for the truth, and it manifests a lack of concern for the truth. It therefore undermines our commitment to the importance of truth. The liar is concerned for the truth, he just doesn't want it. He is taking care to avoid it.

STEWART: But he has to know it. To be able to lie, you need to know what the truth is, to go the other direction.

FRANKFURT: Or at least you have to think you know what it is. Right.

STEWART: But the bullshitter …

FRANKFURT: Doesn't care.

STEWART: At all.

FRANKFURT: He's engaged in a different enterprise.

STEWART: When you say "he," you're looking at me, and it's not right.

FRANKFURT: I didn't say *you*.

STEWART: No, but I see the eyes, with the "he" and the "hmmm" [*looks at Frankfurt*].

FRANKFURT: I'll try to be more careful.

STEWART: I appreciate it.

Stewart then asks about the relative amount of bullshit and lying:

STEWART: Which is more prevalent, do you think?

FRANKFURT: There's a lot of lying, but I think probably bullshit is even more pervasive.

STEWART: Tons and tons of bullshit.

FRANKFURT: Tons and tons of bullshit.

Frankfurt attributes the large and increasing amount of bullshit to the growth of marketing in American culture. Everyone's trying to sell something, and what matters is to get the customer to believe whatever is needed to make the sale. Unfortunately it's not just in used car lots, advertising, sales, or finance where we find unsavory characters. We're being sold bullshit bills of goods in politics, higher education, and journalism.

Frankfurt was intrigued by Stewart's observation that we seem to tolerate bullshit more than lying, and the media play right along. That's perhaps why Frankfurt suggested to Stewart that our tolerance of bullshit might depend on the inevitability of bullshitting. We just can't help it. We seem inescapably drawn to the tawdry and the scandalous. Everywhere we turn, publications and broadcast stations bombard us with ne'er-do-well content: "If it bleeds, it leads." As responsible citizens, we're expected to know something about the more important stuff, but the sheer amount of information in a 24/7 news world makes it impossible to have informed views on all matters. So when push comes to shove, we're forced to bullshit our way through. So too for government officials (at least the ones who aren't busy lying). As for the supposed watchdogs, the news organizations, they want us to believe that they have the equivalent of built-in "bullshit detectors." But the plain fact of the matter is that there exist fewer and fewer news organizations today as newspapers fold, news channels get retuned as shopping channels, and reporters leave the profession for the greener and more lucrative fields of public relations (we'll come back to PR in just a minute). Maybe, just maybe, bullshit is a necessary evil in this "Golden Age of Information." And maybe, just maybe, this necessary evil, and its distant cousin that ol' political spin, is what keeps shows like *The Daily Show* (and its next-of-kin *The Colbert Report*) in business.

A New Spin on an Old Art

We can now take up Stewart's questions to Frankfurt about political spin. Like a good practitioner of the Socratic method, Stewart already knew the answer to his own question.

STEWART: Let me ask you—political spin. What would you categorize that as? You know, the spin that has enveloped political discourse.

FRANKFURT: Yeah, I've thought about that. I haven't got very far, but it is a form of bullshit. I think it's a—.

STEWART: A subcategory.

FRANKFURT: A subcategory, a subset, right. And I haven't been able to put my finger on the distinguishing characteristics of spin, but it's an interesting question.

STEWART: Is spin a subset of bullshit, but because there's an agreement not to call "bullshit" on it? In other words, within the media, they go to Spin Alley. After a debate, they all go to Spin Alley. They would never say, "Hey, let's go over to Bullshit Street." Is maybe the difference that there is sort of an implicit agreement with those who are all bullshitting each other not to call it?

Frankfurt took up Stewart's question and, in a good natured way, allowed his protégé to put him through his Socratic paces.

STEWART: Do you think that the people in political spin think they're lying? Do you think they care about the truth, or do they care about the result of what their spin gets them?

FRANKFURT: Yeah, it's the last I think. They don't care particularly about the truth. They care about producing a certain impression in the minds of the people to whom they're addressing their speech. And they're engaged in the enterprise of manipulating opinion, they're not engaged in the enterprise of reporting the facts.

Facts are what we appeal to in order to determine whether beliefs or statements are true or false. Journalists are in the business of simply reporting the facts. They're supposed to avoid editorializing and avoid inserting their opinion or subjective point of view into the story. Failing to do so gives rise to spin. We can distinguish people engaged in reporting the facts—the who, what, where, when, why, and how of a story—from those who spin the facts, such as a spokesperson for a presidential candidate who's trying to create a certain impression in the minds of voters. Journalists are supposed to be engaged only in reporting the facts, so they're supposed to be devoted to, and thus have a respect for, the truth.

Let's turn some attention to George W. Bush. We'll frame our discussion with the liberal assumption that the watchdog press failed the country in the build-up to the Iraq War in 2003. Weren't the "good guy" journalists supposed to be in wait and ready to pounce on the spin, penetrate the bull, and proclaim truth throughout the land? Well, strangely, they were relatively quiet and acquiescent, at least according to the liberal spin. Ann Coulter and her ilk can wail and cry all they want about the liberal bias in the media, but it was this same media that allowed the administration to wrap itself in the banner of 9/11 and hint that opposition to the war in Iraq was akin to giving aid and comfort to the enemy. The word "terrorist" was bandied about with all its ugly connotations of innocent lives snuffed out in a horrific public moment.

This example would buttress Frankfurt's claim that spinners don't care about the truth, but more about producing certain impressions in the minds of the public. In the case of Bush-Cheney and the war in Iraq—and unlike Clinton's extramarital affair with Lewinsky—it seems that government officials didn't even go to the trouble of lying to the American public. It also seems that the "watchdog media" didn't care enough about what the government was up to.

Was Frankfurt BS-ing about Spin?

Frankfurt claimed that spinners and bullshitters share in common an indifferent attitude toward truth. Liars, by contrast, care about the truth, and willfully express the opposite of what they know or believe to be true. But don't spinners—unlike bullshitters (and more like liars)—*have* to care about the truth?

In the case of a lie, the aim is to deceive people about what's true. For this to happen, liars must have formed a belief about what's true, even if they end up being wrong. Likewise bullshitters aim at deceiving the listener about what the bullshitter does or doesn't know, yet can succeed without actually going to the trouble of forming a belief either way. The same can't be said for the spinner. Like the liar, the spinner must know what's true in order to be able to spin it. Moreover the spinner, again *like* the liar, aims at making it very difficult, if not impossible, for listeners to figure out the truth. Contrary to Frankfurt's claim, then, the spinner doesn't seem to share the bullshitter's lacka-daisical attitude toward the truth, which calls into question Frankfurt's contention that spin is a subset of bullshit. In Frankfurt's defense, he may not have been bullshitting in response to Stewart's question about the difference between bullshit and spin because he does admit that he is still thinking through this issue. Instead, Frankfurt might be engaged in a bull session with Stewart, not bullshit.

In case your head is spinning, let's review. We may distinguish bullshit and spin in the same way we distinguished bullshit and lies, which is in terms of the spinner's *attitudes* (toward the truth) and *intentions*, which is to avoid telling a falsehood (or at least getting caught telling a falsehood). Having gone to the trouble of forming a belief about what's true (like a liar), good spinners go to the further trouble of manipulating a listener's opinions to persuade the listener that their spin is true (like a liar). This tactic is clearly much more involved, and requires much more finesse than mere bullshitting. Consider, for example, a tobacco company CEO who wants to hire someone in PR to convince the public that smoking is pleasurable or cool. The CEO doesn't want to get the company in trouble (read litigation) by having a spokesperson lie, stating for example that there's no causal connection between smoking and lung cancer. To avoid telling a lie, the PR agent needs to know what's true—that there is a connection between the two. If called to action, the spinner might actually be able to convince people, without coming right out and saying so, that lung cancer is just a matter of bad luck, so smoke away! Ka-ching.

Like liars, spinners do, if only of necessity, care about, and so respect the truth. And this might mean that Stewart is on to something when he suggests that the difference between bullshit and spin is that we're more willing to call spin "spin" than bullshit "bullshit."

PR-ization of the Media

The fact that spinners care enough about the truth to know (or believe they know) what it is, and then go to the added trouble of manipulating our opinion about it, helps to explain why we tolerate spinners more than bullshitters. But why should liars, and not spinners, be more vilified than bullshitters? Both spinners and liars share a concern for the truth and must know what is and is not true. Unlike liars, however, spinners don't try to *deceive* us about what the facts are. Instead, spinners try to *color* the (commonly known) facts. Mere bullshitters would never even bother with the facts. It's not that spinners are engaged in reporting the facts, as if they were journalists.

But at least they do care about what is and isn't true. The purpose of spin isn't to change our sense of what the facts are, which is what liars attempt to do, but to put their own particular slant on the relative *significance* or *meaning* of those facts.

As we suggested earlier, spin grows well in the area of PR. But what happens when PR becomes part and parcel of journalism? News organizations, the supposed bullshit-detectors, want reporters out in the street to gather up nuggets of information, which they are then to turn into news stories that will fill column inches or air time. But as we said before there are fewer news organizations than ever before, and advertising revenue is moving away from the traditional print and broadcast media (called "legacy media" in the biz), and toward trendier Facebook, YouTube, and other social media outlets. As a result, investigative pieces are becoming extinct as more and more reporters are tied to their desks doing more and more administrative and clerical work. Yet if productivity is tied to generating news stories then where do reporters increasingly turn? Answer: The ubiquitous press release, which may be full of spin meant to shed positive light on the PR pro's client.

Here is an example of how PR is influencing the truth-seeking enterprise of journalism. British journalist Nick Davies, in his 2008 book *Flat Earth News*, had researchers from Cardiff University do a study on sources in five of Britain's best newspapers. The results showed that 60% of the stories that were studied came in whole or in part from PR agencies or from wire copy; 41% of wire copy had its genesis in a PR agency; and PR pros had a hand in 54% of the stories. Research showed that reporters on their own initiative generated just 12% of the stories. Moreover, Davies wrote that staffing levels were lower than a generation ago even though the news hole had increased. (A news hole is the space left over after the ads are in; traditionally, an average paper is about 60 to 70% advertising and 30 to 40% news, including sports, comics, and so on. By the same token, a traditional local TV newscast is about 22 minutes out of 30, which includes time for sports and weather, consumer reports, and so on.) By the way, just so that this isn't painted as a Brit problem, a *Columbia Journalism Review* study reported that more than half the stories in a *Wall Street Journal* edition were press releases reprinted "almost verbatim or in paraphrase." Simply put, there now exist more PR practitioners than reporters as PR has now gone in-house at major and mid-size corporations and non-profit organizations.

If you were to ask your friendly neighborhood journalists what they think about Davies' finding they would curse the day Hearst was born and say they are part of the solution and not part of the problem. Ah, but ask where their own stories come from and chances are they'll mumble something about the friend at the PR agency who called with a tip. Independence? Objectivity? Well, they say, they called around and talked to other PR folks. But is getting different versions of what could be mere spin really the same as reporting the truth?

This recent phenomenon is what is referred to as the PR-ization of the media. Think of it this way: A PR pro tries to persuade an editor or producer to give his/her client's side of a story, or to report on a product. The editor or producer—that so-called "gatekeeper"—has to decide whether to invest time and money in assigning a reporter to cover the more-or-less manufactured story. The journalist assigned to the story, full of zeal about reporting the truth, is overworked and, although he or she cares about the job, is also juggling worries about declining ad revenue or ratings. So the journalist's temptation is to do a good job on the assignment, at the same time pitching an exposé on a crooked poll to the bosses. But today he/she has the assignment about the company on the other side of town that has perfected the perpetual motion widget that the editor's neighbor's former brother-in-law in PR is pitching.

Remember earlier that we said the news hole has tripled. Do you think the increased space or airtime is devoted to "hard" news? Well, look at shows like *Entertainment Tonight*, or at the programs on the History Channel or the Weather Channel, or at the newspaper sections and niche magazines and websites and social media devoted solely to fashion, food, sports, leisure, travel, finance, and so on. Not to mention *The Daily Show*, which Stewart himself refers to as "fake news."

Spin Alley

It's not that *The Daily Show* is contributing to the PR-ization of the media, because this will happen with or without Jon Stewart. But this latest phenomenon does help to explain Stewart's apparent mission—to establish a true No Spin Zone. Instead of, or maybe in addition to, worrying about BS, Stewart is increasingly turning his attention to spin. As Stewart suggested to Frankfurt, spin may be easier to detect since spinners are up front about what they are up to. But the sheer volume of, and acquiescence to, spin, which is helped along by the increasingly lucrative profession of PR, might make it harder to get rid of than bullshit.

Take, for example, *The Daily Show*'s hilarious segment aired June 4, 2012, "Polish that Turd." Following the disappointing unemployment news, the Obama administration (perhaps master spinners) played another round of "America's most fragrant game show, "Polish that Turd." Likewise, back in 2010, Stewart ran another episode titled "Adult Spin" in which he addressed the rhetoric of the new Republican Congress that was committed to having "adult" conversations about the economy (November 17). Stewart concluded that Republicans are the adults, the media the needy brats, and the Democrats the indulgent step-parents who do anything to keep the peace.

The troubling fact that spin is increasingly taking over political discourse is evidenced by the acclaimed PBS teen program, *In the Mix*, which devoted one of its episodes to spin, "Political Literacy: Sifting Through the Spin." In this program, teens interviewed Jon Stewart, Larry King, and self-proclaimed expert at spin Mary Matalan, who all admitted that spin—which is "nothing more than presenting your position and your candidate in the most favorable light"—has become part and parcel of politics. Stewart tells the teens, "Politicians, at this point in American history, are no different than advertisers." One savvy teen reporter observes, the "problem with politics is that it's fake and you don't know what's real and what's not. You know, it's called spin."[6]

Even if spinners are more "honest" about what they are up to than their ne'er-do-well step-siblings the bullshitters, Stewart's war on spin might be more crucial than his battle with BS. This is because on some level we condone spin, which is not the case for bullshit. Even if spin doctors do care about, or respect, the truth more than bullshitters, it is still the case that they are deliberately discouraging the public from deciding for itself what is true and what is false. In a YouTube interview (May 18, 2007) after appearing on *The Daily Show*, Frankfurt suggested that one way to rid society of bullshitters is to make fun of them—to humiliate and laugh at them to show that we do not take them seriously. Frankfurt thinks that *The Daily Show* serves this purpose through satire. Our best defense against spin might be the same as that against bullshit: ridicule. It would seem that here as well *The Daily Show* does its part.

Truth Matters

What happens to a culture that bandies bullshit as artistry and promotes spinners to the rank of doctor? We end up being more easily confused about distinctions between true and false, right and wrong, reality and appearance. Look at *Crossfire*. They chastised Stewart for not asking Presidential candidate John Kerry tough questions during Kerry's "Indecision 2004" appearance on *The Daily Show*, to which Stewart understandably retorted: "That's not my job. I work for Comedy Central." Many viewers might not have known what to make of Stewart's response. If not his, whose job was it? Well, journalists, of course. Unfortunately, often failing as watchdogs, they've become the tools of able spin doctors. So where can we go for even a snippet of truth? Many young people get their news from alternative sources such as *The Daily Show*. But this seems problematic, since in Stewart's view, providing politically relevant information isn't his job. Instead he says his job is to comment on the news media—to watch the watchdogs.[7]

By bringing up the issue of political spin to his guest expert on bullshit, Stewart points to the near failure of political systems in which image means more than message, a lesson learned from Marshal Mcluhan, the "Oracle of the Electronic Age." Frankfurt and Stewart agree that there's a growing and pernicious prevalence of both bullshit and spin. We need the media as an institution—and individual reporters, broadcasters, editors, directors, producers, and publishers—to take responsibility and renew their commitment to discovering and transmitting truth. This is because the truth is important.

Stewart invited Frankfurt back to *The Daily Show* (January 9, 2007) to talk about his sequel to *On Bullshit*, *On Truth*, or what Stewart refers to as "the Romulus to your Remus." Once again, Frankfurt comes off as terribly likeable and it's very clear that Stewart enjoys his company and chosen subject matter. After a light-hearted exchange in which Frankfurt is slow to answer some of Stewart's questions, Stewart has some fun with Frankfurt.

STEWART: Are you high? What is the lag time here? What's going on? [*Audience laughter*] Here's what I like about you, you actually seem like you are considering what I am saying. No one does that. Not even my family.

FRANKFURT: [*Pauses*] Well, I'm still thinking about why there isn't any chocolate in the book? [*Stewart and audience laughter*]

Throughout the interview Stewart listens to what Frankfurt has to say about truth. It's also apparent that Stewart took the trouble to read Frankfurt's book.

STEWART: Does it [the truth] set our parameters. Does it let us know what reality is? Is that it?

FRANKFURT: Well, that certainly is it. It lets us know what reality is. Exactly.

Stewart then asked Frankfurt whether a society can function without truth:

FRANKFURT: I don't think a society can survive very long without the truth. It doesn't know how to conduct its business. It doesn't know what to do. It doesn't know how to deal with the problems that arise unless it knows some facts ... Truth is very difficult to cope with because reality is difficult to cope with ... [*Brief pause*] You get that?

STEWART: You just blew my mind brother. I love this kind of stuff ...

Frankfurt and Stewart seem to share a genuine admiration for each other. Not only do they share in their commitment to the truth, but also in their common understanding about the nature of political reality in this "Golden Age of Information." And the fact of the matter is that bullshit and spin are on the rise.

Of course today's bullshit artists and spin doctors are the figurative descendants of the Sophists, teachers of rhetoric, the art of manipulating public opinion. Back in ancient Greece, before journalism as we know it ever existed, ordinary citizens relied on another group to keep the Sophists in check. They were the philosophers, doggedly devoted to, and respectful of, the truth. Seeking neither fame nor fortune, Socrates helped found a discipline that would be devoted to seeking truth and calling out bullshit and spin.[8] Harry Frankfurt serves as an exemplary heir to this tradition. But in a culture and age that little respects philosophers and intellectuals in general we turn to the media to be our gadflies, only to find they too have feet of clay. The youth, "corrupted" by Socrates over 2,000 years ago, today see few alternatives but to turn to *The Daily Show* and look to comedian Jon Stewart to be the gadfly to those who should be the gadflies. Parody has become reality. And *that* is bullshit.

Notes

1. John Colapinto, "The Most Trusted Name in News," *Rolling Stone* (October 28, 2004), quoted in Rachel Joy Larris, "The *Daily Show* Effect: Humor, News, Knowledge and Viewers," MA thesis, Georgetown University (2005).
2. Harry G. Frankfurt, *On Bullshit* (Princeton, NJ: Princeton University Press, 2005).
3. Harry G. Frankfurt, *On Truth* (New York, NY: Alfred A. Knopf, 2006).
4. Ibid., 4.
5. Frankfurt, *On Bullshit*, 55–56.
6. *In the Mix*, PBS [Video], www.pbs.org/inthemix/politics_index.html, accessed February 5, 2013.
7. For more, see Rachael Sotos, "*The Daily Show*: An Ethos for the Fifth Estate," in this volume.
8. For more, see Judith Barad, "Stewart and Socrates: Speaking Truth to Power," in this volume.

Chapter 11

The Senior Black Correspondent
Saying What Needs to Be Said

John Scott Gray

From its inception *The Daily Show* has consistently satirized political and cultural figures and institutions across the spectrum. Stewart often delivers the satire himself, but nearly every episode also features at least one of *The Daily Show*'s numerous correspondents. Ed Helms, Rob Corddry, John Hodgman, Stephen Colbert, and Steve Carell are among the best known correspondents in the history of *The Daily Show*. But other correspondents have become beloved for their ability to satirize the media's portrayal of minority or underrepresented populations. Just think of Aasif Mandvi's appearances as the Senior Muslim and Middle East Correspondent, Al Madrigal as the Senior Latino Correspondent, Jessica Williams as the Senior Youth Correspondent, and Kristen Schaal and Samantha Bee as Senior Women's Correspondents.

Our focus in this chapter will be Larry Wilmore, who as Senior Black Correspondent is able to discuss issues of race in ways that a white correspondent probably could not. For example, Wilmore has discussed how the election of Barack Obama could be perceived by the African-American community in the United States, proposing that peer pressure creates a monolithic voting block among African-Americans. Other issues discussed by Wilmore include the Trayvon Martin case, whether the Congressional Black Caucus has "maxed out" the race card, and how Obama should "go blacker" in response to the US credit downgrade.

The Ultimate Daily Show and Philosophy: More Moments of Zen, More Indecision Theory,
First Edition. Edited by Jason Holt.
© 2013 John Wiley & Sons, Inc. Published 2013 by John Wiley & Sons, Inc.

Satire: A Tradition of Cultural Criticism

Satire dates back over 2000 years and is associated with literary works that critique society by ridiculing its shortcomings. Although more easily recognized than defined,[1] "satire reflects society ... helps people to view others differently ... "[2] aiming "to expose foolishness in all its guises—vanity, hypocrisy, pedantry, idolatry, bigotry, sentimentality—and to effect reform through such exposure."[3]

Best known for his *Gulliver's Travels* and "A Modest Proposal," Jonathan Swift (1667–1745) used satire to make his readers reflect on the social and economic structures of Ireland as well as the nature of humanity. In "A Modest Proposal" (subtitled "for Preventing the Children of Poor People in Ireland Being a Burden on Their Parents or Country, and for Making Them Beneficial to the Publick"), Swift suggests that an excellent solution to the ills of the growing population of hungry poor in Ireland would be for them to sell their children to the rich as *food*. He even kindly offers suggestions for how children should be prepared, calling them "a most delicious, nourishing, and wholesome food, whether stewed, roasted, baked, or boiled ..."[4] Swift's call to eat children sounds disgusting and morally repugnant. But once one realizes that his true aim in offering this absurd solution is to reframe our thinking, we notice that he slyly proposes other options that he thoroughly rejects, or seems to, elsewhere in "A Modest Proposal." Among other things, he suggests not wasting money on furniture that's not manufactured in Ireland, rejecting other foreign luxuries, and "teaching landlords to have at least one degree of mercy towards their tenants ... [and] putting a spirit of honesty, industry, and skill into our shop-keepers"[5] instead of seeking overseas goods. Of course, these would be better options than selling the children of the poor as food for the rich.

Satire is not limited to literature, of course. It is also found in the visual arts and popular culture, as exemplified by *The Daily Show* and *The Colbert Report*, which illustrate how political satire still thrives well into the twenty-first century. In fact, satire is so central to *The Daily Show* that Geoffrey Baym "concludes that *The Daily Show* can be better understood not as 'fake news' but as an alternative journalism, one that uses satire to interrogate power, parody to critique contemporary news, and dialogue to enact a model of deliberative democracy."[6] By offering alternatives to the dualistic and partisan perspectives commonly found in politics, *The Daily Show*, like "A Modest Proposal," opens up new avenues of thinking.

Operating at the Border

In the landmark work *Performing Marginality: Humor, Gender, and Cultural Critique*, Joanne R. Gilbert studies the ways female and feminist stand-up comedy offer a lens to examine the ways we construct our personal identity, in particular looking at gender and race.[7] Gilbert highlights the marginal status of comics whose very existence as women or racial minorities opposes the prevailing white male structures of society. Comic entertainers performing from perspectives other than that of the white male serve as critics of that mainstream, because

> marginalized individuals are afforded a freedom unique to their insider/ outsider position; in the context of stand-up comedy, women who perform their marginality may offer a potentially subversive critique of the hegemonic culture while simultaneously eliciting laughter and earning a living.[8]

The topics presented for discussion on *The Daily Show* become part of the mainstream conversation, being seen by a wide array of citizens across demographic lines. While the show enjoys mainstream acceptance, and so counts as an insider in that sense, the sensitivity of some of the topics it raises makes it a kind of outsider as well.

This insider/outsider dichotomy is seen, in particular, when *The Daily Show* overtly places itself in a marginalized position, for example when highlighting Stewart's Jewish heritage when commenting on religious matters,[9] as well as highlighting—in their very designations—the race, ethnicity, class, or gender of its correspondents. These moves are attempts to critique mainstream perspectives in culture and politics. Female and minority comics operate from a perspective at the margins of society, allowing them, as comics, to "heckle" the status quo.[10] These comics "perform their marginality" and exercise "judo rhetoric" against their mainstream opponents (using their weaknesses against them). In this way, humor, Gilbert says,

may serve a democratizing function … playing a crucial role on the
sociopolitical stage. When issues of control, domination, and access to
resources are foregrounded, performing marginality in an aesthetic
entertainment context (that is, stand-up comedy) becomes an important
form of social criticism, a barometer of values and beliefs.[11]

The comic as status quo heckler exposes audience members to the
practice of being critical of the values presented by more mainstream
sources, a job that will be further highlighted when our discussion
turns to the philosophy of Cornel West.[12]

Because these comics are performing on the border between the
mainstream and outright criticism of it, culture itself becomes "both
the grounds of negotiation and its object: it sets the terms of the
encounters, but it is also what is at stake."[13] As an example from *The
Daily Show* that occupies this borderland consider the January 31,
2007 segment with Wilmore and Stewart debating the merits of Black
History Month. Stewart asks if Black History Month serves a purpose,
and Wilmore replies that it does—making up for centuries of oppression with 28 days of trivia. Wilmore remarks, "You know what? I'd
rather we'd gotten casinos." Stewart tries to argue for the importance
of Black History Month, questioning the degree to which this
information is actually trivial. Wilmore responds by asking him to
name the important stuff, Stewart can barely get past the Underground
Railroad and the Tuskegee Airmen when Wilmore calls for honesty,
declaring that Black History Month is a drag. He describes February
as a time when white people have to pretend that they care about black
people, and black people have to pretend that they care about history—
a "lose–lose" proposition!

The dialogue between Stewart and Wilmore clearly inhabits the
borderland between the mainstream and critique of the mainstream;
it criticizes an accepted practice and questions its place in our society.
We must recognize that the point of the segment isn't, of course, to get
rid of Black History Month, but to reflect seriously on its meaning,
particularly given that some people see African-American issues as
being something only worthy of being discussed one month a year,
and the shortest month at that. We must also think about the degree
to which Black History Month must be about more than just King,
Tubman, and Douglass; it needs to be a celebration of the depth and
breadth of the African-American experience, an appreciation that
may currently be lacking in many quarters.

Wilmore looked at Black History Month again in 2012, but this time for very different reasons. In a February 16 segment discussing the basketball player Jeremy Lin, who was then making headlines for his amazing play, Wilmore made clear his disgust: "In the middle of black history month—an Asian-American excels at a traditional African-American sport?!?" When Stewart tried to interject, Wilmore responded, "Don't reduce this to a discussion about my race—this is about *his* race." Wilmore expressed sorrow that this was simply something else being taken from the African-American community, in the tradition of jazz and Ebonics—both stolen! This feeling was only compounded by video of Lin stating how it had always been a dream of his to play in the NBA. Wilmore responded: "*You* have a dream? Knickerbocker please—slow down Martin Luther Kung-Pow." Wilmore considers, however, that this may not be an Asian bid to take over the NBA, but simply revenge for noted astrophysicist Neil deGrasse Tyson—"What was he thinking? Science? That's Asian's turf!" He proposed that the African-American community simply needs to come together and ask Tyson to stop it. Beyond the jokes, however, the real issue raised here is the degree to which stereotypes demarcate certain turfs, and that these stereotypes might hinder our ability to see what is possible. Lin's success helps undermine stereotypes on the basketball court, Tyson's those in the science lab.

The philosopher Simon Critchley furthers the discussion of the role that comedy can play in helping us re-evaluate the borderlands between mainstream and marginal communities: "The comic world ... [is] the world with its causal chains broken, its social practices turned inside out, and the commonsense rationality left in tatters."[14] *The Daily Show* has continued to examine the narratives provided by political spin-doctors and mainstream news outlets who purport to explain the who, what, where, when, and why of the news in a fair and balanced manner. Their reportage is scrutinized by Stewart and company, often revealing inaccuracies, hidden agendas, and even contradictions in their accounts. Doing so, they help us re-examine others' claims about the way things are and why, and what we ourselves should think.

For example, let's consider the very first appearance by Larry Wilmore as Senior Black Correspondent on *The Daily Show* (August 22, 2006). This segment focused on the current status of race discourse. Wilmore condemned what he referred to as "lazy racism." He was greatly disappointed, for example, by former White House Press Secretary Tony Snow's use of the term "tar baby," former Virginia Senator George Allen's use of the term "macaca" in reference to an Indian-American who was filming an event where he was speaking, as well as the comment made by a Florida congressional candidate that blacks aren't the greatest swimmers. His irritation was due to his expressed belief that "we can do better"—that these examples of racism are simply lame. Wilmore pointed out that "everyone knows that blacks can't swim," saying that we've all known this since 1973, when heavyweight boxing champ Joe Frazier finished last in the swimming section of the televised Superstars competition, being beaten even by a member of the *Love Boat* cast! As Wilmore put it, these examples of "lazy racism" pale in comparison to the racism America was founded upon—the enslavement of one race and the eradication of another. Wilmore quipped that racism is in "sorry shape," yet America needs it now more than ever, in fulfillment of Dr. King's dream of whites and blacks coming together and focusing their racism upon—Arabs! Stewart attempted to clarify things, not realizing that Wilmore wasn't talking about MLK, but instead Dr. Lyon King, his podiatrist!

This reference to Dr. King's dream, and Stewart's confusion about which King Wilmore was referring to, shows us how satire can get us to rethink race in America. After 9/11 there was a great deal of backlash toward Arab-Americans. The calls for racial profiling even came from minority communities, where the potential injustice of racial profiling should have been appreciated all too well. By referencing *a* Dr. King, Wilmore gets us to think about *the* slain civil rights leader. One might wonder how Rev. Dr. Martin Luther King, Jr. would have reacted in the aftermath of these attacks had he been alive. Wilmore raises questions like this indirectly. In this segment, several statements might be seen as offensive had they been offered by other people in other contexts. For example, the assertion that everyone knows that black people can't swim could easily be viewed as racist, but in this case Wilmore was clearly using satire to suggest the absurdity of the position in question (racism toward Arabs and Arab-Americans), leading us to acknowledge that this new racism might be as harmful as the older, more virulent versions in America's recent and distant past. Furthermore, the humor surrounding the stereotype that black people can't swim belies a real problem, one that the HBO series *Real Sports* with Bryant Gumbel focused on during a September 15, 2009 segment titled "The Swim Gap." That story, which focused on Olympic Gold medal winning swimmer Cullen Jones, looked at the fact that until a 1971 Supreme Court decision, pools and beaches could still legally practice segregation. It was also reported, furthermore, that black children drown at a rate more than three times that of white children. More must be done to get beyond this stereotype and help turn the tide on statistics such as these. Wilmore's satire helps us recognize this issue.

Heading West

Cornel West has spent his life talking and writing about the injustices faced by marginal populations, writing about a "new cultural politics of difference." In capitalist culture, this new politics is rooted in "escalating xenophobias against people of color, Jews, women, gays, lesbians and the elderly."[15] West agrees with Stewart's repeated assertions about the important social role of the news media. This makes us think of Stewart's famous conflict on CNN's *Crossfire* in 2004 when he asked the partisan hosts to "stop, stop, stop, stop hurting America."[16] As West laments in *Race Matters*, "American intellectual life has few places or pockets to support serious scholarly work outside of the Academy and foundations ... The major intellectual alternatives to the Academy are journalism, social support communities ... or self-supporting writers."[17] The role of *The Daily Show* may not exactly be to report the news, but at least the show does an excellent job of reporting on the reporting,[18] while also using comedy to get the audience to reflect on significant cultural and social issues.

The Trayvon Martin case provided an excellent opportunity for *The Daily Show* in general, and Wilmore in particular, to use satire to re-think the resulting cultural responses to a racially charged incident. On April 4, 2012, Wilmore called for a "racist timeout," as the tragic death of a 17-year-old kid had been turned into an opportunity to score ideological points. According to Wilmore, the right saw Zimmerman (who was accused of shooting Martin) as an unfairly victimized Dudley Do-Right, while the left saw him as an Elmer Fudd character hunting down black people. Wilmore even included an uncanny impersonation of Fudd, saying "be vewy quiet—I'm wacially pwofiling Negwos." The problem, said Wilmore, is that the case was being heard in the Court of Public Opinion, which at the time was the only one that would hear the case. Beyond this, Wilmore questioned the Stand Your Ground law because it seems to give Zimmerman the benefit of the doubt. Wilmore even remarked that the benefit of the doubt is "the one entitlement black people *can't* get from the government."

Wilmore's calling for a "racist timeout" and his attempt to get beyond the partisan rhetoric about the case is a model worth following. Trying to get beyond partisan yelling to start thinking about the issues in an unbiased way is exactly the kind of examination central to the work that West believes we should do. West writes that we should be willing to talk honestly about culture, about "the realm of meanings and values,"[19] adding that "we must delve into the depths where neither liberals nor conservatives dare to tread, namely, into the murky waters of despair and dread that now flood the streets of black America."[20] As an example of *The Daily Show* taking on these issues, consider its discussion of the race card on August 5, 2010. At the time, Maxine Waters and seven other members of the Congressional Black Caucus were under investigation for corruption, and Wilmore tried to use the race card to say that they were being investigated because they were black. However, when he "took out" the race card (in the form of a credit card) and tried to run it through the machine, it was denied. Finding the small print on the back of the card, he read, "Void during a black presidency." No matter, there were lots of other cards Wilmore could use, including the old card, the gay card, the Christian card, the fat card, and so on, saying that there are "all kinds of cards you can use to avoid accountability." Accountability is one of Cornel West's concerns as well, in that he advises us to look at racially charged situations from both perspectives: how social structures impact real possibilities for marginalized communities, and how behavior patterns within those communities can serve to sustain these problems.

On a lighter note, Wilmore tried to help clarify racial reactions to O.J. Simpson, just after O.J. was arrested on robbery charges in 2007. Wilmore began by defending O.J., saying that instead of robbery, it just "sounds like a brother trying to get his shit back." His mood quickly changed, however, from defense to dismay, as he admitted, "I can't do this—I can't defend this crazy man any longer" (September 9, 2007). He added that it was hard to support O.J. the first time around, because "everyone knew he was guilty." Stewart asked why, if everyone knew he was guilty, there was so much celebration among African-Americans when he was found not guilty? Wilmore answered, "For once, the rich white guy who got off was black!" When Stewart asked why stand by someone of the same race just because they're the same race, the reply was, "Habit, Jon." Wilmore then decided it was time for a change in policy: "Attention all black people who watch *The Daily Show*. The three of you need to listen carefully. We're calling off the O.J. thing. It's now officially OK to tell white people that you think he's guilty. No, it doesn't make you an Uncle Tom." Of course, Wilmore had to specify that the other things on "the list" still apply, like hockey (it may be a fun-looking sport, but it's still too soon)! Using satire in this way, Wilmore is able to raise to the surface issues of racial injustice and the idea of what it means to be an Uncle Tom—serious issues—in between the laughs.

Larry Wilmore's Jazz Hands

Cornel West employs a metaphor at the end of *Race Matters* that captures the role that Wilmore in particular, and *The Daily Show* in general, play in instigating a cultural conversation about values in America: the metaphor of jazz. West says "I use the term 'jazz' here not so much as a term for a musical art form, as for a mode of being in the world ... and flexible dispositions toward reality suspicious of 'either/ or' viewpoints, dogmatic pronouncements, or supremacist ideologies."[21] Whenever *The Daily Show* observes extremism or partisan bickering in public discourse, it's on guard for ways to use satire to undermine that rigidity and seek alternative ways of thinking about the issues. Part of the role of West's "jazz freedom fighter" is to "energize world-weary people into focus," in the hopes of fostering reflection and an exchange of ideas. By helping to awaken viewers from their dogmatic slumbers, *The Daily Show* serves a vital role in creating a more informed and socially aware populace.

While *The Daily Show* allows for these opportunities for enlightenment in general, it is Wilmore's role as Senior Black Correspondent in particular that allows for the discussion to turn to many important issues concerning race. In a June 8, 2011 segment on the economy and its impact on the black vote, Wilmore pointed out that Obama, who earned 96% of the black vote, might lose that margin in the 2012 election if things don't turn around (by lose, he meant "goodbye 96%, hello 94%"). Wilmore said he voted for Obama because he was black, and since he is still black … The issue, says Wilmore, is loyalty, and since the Democrats passed the civil rights acts, they have enjoyed black support—mostly by peer pressure. The issue here is whether blacks should vote as a monolithic block, and for what reasons, especially since issues of slavery and equality are no longer directly driving electoral concerns. As Wilmore put it, these days class is more important than race. "It's time that the black community's political structure reflected the diversity of the black community. If you are a black conservative, a little gun-shy of joining the Tea Party, start the Sweet Tea Party. I don't care." He continued by saying that the black community should vote for its individual interest, saying that he could support Herman Cain, since he still has access to the pizzas (especially if he "threw in a two liter"). The larger point in this satirical observation that a vote might be bought so cheaply is that people should take personal responsibility and reflect on their reasons for supporting the candidates they support, instead of just going through the motions and following the patterns of their parents or neighbors. This realization would help truly realize Dr. King's historic dream: judging candidates not by the color of their skin but by the content of their character.

The flipside of this rejection of stereotypes is to recognize that they remain powerful. When the United States' credit rating was downgraded, it was often called "Obama's downgrade" in certain media, including both Fox News and CNN. In an August 10, 2011 segment, Wilmore lamented: "America finally gets its first black president and our credit goes bad!" Wilmore's advice? If you're already in the red— "go blacker!" He continued, "If he is going to be labeled black, he should own it, and by own it, I mean rent it … rent to own it." Tricks that Wilmore said "brothers" have for handling debt include not paying on the first notice, opening up a line of credit by stealing someone else's identity (the US might steal Canada's, perhaps), and letting the kids get the door when China comes asking for their money. Wilmore pointed out earlier in this piece that racial stereotypes like these are used against Obama all the time, as when his playing basketball is overemphasized in the media, or when his birthday party is referred to as a "Hip Hop BBQ."

Wilmore exposes stereotypes that need to be discussed and thereby advances our conversation about their meaning in the 21st century.

In line with this, West says that the overarching aim of his book *Race Matters* was "to revitalize our public conversation about race, in light of our paralyzing pessimism and stultifying cynicism as a people."[22] In satirizing racial stereotypes, Wilmore shares West's aim. In using humor to say things that most media pundits and politicians can't say, Wilmore helps create a deeper level of discourse about race. As Wilmore said when asked whether he thought people would vote for another black president (September 27, 2011), "white voters have finally learned what white women have known for a long time: Once you go down the road of diversity, it's impossible to change course and return to one's previous misconceptions."

Notes

1. "Satire," *Columbia Encyclopedia* (2008), par. 1, http://education. yahoo.com/reference/encyclopedia/entry/satire, accessed February 7, 2013.
2. Jane Ogborn and Peter Buckroyd, *Satire* (New York: Cambridge University Press, 2001), 12.
3. "Satire," *Columbia Encyclopedia*, par. 1.
4. For the full text of "A Modest Proposal" (1729), see www.gutenberg. org/files/1080/1080-h/1080-h.htm, accessed February 5, 2013.
5. Ibid., par. 29.
6. Geoffrey Baym, "*The Daily Show*: Discursive Integration and the Reinvention of Political Journalism," *Political Communication* 22 (3), (2005), 259–276.
7. Joanna R. Gilbert, *Performing Marginality: Humor, Gender, and Cultural Critique* (Detroit, MI: Wayne State University Press, 2004).
8. Ibid., 3.
9. For more on Stewart's Judaism, see Joseph A. Edelheit, "'Jews! Camera 3': How Jon Stewart Echoes Martin Buber," in this volume.
10. Gilbert, *Performing Marginality*, 22.
11. Ibid., 14.
12. Cornel West has himself appeared on *The Colbert Report* on multiple occasions.
13. Sherry B. Ortner, *Making Gender: The Politics and Erotics of Culture* (Boston, MA: Beacon, 1996), 182.
14. Simon Critchley, *On Humour* (New York, NY: Routledge, 2002), 1.
15. Cornel West, "The New Cultural Politics of Difference," in *The Cornel West Reader* (New York, NY: Basic Civitas Books, 2000), 119.

16.   *Crossfire*, CNN (October 15, 2004).
17.   Cornel West, *Race Matters* (New York, NY: Random House, 1994), 63–64.
18.   For more on this, see Rachael Sotos, "*The Daily Show*: An Ethos for the Fifth Estate," in this volume.
19.   West, *Race Matters*, 20.
20.   Ibid., 19.
21.   Ibid., 150.
22.   Ibid., 158.

Chapter 12

The Daily Show's Exposé of Political Rhetoric

Liam P. Dempsey

In no area of human life is the purposeful misuse of reason more pervasive than in politics. Rhetoric, you might say, is the bread and butter of political discourse. It's also the mainstay of *The Daily Show*'s humor. Through purely informal means, the program brings to light various uses of political rhetoric for their recognition and due ridicule. *The Daily Show*'s incisive satire makes these attempts at rhetorical manipulation (literally) laughable.

In this chapter we'll consider *The Daily Show*'s unique capacity to demonstrate, through satire, misuses of reason in politics and the media. We'll consider examples taken from "Indecision 2004," more recent examples from "Indecision 2012,"[1] and some from *The Colbert Report*. We'll begin by considering *The Daily Show*'s treatment of the more common logical fallacies employed by politicians and their exponents. Next we'll discuss various political appeals to emotion exposed by *The Daily Show*. Then we'll consider some of *The Daily Show*'s many forays into the alternative universe of political spin, the systematic, politically motivated use of persuasive language, including "talking points." We'll conclude by briefly considering some of the different comedic devices used by Jon Stewart and Stephen Colbert to expose and satirize these kinds of political rhetoric.

The Ultimate Daily Show and Philosophy: More Moments of Zen, More Indecision Theory,
First Edition. Edited by Jason Holt.
© 2013 John Wiley & Sons, Inc. Published 2013 by John Wiley & Sons, Inc.

A Cavalcade of Fallacies

Fallacies are errors in reasoning, which appear correct, and which often distract people, one way or another, from the real issues. Arguably the most common fallacy used in political discourse is the *ad hominem* argument. This fallacy is committed when, rather than addressing the argument or position a person offers, one simply attacks the person. Similarly, one might try to make a person's argument or position look strong, not by giving reasons for it, but by praising its advocate.

Colbert gives a nice example of the *ad hominem* fallacy by "praising" partisan attacks on a ruling that the Bush administration's warrantless wiretapping program was unconstitutional. Rather than addressing the merits or the details of the ruling, partisan attacks simply dismissed the decision on the grounds that the judge, Anna Diggs Taylor, was appointed by Democratic President Jimmy Carter. Of course, her political affiliations are irrelevant to the cogency of her arguments. Her decision stands or falls by the logical force of her reasoning, not some aspect of her personality or history. The reasons for her decision are (conveniently) ignored by partisan critics.

Also common in political rhetoric is the straw-man fallacy, in which someone attacks a misrepresentation or weakened version of an opponent's argument, preferably one casting the opponent in a negative light. Consider, for example, the claim that Democratic Representative John Murtha advocated a "cut and run" policy in Iraq. Not only is this claim demonstrably false—Murtha advocated a staged re-deployment of troops out of Iraq while keeping them within the region broadly—it also trades on negative language. "Cut and run" is used to insinuate that he, and anyone who agrees with him, are irresponsible cowards. Note well that this phrase in no way addresses Murtha's *actual* position.

The Daily Show exposes similar examples of both of these fallacies in its coverage of Democratic Senator Zell Miller's vitriolic speech against Senator Kerry (Republican National Convention, 2004, Day 3). Indeed, Senator Miller provides a number of examples of fallacies. Not only does he engage in *ad hominem* attacks, many of these attacks are attacks against straw men. Take, for example, his claim that, as president, Kerry would "let Paris decide when America needs defending." The claim is, of course, preposterous. Other examples of the *ad hominem*/straw-man blend are easy enough to find. After Hurricane Katrina, a popular Bush Administration talking point was the plea that the press shouldn't "engage in the 'blame game'" by questioning the timeliness or adequacy of the government's response to the crisis, as if the press doing the important job of asking questions were somehow the real problem. More recently, President Obama's economic policies have been repeatedly described as "socialist," with all the rhetorical baggage this label carries. On the April 3, 2012 episode of *The Daily Show*, Stewart offers a "failed socialist policy" montage which includes Sarah Palin calling President Obama's policies "socialist" and then, not a few minutes later, complaining that only "Fat Cats" benefit from said "socialist" policies!

Consider too the notorious "freedom fries" and "freedom toast" incident, an *ad hominem*/straw-man response to France's arguments against invading Iraq. When Capitol Hill cafeterias finally dropped "freedom" from their menus, Colbert bemoaned it in typical hyperbolic fashion, insisting that the change to "freedom fries" was the finest achievement of the Republican-controlled Congress, that without it, we're left with "surrender fires." Or consider former Governor George Pataki's speech in which he asks the audience, "What is this election about if it isn't about our love of freedom?" implying that only one party, the GOP, loves freedom, while Democrats and others don't (RNC, 2004, Day 4).

This brings up the false dilemma, the fallacy where a complex topic is oversimplified to two options. Consider this remark on a cable news station. To paraphrase: "Sure it's not great having the government collect our telephone records, but it is better than having them collect our body parts!" The argument is, in effect, that we have two choices: either we allow possibly unconstitutional and invasive government surveillance, or we all die! Another famous example of false dilemma, "Either you're with us, or you're with the terrorists," trades on an appeal to patriotism. Satirizing this twisted logic on *The Report*, Colbert concurs with President Bush, insisting, "Either you're for the war [in Iraq], or you hate America. It's that simple!" (August 29, 2006). These false dilemmas have become quite laughable. With President Bush's then struggling poll numbers, it's especially absurd to think that over half the country supported the terrorists! Even so, the use of this sort of false dilemma is all too common. For instance,

Stewart lambasted Vice President Cheney for suggesting that anti-war Democratic candidate Ned Lamont's primary victory over Senator Joseph Lieberman was a victory for Al Qaeda (August 15, 2006). Again, the implication is that one either supports the war or one supports the terrorists, and so Lamont's criticism of the war puts him in league with the terrorists. Picking up on this ridiculous suggestion, Colbert began talking about Lamont as if he and Bin Laden were old friends!

It's worth noting that *The Daily Show* correspondents often use false dilemma questions. Samantha Bee, for instance, satirizes the rhetorical theatrics of the 2004 Republican national convention with the following: "Is tonight the night that they exploit 9/11, or is tonight inspired empty promises for the future?" (RNC, 2004, Day 3). It's fairly common practice on *The Report* for Colbert to ask the Congressional representatives he interviews (in his "Better Know a District" segment): "George W. Bush: *great* president or the *greatest* president?"

The slippery-slope fallacy is committed when someone claims that a seemingly harmless action, if taken, will inevitably lead to a disastrous outcome. On the June 28, 2012 episode of *The Report*, Colbert highlights slippery-slope arguments against the Affordable Care Act. For not only has it been argued that it will lead to "death panels," but also that if the individual mandate is deemed constitutional by the Supreme Court, the federal government will be able to mandate *any* conceivable behavior. As Colbert puts it, "if healthcare can be mandated, what's next, the government telling us we must eat broccoli?" The slippery-slope fallacy is also prevalent in discussions of same-sex marriage. Noting a report of a woman in India allegedly marrying a snake, a Fox News commentator challenged same-sex marriage advocates to give principled reasons for why we ought to "draw the line" at snakes. The implication is that there's a slippery slope from same-sex marriage to *any* conceivable union, however ridiculous. There's also an *ad hominem*/straw-man element here, as if homosexuals were no different from those who practice bestiality, when, of course, it is impossible to form a contract—marriage or otherwise—with a snake. Colbert's response to this argument is to "agree" that homosexuals *should* have to justify this purported marriage to a snake. Having said this, however, Colbert continues:

I don't see gay marriage as a slippery slope down to people marrying snakes. I see people marrying snakes as a step up the slope from gay marriage. I've got no problem with people marrying snakes—as long as they're not marrying *gay* snakes. We must marry limbless reptiles of the opposite sex. Otherwise, it's just unnatural. (June 20, 2006)

On the May 9, 2012 episode of *The Daily Show*, Stewart considers a similar appeal to this fallacy from a politician who argues that if we allow same-sex marriage, the next thing we know, people will be marrying their favorite kind of ice-cream. Mocking this well-worn but facile reasoning, Stewart wonders whether this politician's wife realizes that her husband "cannot see the difference between a consensual love that leads to matrimony and the pleasure you get from a Dairy Queen Blizzard?"

The fallacy of equivocation is committed when someone uses a key word in two or more senses in the same argument and the apparent success of the argument depends on the shift in meaning. A statement from Bush Administration Presidential Press Secretary Tony Snow, satirized on *The Daily Show* (August 2, 2006), provides a humorous example. In response to questions about President Bush's medical exam, Snow proudly proclaims that President Bush was "fit for duty." As a rhetorical device, this proclamation trades on an ambiguity between physical fitness, which a doctor assessed, and professional *competency*, which wasn't tested, and lies beyond the doctor's medical expertise. Stewart illustrates this equivocation by displaying a picture of an overweight William H. Taft who might have been fit for duty (competent) despite his apparent lack of physical fitness.

Finally, there's the fallacy of begging the question, which is committed when an arguer states or assumes the very things he or she is trying to prove as a conclusion. Consider *The Daily Show*'s satirical take on Senator Sam Brownback's argument against state-sponsored embryonic stem cell research (July 19, 2006). Brownback's presentation included a series of pictures following the development of a child, the result of a discarded embryo, a so-called *snowflake* baby. The first picture depicts the frozen embryo in question. During this presentation, Senator Brownback refers to the frozen embryo as the *same person* as in the other pictures. This reasoning is fallacious in that Senator Brownback assumes the truth of the very point at issue. He assumes that an embryo is a person in arguing that the state should treat it as a person. Thus, he begs the question against the proponents of embryonic stem cell research who don't accept the premise that embryos are persons. Indeed, Brownback goes even further, displaying pictures drawn by the child in question, of herself as a "happy" embryo—with a smiley face—juxtaposed with "sad" embryos that haven't yet been adopted. Not only does this beg the question, it also attempts to "tug at our heartstrings," trading on the very strong feelings we have for the welfare of children. As Stewart concludes with a chuckle, if research reveals that some embryos are capable of speech and emotions, they should, indeed, be exempt from research!

Tugging at the Heartstrings

It's common—all too common—for politicians to make direct appeals to listeners' emotions. These include appeals to fear, outrage, and patriotism. Since 9/11, fear has become a powerful rhetorical device in North American political life. Not surprisingly, fear-mongering— causing or using fear in your audience in order to persuade them—has become quite common. In fact, it's fear that often "justifies," in the public mind, both military interventions abroad and limitations on civil liberties at home.

Some of these appeals to emotion are brought out nicely in *The Daily Show*'s treatment of the 2004 Democratic and Republican national conventions. Both parties make ample use of these rhetorical devices to secure support. For example, as Stewart highlights, there were numerous references to Senator Kerry's (comparatively impressive) war record in an attempt to harness the fear, outrage, and patriotic fervor of post-9/11 America.[2] Recall Senator Kerry's salute to the audience and his exclamation: "I'm John Kerry and I'm reporting for duty!" The take-home message: the world is a very scary place, fraught with danger and hidden enemies, but John Kerry, a decorated war hero, will protect us from these dangers.

The Republicans, on the other hand, went so far as to have their convention in New York City, just miles away from Ground Zero. The *continual* references to 9/11 and the threat of terrorism in its delegates' speeches are difficult to overstate. As Stewart notes, not only were "September 11th" and "terrorism" frequent refrains in the speeches of the participants, "September 11, 2001" was displayed on the backdrop to the speaker's podium (RNC, 2004, Day 1).

Colbert summed up these rather obvious—but apparently effective—rhetorical ploys as "crass-tastic."

Appeals to outrage can take at least two forms: trying to harness listeners' outrage in order to persuade them, and simply displaying outrage at something for the same purpose. In the latter case, outrage suggests conviction. If so-and-so is *that* upset about such-and-such, there must be something *really* objectionable about it. Democratic Senator Zell Miller's angry speech at the 2004 Republican national convention (RNC, 2004, Day 3) provides a nice example of the rhetorical use of outrage: "Today's Democratic leaders see America as an occupier not a liberator. And nothing makes this marine madder than someone calling American troops occupiers rather than liberators!"[3] Miller's suggestion is that it's outrageous, even unpatriotic, to describe the American military presence in Iraq as an occupation. The choice of "occupier" over "liberator" infuriates Senator Miller! But notice that Miller hasn't given us any *reason* to view "liberator" as more fitting than "occupier." He's just expressed patriotic outrage, without in any way justifying it, much less his conclusion. What's more, as Stewart humorously points out, President Bush himself had only recently referred to Iraqis as living under "occupation."

The ubiquity of fear-mongering and appeals to outrage and patriotism has also been picked up on by Colbert in his *Report*. In an exchange with Stewart at the end of one episode of *The Daily Show*, Colbert actually fear-mongers about fear-mongering, using fear to draw attention to the dangers of fear-mongering (August 16, 2006). To take another example, Colbert satirizes fear-mongering in cable news reports on the Middle East by enthusiastically embracing the potential outbreak of "WWIII," complete with graphics of explosions and allusions to Armageddon. Similarly, in his regular segment "The Threat Down"—introduced with a siren!—Colbert satirizes the popular use of fear-mongering with lists of things (such as bears) to be afraid of.

Likewise, Colbert makes frequent appeals to patriotism, "wrapping himself in the flag," sometimes literally, in his rants against liberals.[4] Those who criticize the policies of the Bush Administration were seen as part of the "blame America first crowd," and those critical of the Iraq war, or who want to bring American troops home, "refuse to support the troops," or in other words support "terrorists" against

American forces.[5] According to Colbert's twisted logic, criticizing the Bush Administration is tantamount to criticizing America itself and abandoning its troops to the terrorists.

Spin: The Systematic Use of Persuasive Language

Political spin relies primarily on the emotional impact of word choice and selectively highlighting some facts while ignoring others. To spin a political story in one's favor involves using language and imagery intended to produce the most favorable emotional response in the listener, regardless of the reality of the situation. One might recall *The Daily Show* correspondent Ed Helms's look at the second Presidential debate between President Bush and Senator Kerry ("Extras"). As he shuttles back and forth between Democratic and Republican operatives looking for the truth about what happened in the debate, Helms becomes exasperated, recognizing that the he's being told contradictory things. After all, they couldn't have both won the debate! Eventually he comes to the "startling" revelation that their assessments were empty and manipulative attempts at persuasion.[6]

In general, the numerous political "gunslingers" and "spin doctors" who now populate 24-hour cable news can be relied on to spin just about any development in favor of their preferred candidate or party. On the June 4, 2012 episode of *The Daily Show*, Stewart considers Democratic reaction to May's disappointing jobs numbers. Casting it as a sort of game—"Polish that Turd"—Stewart shows a number of the surprisingly different ways in which Obama surrogates spun the news, from calculating job growth without taking into account population growth to the red herring of pointing to Mitt Romney's less than stellar jobs numbers when Governor of Massachusetts. During his June 25, 2012 *Wørd* segment, Colbert likewise satirizes some of Obama's critics who not only spin any bad news for the administration against him—by, for example, saddling Obama with the entire responsibility for things over which he may have very little control—but also by spinning any good news in such a way that he deserves none of the credit. Or even worse, they spin good news—like strong jobs numbers in individual "swing states"—to make it seem like bad news. As

Colbert bemoans in his typical exaggerated fashion, "having a job means I have to go to work tomorrow. Thanks a lot, Obama!"

Informed and educated citizens must be able to separate the logical force of a set of claims from the emotive force or "slant" provided by a political advocate's choice of words. This often involves recognizing the use of euphemisms (language which makes things seem better than they are) and dysphemisms (which makes them seem worse than they are). Euphemisms trade on positive associations, dysphemisms on negative associations.[7] For example, in the sphere of politics a homicide may be referred to as an "assassination" (with its negative connotations) or (with far less negative, almost clinical, if not positive associations) a "neutralization." It matters whether people involved in political conflicts are labeled "terrorists," "insurgents," "guerillas," "partisans," "freedom fighters," or "heroes," whether a military action is referred to as "liberation," "invasion," or "illegal aggression." In many cases, some word choices are neutral, and so are more appropriate than others. To avoid being susceptible to the manipulations of spin, people must be able to distinguish the spin of a claim—positive or negative—from the logical force of the actual reasons given for it.

One currently popular dysphemism is, as we saw above, the use of the term "socialist" to describe government programs that one doesn't like. The use of this emotionally evocative label is nicely satirized on the May 29, 2012 episode of *The Daily Show* with a montage of politicians referring to government programs they don't like—say, the Affordable Care Act or subsidies for solar energy research—as socialist, while comparable programs they do like—say, corn subsidies and Medicare—somehow fail to be socialist. Similarly, the phrase "the war on _____" carries with it an appeal to patriotism and the implication that the one who is waging the "war" is anti-American. An April 16, 2012 montage on *The Daily Show* juxtaposes Fox News's outrage at the Democratic suggestion that the Republicans are waging a "war" on women with a surprisingly large number of examples of Fox's claims of "wars on _____," including the War on Christmas, Hanukkah, Halloween, food, salt, and conservative women.

A closely related spin technique is rhetorical definition. Take for example the (rhetorical) definition of "abortion" as "the murder of an unborn baby." This definition attempts to smuggle in *loaded* words. Defining "abortion" as the *murder* of a *baby* begs the question against those who deny that abortion is murder.[8] The question of whether or not abortion is murder is the very point in dispute, and so can't legitimately be assumed as a basis for debate. Loading a definition in this way can be a very effective rhetorical device despite being unjustified. After all, few would disagree that murdering babies is wrong!

The use of so-called talking points is the *systematic* use of spin by a group or party. In the case of political parties, particular words, phrases, subjects, and emphases are disseminated to the party faithful. When presented with an argument that uses talking points, we must be able to recognize and evaluate them to avoid being unduly influenced by them. *The Daily Show*, particularly through its use of montages, does a nice job of revealing the use of talking points. By showing, in rapid succession, numerous political figures (and reporters) repeating the exact same phrases, the systematic and coordinated use of spin is laid bare. Having been exposed, their virtual vacuity revealed, the talking points lose their rhetorical power.[9]

When successfully employed, talking points are sometimes even adopted by journalists in their supposed objective coverage of the news. In fact, as Stewart notes on February 28, 2012, GOP talking points on how to spin any improvements in the economy were disseminated to sympathetic journalists. They were to stress continuing high unemployment numbers, high gas prices, and the national debt. Stewart's montage shows Fox News pundits hitting these talking points again and again as some good economic news emerges toward the end of February. Indeed, one host is even shown reading the memo itself on air and then proceeding to push the high price of gas, asking his audience the question, what are you doing to pay for gas?

To demonstrate striking double-standards in policy and talking points, Stewart displays a montage of competing and contradictory rhetoric from President Bush concerning Iraq and North Korea (July 11, 2006). In the first case, the (arguably baseless) fear of Iraqi involvement in future terrorist attacks was said to warrant *immediate* military action—time had "run out" for Saddam Hussein. In the second case, the (actual) nuclear threat posed by North Korea was taken as a cue for *diplomacy*, *patience*, and international *consensus*! In his 2002 State of the Union address, President Bush declared that he wouldn't permit the world's most dangerous regimes (the "axis of evil," including North Korea) to threaten the United States. It now seems clear, however, that the main target was Iraq. In the case of Iraq,

Bush presented a false dilemma: "I had a choice to make: either take the word of a madman [Saddam Hussein] or defend America. Given that choice, I will defend America every time." But when faced with the arguably worse threat posed by then-leader of North Korea, Kim Jong Il, President Bush didn't present the situation in terms of this sort of dilemma. So while North Korea continued to threaten America with tests of ballistic missiles and nuclear warheads, the rhetoric about North Korea remained markedly different from the rhetoric that swirled around the invasion of Iraq. The talking points on North Korea emphasized diplomacy and the need for patience, not the imminent threat of a "madman."

To consider another example, then correspondent Colbert's "Words Speak Louder Than Actions" presents the evolution of some of the Bush Administration's more inflammatory rhetoric, demonstrating a striking difference between the talk talked (rhetoric) and the walk walked (action) (RNC, 2004, Day 2). It begins with President Bush's now infamous declaration that his administration wanted Osama Bin Laden, and the other members of Al Qaeda, "dead or alive." Recall that he was "going to smoke them out of their caves" and bring them to justice. As the invasion of Iraq approached, however, the rhetoric changed. Capturing Bin Laden was marginalized—"the objective is not Bin Laden"—and the supposedly growing danger posed by Saddam Hussein was emphasized. Terrifying words and phrases were used: "anthrax," "rape-rooms," "weapons of mass destruction."[10] What's more, Hussein, who apparently wasn't at all involved in the 9/11 attacks, was increasingly and misleadingly associated with Al Qaeda. But with the failure to find weapons of mass destruction in Iraq, the administration's rhetoric once again changed. Rather than claiming that Iraq actually had "weapons of mass destruction," the administration claimed that Hussein was involved in "weapons of mass destruction related program activities." Note that the latter, rather ineloquent, characterization of the Hussein threat, while consistent with the lack of actual weapons of mass destruction, fails to convey the sense of imminent danger which was supposed to justify invasion in the first place.

Imagery and context can also play an important role in political rhetoric, as is illustrated by *The Daily Show*'s "Indecision 2004" coverage of both Democratic and Republican national conventions. Both parties display many examples of stagecraft and pageantry to move viewers to support them. Rather than relying solely on the content of their arguments and positions, both parties make ample use of marketing techniques to persuade the voting public. *Daily Show* contributor Lewis Black comments on the more ridiculous production details of the Democratic convention, like its numerous musical performances and its award-show-style format, with some-times silly or inappropriate theme songs (DNC, 2004, Day 1). Then-correspondent Colbert, by way of trying to excuse his skipping out on the Democratic convention, calls it "a farce, a scripted, stage-managed event. It's not news. It isn't even fake news!" (DNC, 2004, Day 3). In a subsequent episode, Colbert compares what he euphemistically calls his "protest" with what his executive producer refers to as "grounds for dismissal."[11]

Satirized for Your Protection

Exactly how does *The Daily Show* use humor to reveal political rhetoric? Does it use humorous editing techniques to expose attempts at rhetorical persuasion, or does the humor emerge from the rhetoric itself? If you've been paying attention, you should recognize this as a false dilemma. Among the various strategies in satirizing political rhetoric, the montage, as we saw, is ideal for exposing the use of talking points. Half a dozen political operatives (or even reporters) using the exact same phrase is no coincidence, and when put together into a montage, this becomes all too obvious. We've also noted how montages are useful in charting the evolution of talking points as rhetoric changes to suit changing political needs. In general, Stewart's careful selection of footage can reveal many chimaeras of reason. Rhetoric offends the intellect, and when highlighted, humor is the predictable result. Satirizing the excesses of personality-driven cable news show hosts with the most gratuitous examples of rhetoric, Colbert *embodies* the kind of bad reasoning that Stewart merely exposes. Colbert's character embraces the irrational fully, and makes explicit the biased agendas of those he satirizes.

Given the widespread use of political rhetoric, it's clear that many politicians have a rather cynical view of human nature. The popular use of manipulative persuasion techniques suggests that, from the perspective of the political elite, the average citizen shouldn't be trusted with the truth, but should rather accept beliefs handed down from on high. The democratic ideals that help shape and define Western culture reject this elitism, and so it's of the utmost importance that we avoid adopting and maintaining our beliefs uncritically, that we don't fall prey to the rhetorical machinations of our political leaders. A critically informed and thoughtful citizenry is essential to the health of the democratic institutions that are intended to ensure liberty. *The Daily Show*'s ability to expose and satirize political rhetoric makes it both enlightening and, oddly enough, enjoyable too.

Notes

1. Some of these segments are collected in the DVD, *The Daily Show with Jon Stewart: Indecision 2004* (Comedy Central, 2005) while others are taken from episodes which can accessed the Comedy Network website (http://watch.thecomedynetwork.ca/the-daily-show-with-jon-stewart/full-episodes). References will be made parenthetically in-text to specific conventions' and days' coverage.
2. Stewart also considers more familiar sorts of Democratic pandering. In an effort to "relate" to their working-class base, several speakers recounted stories of their difficult upbringings and working-class backgrounds, from being the son of a mill worker to being the son of a goat farmer.
3. After the speech, Senator Miller did an interview on Chris Matthews's show *Hardball* (MSNBC) in which he lamented that they didn't live in a time when he could challenge Matthews to a duel!
4. As viewers of the show will have noticed, the show's mascot is a bald eagle, and the stars and stripes, and other bits of patriotic symbolism, are ubiquitous.
5. More than one of his guests who are critical of the Iraq war has faced the (loaded) question: "Why do you hate our troops, sir?"
6. Post-debate spin has a significant impact on public perceptions of political debates. Winning a Presidential debate in the public's mind often means having advocates that effectively persuade the viewing public that the candidate has won or done a good job, regardless of whether this is so. Obviously the quality of a candidate's performance makes the job of spinning more or less difficult. But even disastrously poor showings can sometimes be effectively spun, and so it's important to recognize the influence of post-debate "spin doctors."
7. On the use of euphemisms and dysphemisms in political rhetoric, see Brooke N. Moore and Richard Parker, *Critical Thinking* (7th edn.) (New York, NY: McGraw-Hill, 2004), 124–128.

8. Alternatively, one might give a rhetorical definition of abortion which begs the question against the pro-life position by, for example, defining "abortion" as "the termination of a fast-growing tumor." A relatively neutral definition is "the termination of an embryo or fetus," which describes abortion without begging the question against either position on its moral status.

9. Likewise, a montage of different reporters who are, for example, leveling *loaded questions* against a person, party, or group brings to light potential biases in the press.

10. "Weapons of mass destruction" is a nebulous phrase including a variety of weapons which can differ widely in their potential destructiveness, while other weapons which seemingly possess the potential to cause mass or indiscriminant destruction (napalm, white phosphorous, depleted uranium munitions, and cluster bombs) may or may not be included. Note as well that large munitions (such as 2000-pound "bunker busters") used on urban targets are quite capable of causing mass and, in some cases, indiscriminate destruction.

11. For a somewhat different slant on spin, see Kimberly Blessing and Joseph Marren, "More Bullshit: Political Spin and the PR-ization of Media," in this volume.

Chapter 13

The *Daily Show* Way
Critical Thinking, Civic Discourse, and Postmodern Consciousness

Roben Torosyan

> *If you want to become whole,*
> *let yourself be partial ...*
> *If you want to be given everything,*
> *give everything up.*
>
> Tao Te Ching[1]

For many 20-somethings and grandmothers alike, *The Daily Show* taps a human longing for questioning, conversation, and fun that is generally neglected in civic discourse. The show can also help us at once give up being locked into our own assumptions and biases, while owning just how *inevitably* partial any view is.

Civil Disservice

Despite Stewart admitting his own "socialist" sympathies, *The Daily Show* often critiques not only right-leaning but left-leaning language. After Froma Harrop, the president of the National Conference of Editorial Writers and its Civility Project, labeled Tea Party "patriots" as "terrorists," John Oliver interviewed her. Harrop had written, "The tea party Republicans have engaged in economic terrorism against the

The Ultimate Daily Show and Philosophy: More Moments of Zen, More Indecision Theory, First Edition. Edited by Jason Holt.
© 2013 John Wiley & Sons, Inc. Published 2013 by John Wiley & Sons, Inc.

United States—threatening to blow up the economy if they don't get what they want."[2] Oliver sought "to find out how to restore civility to America's public discourse" in a report entitled "Civil Disservice" (January 12, 2012).

Midway through the piece, Oliver said, "I really admire how understanding you are to people who have different opinions to you … such as yourself." Harrop paused, then replied, "Yeah." Oliver pushed further, "So apparently, there are a lot of people out there that are just name-calling for no real reason. How can I get them to tone down the language?" Harrop failed to engage his point. Oliver then asked, "What if they don't fight back, they just get into this weird displacement?" Harrop replied, "Meaning?" And Oliver said, "Meaning that they kind of don't engage in what I've just said to them." Harrop answered, "Well you chain them up in a room." Oliver then confined Harrop to an elevator but similarly failed to get her to acknowledge her rhetoric.

After the airing, Harrop subsequently wrote in a follow-up blog, "Of course it was staged. 'The Daily Show' is comedy, not journalism. This was a comedy sketch in which the participants played out a parody of themselves, just as the guest hosts of 'Saturday Night Live' are sometimes cast in self-deprecating situations. But you already knew that, didn't you?"[3] In other words, Harrop tried to claim that contradicting her own desire for civility was deliberate, that she caricatured herself. Yet in neither her so-called parody nor her blog did she ever retract her use of the labels "terrorism" and "terrorists."

In contrast to Harrop's cynicism, extreme language, and denial, *The Daily Show* promotes language that's more moderate and accurate. Interestingly, despite the show's ironic satire, it aims at greater accuracy as a means to the larger end of truth in general, a stream of thinking termed "modernism." But in "postmodernism," truth is seen more as both a continuum (from less true to more true) and as a process (given that there is no unbiased perspective out there, the point is to question everything). Despite its modernist message that there is truth, the show's constant questioning makes us more self-conscious about our own thinking habits. *The Daily Show* and its writers "teach that deliberation is not a means to an end but an end in itself. Discussion, dialogue, provocation, and questioning are valued for their own sake—not because they lead to truth but because they foster a community able to discern untruth."[4] Better, I believe the show does lead to *truer* understanding. But more than information, the show promotes transformation—from knee-jerk habits of mind to mindful self-awareness. One way it does so is by catching how people try to manipulate opinion using the red herring tactic.

The Red (Herring) Menace

In a segment entitled "Are You Prepared?!?" (May 16, 2006) correspondent Samantha Bee begins, "Recent events have shown that Americans face certain death. Death that will kill you." Like many of the show's fake news items, the report caricatures the way the nation's leaders and television media tend to sensationalize stories, appealing to emotion rather than disciplined reason.

Bee interviews one suburban couple about their emergency preparedness:

BEE:	Homeland Security says you need duct tape and plastic sheeting to protect your home. I assume you have that?
COUPLE:	No.
BEE:	Communications gear?
COUPLE:	No.
BEE:	(*lowering her voice as if embarrassed*) Do you at least have a large tarp with which to collect the corpses of your friends and family?

While exaggerated for comic effect, Bee's parody of loaded media questions conveys a serious message: Civic discourse is often driven more by emotion and dogma than by reasoned dialogue. By reducing the entire issue of emergency preparedness to "either protect yourself or die," Bee lampoons how such false dichotomies (false either/or choices) do anything but promote safety (much less a *feeling* of safety), which requires even-tempered, reasoned planning, preparation, and prevention.

Hysteria makes a great red herring. As Stephen Colbert says, "There's fear out there; someone's gotta monger it." The tactic of redirecting attention away from corruption, wasteful government spending, and other serious problems is just one way Stephen Colbert's character regularly exudes the very *opposite* of seven critical thinking attitudes.[5] In contrast, Stewart and team regularly enact them all:

(1)   inquisitive
(2)   open-minded
(3)   truthseeking
(4)   systematic
(5)   analytical
(6)   judicious
(7)   confident in reasoning[6]

To illustrate the show's "judicious" undercurrent: After the 2005 London terrorist attacks, Stewart mused, "The attacks happened overseas, yet 62% of Americans are worried about similar attacks here. I wonder why Americans are so nervous about it." Glaring news headlines then flashed with ominous voiceovers: "London Terror," "Attacks in London," "Who's at risk? How prepared are we?" Wide-eyed, Stewart said, "Oh, I see. But I'm sure the on-air cable hosts will bring some perspective, context, and understanding to the coverage." Clips then showed hosts saying: "Are we next in America?" "How safe are we in America?" "Can we prevent a subway or a bus attack in the US?" "Why are they doing this?" and "You have to wonder, will we ever *truly* feel safe again?" Such clips highlight our tendency to focus egocentrically on our own safety when people suffer elsewhere. They also show the failure of news organizations to act in the traditional, time-honored role of judicious watchdog, arbiter, and protector.

Daily Show humor presupposes that news organizations have a responsibility to the public, much as Jean-Jacques Rousseau (1712–1778) conceived a government and its citizens to be bound by a social contract. Government should provide people "a form of association which will defend and protect with the whole common force the person and goods of each associate."[7] News organizations, similarly, should function in ways that benefit people, not use scaremongering to gain audience share. Likewise, Stewart and company show how politicians appeal to voters' basest instincts to rally support for their own ideological positions.

"Diss" Ingenuous Bullshitting:
Scapegoating and Leaping to Judgment (Day)

When the Republican-dominated House passed a resolution to continue the Iraq War (June 19, 2006), Stewart underscored the event:

> STEWART: Representative Tom Cole encapsulated how the Republicans had once again succeeded.
>
> COLE: (*video clip*) Whether we are right or wrong on our side of the aisle, we do have a common position and it's expressed in this resolution.
>
> STEWART: That's right: He's right. Or wrong. But either way, people agree with him.

The congressman's assumption here seems to be that we shouldn't focus on the adequacy of such positions, let alone whether they would help or harm. Interestingly, this is the mark of neither honesty nor lying, but bullshitting, which involves making assertions without caring about their truth or falsity.[8] Worse yet in this case, we only need agreement among the party in power, regardless of consequences, because the majority is presumed to represent the will of the people. Such an epistemology (or framework for knowing what's true) devalues thinking through decisions, compromises democratic deliberation, serves only the interests of those in power, and reduces everything to either–or absolutes. As Stephen Colbert says (in one installment of "The Wørd"), "You're either for the war, or against America. There's no gray area." ("Or gray matter, apparently," as the explanatory side-text reads onscreen.)

Stewart has said most politicians probably do truly believe they'd do a better job than their opponents. But they tend to neglect making honest arguments to justify that belief. They don't consider enough information honestly to arrive at the best course of action. Instead, they often follow Niccolò Machiavelli's (1469–1527) advice "to learn how not to be good, and to use this knowledge and not use it, according to the necessities of the case."[9] Such reasoning leads to thinking that the ends one presumes to be good "justify" any means, no matter how destructive.

With a postmodern focus on process, Stewart often disagrees less with what politicians actually believe, and more with the way they suppress respectful and possibly fruitful exchange. Many leaders go from duplicitously manipulating rhetoric to outright dissembling and lying. Worse still, the media often appear to collude in the deception, failing to provide appropriate context or perspective. For example, when former Defense Secretary Donald Rumsfeld gave a speech (May 9, 2006), he was interrupted by hecklers. Then he took a question.

QUESTIONER: I'm Ray McGovern, a 27-year veteran of the Central Intelligence Agency. Why did you lie to get us into a war that was not necessary, that has caused these kinds of casualties?

RUMSFELD: First of all, I haven't lied.

STEWART: Oh, he didn't lie. Well, that settles it. There's pound cake in the back, we can have a good time, and uh—

RUMSFELD: It appears that there were not weapons of mass destruction.

MCGOVERN: You said you knew where they were.

RUMSFELD: I did not.

STEWART: See? He never said he knew where they were.

RUMSFELD: (*earlier video from March 2003*) We know where they are. They're in the area around ... Baghdad.

STEWART: Well to be fair, Rumsfeld probably never saw that episode of *Meet the Press*.

Stewart begins his comments, as he often does, in the guise of a hopeful, if somewhat gullible, citizen. He then pretends to believe that the media will dutifully investigate such doubletalk: "So, the Secretary of Defense, caught, in a contradiction, about weapons of mass destruction. Surely that will be a big story." Clips instead show CNN's Paula Zahn accusing McGovern of having "an axe to grind," Tucker Carlson calling him "not just any heckler," and Anderson Cooper asking McGovern irrelevantly "Were you nervous?" Carlson continued:

CARLSON: Isn't it enough that he was wrong and had bad judgment? Why does he have to be a liar too?

MCGOVERN: Well, that's the question you'll have to direct to him.

STEWART: But won't.

Stewart then showed clips from what he called "a Fox News unvestigative report" [sic] about Rumsfeld entitled, "Why He Fights." The reporter interviews General Paul van Riper—who called for Rumsfeld's resignation—and asks accusingly:

FOX NEWS REPORTER: What are you trying to accomplish by doing this? And you don't think this debate threatens the civilian leadership of the military? Does that hurt the war effort?

STEWART: (*sniffing deeply*) Mmm, I can't tell if I'm smelling the fairness (*sniffs*) or the balance.

Alluding to the Fox News tagline "Fair and Balanced," Stewart draws attention to how such loaded questions support a one-sided agenda, rather than providing an even-handed and honest investigation or discussion. By allowing such contradictions to speak for themselves, *The Daily Show* implicitly invites us to notice when we too resort to deception—keeping *us* honest when we believe, say, that we ourselves deserve to succeed by any means necessary.

In the Line of Ire: Reframing the Debate

One way to fight Machiavellian manipulation, the show implies, is to reframe the terms of debate. In interviewing William Bennett, author and former Secretary of Education under Ronald Reagan, Stewart questions the apparent inconsistency between Bennett's claim to affirm America's belief in freedom and his attempts to limit freedom by a ban on gay marriage.

STEWART: Why not encourage gay people to join in in [sic] that family arrangement if *that's* what provides stability to a society?

BENNETT: Well I think if gay ... gay people are members of families, they're *already* members of families.

STEWART: And that's where the buck stops, that's the gay ceiling.

BENNETT: Look, it's a debate about whether you believe marriage is between a man and a woman.

STEWART: I disagree. I think it's a debate about whether gay people are part of the human condition or just a random fetish.

Stewart rejects Bennett's framing of the debate. He doesn't just contradict him by saying, "Marriage isn't *necessarily* between man and woman." Rather, he suggests that the debate isn't about how to define marriage, but instead about who counts as human, and how to understand the human condition.

> BENNETT: The question is how do you define marriage? Where do you draw the line? What do you say to the polygamist? What do you *say* to the polygamist?
>
> STEWART: You don't say anything to the polygamist. That is a choice, to get three or four wives. That is not a biological condition that "I gots to get laid by different women that I'm married to." That's a choice. Being gay is part of the human condition. There's a huge difference.

Stewart first shows that calling homosexuality a *mere* choice ignores that it's a much more basic condition of who someone is; he thus undercuts superficial versions of the determined/chosen dichotomy. Stewart then speaks to the larger question of what it means to be human. While Stewart seeks to foster respect for the freedom to be our fully human and different selves, Bennett treats differences of human condition as subject to choice and hence, regulation.

> BENNETT: Well, some people regard their human condition as having three women. Look the polygamists are all over this.
>
> STEWART: Then let's go slippery slope the other way. If government says I can define marriage as between a man and a woman, what says they can't define it between people of different income levels, or they can decide whether or not you are a suitable husband for a particular woman?
>
> BENNETT: Because, gender *matters* in marriage, it has mattered to every human society, it matters in every religion, uh, it has mattered in …
>
> STEWART: Race matters in every society as well. Isn't progress understanding?

Bennett's appeal resembles the warning of conservative orator Edmund Burke (1729–1797) against interfering extensively with habit and tradition, because society needs stability. Stewart suggests, on the other hand, that to avoid stagnation, society also needs change and progress—which require that we become more inclusive of greater variety and difference over time. To learn first requires admitting that one's perceptions may be limited. As the *Tao Te Ching* puts it, "The mark of a moderate man is freedom from his own ideas."[10] To free our minds, we must if not actually shift frames of reference then at least try honestly to understand frames different than our own.

Look Who's Not Talking Now:
Going Beyond Experience

Our experience both opens and closes our perception of the world, like a lens that brings some things into focus while blurring others. As the philosopher Hans-Georg Gadamer (1900–2002) wrote, "If a person is trying to understand something, he will not be able to rely from the start on his own chance previous ideas."[11] If Bennett fails to question the source of his moral indignation—how, for instance, family influence or a distaste for gay sex may influence his viewpoint—he can't truly understand either the issue or his role in debating it.

In his interview, Bennett went on to target "activist" judges, saying that gay marriage is coming because "the courts have decided it." He continued by associating being gay with a devaluing of marriage in Western culture:

BENNETT: In Holland and Norway, marriage is taken less seriously. When you define it out, when you start to say it can involve anybody, then I think, any grouping, anybody who loves anybody, it has serious problems.

STEWART: It has serious problems. And you know divorce is not caused because fifty percent of marriages end in gayness.

Deliberately associating being gay with "taking marriage less seriously" is a similar form of scapegoating. Bennett's argument seems similarly aimed at blaming an innocent target (here, homosexuals) and gives no reason for his prejudice.

Stewart puts the obsession with the issue of gay marriage, and its abuse by politicians and pundits, in perspective by identifying divorce as not the result but the greater concern. As with all humor, the joke first gives a context (marriage), then sets up an incongruity or problem (what ends a marriage), and finally leaps to an unexpected resolution (marriage ends in gayness). The structure of such jokes resembles that of serious problem-solving. To make sense something, we need to put it in appropriate context then build a new understanding. Stewart's juxtaposition clarifies that the institution of marriage is threatened not by homosexuality but by choices people make.

Show Me the Meta

America (The Book) contains an image of colonists meeting Native Americans.[12] The caption reads, "America's path to democracy was cleared by the colonists' generous giveaways, like the much sought-after 'Smallpox Blankets.'" The line makes us laugh at an agonizingly tragic fact about colonial history. Such sharply tinged satire in *The Daily Show* derives from the very nature of tragedy and comedy. According to Friedrich Nietzsche (1844–1900), tragedy combines both Apollonian and Dionysian tendencies, reason and recklessness, restraint and excess, going back and forth between the two, never resting at either.

Such a dynamic relationship is the theme of correspondent Ed Helms's visit to one of the great battlegrounds of what *The Daily Show* terms the "evolutionary" war. He stands in front of Ray County Courthouse, in Dayton, Tennessee, the site of the infamous 1925 Scopes Monkey Trial, where John Scopes was convicted for teaching evolution to high school students. That trial "gave Dayton a reputation for closed-minded ignorance," as Helms says. But, he then implies, it's really just a reenactment town.

HELMS: (*voiceover*) Just like Colonial Williamsburg, the town is populated with costumed performers who reenact the quaint attitudes of the good old days.

HELMS: (*to resident June Griffin*) What is your take on the Scopes trial?

GRIFFIN: Evolution is a total fabrication and a lie. Evolution distorts faith, destroys faith, and builds an economic market that is contrary to our American way of life.

HELMS: That's good stuff.

HELMS: (*voiceover*) In addition to the skilled actors, Dayton's attention to detail is staggering. The town has gone so far as to erect this elaborate set of a fully functioning college. Named after William Jennings Bryan, the prosecutor in the Scopes trial, the college keeps things authentic. Store owner Tim Cruver, whose daughter plays one of the college students, explains.

HELMS: (*to Cruver*) What does their science department teach regarding evolution v. creationism?

CRUVER: Well it's a fact that they're going to be teaching creationism up there because they don't believe in evolution.

HELMS: When the tourists aren't, ya know, milling around, watching the classes and stuff, then what do they teach?

CRUVER: Well, the same thing.

According to a 2005 Pew Forum survey, nearly two-thirds of Americans support teaching creationism alongside evolution. Yet doing so treats faith and prejudicial belief on par with scientific truth. Science requires observation, testing, data, analysis, and verification. And these can't simply be forced to fit one's values, important as values are in deciding what questions to pursue.

Dayton's opposition to evolutionary theory, as Helms puts it, "would be terrifying if it were real"—which it is! It rightly scares us that so many people ignore or defame the scientific community's consensus that humans evolved from non-human primates. An extra irony comes when Griffin says that she despises actors, apparently not realizing that Helms himself is an actor:

HELMS: June, you're very good, you're very good. Do you have a
            background in acting?
GRIFFIN: No, I despise actors.
HELMS: Really?
GRIFFIN: Yes.

Griffin's "character" is unaware of the difference between a faith-based view (such as creationism) and a verifiable, scientific account of human origins (such as evolution), and is equally unaware that an actor has conned her into being the butt of a joke.

While the entire "Evolution, Schmevolution" series implicitly supports evolution, Stewart himself is usually concerned less with *what* people should think and more with how to engage in productive dialogue.[13] In addition to reframing the terms of debate, he shows how to "go meta," or get above it all, and improve the process itself, be it political argument or media reportage.

For example, when interviewing Ramesh Ponnuru, author of *The Party of Death*, Stewart begins with meta-commentary:

STEWART: It seems like rhetoric like *The Party of Death* puts people
            on—I guess what I would call—the *defensive*, in some
            respects.
PONNURU: Yeah. I can't really present the argument against things
            like abortion by pretending it doesn't have something to
            do with death. I guess that's part of the argument.
STEWART: Could you agree there is maybe sanctimony on both sides?
PONNURU: Yeah, absolutely.
STEWART: Now, what's the sanctimony on your side?

By referring to sanctimony, Stewart targets the false righteousness in many debates. When pro-life advocates call abortion "genocide" and its defenders "murderers," they ignore important issues, such as women's right to protect their bodies. Likewise, when pro-choice advocates use language such as "products of conception" or "termination of pregnancy," they dehumanize the issue as one of cold, impersonal science. Ponnuru goes on to claim, "I try very hard to argue for a rational case," but rather than granting that his opponents have a reasoned defense with whom he disagrees, he reduces them to mere proponents "of death."

Stewart's approach to discourse, on the other hand, avoids the common attack-and-defend interview model, and instead endorses problem-solving values of conflict resolution.[14] As Stewart illustrates, this model prefers rationality to reactivity, sincerity to disingenuousness, authentic representation to dissembling, meaning to absurdity, and recognition to cynical suspicion. Even when the show's writers use sarcastic or cynical humor, they do so not to make empty jokes, but to recognize more honestly what is otherwise ignored.

Self-Effacement and Good Faith

STEWART: I disagree with a lot of people. I think the whole problem with this debate is it's being waged on both extremes. If you extend it out it becomes: Do you condone what some would call rape to prevent what some would call murder? Because women are, I think rightly so, protective of what we call their p*$#ies. I don't know the scientific terms. But that's the part that's missing from the book. Can I tell you something?

PONNURU: Yeah.

STEWART: I am very unprofessional.

No sooner does Stewart seriously summarize the abortion debate than he irreverently uses a word he knows will be censored and then derides his own behavior. Much as post-modernism frees us up to value ruptures and bursts of irrationality, Stewart's interruption functions "momentarily breaks, but does not derail, the otherwise linear, logical flow of the discussion."[15] Moreover, Stewart's style seems aimed at putting interviewees more at ease, giving them a relatively free and uninhibited venue for expression. Adding unexpected taboo provides further lighthearted relief from the tension of serious discussion. Despite disagreeing with guests like Bennett and Ponnuru, Stewart will often efface himself to provide his guests with a face-saving out. For example, Stewart backed off Bennett at one point and said, "I'm just grasping at straws," taking responsibility for his own limited perspective, and even putting himself down.

Strikingly, Stewart will also often put down audience ridicule of a guest. When Ponnuru hesitated and stumbled at one point, and the audience began to cheer, Stewart cut them off, saying, "No, no, no." Then he said to Ponnuru, "And I want this, honestly: for us to have a conversation, because you're a smart guy, and you've made a lot of smart arguments." Stewart's shtick is at once an act and at the same time implies, as a tee-shirt from the Stewart-Colbert Rally read, "I may not agree with you, but I'm pretty sure you're not Hitler." In effect, Stewart extends a presumption of good faith to his interviewees rarely seen in the media.

When actor Kevin Spacey told Stewart he wished "Congress and the Senate would go at [the president] every day" and added, "or maybe it should just be you ... You should go, and every day ask him questions," Stewart replied, "I could barely get myself to work in the morning." As usual, Stewart portrays himself as a mere clown. When he himself is interviewed, he denies that *The Daily Show* is anything but comedy or at best, political and cultural satire. Such denials only reaffirm that Stewart's self-inclusive way of poking fun embodies a powerful way of being in the world—one of thoughtful, self-reflective, and modest engagement.

In the Ponnuru interview, for instance, Stewart ultimately begs to get beyond heated provocation: "Isn't there a rational conversation to be had in the country ...?" Stewart's repeated call to overcome mutually exclusive oppositions often helps viewers to clarify their own thoughts and feelings, whether they agree or disagree with him or his guests. One rhetorician sees an "agonistic aesthetic" in the way the show aims at a "healthy pluralism that resists reducing antagonists to enemies, and looks to articulate similarities and points of contact and convergence."[16] Stewart thus seeks to find common ground across political and ideological lines of debate.

Good faith, such as Stewart extends to most of his guests, relies on an implied promise that parties will participate sincerely in open dialogue and assume that progress can be made. By contrast, politicians and celebrities alike often act from bad faith, characterized by hidden agendas, closed discussion, and pessimism about, or indifference to, the genuine progress that open discussion might foster. Hence Matt Lauer delivers straight-laced reports like "Countdown to Doomsday," which Stewart called a "two-hour investigation into your pants and why you should crap them."

When President Bush spent part of his vacation reading—and reportedly *liking*—Albert Camus's (1913–1960) philosophical novel *The Stranger*, Stewart hinted at the irony of timing this choice during the Iraq War: Bush chose "a classic novel about a Westerner who kills an Arab for no good reason and dies with no remorse. Why that would strike a nerve, I don't know." *Daily Show* correspondent Jason Jones then "quoted" a response Bush might have to the work: "If the unexamined life is not worth living, then the soul not delved into is not worth being." Jones wishes that Bush were a kind of "philosopher king," Plato's ideal ruler, always acting rationally in the state's best interest.

Stewart similarly demonstrates how to act in good faith when he adopts the persona of a serious reporter providing much-needed perspective in place of mere sensationalism:

STEWART:	Obviously what is going on in the Middle East is awfully complicated. The fuel that fans the flames: The rival factions within Islam, both of them seem to have antipathy towards the US, Israel. It seems like there are some authoritarian regimes that are using proxy countries to fight their wars. It's a very difficult situation to grasp. Luckily, news organizations are on hand to give us context and ask the important questions.
PAULA ZAHN:	(*CNN graphic*: "Armageddon?") Are we really at the end of the world? We asked faith and values correspondent Delia Gallagher to do some checking.

By juxtaposing the complexity of current global crises with the crassly commercial way they're covered, *The Daily Show* lets misleading statements and images be their own undoing. The effect can be more powerful than a detailed critique by an academic.

Encouraging us be critical of what we take in, *The Daily Show* forces us to "be partial" (as the *Tao* counseled in the epigraph at the start of this chapter), or own up to our subjectivity—and at the same time to "give everything up," or surrender our beliefs, and thus keep learning and questioning. Further, while forcing us to reckon with how disturbingly easy it is to be manipulated, *The Daily Show* also provides a cathartic laugh in the face of such seemingly inevitable pain and disappointment.

Who knew thinking could be so fun and instructive at the same time?[17]

Notes

1. Lao-tzu, *Tao Te Ching*, trans. Stephen Mitchell (New York: Harper-Perennial, 1992), 22.
2. Froma Harrop, "Democrats Also Need a Presidential Primary in 2012," www.realclearpolitics.com(August 2, 2011), last accessed February 2013.
3. Froma Harrop, "To the Angry and the Confused ...," www.fromaharrop.com (January 17, 2012), last accessed February 5, 2013.
4. Joanne Morreale, "Jon Stewart and *The Daily Show*: I Thought You Were Going To Be Funny!" in *Satire TV: Politics and Comedy in the Post-Network Era*, eds. J.A. Gray, J.P. Jones, and E. Thompson (New York: New York University, 2009), 121.
5. See Roben Torosyan, "Things That Make You Go 'What?': Colbert as Anti-Critical Thinker," in *Stephen Colbert and Philosophy: I Am Philosophy (And So Can You!)*, ed. A.A. Schiller (Chicago, IL: Open Court Press, 2009), 29–49.
6. Most of these are drawn from American Philosophical Association, *Critical Thinking: A Statement of Expert Consensus for Purposes of Educational Assessment and Instruction*, "The Delphi Report," Committee on Pre-College Philosophy (ERIC Doc. No. ED 315 423) (1990), 13.
7. Jean-Jacques Rousseau, *The Social Contract*, trans. G.D.H. Cole (Amherst, NY: Prometheus Books, 1988), 23.
8. For more on bullshit, see Kimberly Blessing and Joseph Marren, "More Bullshit: Political Spin and the PR-ization of Media," in this volume.
9. Niccolò Machiavelli, *The Prince*, trans. Luigi Ricci, rev. E.R.P. Vincent, (New York: McGraw-Hill, 1950), 56.
10. Lao-tzu, *Tao Te Ching*, 59.
11. Hans-Georg Gadamer, *Truth and Method*, trans. and eds. Garrett Barden and John Cumming (New York: Seabury Press, 1975), 238.

12. Jon Stewart, Ben Karlin, and David Javerbaum, *America (The Book): A Citizen's Guide to Democracy Inaction* (New York: Warner Books, 2004), 18.

13. For more, see Massimo Pigliucci, "Evolution, Schmevolution: Jon Stewart and the Culture Wars," in this volume.

14. Jay Rothman, *Resolving Identity-Based Conflict in Nations, Organizations and Communities* (San Francisco: Jossey-Bass, 1997), 17, 40, and 47.

15. Geoffrey Baym, *From Cronkite to Colbert: The Evolution of Broadcast News* (Boulder, CO: Paradigm, 2009), 116.

16. Kelly Wilz, "Models of Democratic Deliberation: Pharmacodynamic Agonism in *The Daily Show*," in *The Daily Show and Rhetoric: Arguments, Issues, and Strategies*, ed. T.G. Knapp (Lexington: Lexington Books, 2011), 79.

17. My deepest gratitude goes to Melanie Torosyan, Chris Worsley, Kohar Gumusyan, and Michael Allen, each of whom continues to help me both express myself fully and not take myself too seriously.

Segment 4
INTERVIEW
RELIGION AND CULTURE

Chapter 14

GOP Almighty
When God Tells Me (and My Opponents) to Run for President

Roberto Sirvent and Neil Baker

Every good politician knows the value of a solid endorsement. Securing the support of a big name in your party might just be the factor that can tip the scales in your favor, and going into a primary you'll want every advantage you can get. Influential organizations like the AARP and the NRA also make for powerful friends on the campaign trail, as do popular activists and even movie stars. Still, while it can be great to have the backing of conspicuous figures like Oprah or Angelina Jolie, the most valuable political endorsements are the ones that come straight from the top—so why not try to swing one from the big man himself? After all, Rick Perry and Michele Bachmann seem to have managed it.

But if you're like us, you have a habit of asking questions, and for just this reason you tend to get suspicious whenever politicians start talking about their "in" with God. You're probably an avid viewer of *The Daily Show*, too. (You're reading the book, in any case.) If any of this sounds like you, we invite you to join us as we take a few lessons in healthy skepticism from one of the masters, Jon Stewart. In the next few pages we'll show how *The Daily Show* targets those political and religious leaders who claim to receive clear revelations from the divine, either by their own particular religious experiences and practices or through sacred texts. As we do,

The Ultimate Daily Show and Philosophy: More Moments of Zen, More Indecision Theory, First Edition. Edited by Jason Holt.

we'll consider some of the ways Stewart calls into question their apparently unquestionable grasp of the mind of God.

Here's where a little philosophy can help us. Philosophers like the famous English thinker John Locke (1632–1704) have made their living by carefully examining not only the nature of the world around us, but also the more puzzling aspects of human behavior. For instance, Locke describes and critiques the sort of "enthusiasm" we saw at the opening of this chapter by recognizing that such religiously convicted individuals: "persuade themselves that they are under the peculiar guidance of heaven in their actions and opinions, especially in those of them which they cannot account for by the ordinary methods of knowledge and principles of reason."[1] In similar fashion, our goal in this chapter will be to describe the behavior of those who profess a unique or superior access to God. Rather than attempt to say whether or not these experiences are genuine or "real," or whether any candidate really has received the divine endorsement, we'll be asking how philosophy might help us appreciate the commentary that *The Daily Show* has to offer.

Newt Gingrich on a Potato

If Michele Bachmann had been feeling any pre-election jitters in the days leading up to the Iowa Republican caucuses, you certainly wouldn't have known it by looking at her. On January 4, 2012, the day after the caucuses, Stewart pulled up a clip that had aired on CNN earlier in the week to remind viewers of the confidence she'd shown her constituency. In it, Representative Bachmann trumpets her conviction that supporters at home were "gonna see a miracle happen on Tuesday"; she had "absolutely no doubt" of it. Seemingly she had it on divine authority that there was a victory in her future. She lost of course, coming in dead last out of six candidates, but what confused Stewart even more than God's apparent miscommunication is the fact that despite her loss, Bachmann went on to affirm that her faith in "the Lord God Almighty" remained "unshakable." Bachmann really didn't get the miracle she was expecting, yet her certainty that her efforts were somehow intertwined with God's will went entirely unaffected. Strangest of all, many of Bachmann's opponents also expressed sentiments indicating their faith in some kind of divine power behind their respective campaigns.

To help shed some light on just why God seems hesitant to come out with his actual Presidential pick for November 2012, Stewart appealed to his correspondent, Wyatt Cenac, who was on location in heaven. And not surprisingly, heaven looks a lot like a Las Vegas sports book. After all, Representative Bachmann isn't the only one who talks about her goals and aspirations in terms of divine providence. As Cenac reminds us, "God's got his hands in a lot of human pies: football, the Grammys, Latin Grammys … "; the list goes on. So if the man upstairs has such a stake in all these human affairs, why doesn't he throw us a bone here?

Well sure, Cenac agrees, it would be easy enough for God to give us some sort of sign: "Maybe put Newt Gingrich's face on a potato?" Cenac asks us to keep in mind, however, that we're talking about the same guy who evidently doesn't see any need to resolve the whole Judaism/Christianity/Islam thing. He's the guy who creates a highly populated, low-lying Asian archipelago, only to destroy it with a freak tsunami. "The dude works in mysterious ways, man!" If we're really going to speak with Bachmann's certainty then in saying that heaven's running every show, Stewart's conclusion starts to makes sense: God "just kinda loves the game of it all."

What Stewart has done in this segment is highlight the arrogance and foolishness that lies at the heart of Bachmann's view of God. Recall for a moment Locke's criticism from the previous section. One of the problems he has with religious enthusiasm is that the "enthusiast," taking his own intuitions for divine direction, doesn't always find it necessary to weigh his opinions against the "principles of reason." As such, it can be very difficult to convince him that some of his beliefs may be false. More importantly, however, when someone starts believing his perspectives are unquestionable, his "convictions" often tend to become somewhat self-serving. Locke warns that religiously convinced individuals risk this type of arrogance whenever they have "flattered themselves with a persuasion of an immediate intercourse with the Deity and frequent communications with the Divine Spirit."[2] While he is careful not to deny that God does sometimes "enlighten men's minds in the apprehending of certain truths," Locke cautions that this way of being religious carries with it a number of dangers.[3]

Clearly, Locke's criticisms apply to Bachmann and her fellow candidates. Stewart's commentary highlights just how irrational it is for one politician to claim with absolute certainty that God favors her above her opponents, even—especially—as her opponents are simultaneously issuing similar claims. Surely their beliefs cannot *all* be true. Yet this *Daily Show* segment is getting at a problem that runs even deeper than this, and Locke's insights can help us see what it is. The arrogance of religious enthusiasm, we learned, is the idea that the "enthusiast" plays a special role in the divine plan; in fact this is exactly what seems to be happening in Bachmann's case. The way she sees it, her own political career is so crucial within God's design for world history that her success is sufficiently important to necessitate a miracle from the hands of the Almighty himself. But the logical implications of Bachmann's deterministic theology should not go unnoticed. For if God has the ability to run her campaign—and assuming he actually cares about it in the first place—then Stewart and his wise correspondent Wyatt Cenac are right to wonder one thing: if God is so willing to direct his favorite Republican presidential candidate to victory, then why does he find so little urgency in addressing issues like religious conflicts and natural disasters? You know, things that *really* matter.

Pious Politickin'

During the May 17, 2006 segment of "Back in Black," Lewis Black felt "called" to talk to *Daily Show* viewers about Jesus. Hands solemnly folded below a gentle countenance, Black's demeanor was altogether pleasant and inviting—we hardly needed to wonder what his next words would be. "Have you taken him as your personal lord and savior?" The thunderous laughter echoing from the studio audience indicated the negative. Black continued, "No? Then you're probably not in politics!"

Black is commenting of course on the astonishingly important role that religious enthusiasm has come to play in American politics. He goes on to explain that: "In recent years religious fundamentalists have evolved—I'm sorry, "intelligently designed"—themselves into a force to be reckoned with." Indeed, it's probably not too strong to say that success in a Republican primary today depends at least in part on a candidate's professed faith. But this doesn't mean that just any ol' religion will do. No, to pass muster in the contemporary political climate you'll need to show a particular kind of religiosity, the *fundamentalist* kind. This is because for many religious fundamentalists, if you're not their particular kind of "religious," you're not religious at all.

This matter raises questions about the rhetoric of the politicians we've already discussed: to what extent do they really *believe* what they say, and to what extent are they merely saying what they have to in order to satisfy their political base? Obviously, these are impossible to answer in any definitive way. It's worthwhile however to consider the possible negative effects of religious fundamentalism having so much sway. The dangers involved are made frighteningly clear by the prodigious amount of political power we find in conservative Christian organizations such as James Dobson's Focus on the Family. Black calls attention to this problem by referring viewers to a clip from *Hannity & Colmes*. In it, Dobson confronts a few select conservatives who made the unfortunate mistake of disagreeing with him. Before millions of devoted followers, he issues them the stern warning that there's "going to be some trouble down the road if they don't get on the ball." "In other words," Black translates, "you're my brother and I love you, but don't ever take sides against Focus on the Family again."

As Black makes clear, appealing to fundamentalist sensibilities seems to make perfect political sense in a climate where religious leaders like James Dobson and Pat Robertson exert such influence over the voting public. Not only will you have the support of a few of the most powerful voices in the country, you'll have convinced a significant percentage of Americans that should you take office, God himself will be there directing your every political move. Under such circumstances, it's almost impossible to imagine how a conservative candidate who opposes the tenets of religious fundamentalism might win the nomination for President, much less the Presidency itself. At the end of the day then, it's difficult to say who deserves harsher criticism: the candidate who claims to have God's endorsement, or the voter who believes him.

Thus Saith Pat

OK, we've been sympathetic. We've recognized just how tough it can be to win a Republican primary without playing to the fundamentalist base. Let's start getting a bit cynical, shall we? Pat Robertson, founder of the Christian Coalition and the Christian Broadcasting Network, is always ready to throw a foot or two into his mouth, and from this we can only guess that he secretly enjoys criticism from skeptical minds like ours. And with some help from *The Daily Show*, we'll be all too happy to oblige.

When the Supreme Court voted to decriminalize sodomy in 2003, Robertson let loose a few words that give us a glimpse of the motives that drive the formidable political machine of religious fundamentalism. Stewart aired the clip during his show on July 17: "This Supreme Court has, in my opinion, been weighed in the balance of God's judgment and found wanting. And what we're doing is praying that God will move in his way against them. It's up to the Lord to decide what to do." But Stewart smells something fishy—who's really calling the shots here? He fills in the gaps with a bit of commentary: "It's up for the Lord to decide. Pat Robertson just *identifies* who to crush. The Lord does the crushing. It's a little thing called teamwork. Robertson sets, the Lord spikes." American theologian Reinhold Niebuhr (1892–1971) once quipped that many religious people are in the habit of looking at God "as the sanctifier of whatever we most fervently desire."[4] As Stewart demonstrates, Robertson's comments seem to be excellent examples of what Niebuhr is talking about. It is as if Stewart were saying, "Go ahead Pat, pick your political target; God will make sure that evildoer gets what's coming to him." Such a strategy effectively allows the fundamentalist to speak with divine authority, and in this way he is able to equate God's agenda with his own.

We've yet to acknowledge however what is probably the most rhetorically advantageous aspect of Robertson's approach. Consider for a moment what's implied by the belief that an individual speaks for the divine: to disagree with such a person is really to disagree with the Almighty himself. This does more than signal the end of what might otherwise have been constructive debate; in an insidiously literal sense, it serves to demonize all dissenters and would-be dialogue partners. We need only think about the rhetorical effect of Robertson's concluding words to get a sense of the "righteous anger" his followers are likely to develop toward the Supreme Court Justices he denounces: "We ask that we might see freedom from what this institution has done to this nation. Let your hand rest heavily upon them. We pray in Jesus' name. Amen." Using this sort of language, Robertson all but removes the possibility that there may indeed be valid perspectives other than his own that should be considered. After all, like other religious fundamentalists, he has no doubt about the special access to God that he enjoys, and as such he simply cannot be wrong.

No Really, It's in the Bible

While we're on the subject of getting things wrong—Glenn Beck. As you may know, his show was pulled (although some called it a "parting of ways") from Fox in 2011, despite its sizable viewer base. Why, you ask? Well some have suggested that he was beginning to strike a few of the higher-ups in the Fox News Channel as something of a religious fanatic. But Jon Stewart isn't interested in hearsay. "That may be what the mainstream media and 'professors' and 'facts' and 'evidence' would like you to think," Stewart says, mimicking Beck's paranoia. "So what's *really* going on here?"

To find out, Stewart goes right to the source. In his April 7, 2011 episode he plays for us a number of telling clips from Beck's show. In the first segment we find Beck warning of the "coming insurrection," that is, the apocalyptic storm that's spreading "chaos" and "evil" across the globe. In the next, he's informing his audience that there are "signs in heavens and earth," and that "people have been paying attention to them for two thousand years." Finally, we hear Beck ridiculing the "other network," the one telling us all that the biblical apocalypse of Revelation is nonsense, that there's "not a lick of truth to it." He urges us instead to "search our feelings and know what's true."[5]

All right, this does seem to border on the extreme. Stewart "wants" to believe Beck when he says that we're living in the most turbulent and tumultuous point in history, the era predicted in biblical times that would signal the end of the world. But what about the generations that lived through world wars and depressions? What about periods in history in which families could expect six of ten children to die from what we now refer to as a sinus infection? Beck seems to believe that the meaning to be drawn from the apocalyptic texts of the New Testament is crystal clear, and as such, the only reason he can come up with as to why we might disagree with his conclusions is that we've decided to ignore the writings entirely. Certainly some choose to pay the Bible more attention than others do. Even so, given that contemporary readers are separated from the biblical authors by a cultural gap of nearly 2000 years, is it possible that the modern-day significance of the New Testament might be less clear than Beck lets on?

We've come to recognize that a significant aspect of the problem we confront is bound up with the issue of interpretation. To help us make sense of the situation then, we'll take a lesson from the branch of philosophy that deals entirely in interpretation: hermeneutics. And we simply can't talk about philosophical hermeneutics in any adequate way without making reference to its champion, the eminent Hans-Georg Gadamer (1900–2002).

One of the concepts that Gadamer argues most vehemently against in his famous *Truth and Method* is the idea of "objectivism."[6] This is the belief that once an author composes her text, the meaning of what she has written acquires its own independent existence; the objectivist maintains therefore that no matter who happens to be reading the author's text, its meaning remains fixed. Gadamer asks us however to consider the significance of our prejudices within the process of interpretation. (When Gadamer speaks of "prejudice," he means our unspoken assumptions, or "pre-judgments.") He reminds us that no reader has the ability to remove himself from his own situation in culture and history, and that both of these factors play fundamental roles in determining what assumptions and beliefs the reader will bring along when reading. Neither is there an author who possesses the ability to write in a cultural or historical vacuum. (Think about it for a moment—when you want to convey a message, don't you make use of a *preexisting* language? It would be a real pain if we had to create an entirely new system of shareable meaning every time we wanted to communicate.) At the very least, this shows just how difficult it is to defend the notion of a single "essential" meaning.

Once we admit the real ambiguity and uncertainty involved in all interpretation, Glenn Beck's arrogance in holding up his own interpretations as "gospel truth" becomes very hard to miss. Not only does he blindly assume that of all the generations that have read and cherished their sacred scriptures, it's to *his* generation that the texts actually speak; he also seems entirely unwilling to acknowledge that his interpretation is conditioned by culture and history. Otherwise, he would need to admit that there might be legitimate alternative readings to take into account. Beck of course would likely respond to these criticisms with the all-too-common assertion that "true" followers are gifted with a special clarity of understanding. If only the rest of us knew God like Glenn.

Pat "Gay People Cause Hurricanes" Robertson

When you've spent as much time commenting on politics and public affairs as Jon Stewart has, you start getting to the point where not much can surprise you anymore—except of course when it comes to Pat Robertson. Stewart tells us about a recent Robertson shocker in his October 25, 2011 episode, around the time the candidates competing for the Republican presidential nomination were in the midst of hot debates. At this point we should remind ourselves that few people have a better knack for extremist language than Pat "Gay People Cause Hurricanes" Robertson (as Stewart refers to him). As such, it caught Stewart entirely off guard when Robertson dared to come out with criticisms concerning the extreme language of the Republican candidates.

Indeed, this *is* rather incredible. Now critiquing the many problems with extremist rhetoric would move beyond the scope of this chapter. However, we do want to look at the absurdities that result when extremist rhetorical strategies are used to make absolute statements about God. We've already alluded to some of Robertson's more outrageous comments, and Stewart reminds us of a few more in this segment: for instance, he asks us to consider Robertson's argument that the 2010 Haitian earthquake was the result of a deal with the devil. Then there's his belief that "Islamist people" are bent on having foot-washing areas constructed in airports. And who could forget his question about whether or not a man who desires to have sex with ducks is, as he puts it, "protected under hate crime." But while each of these examples would provide plenty of material for our analysis, we'll focus on one statement in particular that can help shed some light on Robertson's particular approach to God and God's will for humankind.

In a clip that had aired in 2009, Pat Robertson offers his viewers what is known as a "slippery slope" argument against same-sex marriage: "If we take biblical standards away in homosexuality ... what about bestiality? And ultimately, what about child molestation and pedophilia?"[7] One would be hard-pressed to find a clearer example of extremism spoken in the context of moral debate, or one more offensive. But what exactly is it about Robertson's moral reasoning that brings him to such outlandish opinions? We suggest that despite his particular commitments to the moral authority of the Christian scriptures, his problem is in essence no different from that of any other extremist rhetorician: Robertson suffers from an unwillingness to admit life's real ambiguity.

Let's take a moment to analyze Robertson's argument. The "biblical standards" which he holds up as divine commandments are undoubtedly grounded in one of the exceedingly few New Testament passages that refer to same-gender sexual activity—passages like Romans 1:26–27. For argument's sake, let's ignore the controversy that has long raged among biblical historians over whether the writings of the Apostle Paul ever actually refer to the homosexual orientation that we speak of today. What's more important for us to recognize in this context is that we've once again caught Pat red-handed in the act of practicing objectivist hermeneutics. As we saw in our discussion of Gadamer, it's nonsense to assert that the meaning of this or that text fell directly from heaven; rather, a text will always be borne upon and reflect an interaction with the cultural assumptions of its day. Thus, by appealing to the Bible as an unambiguous and unquestionable rulebook from God, Robertson finds clarity where clarity is lacking.

Reinhold Niebuhr phrases it this way: "Biblical observations upon life are made in a living relation to living history. When they are falsely given an eminence which obscures this relation, they become the source of error and confusion."[8] Looking to the Bible for support in finding an appropriate approach to today's moral problems is no easy business, and it simply cannot be done using extremist or absolutist reasoning. Of course this shouldn't be taken to mean, merely because the biblical authors wrote in an earlier time, that they therefore have nothing important to say to us.[9] We can however use what we've learned from *The Daily Show* to recognize that statements like Robertson's only serve to muddy the waters, and as we've tried to show here, the waters are muddy enough to begin with.

Remember, You're Only Human

If the beliefs associated with religious fundamentalism are to be taken seriously, it would indeed seem that God works in some very mysterious ways. Michele Bachmann had absolutely no doubt that a miracle was waiting for her at the 2012 Iowa caucuses—it wasn't. Glenn Beck read the signs of the times and discovered that we're currently living in the apocalyptic tumult foretold in Revelation. Yet despite the seemingly unanswered prayers and unfulfilled prophecies, despite all of the evidence and the conclusions to which they may point, our fundamentalist friends haven't relented in their belief. After all, who are we to question the unsearchable ways of God?

Of course the true irony here is that for these religious fundamentalists, God's ways really aren't that mysterious at all. On the contrary, everyone discussed above and criticized by *The Daily Show* has been all too *certain* that he or she knows the true mind of God. Niebuhr cautioned us against this type of pretension in matters of faith, and for this reason he was a tireless critic of politicians and religious leaders alike who sought to claim divine sanction for their own particular standpoints. Any institution professing "unconditioned truth for its doctrines and unconditioned moral authority for its standards," he argues, cannot help but develop into "just another tool of human pride."[10] Instead, it's Niebuhr's understanding that profound religion

> must recognize the difference between divine majesty and human creatureliness; between the unconditioned character of the divine and the conditioned character of all human enterprise ... Religious faith ought therefore to be a constant fount of humility; for it ought to encourage men to moderate their natural pride, and to achieve some decent consciousness of the relativity of their own statement of even the most ultimate truth.[11]

If Niebuhr is correct, then it seems that Wyatt Cenac was right after all: God's ways *are* mysterious. But it's at this point that people like Michele Bachmann and Pat Robertson start to get it wrong. The religious fundamentalist does not tolerate mystery, but instead seeks to overcome and conquer it with certainty, even if the certainty is only superficial. Jon Stewart won't let us off that easy. He asks instead that we be good skeptics, that we ask the difficult questions and be willing to accept difficult answers. Now it may be that with this approach we'll never really know for certain who's getting the "God endorsement." Still, perhaps it's precisely this uncertainty that will finally begin to spark in us the sort of humility that Niebuhr has in mind.

Notes

1. John Locke, *An Essay Concerning Human Understanding*, Book IV, chapter 19, par. 5.
2. Ibid.
3. Ibid.
4. Reinhold Niebuhr, *The Irony of American History* (New York: Charles Scribner's Sons, 1952), 28.
5. Note the similarity to Stephen Colbert's notion of truthiness. See Amber L. Griffioen, "Irrationality and 'Gut' Reasoning: Two Kinds of Truthiness," in this volume.
6. Hans-Georg Gadamer, *Truth and Method* (New York: Continuum, 2006). For a more technical discussion of Gadamer as well as the historical development of philosophical hermeneutics, see Jean Grondin, *Introduction to Philosophical Hermeneutics*, trans. Joel Weinsheimer (New Haven, CT: Yale University Press, 1994).
7. For more on such fallacies, see Liam P. Dempsey, "*The Daily Show*'s Exposé of Political Rhetoric," in this volume.
8. Niebuhr, *The Nature and Destiny of Man*, vol. II (Louisville, KY: Westminster John Knox Press, 1966), 271.
9. Philosopher of religion Keith Ward has written a great deal about this and other related issues. If you're interested in exploring them further, a great place to start would be his *God: A Guide for the Perplexed* (Oxford: Oneworld Publications, 2002).
10. Niebuhr, *The Nature and Destiny of Man*, vol. II (Louisville, KY: Westminster John Knox Press, 1966), 201–202.
11. Niebuhr, *The Children of Light and the Children of Darkness* (New York: Charles Scribner's Sons, 1972), 94.

Chapter 15

Profaning the Sacred
The Challenge of Religious Diversity in "This Week in God"

Matthew S. LoPresti

What's so funny 'bout peace, love, and understanding?

Elvis Costello

The God Machine and its avatars—Praise be upon that which is both many and one!—have revealed the three major philosophical responses to religious diversity: exclusivism, inclusivism, and pluralism. These *isms* reflect distinct philosophical attitudes and presuppositions held by religious zealots, secular heathens, and all those wimpy fence-sitting agnostics in between. To make their significance available to the uninitiated, let's explore these philosophical positions through the wisdom of the God Machine's high priests: Stephen Colbert, Rob Corddry, and Ed Helms. By examining the philosophical responses to religious diversity, we can begin to understand how the responses often hinder—but sometimes help—attempts to reconcile contentious differences between the world's major religious traditions.

A quick look at the philosophical problems presented by religious diversity might incline us to seek some sort of integration of the various religions. However, merging the different traditions into one mega-religion, where everyone is welcome and everybody gets saved, regardless of whether they follow Jesus, Buddha, or the Flying Spaghetti Monster, is not a plausible solution. Despite the warm, cuddly feeling we might get imagining people of all creeds holding

The Ultimate Daily Show and Philosophy: More Moments of Zen, More Indecision Theory, First Edition. Edited by Jason Holt.

hands and singing "Kumbaya," any attempt to unify the religions of the world under one banner would do tremendous violence to the individual traditions themselves. Such violence would not be physical, of course, but intellectual. The philosophical differences that separate religious traditions are far too complex to allow full integration, and many of the differences are fundamental to the identities of the individual traditions.

The distinct lineages and teachings of different religions should be respected and honored for the unique insights into human existence that they provide. Some religions address facets of human existence that do not concern other religions. For example, we can't just say that each religion is a different response to the divine, because some religions have neither gods nor a concept of transcendence. People who wish for inter-religious harmony too often overlook such details, for while the ideal of harmony may suggest unification, it absolutely *requires* difference. Nothing would be more detrimental to promoting harmony *among* world religions than to eliminate the defining differences between them. Identity isn't harmony. However, if we do preserve the integrity of these various religions and their respective claims to truth, this will give rise to significant philosophical problems. To help resolve these differences, let's *bring out the God Machine*!

"Who's your daddy!?" [*Smack*!]

[*"Bebobobebobobebobebobobebobobebo … be … bo … bo."*]

Exclusivism!—There Can Be Only One

You know what that means, people. Oh yeah! Time for a "faith-off!" In "This Week in God: Alt God Machine" (April 6, 2006) Ed Helms offers play-by-play commentary on two religious practices as if they were pitted against each other in head-to-head competition. Helms calls it a "faith-off," guided by the simple exclusivist dictum: "Only one can be right!" The contenders: Hindus in India celebrating *Holi* (the Festival of Colors) and the descendents of the Ancient Mayans in Mexico welcoming the new spring. Now religious exclusivists aren't so meek as to stake some small claim of truth and stand silently by while others hold ostensibly competing views. On the contrary, exclusivists claim that one tradition alone exhausts any and all religious truth, coincidentally, *theirs*. Hence the name "exclusivism." They claim *exclusive* rights to religious truth, declaring the claims of all other religions to be false, and hence the faith-off where *only one can be right*.

In a side-by-side camera shot the Mayans and Hindus begin their rituals rather timidly. Both practices seem pretty dull until, as Helms comments, the Hindus make their move: "Oh, Doctor! The Hindus throw some kind of colorful powder! There's more! Colors just keep comin'. The Mayans cannot hold on! This is over people! It is over. Hinduism wins! Down goes Maya! Down goes Maya!" Both the humor and the exclusivist rules of the faith-off rely on this being a zero-sum competition, where only one practice can be effective, only one tradition true, meaning that all other practices are ineffective, and all other traditions false. This kind of exclusivist view really lays an intellectual smack-down on other religions, claiming title to what I call here the triple-crown of religious truth. This triple-crown consists of the following major categories of religious dogma: religious praxis (rituals, practices), soteriology (theories of salvation), and religious ulti- mates (objects of greatest religious worship or concern, such as God, Brahman, Dao, and so on). It's difficult to sort the pretenders from the contenders here. Naturally, we could just lazily rely on what Stephen Colbert would call the "truthiness"[1] of each and call it a day; how- ever, a responsible philosophical examination would be troubled by the remarkable lack of *objective* evidence favoring one religion over others in these areas.

The most prominent philosophical problem that arises whenever different religious traditions are compared, and which serves as a setting for the three jewels in the triple-crown, is the problem of conflicting truth claims.[2] Religious pluralism, which will be discussed later, questions whether different religious traditions actually produce conflicting truths claims in these areas, while religious exclusivism, and to a lesser extent, religious inclusivism affirms that if one is true then all the others are false. However, even if exclusivism is right and it's true that only one religion could be right, this should in no way lead us to believe that any one of the religious traditions that exist in the world today is *the* one.

It's difficult to imagine inter-religious conflict occurring if those involved didn't think that they *alone* were in the right. The implica- tions of such monopolistic claims can clearly make inter-religious communities divisive and hostile to one another. While most religions don't operate as spectator sports where faith-offs determine what's true or what's right, exclusivist followers are much more likely to work to convert and assimilate or marginalize others. The former is hardly ever benign, and the latter can easily foster ill will, intolerance, and even genocide. But religion is about much more than being nice to one another; it's unavoidably and unmistakably invested in being *true*! Clearly this concern for truth can be the root of more than just academic disputes. These difficulties can be exacerbated when exclusivists take a zero-sum approach to truth when comparing their tradition to others. But this also seems to be cause for laughter when the issue is presented as a literally competitive faith-off. For a slightly more enlightened reaction to perceived competition for the triple-crown, we must, once again, *bring out the God Machine*!

"The power of Colbert compels you!" [*Whack!*]

[*"Bebobobebobobebobebobobebobobebo … be … bo … bo."*]

Inclusivism!—One of Us

One of the hallmarks of a genuine Christian is a determined commitment to the salvation of others. This goes for both exclusivist and inclusivist Christians. Both are forms of religious absolutism, considering their own version of religious truth to be the only correct one. The difference is that while an exclusivist may attempt to convert everyone to her precise way of thinking, the inclusivist will consider conversion unnecessary for those who hold different but sufficiently similar views. These sufficiently similar views and practices can be explained as deficient manifestations of Christianity. For example, one can argue, as Catholic theologian Karl Rahner (1904–1984) has, that members of certain religious traditions are actually, unbeknownst to them, "anonymous Christians." The benefit of this way of thinking is that one doesn't have to feel bad for people who've never even heard of Jesus. They won't go to hell as a result of not accepting him as the alleged "one true God" he's supposed to be for Christians. So long as these Godless heathens are good *anonymous* Christians, they can still make it through the pearly gates without ever having to say "Amen." I like to think of this view as "armchair evangelism." Academic theologians are particularly adept at this, saving souls without ever having to leave the ivory tower by merely redefining what it is that other religions *actually* believe and whom they're *really* worshipping. This often means holding views and beliefs that are completely detached from reality.

Although this explanation of religious diversity might avoid the hands-on cultural imperialism that comes from overzealous evangelical missions, it still results in harmful intellectual imperialism, since it forgoes a genuine attempt to understand and appreciate other religions, seeing them instead from a limited if favorable perspective. Though now a High Priest Emeritus of "This Week in God," Stephen Colbert employed just this sort of absurd reasoning in his insightful roast of President Bush during the 2006 White House Correspondents' Dinner. Colbert's witty repartee lit the way of his evangelical ministry when he spoke from the pulpit: "Though I am a committed Christian, I believe that everyone has a right to their own religion. Be you Hindu, Christian, or Muslim, I believe there are infinite paths to accepting Jesus Christ as your personal savior."[3] Displaying great confidence in the power and truthiness of his own religion, Colbert's is a very thoughtful and sweet gesture, trying to make room for the salvation of Hindu and Muslim souls. But how can this inclusion be achieved? Are Colbert's views to be broadened so as to accept the teachings of others as conveying truthiness too? Not quite. We can see at the close of his statement of faith that his is an expression of naïve religious inclusivism, ignorantly and erroneously reducing other traditions to different manifestations of Christianity itself.

Colbert's satire of Bush's naïvely simplistic view of the world demonstrates an inclusivist attempt to co-opt or explain unique traditions solely in terms of something familiar, in this case Christianity. Inclusivist claims that other religions are "OK" often result from an incorrect understanding. The thought for instance that "Christians and Buddhists worship the same God" is patently false. They don't; in fact, many Buddhists are *atheists*. The ideas that inform Buddhism, like *impermanence* and *no-Self* (Emptiness), are central and unique to the Buddhist tradition. So too are *Atman* and *Brahman* unique to South Asian traditions, *Dao* to Daoism, and so on. These religious concepts are unique, and tend to be completely foreign to other traditions (even if, in the end, they imply similar views of loving one's neighbor as oneself, nonviolence, and compassion); they tend not to be understood by off-the-cuff inclusivists, and are essentially ignored by intellectually irresponsible inclusivists who are better informed.

These inconvenient facts don't discourage well-intentioned armchair evangelists from casting entirely different traditions as variations on their own. For example, Colbert's description of Hinduism as a path to accepting JC as one's personal Lord and savior assumes that Hinduism is, at base, just another type of Christianity—although one that's several millennia older, with a pantheon of divinities, both male and female, and a multiple-life system of karma and rebirth instead of a one-chance shot to avoid sin and eternal damnation.

So what's wrong with that—especially if it can lead to fewer incidences of religious violence? It seems that American ignorance of foreign cultures can be useful after all! The problem is that implying that another tradition is right or true, only to the extent that it resembles one's own, denies the native version of the tradition a legitimate explanation of itself.[4] If successful, however, the inclusivist approach could conceivably reduce religious violence motivated or rationalized by perceived differences, but it fails utterly at even approaching a true understanding of other traditions. This failure would rightly be seen as offensive by adherents of these religions, and would lead to blatantly erroneous interpretations of their traditions, beliefs, and intentions.[5] At its best, such inclusivism is a naïve attempt to cast other religious traditions as having access to the truth, the way, and the light *as you and your religion define it*. At worst, this sweet, seemingly innocent intention can be a form of intellectual imperialism, attempting a hostile takeover of an entire belief system.

The ultimate irony of inclusivism is that, despite its seemingly good-natured intent to be *a uniter, not a divider*, it actually works to marginalize and isolate religious traditions by the very means by which it intends to be more open to them. No one wants to be subject to some "triumphalist" philosophy that reduces their identity and professed self-interests to something they think, believe, and dare I say, *know* they're not. Yet so many seem eager to do this to others as a way of demonstrating the alleged universality of their own beliefs. As a result, religious inclusivism tends, in spite of itself, to antagonize and exacerbate the tensions that may already exist between religions.

As explained earlier, religious exclusivism and inclusivism are types of religious absolutism, which judge other religions solely in terms of one's own foreign values, goals, and dogmas. The move towards genuine and mutually open dialogue isn't so obvious a step if one has either of these attitudes. After all, what need is there to learn from or about other religions when one's own is presumed to be the correct cipher for interpreting the meaning and value of all others? From an exclusivist point of view, inter-religious dialogue is an even less obvious step since inter-religious engagements would be warranted *only* for the purpose of conversion. Jeffery Long, a Hindu religious pluralist, writes that

> the problem with both inclusivism and exclusivism is that they do not take with sufficient seriousness the possibility that other religions may teach important truths that are not already contained within their own traditions ...." Both ultimately deny the "*legitimacy* of all other religions ... *as* other religions.[6]

Naturally, these philosophical responses to religious diversity tend to problematize inter-religious harmony and squelch any genuine attempt at inter-religious dialogue. If dialogue is to take place at all, then all sides must be open to the possibility of change while remaining confident enough in their own positions to avoid feeling intimidated or threatened by other traditions.

Given the unquestionably vast history of inter-religious violence, it's nice every so often to hear about the ways that people of different faiths can come together under the banner of dialogue and moral unity. To help us figure out more appropriate responses to religious diversity, we once again *bring out the God Machine*!

"You are healed!" [*Thud*!]

[*"Bebobobebobobebobebobobebobobebo ... be ... bo ... bo."*]

Pluralism!–Inter-Religious Harmony (Against Gays) in Jerusalem

Over the centuries various religious groups have been able to cooperate in forming societies of great learning, wealth, and power. It seems that a similar kind of peaceful dialogue is desperately needed these days, and so it seemed to be cause for celebration when Stephen Colbert reported in "This Week in God: The Manife-station" (April 18, 2005) that such pluralistic unity may have already begun in the Middle East, when religious leaders sat down together to discuss their common interests. What motivated such an unprecedented display of unity between religions that preach compassion and love in one of the most religiously violent places on Earth? Good ol'-fashioned intolerance of course! Jews, Christians, and Muslims of the holy city of Jerusalem banded together in a show of solidarity—not for peace, social justice, or some other wacky idea, but *against* a gay-pride parade. Despite the wide swath of social justice issues these PRIHK's could have addressed,[7] I suppose in some demented way that their coming together to face the supreme domestic terror of the day for religious conservatives—their own homophobia—could still be cited as a step in the right direction as far as inter-religious harmony is concerned. This is because inter-religious dialogue is more than just a good idea, it's necessary for the development of a satisfactory response to religious diversity. But is this really the kind of harmonious pluralism we need?

Scholars and theologians have discussed shared interests between religions for centuries, and so finding common ground among various traditions (for good or ill) on external issues isn't all that uncommon. The superficial ecumenical harmony Colbert brings to our attention is light years away from having anything to do with developing interfaith understanding, much less offering the possibility of a common ground of doctrine and belief. It's thus unfortunate, but also unremarkable, that these PRIHK's are only superficially pluralistic and don't go any further to explore how their foundational beliefs or practices might complement one another in more spiritually productive ways.

By "religious pluralism," we don't simply mean a tolerant attitude towards the many different religious traditions of the world. Religious pluralism abandons the zero-sum view of religious truth (recall the "faith-off") found in religious absolutism, attempting to account for the world in such a way that many religious claims from various traditions might be able to be simultaneously true. This is a pretty tall order. First, one has to respect—and therefore understand—individual traditions' belief systems, theories of salvation, objects of worship, rituals, and practices, so as to avoid conflating those that are distinctly unique. At the same time one must be able to explain how these vastly different systems might still be simultaneously true without falling into the pitfalls of a debilitating relativism. Religious relativism is the view that "all religions are equally true," but this also implies that they're all equally false. Why? Because if all belief is true, then there is no way to define what "true" means in this instance. Something must be identifiable as false if something else is to be identifiable as true. So, unfortunately for relativism, any suggestion that "all religions are equally true" strips the concepts true and false of any discernible meaning with regard to religion. Since relativism is incapable of offering a standard for determining truth, it also lacks any meaningful explanatory power.

The most basic minimum standard that distinguishes pluralism from relativism is the former's basic adherence to the law of non-contradiction. David Ray Griffin writes that in its generic form, religious pluralism is even further distinguished from other isms by its adherence to two basic assumptions, one negative, the other positive.

> The negative affirmation is the rejection of religious absolutism, which means rejecting the a priori assumption that [one's] own religion is the only one that provides saving truths and values to its adherents, that it alone is divinely inspired, that it has been divinely established as the only legitimate religion, intended to replace all others. The positive affirmation, which goes beyond the negative one, is the acceptance of the idea that there are indeed religions other than one's own that provide saving truths and values to their adherents.[8]

Many philosophers of religion argue that there's no good reason to think that any one religion has a monopoly on truth; indeed, there seem to be elements of truth or authenticity in many different aspects of divergent religious traditions.[9] This *doesn't* imply however that all aspects of all religions are somehow correct. Rather, it means that no *one* religion has the *whole* story. Pluralism walks the middle ground between relativism and absolutism by suggesting that there are elements of truth to be found throughout the landscape of religious thought. Does this mean that all religions are somehow equally false? The absolutist might object to his particular tradition losing its luster of pure, complete veridicality under the pluralist hypothesis, but just because another tradition might be appropriately sensitive to some truth not emphasized in one's own, doesn't imply that one's own tradition is false, even in part. Despite undeniable areas of overlap, it is quite clear that the problems of human existence that religions address vary significantly from one tradition to the next.

A Plurality of Pluralisms

The Hindu Festival of Color and the Mayan welcoming of spring in Ed Helms's faith-off are two entirely different rituals, yet both celebrate the change of seasons. But celebrating the cycles of the earth needn't be tied to any specific doctrine or religious intentions beyond a basic awareness of life, death, and renewal. These celebrations needn't conflict with the doctrines and dogmas of other religions, nor does the one religious celebration challenge or negate the validity of another. This goes double for partaking in the Christian sacraments or practicing Buddhist meditation. These are neither competing nor necessarily conflicting responses to the divine. Rather, they are two entirely different practices that have entirely different aims. The effectiveness of one would in no way diminish the possible efficacy of the other.

In "This Week in God: Divine Right" (February 7, 2006), Rob Corddry endorses the effectiveness of different practices in his "Thank you Lord, may I have another" sketch, in which he briefly presents Shinto, Russian Orthodox, Indonesian Muslim, Thai Buddhist, and Shiite Muslim rituals, all meant to "please God" through spiritual purification. Though it too is a superficial type of pluralism (after all, this is comedy), Corddry's example offers an excellent transition between praxis and salvation. More often than not, the practices of different traditions, when properly understood, are *not* in conflict, so long as it isn't assumed (as an exclusivist would), that at most only one of the various rituals could be effective.

The brand of religious pluralism developed by the contemporary philosopher John B. Cobb, Jr. can account for multiple theories of salvation, arguing that "there is no contradiction in the claim of one that problem A is solved by X and the claim of the other that problem B is solved by Y .... The claims are complementary rather than contradictory."[10] Cobb uses this basic logical truth to attempt to reconcile contradictions that ostensibly plague inter-religious dialogue between Christians and Buddhists in particular.[11] Christians can seek transcendent salvation through Christ, while Buddhists can realize immanent epistemic awakening. These aren't mutually exclusive, because the salvation sought in each case is of a *different* kind. According to this type of pluralism, not only are there different ways of achieving a similar religious objective, there are also different legitimate goals. To see how this might work, we'll turn to what's often called "process" metaphysics, which also allows for obeisance to a plurality of different religious ultimates.

The process metaphysics of Alfred North Whitehead (1861–1947) describes the world as being in a constant state of flux, and ruled by a multiplicity of ontological "ultimates." Two of the ultimates most commonly identified in Whitehead's theory of reality are what we will call here "Creativity" and "Deity." Creativity is the universal force that propels dynamic change, and the other ultimate is a personal being who works with the world, guiding its creative flow towards ever-increasing moral and aesthetic ends. Neither ultimate is in complete control. Instead, the two work together to carry the world forward. This generic notion of a deity differs in important ways from other characterizations of God in the Abrahamic tradition. Among other changes, the meaning of "omniscience" and the manner in which God can act in and react to the world are altered in ways that make God a bit less fantastic, and thus more plausible than the deity of traditional Western theology, which is wrought with contradictions. Traditional theists are loath to accept this "process" conception of God, even though it's still a uniquely powerful and omniscient, good and caring being. It is, to this extent, compatible with the sacred texts of the three major theistic faiths of the West (though not necessarily with all of the hundreds of widely diverse sectarian dogmas of every single denomination that stems from these faiths). Creativity, on the other hand, works as a generic category that can include non-theistic, non-personal, non-dualistic religious ultimates such as the nameless, formless *Dao* of Daoism, the blissful Emptiness (*sunyata*) of Buddhism, and the unqualifiable *nirguna Brahman* of Hinduism. Creativity drives "the becoming of the world," the divine being shapes it, and inspires us towards moral and aesthetic improvement. In Whitehead's philosophy, the world couldn't exist as it does without both of these ultimates working together, and Cobb argues that it's precisely these *two* ultimates (and possibly more) that underlie the objects of religious worship or concern of the various traditions around the world. (An ontological ultimate is an aspect of reality that is not reducible or explainable in terms of any other aspect of reality. Rather it is the aspect in terms of which other things are ultimately explained.)

"The God Exchange" Is Now Closed

In "The God Exchange" (November 10, 2005), Rob Corddry highlights the triumphs and woes of the world's religions in terms every capitalist can understand—fluctuating stock prices. In a jaded consumer market where religious recruitment and retention is almost as paltry as US military reenlistment rates, it's important for religious leaders to keep abreast of the almost daily fluctuations of "religious market value," the highs and lows of religious morale, and "convert-futures" rocked by scandals, natural disasters, and religiously fueled political unrest. It's a competitive market of ideas and religious life-styles these days, and forces that push and pull people to identify with (or against) certain faiths are a sad indication of just how fickle some people are when it comes to reality.[12] It should be a great relief that reality itself isn't actually subject to change from person to person, faith to faith, or due to the whimsical market forces dictated by what-ever religious ideas are currently in vogue. The plausibility of a pluralistic view of religion greatly depends on the underlying theory of reality (or metaphysics) that informs it. Fortunately, Cobb's deep religious pluralism offers us a metaphysical platform with broad enough explan-atory power to accommodate widely divergent belief systems. No matter which religious robe we don, we can see a multiplicity of them as being cut from the same metaphysical cloth. Hopefully this view can help the competitive and combative emotions, which have dominated inter-religious relations for so long, slowly become a thing of the past.

The satire of *The Daily Show* not only amuses but also enlightens its audience. Often the comedy, especially when it focuses on religion, stems from the fact that the subject matter itself resists full compre-hension.[13] It should be no mystery why competing notions of the sacred can be so damned funny. Where understanding stops in a sub-ject such as religion, emotion fills in the rest. Be it anger and even hatred of the zealot, the righteous indignation of the evangelical, or the amusement and LOL reaction of the un-indoctrinated, these responses—the destructive and the creative—are natural, human. The destructive ones can be eschewed, however, when we develop a greater understanding of philosophical solutions to the problem of religious diversity, as outlined in this chapter and illustrated by "This Week in God." The response that best enables genuine inter-religious dialogue and harmony is pluralism.

If, for whatever reason, pluralism *doesn't* turn out to be viable, it's my sincere hope that people, fallible and far from omniscient as they are, will increasingly abandon monopolistic answers to questions about the meaning of life, our place in the universe, and how we ought to orient ourselves in the face of life's mysteries. A good sense of humor at our own expense, and recognition of the often palpable absurdity of being thrown into the mystery of this world, goes a long way in helping us attain the healthy degree of humility required of us when making claims and arguments about religious truth. In the end, I'm in agreement with Whitehead:

> There remains in the final reflection, how shallow, puny, and imperfect are [our] efforts to sound the depths in the nature of things. In philo-sophical [or religious] discussion, the merest hint of dogmatic certainty as to finality of statement is an exhibition of folly.[14]

Indeed, it's only with such overt humility that any attempt to under-stand the world's religions must begin.

Eulogy: The Safe Turn to Politics

I, myself, actually owe a lot of religious people an apology—not for making jokes at their expense, but for not appreciating and thanking you for how well you've handled it.
                                        Jon Stewart (April 22, 2010)

Just before its fourth birthday, the segment "This Week in God" uncer-emoniously shed its mortal coil and ascended into heaven. God loved it so much, he couldn't bear to watch it anymore. As with most of our earthly problems, there is reliable biblical precedence of blaming a woman for its demise. Samantha Bee was, after all, the last corre-spondent to, shall we say, engage the God Machine's phallic button (September 13, 2007). If we don't want to blame a woman, perhaps we can just say it was pre-determined. The segment was something of a Colbert creation, and despite others taking over the segment, it inev-itably became a casualty of his departure. "This Week in God" clearly wouldn't work in the *Colbert Report*'s format and shortly after the *Report* began, our conservative hero came on at the end of the *Daily Show* to ask why the recording of his voice making the silly game show noises was still being used for the God Machine segment—noises exquisitely reproduced between sections of the original chapter above. Soon afterward, the feature saw its final installment.

Following the ascension of the God Machine, there has been less and less religion-based humor on both *The Daily Show* and *The Colbert Report*, except when it has been cleverly tied in to the ubiquitous political humor of both shows. The entire premise of Colbert's show rests upon an aggressively dumb egomaniac spewing *O'Reilly Factor*-esque political drivel (a.k.a. "punditry"), whereas *The Daily Show* has no such conceptual restraints. The closest thing to "This Week in God" has been Colbert's "Yahweh or No Way" segment on the *Report*, but even this is used typically to safely poke fun at his own Catholic faith and runs maybe three times a year if we're lucky. Although there's probably no single cause for the decrease of politically unrelated religious humor, we can perhaps point to the violence and threats from religious extremists in recent years as putting a sobering chill on otherwise humorous takes on religious issues on both *The Daily Show* and *The Colbert Report*.[15]

Religious topics seem to be pretty much out of bounds these days. One notable exception was Stewart and Colbert's mutual coverage of the 2012 Democratic National Convention, during which religious conservatives called liberals to account for removing any reference to "God" from their political party platform. (This issue was raised in an attempt to "win the news cycle" by directing attention away from Michelle Obama's stellar convention speech.) Ever the model of thick skin, unity, and order, liberals dutifully caved under the immense pressure of a conservative talking point barely covered by genuine news agencies over the course of single news cycle. What followed was surely a sign of the impending apocalypse as Democrats loudly denied God three times on national television. The focus of the humor here though was on the political process of the vote and its conclusion rather than on religion, religious belief, or believers. Although Stewart did at least ponder how absurd it would be for God to care about something so trivial as his name in a political platform: God's not the sort of guy, Stewart says, to pick up a book on the natural world and immediately scan the index for references to the Tetragrammaton. Perhaps not, but the last time God was denied three times so publically the Messiah was tortured, executed, and mutilated.[16]

In fairness, this particular opportunity for religious humor, like so many others, came in the context of a piece of political theater. The ties that bind religion and politics are far from exclusively

American; indeed, according to the Liberal/Socialist idol Karl Marx (1818–1883), this relationship is no less ancient than the social phenomenon of religion itself. Religion, Marx says, is a mechanism for controlling the masses. Politics and religion therefore are natural bedfellows in the quest for power.

Religious fervor, however, has a less than opiate-like effect, and the current merger of religion and politics in some parts of the world is having a real effect on comedy shows. Religious humor loses its luster in the face of real violence, and our comedic heroes do have real lives with real families to care for. At one point when Colbert was covering a topic that related to Islam, he paused to make an aside to the camera, that there is indeed nothing whatsoever funny about such a wonderful world religion as Islam. This comment elicited chuckles before Colbert went on to tell his joke. I don't remember the joke, but I will never forget the comment, which despite Colbert's smile and the audience laughter struck me as a deadly serious disclaimer.

It's not funny if you have to consider whether you're crossing a line that might make you, your family and friends, your staff, your company, and so on, "legitimate" targets for mass-murder in some people's demented minds. Given the choice between being a martyr for free speech and living a life of comedic luxury, there aren't many incentives for Stewart and Colbert going down the rougher road.[17] Religious humor can give you pause for thought, but at what point does simply pointing towards what *others* do and waxing philosophically about it make one complicit in the activity and thus a possible target? I can't imagine. The whole point of this eulogy is that we don't know, because trying to rationalize irrational extremism is a futile, and possibly dangerous, task.

As a fan and as a philosopher of religion, I cannot decide if the *Daily Show* and *Colbert Report* writers are cowardly for willfully avoiding religious humor (unless it's tied to politics), or if they're geniuses for tying religious topics to political humor so they can more safely engage their audience. Why? Because political belief is understood to be a matter of personal (or Fox News-received) opinion. Everyone has a political opinion. This is the realm of the subjective, and the subjective is always rife with humor. Humor in politics is hardly ever offensive, because everyone knows that no one person has a truly objective political view on things. People's religious sensibilities, on the other hand, tend to be much more sensitive. The realm of the sacred is thought not to be subjective at all, but rather the ultimate reality. When we mock religious belief, then, we play a dangerous game of insulting narratives and identities that, for their adherents, are sacred and thus hardly even comparable to the mundane matters of this world.

When something religious comes up as a topic for satirical coverage or hilarious analysis on either show, the easiest and safest thing to do is take a political angle. The sacredness of religion seems neutralized when presented to an audience through the lens of politics; in other words, when we look at religion *as* politics, the "objective" is relativized and made subjective and thus the sacred can be safely profaned.[18] It's not only easier to avoid taking offense, it becomes easier to laugh at one's own limited understanding of the sacred, one's own belief system, even oneself. When we position the sacred (religion) as profane (politics) we remove the offense people might see leveled against their tradition and instead level it against the politicization of religion. This neutralizes our otherwise overly tender religious sensitivities by making the joke about the interplay between religious adherence and political agendas.

Honest and uncensored religious humor, while funny for believers and non-believers for different reasons, is especially valuable for believers. The apparently increasing restraint on religious humor is unfortunate, because such humor forces a critical reorientation toward important religious matters. The appeal of such humor causes philosophical reflection, moving us to question things we aren't used to questioning. Both humor and philosophy can expose and scrutinize underlying assumptions. A playful approach to issues as serious as mortality and the destiny of the human soul (if there is one) gives us an *unpreachy* pause of reflection to consider how utterly brief and precious our time is on this planet. Such humor is most powerful when it simultaneously calls into question how seriously we take ourselves in light of the many minor or major imperfections of this life.

Although Stewart and Colbert give a more limited role to religious humor than they used to, even without the God Machine they still lead us (intentionally or not) to deeper insights and wisdom that move us, in religious pluralist John Hick's (1922–2012) terms, from an ego-centered to a reality-centered existence.[19] They do this by helping us to laugh at ourselves, even at our deepest beliefs, which we so often identify with to such an extent that we confuse our personal identity with dogma itself. As a philosophy professor I can encourage my students to consider the dark truth that a time will come when no one alive will know they ever existed, but the humorist can deliver more subtle ways of encouraging people to get over themselves and learn to laugh about otherwise serious things. Such laughter produces space for deeper consideration, especially when the humor rings true. This is particularly important today, as we seem to have less and less space for safe critical consideration of the effects of religious zealotry on our open, pluralistic society and the challenges and opportunities religion poses to the emerging global community.

It's probably too simple to say that the hosts and writers of *The Daily Show* and *The Colbert Report* are either cowardly or ingenious to eschew religious humor without the lens of politics. Again, these arenas overlap in our everyday lives, forming the social fabric out of which we make sense of where we have been, the choices before us, and where we are going. So to some extent this is unavoidable, and it's the safe way of doing religious humor (safe for the network's ratings, and physically safe for those involved, as there's less chance of suicide bombers targeting them). Still, I think it's better to err on the side of charitable interpretation and say that there's an undeniable degree of ingenuity in the clearly successful formula of both shows for gently making the sacred profane with a twinkle in their eye.

In the end, articulating the religious in terms of the political, takes what may otherwise be an off-limits sensitive topic and turns it into a comparatively safe target for satire and even mockery. There have been some great examples of this in recent years but the art of profaning the sacred has become increasingly rare.[20]

The God Machine
RIP
October 27, 2003 – September 13, 2007

Notes

1. Truthiness is a term Colbert gives for "gut thinking," which is a variety of individual relativism, the bane of Philosophy professors everywhere. David Kyle Johnson gives a good introduction to what's wrong with such thinking in his "Colbert, Truthiness, and Thinking from the Gut," in *Stephen Colbert and Philosophy: I Am Philosophy (And So Can You!)*, ed. Aaron Allen Schiller (Chicago: Open Court, 2009), 3–18. See also Amber L. Griffioen, "Irrationality and 'Gut' Reasoning: Two Kinds of Truthiness," in this volume.

2. The challenge posed by the diversity of religious or mystical experience comes in a close second and is intimately related.
3. White House Correspondents' Dinner, C-SPAN (April 29, 2006).
4. It would be similarly absurd to reduce the humor of all Comedy Central programs as being funny only to the extent that they resemble the satire of *The Daily Show*, even if they preceded its existence or rely on entirely different kinds of humor.
5. Imagine a Buddhist being so daft as to try to explain to a Christian that the teachings of Christ are really just skillful lies (this is an actual compassionate pedagogical tool used by enlightened teachers in Buddhism) to help them be a better (*"anonymous"*) Buddhist and become wise enough to be receptive to the teachings that all things are Empty and that there really is no God or soul after all.
6. Jeffery Long, "Anekanta Vedanta: Towards a Deep Hindu Religious Pluralism," in *Deep Religious Pluralism*, ed. David Ray Griffin (Louisville, KY: Westminster John Knox Press, 2005), 140.
7. These religious leaders are members of an informal organization I like to call the Pan-Religious Israeli Homophobia Koalition, or PRIHK, formally known as No-NAMB.
8. David Ray Griffin, ed., *Deep Religious Pluralism* (Louisville, KY: Westminster John Knox Press, 2005), 3.
9. Along with Griffin's *Deep Religious Pluralism*, see, for example, John Cobb, *Beyond Dialogue: Toward a Mutual Transformation of Christianity and Buddhism* (Philadelphia: Fortress, 1982); John Hick, *A Christian Theology of Religions: The Rainbow of Faiths* (Louisville, KY: Westminster John Knox Press, 1995); Paul F. Knitter and John Hick, eds., *The Myth of Christian Uniqueness: Towards a Pluralistic Theology of Religions* (Maryknoll, NY: Orbis Books, 1987).
10. Leonard Swidler, John B. Cobb, Jr., Paul F. Knitter, and Monika K. Hellwig, *Death or Dialogue? From the Age of Monologue to the Age of Dialogue* (Philadelphia: Trinity Press, 1990), 14.
11. Griffin discusses two very helpful quotes from Cobb on this very point in *Deep Religious Pluralism*, 48. See John B. Cobb, Jr., *Transforming Christianity and the World: A Way Beyond Absolutism and Relativism*, ed. Paul F. Knitter (Maryknoll, NY: Orbis Books, 1999), 74, 140.
12. As if the moral quality of publicly declared adherents to one faith or another implied anything about the religion itself. For example, pedophiliac priests and the Spanish Inquisition in no way invalidate the teachings of Christ, nor do the actions of terrorists who wrap themselves in the cloak of jihad in any way diminish the teachings of the prophet Mohammed.

13. For more on the humorous aspect of nonsense, see Alan Richardson, "Tractatus Comedo-Philosophicus," in *Monty Python and Philosophy: Nudge Nudge, Think Think!* eds. Gary L. Hardcastle and George A. Reisch (Chicago: Open Court, 2006), 217–229.

14. Alfred N. Whitehead, *Process and Reality: An Essay in Cosmology*, eds. David Ray Griffin and Donald W. Sherburne (New York: Free Press, 1978 [1929]), xiv.

15. This despite their defiant stance in defense of the free speech of Trey Parker and Matt Stone's "depiction" of *South Park*'s Mohammed in a bear suit. Other factors may include conscious or subconscious censoring by the hosts and staff writers, corporate censorship, maybe even focus groups that tell producers that political humor alone is the way to go these days. Surely not everything needs to be understood in terms of politics to poke fun. Nevertheless, political humor has been a wildly successful focus of both shows, but this pendulum cannot swing much further in this direction as it's increasingly the *only* lens through which anything religious is *ever* made to seem funny.

16. In the Bible's New Testament, the Apostle Peter denies knowing Jesus three times in the events that lead up to his crucifixion.

17. Heck, just writing this eulogy for "This Week in God" led to my having to self-edit a large section on Islamic extremism and humor because I wonder if it's worth drawing explicit attention to the issue in the way that I would have liked.

18. Undoubtedly there are some people who take their political views to be sacrosanct, but I'm willing to go out on a limb here and say that in comparison, people who are politically faithful are nowhere near as devotional as religious extremists. Comparing political faithfulness with a religious devotion so serious that it can't even allow for a humorous perspective of itself is a bit like comparing an extension on your taxes to eternal salvation. No reasonable, successful, or widely accepted political philosophy claims to arrogate the truth on all things. Similarly, no political philosophy requires the evangelical indoctrination of others or forbids its adherents from entertaining other political ideas or perspectives, as do some formal religious traditions and institutions. Therefore, although many people are passionate about their political views, this doesn't usually approach the sort of indoctrination of religious fanatics, and when it does, we commonly characterize such extreme levels of devotion as *religious* in nature. In the end, it's safe to say (that is, it's *reasonable* to say, and thus an unsafe thing to point out) that the religious fanatic is a whole other level of crazy than even your most obnoxious political dittohead.

19. See John Hick, *An Interpretation of Religion: Human Responses to the Transcendent*, 2nd edn. (New Haven, CT: Yale University Press, 2004).

20. I dedicate this revised chapter to Anne Hathaway, who having read the first edition of *The Daily Show and Philosophy* proceeded to wax philosophically on process metaphysics and religious pluralism in her acceptance speech for an award at the 2009 Palm Springs Film Festival. She might have lost her audience, according to some of the entertainment news coverage (www.eonline.com/news/77767/anne-hathaway-s-hot-desert-night-with-new-man, last accessed April 24, 2013), but she won me several invitations to participate in a Philosophy conference and author chapters in related books. Thanks, Anne, for making your own connections between philosophy, film, and pop culture. It's when our students and our readers make these connections independently that we professors know that our efforts have made a difference; it is also the greatest compliment we can receive. Thank you.

Chapter 16

Jon Stewart and the Fictional War on Christmas

David Kyle Johnson

As long our enemies view the words "Happy Holidays" not as a lazy man's way to avoid the time-sucking double holiday saluta-tion "I wish you a Merry Christmas and a Happy New Year," but rather as a sub-textual "Fuck you and your baby Jesus," there can be no peace!

Jon Stewart declaring war on Christmas
(December 6, 2011)

Every December we are told there is a war on Christmas. "Those damn pagan atheist liberals are trying to take the 'Christ' out of 'Christmas' again. Don't let 'em. Jesus is the reason for the season!" Jon Stewart, however, claims that this war is a farce. As he said to Gretchen Carlson, "Since you asked the question, 'Am I nuts to think there's a war on Christmas?' it's only polite for me to offer you a resounding, 'Yes, you're fucking nuts'" (December 3, 2012). But how could he say this? Eliminating courthouse nativities and religious school plays, banning blinking colored lights, and making it illegal to say "Merry Christmas"—isn't it obvious that there is a liberal con-spiracy to eliminate Christmas from all spheres of public life? After all, Stewart himself declared a war on Christmas, asking that "Christmas immediately and unilaterally withdraw to its pre-'67 borders—pre-1667 borders" (December 6, 2011).

The Ultimate Daily Show and Philosophy: More Moments of Zen, More Indecision Theory,
First Edition. Edited by Jason Holt.
© 2013 John Wiley & Sons, Inc. Published 2013 by John Wiley & Sons, Inc.

Of course, he was no more serious than the time he said he would not rest "until every year families gather to spend December 25th together at Osama's Homo-bortion pot'n'commie-jizz-porium" (December 7, 2005). The truth is, the war on Christmas is just another in a string of wars—along with wars on Hanukkah, Easter, fall holidays, Halloween, fossil fuels, the constitution, ladies' night, fishermen, salt, chocolate milk, sugary drinks, food, and spuds—that Fox News has fabricated to feed their "Republicans are victims" narrative. (The only war that Fox News thinks is fabricated is the Republican war on women. [April 16, 2012].)

As we shall see, however, there is a war *for* Christmas—a war fought by Christians to claim the holiday for themselves. What has been labeled as the "war on Christmas" is actually just a reaction to Christianity's efforts to take a holiday that has never been about them, and make it all about their savior Jesus.

There Is No War on Christmas

For God sakes [sic], Fox News itself is located in midtown Manhattan, the epicenter of all that is godless, secular, gay, jewy, and hellbound—and yet even here, all around your studio, it looks like Santa's balls exploded.

Jon Stewart (December 3, 2012)

The war on Christmas, and in fact the phrase itself, was invented by Fox News in 2005. That year, Fox News correspondent John Gibson published *The War on Christmas* and Bill O'Reilly complained about businesses such as Walmart saying "Happy Holidays" to their customers instead of "Merry Christmas." Ironically, O'Reilly thought non-Christians had to be crazy to be offended by a two-word phrase like "Merry Christmas," yet thought the phrase "Happy Holidays" was deeply offensive to Christians. Apparently, Stewart pointed out, "every time you say 'Happy Holidays,' an angel gets AIDS" (December 13, 2005). That year O'Reilly also made one of Samantha Bee's six-second jokes—"Christmas: it's the only religious holiday that is also a federal holiday. That way Christians can go to their services and everyone else can stay home and reflect on the true meaning of separation of church and state"—a part of this war, as a "counterargument" to "public displays of Christmas."[1]

Every year since, Fox News correspondents have bombarded us with examples of how "liberals" are waging the war on Christmas. In fact, "The annual Fox 'War on Christmas'" has even "become a little predictable," lending itself to Mad Libs like: "Last week in [*godless liberal bastion*] a group of [*small group of annoying people with limited control over our culture*] ruined Christmas by forcing the removal of [*a classic Christmas symbol*]" (December 3, 2012). The problem is, nearly all their claims are either exaggerated or just plain false. For example, no school in Plano (Texas), Saginaw Township (Michigan), or Orlando (Florida) banned the colors red and green during Christmastime. The schools themselves proved they offered no such restrictions by posting their guidelines online; Stephen Colbert was smart enough to call out Gretchen Carlson concerning this on the *Report* (December 13, 2010). Ridgeway Elementary School in Dodgeville (Wisconsin) didn't change the lyrics to "Silent Night" to eliminate all references to religion. They performed a Christmas play (that was co-authored by a church choir director) entitled "The Little Tree's Christmas Gift" that changes the lyrics of existing Christmas songs to make them easier for children to learn.[2] And, although it is true that Democratic Rhode Island Governor ("and part-time Steve Doocy impersonator") Lincoln Chafee didn't call the tree in the Rhode Island Statehouse a Christmas tree in 2011, it is false that the former Republican governed called it a Christmas tree for the previous eight years. In fact, when he used the more offensive term "holiday tree" the previous year, Fox News didn't make a peep (December 6, 2011).

It is true that some schools have stopped calling their late-December recess "Christmas break" and Tulsa (Oklahoma) did take the word "Christmas" out of its seasonal parade (a year before Fox complained about it). Further, some retailers did instruct their employees to use the phrase "Happy Holidays" instead of "Merry Christmas" to avoid potentially offending non-Christians. But such events hardly constitute a war on Christmas. In 2005, the Bush White House sent out a "holiday card" that merely wished everyone a "Happy Holiday Season" and Bill O'Reilly himself was selling *O'Reilly Factor* "holiday" ornaments to put on your "holiday tree" (December 13, 2005). Were Bush and O'Reilly waging a war on Christmas? Of course not. As Stewart put it, "I suppose you could say 'Merry Christmas and a Happy New Year' but you probably have shit to do.

You shorten it to 'Happy Holidays.' Not everyone who says that is anti-Christian" (December 7, 2005).

So, no one is waging a war on Christmas—trying to remove Christmas from the calendar, strip it of governmental recognition, or prevent anyone from celebrating it. There are some complaints about how Christmas is recognized by the government—for example, objections to courthouse nativities and public school religious plays. And sometimes those complaints are successful. "Do atheists land an occasional blow? I guess. Even the Washington generals get lucky once in a while" (December 3, 2012). But that's not a war on Christmas itself. (We'll talk more about that later.)

Of course, the fact that Fox News pundits distort facts, get things wrong, and just flat out lie to create the illusion that there's a war on Christmas is no surprise to regular *Daily Show* viewers. On June 21, 2011 Stewart admitted that he was wrong when he said, on "Fox News Sunday," that every poll shows Fox News viewers are "the most consistently misinformed." PolitiFact pointed out that one poll (out of three) merely had Fox viewers close to the bottom. (Unfortunately, that same poll seemed to indicate that Stewart's stoner viewers are "fact fucking" him and placing him close to the bottom as well.)[3] Not offering up a correction would be "irresponsible" and would undermine the "integrity and credibility that [Stewart] tries so hard to care about." So he offered one. But Stewart then went on to point out 21 Fox News statements PolitiFact identified as lies, two of which received a "pants on fire" rating, and two of which won "lie of the year" awards (June 21, 2011). But the lies don't stop there.

The First War *for* Christmas

In the old days, before the "War on Christmas," the celebration of the birth of Christ lasted a day—like birthdays do.
                                        Jon Stewart (December 3, 2012)

Actually Jon, that's not exactly right. The history of Christmas is far more complicated. And, although there is no war on Christmas, there has been a war waged *for* Christmas for centuries—a war waged by Christians to claim late-December celebrations for their own. Ironically, despite its modern-day namesake, Christmas is not a Christian holiday—the main elements of late December celebrations have never had anything to do with Jesus, and the holiday's origins do not trace back to Jesus' birth.

Late-December harvest celebrations—like the Roman Saturnalia—that included extremely raucous parties, feasting, drinking, gift-giving, friend- and relative-visiting, and greenery date back 2000 years before Christ.[4] Back then, the days getting shorter in the fall also made people worry that we might be thrown into perpetual darkness. So, late December was also a time to celebrate the winter solstice and the fact that the days were getting longer. Consequently, late December was also popular with sun worshipers. But early Christians didn't even celebrate their own birthdays, much less Jesus'. It was thought that birthdays were the kind of self-aggrandizing affairs only pagans indulged in. So Christians didn't celebrate Jesus' birth, at all (much less in December), for the first 300 years or so of their existence. And things only changed because of Constantine.

When the Roman Emperor Constantine converted to Christianity in the 300s, he didn't want everyone worshiping and celebrating non-Christian deities and events. So he Christianized the wildly popular late-December celebrations. How? Since the biblical nativity stories don't give a date for Jesus' birth,[5] Constantine simply declared Jesus' birth to have occurred on December 25 (the same day the worshipers of the sun god Sol Invictus were celebrating the birth of their god). That way, all the late-December celebrations that Constantine couldn't prevent would "officially" be in the name of Jesus. Thus the Christian war *for* Christmas—to claim late-December celebrations—began.

This war continued throughout the Middle Ages as the church added a plethora of religious observances on and around December 25, including a mass at dawn called "Aurora" and a midnight mass called "Christ's Mass"—a name that wouldn't be applied to the holiday itself until the 11th century. But their efforts to Christianize the holiday were never fully successful. People did come to believe that Jesus was born December 25 and forgot about the holiday's pagan origins, but religious observances were never the holiday's focus. Staying up past midnight for mass and then getting up again at dawn for mass just couldn't compete; the raucous elements of the holiday's celebration always dominated. Before and after Constantine, late December was primarily a time for gift-giving, visiting, drinking, feasting, and sex. In fact, traditions that included attending orgies before and after Christ's mass continued in Ireland through the nineteenth century.[6]

As historian Stephen Nissenbaum puts it in *The Battle for Christmas*, "Christmas has always been an extremely difficult holiday to *Christianize*."[7] In fact, the Christians' efforts to Christianize Christmas failed so miserably that the Puritans banned the holiday; Christmas celebrations were largely illegal in both England and the Americas during the 1600s and 1700s, where the Puritans had influence.

Stewart got himself into a bit of trouble dealing with this aspect of Christmas history. Fox News often cites the Puritans' desire for religious freedom as a reason that the religious elements of Christmas should be embraced by the government. Stewart did rightly observe that the Puritans "outlawed Christmas celebrations as a sacrilege and declared gifts and Christmas decorations satanical, levying a five-shilling fine on anyone for saying 'Merry Christmas'" (December 6, 2011). But alas, he foolishly trusted *The History Channel* when they (mis)informed him that Congress met on Christmas day for roughly the first 60 years of American history. He should know better than to trust a channel that thinks Nazis had alien technology.

Still, his larger point was accurate. Fox News often clamors for a return to the way our forefathers celebrated Christmas, but Christmas was not celebrated by most Americans for much of our country's early history, and was not even officially recognized as a national holiday until 1870. The only reason Congress didn't meet on Christmas before 1870 was because they took extremely long breaks that happened to overlap with Christmas. For example, the last time Congress met in 1789 was on September 29 and they didn't reconvene again until the first Monday in January.[8] As "Ben Franklin" pointed out on *The Daily Show* (while taking a break from banging second-rate French prostitutes), in 1789 no one said "Merry Christmas" until December 25,[9] and if one did celebrate, it was most likely by "stuffing his face, getting drunk, and wallowing in vomit" (December 12, 2011).[10] Christmas in 1789 was more akin to the modern St. Patrick's Day.

Christmas made a cultural comeback in the early 1800s, but not because of religious influences. Its revival was primarily the work of Charles Dickens, Queen Victoria, and Clement Clarke Moore[11] and resulted in a grand resurgence of the holiday's raucous elements. New York City in particular "suffered" from wassailers—bands of noisy drunken lower-class miscreants parading through the streets demanding entry into wealthy homes to partake of their best food and drink.[12] The upper class eventually succeeded in domesticating the holiday by fooling the poor into thinking that Christmas should be about tricking children into believing that St. Nicholas will bring them presents. Businesses quickly realized that large profits could consequently be had and the commercialization of Christmas began. But religion had nothing to do with it.[13]

The Modern War *for* Christmas

For whatever annoying local ticky-tack Christmas-abolishing story you and your merry band of persecution-seeking researchers [at Fox News] can scour the wires to turn up, the rest of us can't swing a dead elf with without knocking over an inflatable snow globe or a giant blinking candy cane.
Jon Stewart (December 3, 2012)

The holiday's religious elements didn't enjoy a resurgence until it was clear that Christmas was here to stay and Christians renewed their efforts Christianize it. Most prominently this included renewing Constantine's efforts to claim the holiday's origin— "Jesus is the reason for the season"—and declaring that the only correct way to celebrate is the Christian way—"Keep Christ in Christmas. After all, it's CHRISTmas!"

As we have seen, such efforts are fallacious at best and downright dishonest at worst. Jesus is not the reason for the season; he was tacked on to an already existing holiday by Constantine to aid in converting the Roman Empire. Again, historically speaking, we celebrate in late December because the harvest is done and the days are getting longer,[14] and we celebrate on December 25 specifically because that is when the ancients thought the sun was making its comeback.[15] Even if Jesus had never existed, even if Constantine had never converted to Christianity, even if Christians never celebrated the birth of Christ, we would still celebrate in late December.

Christmas is about Christ because the word "Christ" is in "Christmas" as much as Sunday is about the sun because the word "sun" is in "Sunday."[16] Besides, it is only called "Christmas" because the Christians decided to call it that. It would be like me going to your house, calling your dog "Kyle's dog," and then trying to take it home because of "what people have been calling him." Of course, there is nothing wrong with Christians making their December celebrations Christ-centered, but they can't demand that everyone should. After all, they tacked on their religious observances long after the holiday was established. It would be somewhat like me demanding that everyone's Thanksgiving dinner include my grandmother's homemade noodles. Although they are really good, everyone should be free to celebrate as they see fit.

As Stewart has shown us many times (for example, July 27, 2011), Fox News is very good at playing the victimization card. The narrative that Fox News creates includes the assumption that conservatives and Christians are a persecuted minority. "The mainstream media has a liberal bias," they claim, despite the fact that it is Fox News and its conservative bias that is mainstream, trouncing all others in the ratings. The last acceptable forms of discrimination, prejudice, racism, and misogyny—according to Fox News—are against Catholics, Christians, and black and female conservatives. And Fox News plays the victimization card most often at Christmastime. As Stephen Colbert put it, on his "The Wørd" segment on "Xmas," "This war on Christmas is just a part of the larger war on Christianity. Christians in the United States are a persecuted minority (all 80% of them), a minority under siege by the powers that be (except for the President, Congress, and State Legislatures)" (December 5, 2005).

Of course, this is ridiculous. As Stewart pointed out to Mike Huckabee in an extended interview (April 6, 2011), "As someone who is not Christian, it's hard for me to believe Christians are a persecuted people in America … God willing, maybe one of you one day will rise up and get to be President of this country, maybe forty-four in a row."[17] How hard is it to be elected to office if you are a Hindu? Would you admit that you are an atheist in a job interview? Nearly every American church rings hymns from their bell tower every half-hour and no one objects, yet if a single mosque offers up a call to prayer five times a day, all hell breaks loose. It almost seems as if, when something does not have an expressed and obvious pro-Christian or pro-conservative bias—like Fox News—it's considered anti-Christian and liberally biased.

The same is true for Christmas. No holiday enjoys more of a favored status than Christmas; it is a ubiquitous juggernaut that takes over much of the world every year for more than a whole month. Special names are even reserved for Christmas critics: "Scrooge" and "Grinch"; "Christmas seems to be everywhere" (April 16, 2012). Yet Fox News somehow thinks Christmas is endangered and automatically takes any criticism of the holiday to be a criticism of Christianity, even if what's being criticized is the holiday's secular elements, like its commercialization. This helps reinforce the assumption that Christmas is all about Christ, a major weapon in the Christian war for Christmas. Thus a large part of the Christian war for Christmas is being waged by Fox News.

The frequency, magnitude, and severity of "anti-Christmas" efforts are exaggerated. But those that exist are simply a reaction to Christians trying to force the Christian way of celebrating the holiday on everyone else. There is nothing wrong with such a reaction. I should not be forced to recognize or celebrate the religious aspects of Christmas any more than you should be forced to have my grandmother's delicious homemade noodles at your Thanksgiving celebration.

A Wall of Separation between Christians and Christmas

Yes, yes, lady wearing cross on television, religious freedom is on the rocks. The rocks!

Jon Stewart (December 6, 2011)

After World War II, most Americans wanted to distinguish their government from that of the godless communists. Consequently, Congress added "under God" to the Pledge and adopted "in God we trust" as the national motto, adding the phrase to all coins and currency. The general populace followed suit and, among other things, religious school plays and courthouse nativities became ubiquitous.

But objections to such displays soon followed. Critics suggested they constituted a governmental endorsement of Christianity itself which violates the separation of church and state. Those ignorant of Christmas's history replied that it was just the government celebrating Christmas, an already nationally recognized holiday; you can't ban such celebrations without banning Christmas itself. But, of course, we know better. There is more than one way to celebrate Christmas, and nativity scenes and plays about Jesus' birth are clearly religious celebrations. A government participating in them endorses Christianity.

Others defended the displays, however, by pointing out that the phrase "a wall of separation between church and state" is nowhere in the Constitution. Consequently, they argue, governmental favoritism of Christianity is fine. The founders merely meant to prevent the establishment of a state religion—not to prevent government favoritism toward religion—so courthouse nativities and public-school religious plays are perfectly fine.

Such arguments are poor, however. One can invoke a principle without mentioning it, and that is exactly how the Constitution establishes a wall of separation between church and state. It makes clear that there should be no religious test for holding a government office and the First Amendment states that "Congress shall make no law respecting an establishment of religion, or prohibiting the free exercise thereof." A long history of judicial interpretation and application of the Constitution shows it establishes that government cannot favor any particular religion.

Conservatives often suggest that this interpretation of the Constitution is incorrect because our Founding Fathers, like Thomas Jefferson, were diehard Christians. For example, as a guest on *The Daily Show*, David Barton told us that most of what we've been told about Jefferson is a lie—a result of people taking Jeffersonian quotes out of context (May 1, 2012). In his book, *The Jefferson Lies*, Barton claims that Jefferson was not secular, but instead let religion "infect" most of what he did.[18] According to Barton, Jefferson would be on the side of modern-day conservatives—perfectly fine with a government endorsement of Christianity, public-school Christmas plays, and courthouse nativities.

Ironically, however, Barton does exactly what he claims his opponents do: he takes Jeffersonian quotes out of context to support his view.[19] "One side will yell about the other, and they're doing exactly what the other side does" (May 1, 2012). For example, in his chapter "Lie #2: Thomas Jefferson Founded a Secular University," Barton claims that Thomas Jefferson once quipped that Sir William Blackstone's book *Commentaries on the Laws of England*—a book that supposedly praised the importance of Christian influence on law—was as important to American lawyers as the Koran is to Muslims.[20] In actual fact, Jefferson was putting down Blackstone's book. Jefferson was "lamenting" the "opinion" that Blackstone's book was revered like the Koran; this reverence for Blackstone, Jefferson thought, was "deprecating law science."[21] Elsewhere Jefferson bemoans the use of Blackstone's book in law schools saying it has "done more towards the suppression of the liberties of man, than all the million [sic] of men in arms of Bonaparte ..."[22] Unfortunately, Barton's book is packed with similar errors on nearly every page.

Although the Founding Fathers were certainly not modern atheists, they weren't anything like modern-day conservative Christians and would not be on their side in the Christmas debate.[23] Most of the Founding Fathers were a product of the Enlightenment, which viewed most religious claims with a very healthy dose of skepticism. Specifically, Thomas Jefferson was a deist (someone who believes that God exists but does not interact in any way with the world at all) who published a version of the New Testament that omitted all of Jesus' miracles.[24] In fact, it is from Jefferson himself that we get the phrase "a wall of separation between church and state." It came in a letter that Jefferson wrote to the Danbury Baptists who were worried that the religious majority in Connecticut would try to make "their Chief Magistrate ... assume the prerogative of Jehovah and make laws to govern the Kingdom of Christ."[25] Jefferson assures them they have nothing to worry about by quoting and then clarifying the first amendment, saying it built "a wall of separation between Church & State."[26]

I personally don't think the Founding Fathers' intentions matter all that much. I am not a constitutional originalist. I think the constitution should be interpreted in the way that leads to the best government. Even if the Founding Fathers approved of the government favoring Christianity, that wouldn't make it a good idea. Governments favoring one religion over another has led to centuries of conflict and millions of deaths.[27] Think how much more peaceful things could be if the governments of Iran, Afghanistan, Pakistan, and Saudi Arabia did not favor Islam, and the governments of Israel and India did not favor, respectively, Judaism and Hinduism.

If religious conservatives just sat down and thought about it for a bit, they'd realize they want a separation of church and state too. Letting the Lutheran church fire someone because they have narcolepsy, contrary to the Americans with disabilities act, in the name of religious freedom might seem like a cause for a hearty "hallelujah." But, if religious law can override civil law, as Aasif Mandvi pointed out, then Muslims should be allowed to use and favor Sharia law when it comes into conflict with civil law too (January 26, 2012).

Obviously, the government showing favoritism to Christianity is a bad idea. And since a courthouse putting up a nativity scene clearly constitutes an endorsement of the Christian way of celebrating Christmas and thus an endorsement of Christianity itself, that's a bad idea too. The same applies to religious Christmas plays in public schools. Of course, people are free to put nativity scenes on their own lawn—or in front of their vaginas to protect against government mandated and Republican endorsed trans-vaginal ultrasounds (April 16, 2012)—and private Christian schools are free to do all the religious plays they want. That right is also guaranteed by the First Amendment: "the free exercise thereof." But unless the government gives equal recognition to the nonreligious aspects of Christmas or gives nonreligious groups an equal opportunity to erect displays, such happenings violate the First Amendment.[28]

The Original Meaning of Christmas

*There's a war on Christmas? Has anyone told Thanksgiving?
'Cause this year, Black Friday, a.k.a. "Christmas's opening bell,"
got moved back a day to Black Thursday—or as we used to call
it, "Thanksgiving." Christmas is so big now, it's eating other
holidays. Watch your ass Halloween, you're next.*

Jon Stewart (December 3, 2012)

There is no war on Christmas. If there were, it would be the most unsuccessful war of all time. Christmas is the biggest, most recognized, and most cherished holiday of all. The events that Bill O'Reilly and Fox News think constitute a war on Christmas are actually just efforts to correct the effects of the Christian war *for* Christmas— their efforts to claim late-December celebrations for their savior, Jesus, and force their way of celebrating on everyone else. But Jesus is not the reason for the season and you don't have to keep Christ in Christmas if you don't want to.

Conservatives often wish for a return to the way the earliest Americans celebrated Christmas[29] and offer their quest for religious freedom as evidence that the government should endorse the Christian way of celebrating the holiday. But the Puritans were not seeking religious freedom in the conventional sense. They did not seek to establish communities where everyone was free to worship God in the way that they saw fit. They established communities that enforced their specific religious practices in a theocratic manner. Anyone who deviated from that, including anyone who decided to celebrate Christmas, was fined or put in stocks. If you tried to take the day off, you might even end up in jail. As Stewart pointed out (December 6, 2011), if the puritans were alive today, they would decorate their town square at Christmas by putting Fox News correspondents who demand everyone celebrate Christmas in stocks.

Notes

1. To make this claim in 2005, he had to dig back a year in *The Daily Show*'s clips—a fact comically revealed by a very pregnant Samantha Bee realizing the highlights in her hair were different in the clip O'Reilly used, "those are honey, these clearly caramel" (December 7, 2005).

2. Rob Boston, "Is There a 'War on Christmas'? Religious Right Holiday Campaign Raises Money and Members by Distorting Reality," *Church & State Magazine* (2007), www.au.org/church-state/december-2007-church-state/featured/is-there-a-%E2%80%98war-on-christmas%E2%80%99, last accessed February 6, 2013.

3. PolitiFact, "Jon Stewart Says Those Who Watch Fox News Are the 'Most Consistently Misinformed Media Viewers'," www.politifact.com/truth-o-meter/statements/2011/jun/20/jon-stewart/jon-stewart-says-those-who-watch-fox-news-are-most, last accessed February 5, 2013.

4. This is not long enough ago, however, to explain the Flintstones' Christmas special which, apparently, was "celebrating Jesus' birth, thousands of years before the birth of Jesus" (December 3, 2012).

5. In fact, biblical scholars agree, they tell us two totally different contradictory stories. For example, the gospel of Matthew has the holy family living in Bethlehem, fleeing to Egypt after the wise men's visit, and then much later moving to Nazareth for the first time. The gospel of Luke has the holy family originally living in Nazareth, going to Bethlehem for a short time because of the census, and then immediately returning to Nazareth after the birth. For more on these and other discrepancies in the biblical narratives see Bart Ehrman, *Jesus, Interrupted: Revealing the Hidden Contradictions in the Bible (And Why We Don't Know About Them)* (New York: Harper One: 2010).

6. "Even when the Irish rituals were religious, they retained the rowdy old Carnival note—alcohol, sex, and aggressive begging. Take the midnight Mass on Christmas Eve, for example. This event (it was held outdoors, illuminated by great bonfires) was usually preceded and followed by what a nineteenth-century Irish writer termed "jovial orgies," perambulating groups who engaged in heavy drinking that often lead to elicit sexual couplings. By the 1830s, the church itself had largely abolished the midnight Mass." Stephen Nissenbaum, *The Battle for Christmas* (New York: Vintage Books. 1996), 305.

7. Ibid., 8, original emphasis.

8. See the PolitiFact article, "Comic Jon Stewart Says Congress Met Most Christmas Days in Its Early Years," www.politifact.com/rhode-island/statements/2011/dec/09/jon-stewart/comic-jon-stewart-says-early-congress-met-most-chr, last accessed February 5, 2013.

9. Unlike us, who say "Merry Christmas" every day from Thanksgiving to New Year's.

10. Franklin also pointed out that papists did attend church on Christmas day, and in 1789 the Universalists of Boston were holding their first major Christmas church service.

11. See chapters 3–4 of David Forbes, *Christmas: A Candid History* (Berkeley: University of California Press, 2007).

12. This practice was a call back to earlier social inversion traditions in Saturnalia where there was no preference given to those who received the best food and drink and often the wealthy would serve the less fortunate.

13. See Nissenbaum, *The Battle for Christmas*, chapters 2–5.

14. In the most literal sense, the reason for the season is the tilt of the Earth's axis. It's cold every December in the northern hemisphere because that's when it's tilted away from the sun.

15. Technically speaking, the winter solstice is usually on the 21st, but the 25th is when the ancients could notice that the days were getting longer.

16. Sunday bears the name of the sun because it was the holy worship day of sun worshipers. Thursday was Thor's day; Wednesday belonged to Wodin; Monday belonged to the moon.

17. For the extended interview, see www.thedailyshow.com/watch/wed-april-6–2011/exclusive---mike-huckabee-extended-interview-pt--3, last accessed February 5, 2013.

18. See David Barton, *The Jefferson Lies: Exposing the Myths You've Always Believed about Thomas Jefferson* (Nashville, TN: Thomas Nelson, 2012).

19. Barton frequently distorts the facts and outright lies to support his position. In fact, he did this on *The Daily Show*, and it went right past

Stewart. Barton claimed that a five-year-old kid in St. Louis was picked up by the scruff of his neck, yelled at by his teacher, and then later his principal as well, for praying over his lunch at school. This is a common urban myth often cited by Christians in an effort to make them seem victimized. The real story is that 10-year-old Raymond Raines got detention for fighting in the cafeteria. See Kyle Mantyla, "David Barton, Jon Stewart, and the Myth of Raymond Raines," www.rightwingwatch. org/content/david-barton-jon-stewart-and-myth-raymond-raines, last accessed February 5, 2013.

20. Barton, *The Jefferson Lies*, 35.

21. Thomas Jefferson to Jon Tyler, May 26, 1810, in *The Writings of Thomas Jefferson*, ed. Andrew A. Lipscomb and Albert Ellery Bergh, vol. XII (Washington, DC: Thomas Jefferson Memorial Association, 1907), 392–393.

22. Thomas Jefferson to Horatio G. Spafford, March 17, 1814, in *The Writings of Thomas Jefferson*, ed. Andrew A. Lipscomb and Albert Ellery Bergh, vol. XIV (Washington, DC: Thomas Jefferson Memorial Association, 1907), 119–120.

23. For more on how evangelical Christians have distorted early American history, see Chris Rodda, *Liars for Jesus: The Religious Right's Alternative Version of American History*, vol. I (Charleston, SC: BookSurge, 2006).

24. He published it under the title "The Life and Morals of Jesus of Nazareth" and distributed it to native Americans.

25. Letter of October 7, 1801 from Danbury (CT) Baptist Association to Thomas Jefferson, Thomas Jefferson Papers, Manuscript Division, Library of Congress, Washington, DC.

26. Thomas Jefferson, *The Writings of Thomas Jefferson*, ed. Albert E. Bergh, vol. XVI (Washington, DC: Thomas Jefferson Memorial Association of the United States, 1904), 281–282.

27. The sordid history of violence fueled by government endorsed religion is, in fact, good reason to think the Founding Fathers did not want the government to favor Christianity. The history of England, from which they fled, was a history fraught with violence fueled by governmental religious favoritism. Thousands upon thousands had died as a result of religions struggling against each other for power. Oliver Cromwell and the Puritans took things over from the Church of England, blowing a few things up and burning a number of people at the stake in the process, only to have the church of England take over a few years later and burn them at the stake.

28. Some might argue that since the First Amendment only mentions Congress, it does not restrict local governments from favoring

Christianity. But thanks to court rulings on the *due process clause* of the 14th Amendment, the Bill of Rights applies to both local and state governments. Of course, that's not to say that the government is flawless in enforcing the separation of church and state. Clearly "under God" in the pledge and "in God we trust" on our money and as our national motto favors monotheistic religions over polytheistic and nontheistic religions such as Hinduism and Buddhism. And since "God" is what Christians call their deity, and not so much what Jews call their deity (Yahweh) or what Muslims call their deity (Allah), it actually favors Christianity specifically. And don't get me started on The National Day of Prayer or the phrase "God bless America" at the end of every State of the Union address. But two wrongs don't make a right. Fox News lying about healthcare reform including death panels does not justify them lying about Texas eliminating mentions of Christmas and the Constitution in their textbooks (June 21, 2011). In the same way, one violation of the separation of church and state does not justify another.

29.   A true return to the holiday's roots would be quite disturbing. Among other things, we would have to replace Santa Claus with a much more menacing figure named Krampus. Krampus is a centuries-old Austrian folk legend that, as Stephen Colbert taught us, wears sheep skins, ram's horns, and is covered in the urine of small children (because he scares the hell out of them). See *The Colbert Report* (December 9, 2009).

Chapter 17

Evolution, Schmevolution
Jon Stewart and the Culture Wars

Massimo Pigliucci

"Are we characters in a dubious fairy tale written thousands of years ago in the depth of human ignorance, or random globs of cells who got a little luckier than the fucking slime that grows on our shower towels?" This was the opening question in *The Daily Show* series "Evolution, Schmevolution," one of the most daring attempts at exploring a serious and controversial issue in the history of fake news TV. *The Daily Show* appropriately timed the series to air during the momentous trial that took place in Dover, Pennsylvania in the fall of 2005. The plaintiff in the case, "Tammy Kitzmiller v. the Dover Area School District," contended that the theory of "intelligent design" (ID) shouldn't be taught in public schools on the grounds that it's a form of creationism, and that teaching it would amount to a clear violation of the separation between church and state.[1]

Stewart's opening question goes straight to the heart of why there's a controversy between creationists and evolutionists and not, say, between creationists and quantum physicists: people have an intuitive understanding of the philosophical implications of the idea of evolution, while the consequences of quantum mechanics in this context are much more nuanced (another reason why quantum mechanics is usually left alone is that, as Nobel physicist Richard Feynman reminded us, nobody *really* understands quantum physics, not even

The Ultimate Daily Show and Philosophy: More Moments of Zen, More Indecision Theory,
First Edition. Edited by Jason Holt.
© 2013 John Wiley & Sons, Inc. Published 2013 by John Wiley & Sons, Inc.

quantum physicists). Stewart's framing of the problem is reminiscent of another famous source of popular scholarship, Monty Python, in their immortal opus *The Meaning of Life*:

> Why are we here? What's life all about?
> Is God really real, or is there some doubt? ...
> What's the point of all this hoax?
> Is it the chicken and the egg time? Are we just yolks?
> Or, perhaps, we're just one of God's little jokes.

And so on and so forth.

Of course, phrasing the question as an either/or choice may in itself represent a classic example of logical fallacy, the false dichotomy, in which someone presents two options as exhausting all possibilities, when in fact there are more positions that can be reasonably taken. During the "Evolution, Schmevolution" series, Lewis Black, a regular *Daily Show* commentator, points out that presenting an issue as an either/or choice may not be the wisest thing to do, and indeed may lead to rather silly outcomes:

> The scientific method has taken us pretty far: we've cured diseases, sent men to the moon, given erections where before there were none ... Religion has also inspired man to do some pretty great things [*showing image of the Sistine Chapel's ceiling*]. The problem is, when you try too hard to apply science to religion, both come off looking ridiculous.

So, what's the real status of the scientific theory of evolution? And what do people mean by "intelligent design?" More generally, what's the proper relationship between science and religion, not to mention politics, in early 21st century America? This chapter will examine these and other weighty questions through the inquiring minds and sharp tongues of Jon Stewart, Lewis Black, and former *Daily Show* "correspondent" Ed Helms. While the four episodes of the "Evolution, Schmevolution" special may have changed few minds on this topic, the series represents a good example of humorous yet engaging intellectual discourse, addressing complex philosophical questions, even peppered with instances of logical fallacies committed by the host, his correspondents, or some of the guests.

Evolution: The Fundamentals

Scientific theories are complex statements about the workings of the natural world, and they're notoriously difficult to frame in straight-forward and understandable terms. This explains why scientists are famously inept at communicating with the general public (with few remarkable exceptions such as Carl Sagan, Stephen J. Gould, and Richard Dawkins).[2] This ineptness was on display during Ed Helms's interview with primatologist Dan Wharton at the Bronx Zoo. The guy managed to remain as stiff and humorless as the quintessential ivory tower intellectual even when Helms launched into a discussion of the comparative anatomy of human and chimpanzee penises (although, to be fair, *The Daily Show*'s editors did their best to accentuate the effect on poor Dr. Wharton)!

Nonetheless, in the opening monologue to the "Evolution, Schme-volution" series, Stewart gave a succinct but substantially correct summary of the Darwinian theory, using a diagram portraying the classic example of giraffes with necks of different lengths, one of which was clearly more adapted to reaching high tree leaves than the others (there was also a "really cool" but alas unlikely mutant version that could spit fire from its nostrils). Essentially, Darwin's theory is based on two fundamental insights: on the one hand, all living creatures are related to each other by common descent; on the other, organisms differentiate from each other and adapt to the ever-changing conditions of their world.[3] The main mechanism for this latter process is natural selection. Natural selection, in turn, is simply the result of the fact that animals (and plants) differ from each other (because of mutations in their DNA) in transmissible traits that affect their survival and their ability to produce offspring. Those that manage to survive and have more babies will pass more of their winning characteristics to the next generation, where the game will start all over *ad infinitum*. That's pretty much it, though there are a few additional complications, and the whole story can be told in much more precise (and quite a bit more complicated) mathematical terms.

Philosophers of science have sometimes debated the scientific status of Darwin's theory. Karl Popper (the father of "falsification-ism," the idea that scientific theories can't be proven correct, but must be capable of being proven wrong) at one point stated that

"Darwinism is not a testable scientific theory, but a metaphysical research program."[4] This pronouncement is often quoted by creationists, although Popper later admitted that his earlier views on the subject were mistaken: "I have changed my mind about the testability and logical status of the theory of natural selection; and I am glad to have an opportunity to make a recantation."[5] If only such intellectual honesty were more common in these sorts of debates! Popper's error aside, the consensus among philosophers of science is that the theory of evolution is a legitimate scientific theory, characterized by a mix of historical claims (common descent) and experimentally verifiable natural processes (mutation and selection). As Patricia Cleland effectively sums it up, it isn't rocket science, but it's very solid science nonetheless.[6]

What sort of evidence can scientists possibly muster in support of their statements about life forms that are now extinct? In part, the evidence is the sort of inferential logic based on fossil records that Lewis Black highlights in his "Evolution, Schmevolution" commentary. As he puts it:

> Scientific theory is based on observations made in the real world .... [For] little creationists there is "D" is for Dinosaurs, where kids are taught that before the Flood all dinosaurs were vegetarian. Makes sense, especially when you look at this early dino-skeleton [points to a fossil of a meat-eating dinosaur]: those 80 dagger-shaped teeth and huge claws were perfect for chasing down and killing any plants that try to run away!

That, in a nutshell, is the scientific method.

Why, Then, Is There a Problem?

While watching "Evolution, Schmevolution," one could be forgiven for concluding that the theory of evolution ought to be uncontroversial for the simple reason that it makes sense. This would be the same sort of mistake that a politically liberal viewer of *The Daily Show* might make when concluding that, say, it's pretty obvious that the United States shouldn't have invaded Iraq (Stewart's then-long-running series "Mess O' Potamia" is probably worth a book in and of itself). But the fact is that evolution is highly controversial in the

United States. More than 50% of Americans surveyed in various Gallup polls reject the theory entirely, and many more accept it only with the proviso that God is somehow controlling the process. Explanations for the predominant American view include a long and complex history of anti-intellectualism peculiar to the United States and the sorry condition of scientific literacy in the population at large.[7]

The "problem" was clear for everyone to see when Ed Helms visited Dayton, Tennessee, the site of the original "monkey" trial of 1925, during which substitute science teacher John Scopes was tried and eventually convicted of teaching the "false doctrine" of evolution (the only time evolutionists have actually lost a court case).[8] Helms interviewed locals while pretending that they were actually impersonating characters from 1925. As he put it: "So come on down and enjoy Dayton, safe in the knowledge that it's all pretend. Because if it were real, it would be fucking terrifying." Indeed, a woman interviewed by Helms candidly stated an astonishingly common position among the American public: "Evolution is a total fabrication and a lie. Evolution destroys faith and builds an economic market that is contrary to our American way of life."

Of course, the creation–evolution controversy, while not a scientific debate, has several root causes—not just scientific ignorance and religious bigotry. Stewart's crew subtly brought to the public's attention the political element at work. The controversy has been exploited politically ever since three-time Presidential candidate William Jennings Bryan volunteered to be on the prosecution team against John Scopes in 1925, facing the famous (or infamous, depending on your point of view) liberal lawyer Clarence Darrow, activist and prominent member of the newly established American Civil Liberties Union. During the "Evolution, Schmevolution" series, Stewart brought in Chris Mooney, author of The Republican War on Science, to weigh in on the broader issue of the relationship between politics, science, and religion. Stewart pointed out that putting a political spin on scientific findings is nothing new, and that Republican and Democrat administrations alike engage in such practice. Mooney replied that the current situation is different, because "The scientific community [is] coming out and releasing strong statements saying that the [Bush] administration abused science across the board. And I would trust the scientific community to diagnose whether science has been overly politicized."

The second President Bush actually came out in favor of creationism as a competing theory, stating on August 3, 2005 that "That decision [about teaching creationism in public schools] should be made by local school districts, but I [feel] like both sides ought to be properly taught ... I think that part of education is to expose people to different schools of thought." This is the standard (and rather disingenuous) ID line of "teaching the controversy."

Mooney, addressing the broader contention that disagreement within the scientific community implies that we should seriously consider all positions on an issue, said that no matter how ill-supported, "Scientific knowledge is by its nature tentative, so you can selectively say 'Oh, we don't know enough about global warming,' when in fact we know a heck of a lot ... It's the same about evolution ... The war on science is compelled by corporate interests and religious conservative interests." Stewart then pursued this general line by presenting the possibility of a postmodern position on truth: "Will scientific debate, then, become in the same way that a court case becomes, in that ... if you hire the right experts you'll do better ... In the way, let's say, OJ Simpson puts together a nice team and hires guys who say 'DNA means nothing!'"

This point about the alleged relativity of truth and knowledge is a serious one that philosophers have discussed ever since the ancient skeptics argued that there can't be certain knowledge of any kind. The long tradition of rationalism in philosophy, from Plato (429–347 BCE) to Descartes (1596–1650), argued for the milder position that while empirical knowledge (based on what the senses tell us) is unreliable, the mind can access truth by using logic and applying it to first principles (culminating in Descartes's method of "radical doubt"). Then again, empiricists like David Hume (1711–1776) pointed out that there's very little, if anything, about the outside world that we can come to know in this way, and the best we can hope for are rather tentative conclusions based on admittedly incomplete empirical evidence. As a result, science—which emerged as a blend of rationalism and empiricism—is a messy business yielding rather tentative conclusions. According to Mooney, this situation doesn't sit well with the need for relatively simple answers in both the political and religious arenas. In this respect, it's interesting to note the awkward and philosophically untenable position in which religious fundamentalists put themselves when they resort to claiming that scientific knowledge is relative. Surely they don't want to go as far as claiming that *all* knowledge is relative to one's culture or ideological position, since that would undermine their own religious stance. The same applies to the extreme postmodernist position, which is often attacked on the ground that if no point of view has any special claim to truth, why should one regard the postmodern position itself as having more value than any of the many possible anti-postmodernist positions?[9]

What Is Intelligent Design, Anyway?

The "Evolution, Schmevolution" series was prompted, as mentioned earlier, by the trial in Dover. That trial was important in the history of the controversy because it was the first time that the idea of "intelligent design," and not just standard "the earth is 6000 years old" creationism, was being tested in a court of law. But what exactly is ID? Once again, Stewart and his collaborators did a surprisingly good job of getting to the bottom line in a clear and entertaining way. As Stewart said, "Put simply, Intelligent Design says life on earth is too complex to have evolved without some kind of guiding hand. They are not saying it's God, just someone with the basic skill-set to create an entire working universe." This captures the alleged (and clearly disingenuous) distinction between creationism and ID, the very same "distinction without a difference" that made Judge Jones impatient at the Dover trial: "The evidence at trial demonstrates that ID is nothing less than the progeny of creationism ... Compelling evidence supports the Plaintiff's assertion that ID is creationism re-labeled."

To further probe this matter, Stewart convened a panel discussion featuring leading ID proponent William Dembski, historian John Larson, author of *Summer for the Gods*, and New Age spiritualist Ellie Crystal.[10] Dembski opened the discussion with an interesting philosophical move: according to him, ID proponents don't deny natural selection, since "it's not either/or—there can be design that's implemented through [natural selection]." This suggests that evolutionary biologists are guilty of committing the fallacy of false dichotomy that we already encountered at the beginning of this chapter. Of course, strictly speaking, Dembski is correct: science can't rule out supernatural oversight of natural processes, simply because the supernatural is outside the purview of science. Since by definition the supernatural can't be subjected to empirical investigation and experimentation, the possibility advanced by Dembski—usually referred to as theistic evolution—can't be excluded on scientific grounds. This, however, is a somewhat Pyrrhic victory for ID.[11]

ID's proponents, beginning with Dembski himself, repeatedly claim that ID is good science. Stewart highlights the contradiction when he brings up the following example: "Let me ask you this: Intelligent Design, the scrotum, the most painful part of my body. This intelligent designer chose to put it in a bag that anyone can walk across and hit with a baseball bat." To this Dembski could only reply with a rather evasive "ID is not committed to every aspect of reality being the result of intelligence." Well, then, how do we know which bits of reality ID is committed to explaining?

While Stewart clearly meant the scrotum reference as a joke (indeed, he thanked Dembski for considering the question seriously enough to attempt to address the point), he was actually right on the mark. If a supernatural (or, for that matter, natural) intelligent agent is directing evolution from behind the scenes, then that agent is responsible not just for the marvels of biological complexity and success, but for the apparent stupidity and inefficiency that plagues the biological world.[12] This is why I said theistic evolution results in a Pyrrhic victory for ID. Let's not forget, as evolutionary biologist Ernst Mayr observed, that 99.99% of all species that ever existed are now extinct. Not exactly a record to be proud of if one aspires to the title of creator and engineer-behind-the-scenes of the universe!

Of course, a weaker interpretation of Dembski's claim of non-mutual exclusivity is that religion and science aren't inherently incompatible, contrary to what has been asserted on various occasions, for example, by biologist Richard Dawkins.[13] Stewart posed precisely that question to the historian on the panel, John Larson, who pointed out that "we are talking about science here, the problem with divine intervention, a miracle, is that it's not repeatable, it's not testable in a laboratory, it's not falsifiable." In other words, ID proponents simply can't have it both ways: either there's a supernatural designer who works outside of the confines of natural laws—in which case ID isn't science and shouldn't be taught in public schools as such—or ID has to make some claims that are empirically verifiable and so be open to the possibility that such claims may be shown to be false. Once again, Dembski's rebuttal is rather weak: "I'm not talking about the big G,

I'm saying that there are organizing principles." But of course no scientist has ever claimed that there are no (natural) "organizing principles" generating the order and complexity that we see in the universe. Natural selection is supposed to be precisely one such organizing principle!

Stewart saw through Dembski's rhetoric, and promptly asked him "What came first [for you], the religion [sic] conversion or the evidence convincing you?" to which Dembski admitted "the religious conversion came first." Now, strictly speaking, Stewart was very close here to committing the genetic fallacy, rejecting an argument not on the grounds of its weakness, but because of where it comes from. One might also diagnose this as coming close to the *ad hominem* fallacy, rejecting the view because of the view holder. Just because, say, a racist biologist publishes a paper purportedly showing evidence of genetic differences in the cognitive abilities of different ethnic groups, one can't reject the paper simply on ideological grounds. Proper scientific analysis requires the evidence presented in the paper to be assessed on its own merits, regardless of the ideological positions of the author. Nonetheless, the fallacy occurs only if one concludes from the character of a given individual that his ideas are necessarily flawed. Stewart obviously stopped far short of that, simply hinting at the curious fact that while the scientific community includes people of all religions, ID proponents are invariably committed to a narrow range of Christian (or Muslim) conservative positions. It doesn't follow that ID proponents are wrong, but it would be disingenuous or naïve not to be suspicious of their motives and possible biases.

So, Evolution or Schmevolution?

Jon Stewart began the "Evolution, Schmevolution" series by promising (obviously in jest) that the public would finally know the answer by the end of the week. Again this is analogous to Monty Python's promise in the title song of *The Meaning of Life*:

> So just why, why are we here?
> And just what, what, what, what do we fear?
> Well *ce soir*, for a change, it will all be made clear
> For this is The Meaning of Life.

Just as Monty Python didn't really "solve" the meaning of life, neither did Jon Stewart solve the evolution–creation controversy. Perhaps figuring out the meaning of life is a personal matter, something that's up to particular individuals to work out for themselves. One might be tempted to see an analogy between the two questions, and argue that the solution to the evolution-creation controversy is also a personal matter, not an issue that can be resolved by objective external evidence. In a sense, this may be the case; let me explain, by way of a short digression.

Meaning in life is not to be found in external, objective mandates (unless one believes that such meaning can come from a god, and one also has reason to believe that that god's message has been transmitted loud and clear). Rather, individual human beings construct meaningful lives out of their physical possibilities and limits, their cultural biases and practices, and their innate desires. As Aristotle would have put it, "happiness" (although the Greek word *eudaimonia* really has a broader meaning than the roughly equivalent English term) is a work in progress, and we can't assess the outcome until death puts an end to the quest. It's for this reason that it makes little sense to ask the simplistic question: what is *the* meaning of life?

Similarly, it might seem to make equally little sense to seek a resolution to the evolution–creation controversy. Scientists and philosophers of science have convincingly argued that there's simply no *scientific* controversy here.[14] From a philosophical standpoint, ID isn't science, because it doesn't include empirically verifiable statements, and because it invokes a supernatural intervention which is by definition outside the realm of scientific investigation. From a scientific perspective, there's just about as much disagreement among professional biologists on the modern theory of evolution as there is among physicists on the mathematics of quantum mechanics—pretty close to zero. Of course, both theories may eventually be superseded or significantly altered in the future, but certainly not by vague statements about intelligent organizing principles. In this sense, the evolution–creation debate is similar to the debate on global warming, as Chris Mooney pointed out to Stewart: the scientific community increasingly converges toward one answer, but the public is divided on the issue because of the political and ideological muddling that seeps through the media's treatment of it. Perhaps ironically, Jon Stewart's approach to the evolution–creation controversy ranks as one of the best media treatments of the debate in recent memory.

In another—non-scientific—sense, however, the "solution" to the controversy is and can only be personal, in that individuals have to make up their minds about whether they're willing to fully accept a scientific-rationalist worldview, or whether they'd rather pick and choose which aspects of a pre-Enlightenment mentality they wish to retain. One can certainly enjoy the benefits of science—from laptop computers to air travel to modern medicine—while still engaging in mystical thinking about intelligent designers and worldwide floods that never happened, but this comes at the risk of much cognitive dissonance and social strife, not to mention philosophical untenability. Although we're free to choose either side, it is not the case that the two choices are equally wise.

The *Daily Show* series on evolution ended on a semi-sober note, with a brief outline of the matters that should really concern us. Forget supernatural intelligent design, the real problem is that humans have now learned enough about genetics and evolution to actually start tampering with the basic structure of life itself. Stewart and company take aim at genetic engineering and cloning while depicting scientists as aloof, out of touch with what's important to humanity, engaging in intellectual games for their own sake (as in the case of efforts to clone cats, which Stewart characterizes as "making copies of something no one needed to begin with"). Indeed, a basic problem with the creation–evolution controversy is that in one camp we have an army of anti-intellectuals who distrust science, and in the other a small elite band of intellectuals who largely think it beneath them to explain to the general public what they're doing and why (despite the fact that it's the general public that pays their bills).[15] Stewart introduced the "Evolution, Schmevolution" series by saying "The stage was now set for an epic debate between the forces of science on one side and religion on the other. One side says 'You're backwards, and primitive,' the other side says 'You're godless, and love Satan.' Sadly, the debate itself has not evolved in over 150 years." Indeed.

Postscript: After (and Before) Dover

In true mock-journalistic fashion, Jon and his gang did a follow-up on the Dover story, very shortly after the "Evolution, Schmevolution" series. On December 15, 2005 they aired a piece entitled "Until

Hell Freezes Dover," in which they reported on the inane comments of 700-Club host Pat Robertson in the aftermath of the fact that the creationist board members who had engineered the debacle were not reelected.

Special correspondent Samantha Bee covered the story, beginning by showing a clip of Robertson in which he said, apparently in all seriousness, "I'd like to say to the good citizens of Dover, if there is a disaster in your area, don't turn to God. You just voted god out of your city." Of course Robertson had made similar despicable pronouncements before (most notably after the 9/11 attacks) and has done so again since (about any state that showed a hint of lessening discrimination against homosexuals), but it is always sobering to realize that—despite being featured on a comedy show—the quote is meant in a deadly serious way by the "good" reverend.

And speaking of interesting clergy figures, Bee also managed to find a local apologist of the apocalyptic scenario, one Jim Grove, pastor of the Heritage Baptist Church of Dover. He is worth quoting extensively, as little additional commentary is needed (and pretty much none, in fact, is provided by Bee herself):

> I've seen it coming for years. They are teaching in public schools environmentalism, they are teaching anti-sovereignty [presumably referring to civics lessons about the United Nations], they are teaching the gay lifestyle. If you are going to vote god out of your community, we have to suffer the results of that.

The pastor then actually—and, again, without a trace of irony—presented himself as middle-of-the-road and reasonable, as testified by his willingness to compromise and do the Halloween parade, even though it is a clearly "pagan" event. He concluded:

> We live in the last days, I believe, many of the signs are there. I think the computer has a great deal to do with this. We are being controlled more and more and more by computers. It's getting to the point where you can't do anything without a social security number. And I think that's a precursor to the Mark of the Beast, Revelation chapter 13. God turned them over to a reprobate mind, which ultimately leads to moral corruption and moral depravity.

All of this, of course, in a town where a whopping nine churches serve a population barely over 1000.

The Daily Show's "Evolution, Schmevolution" special was not the first time that Jon and his writers took on the issue of creationism (nor, as it turns out, it would be the last—far from it). For instance, on November 14, 2001 they ran a piece called "Tyrannosaurus Redux." Jon began the segment by pointing out that "Luckily, here in our country we have never really faced issues of fundamentalism, so we don't have those kinds of disagreements. For instance, as all of us know, the world and everything in it was created in one week, 6000 years ago. There is no disagreement there. Or, is there?" Which led to a special report by Mo Rocca, focusing on Carl E. Baugh (PhD), of the Creation Science Museum in Glen Rose, TX, who plainly stated that "There is no conflict between true science and the Bible."

The idea that there is a "true" and Bible-friendly science, as opposed to an untrue, materialistic, and atheist science, is a standard trope of creationist propaganda, and Rocca manages to capture the absurdity of the notion perfectly during his interview with Baugh. The stunning "discovery" made by the latter during his research is that "Man and dinosaur appeared on planet earth 6000 years ago, they were created to live together, and they were friends." How does Baugh know this? Rocca manages to get the fellow to actually run a "scientific" commentary on, well, fictional television shows, as an illustration of how "man and dinosaur" once lived together. While they start with a clip of *Land of the Lost* (where Baugh expresses doubts about the depiction of carnivorous dinosaurs-eating martians), by far the most hilarious bit comes with *The Flintstones*: "I am intrigued with the Flintstones," says Baugh very candidly, and goes on to explain a scene featuring Barney using a bird or a Pterodactyl (probably the latter, says Baugh) to trim his lawn. Makes sense, because Pterodactyls are well known to have been herbivores (they were actually carnivores, likely eating fish, insects, and other small animals—but of course that's according to atheistic paleontology). Not content, Rocca points to a scene where Fred is holding a small dinosaur in his arms, which prompted Baugh to comment: "I find that rather plausible and realistic."

The reason I think this is so bizarre is because when I was living in Tennessee and giving talks about evolution I jokingly pointed out that creationists are people who think *The Flintstones* is a documentary. Turns out, I was unwittingly exactly right ... There is also very little to laugh, unfortunately, about Baugh's creationist museum. While

Rocca mocks him for giving tours to both of his visitors, a few years later Australian creationist Ken Ham managed to raise millions of dollars to open a highly successful creationist museum in Kentucky—where men and dinosaurs are indeed featured side by side in friendly interaction. Reality truly is more bizarre than fiction.

The Daily Show has also dealt with controversy within both camps, creationism and evolution, not just across them. In the above mentioned segment by Mo Rocca, for instance, the comedian interviews another creationist, pastor David Auterson, who says about some scenes from The Flintstones, like a large cat carrying Fred outside of his house, "obviously none of those things happened in the real world." Obviously. More interestingly, Jon has made fun of the scientific establishment itself, as in a hilarious segment on August 5, 2009, featuring John Oliver arbitrating a dispute between two paleoanthropologists: University of Pittsburgh's Jeffrey Schwartz and New York University's Todd Disotell, disagreeing about the true relationship between humans and other primates.

Schwartz believes (contradicting the pretty much universally accepted notion in biology) that "our closest relative is the orangutan, not the chimpanzee," as he stated in a published paper in the Journal of Biogeography (which, as Oliver drily observed, "hit selected university bookstores"). "It's utterly wrong, we are more closely related to chimps" was Disotell's uncompromising response to Schwartz.

While this is actually a tempest in a teacup (Schwartz is clearly wrong, according to the available evidence and the consensus of the relevant academic community), the segment captures an actual clash between two academic sub-cultures, those anthropologists who rely mainly on physical traits and those who trust chiefly the molecular evidence. Schwartz belongs to the first camp: "Humans and orangs are the only primates that can grin with a closed mouth. We [and orangutans] are the only primates that have a hairline. Humans and orangs tend to copulate face to face." Disotell is equally clearly a member of the second clan: "It goes in the face of all genetic evidence to date. Our entire genome tells us that chimpanzees are indeed more closely related [to humans]. We share over 99% of our DNA with chimps [the actual figure is 98.8%, but who's counting]."

Oliver (rightly) mocks the two scientists throughout, for instance asking Schwartz (in response to a remark of the latter) whether "interesting" means something different in science than in normal life, managing to capture if not the absurdity certainly the self-contained parochialism of the academic world. At one point he asks Disotell how the dispute is going to unfold, to which the scientist answers that he is writing a paper to counter Schwartz's claims, to which Schwartz will likely respond with a paper of his own, to which Disotell will respond ... You get the drift. "And no one will read any of them," says Oliver, to which Disotell candidly responds: "Probably true, unfortunately."

Finally, it is worth noting that Jon and co. sometimes explore the really big questions about science itself, as in a segment by Aasif Mandvi (October 26, 2011) entitled "Science: What's It Up To?" The segment begins with a series of bizarre anti-science quotes from Republican politicians, all Presidential candidates: Herman Cain says that he doesn't believe in global warming; Rick Santorum absolutely denies evolution; and Michelle Bachman claims that vaccines are harmful to human health. Clearly, says Mandvi, science is up to something.

What, exactly, is "science" up to? Enter yet another former Republican Presidential hopeful, Texas Governor Rick Perry: "There are a substantial number of scientists who have manipulated data, so that they will have dollars rolling in to their projects." (If you watch the clip carefully you can actually see Perry hesitating, as if he expects to be contradicted immediately for the inanity and lack of evidence of what he was saying. Or maybe that's my optimistic imagination playing tricks.)

Much of the rest of the segment features an interview with Republican strategist Noelle Nikpour, which is of course hilarious while—yet again—allowing viewers to get a glimpse of what has come to be known as the Republican war on science (the title of the above mentioned book by journalist Chris Mooney, who was in fact a guest on *The Daily Show* [September 12, 2005]). Nikpour makes wild accusations about scientists scheming the American public for financial gain, which Mandvi follows up with the obvious question: "Now, do you have any, I don't want to say, evidence, not data ..." Without losing a beat (and while flagrantly ignoring the question) Nikpour replies: "I think every American, if they really thought about it, would have a gut feeling that some of these numbers that the scientists are putting out, are not right." Clearly, gut feeling trumps evidence, especially when it comes to science.[16]

Nikpour raises a question I have heard from science denialists very often, and which superficially makes perfect sense: why are scientists the only ones qualified to comment on scientific funding?

The implication, of course, is that science is a cabal of self-serving individuals who rubber stamp anything that members of their own community say, for both glory and financial gain. But Mandvi immediately replies with the equally obvious counter to this argument: "It's like why are surgeons the only ones allowed to perform surgeries, and other surgeons are the only ones who get to say whether or not this surgery is necessary or not, right?" "Absolutely." "It doesn't make any sense." "It never makes any sense."

Mandvi cunningly manages to capture on camera yet another common (and so fallacious it really shouldn't be funny) "argument" by science denialists. Here is the full exchange, for your amusement and chagrin.

NIKPOUR: It's very confusing for a child to be only taught evolution, to go home to a household where their parents say "wait a minute," you know, "God created the earth."

MANDVI: What is the point of teaching children facts if it's just going to confuse them?

NIKPOUR: It confuses the children when they go home. We as Americans, we are paying tax dollars for our children to be educated. We need to offer them every theory that it's out there. It's all about choice. It's all about freedom.

MANDVI: I mean it should be up to the American people to decide what's true.

NIKPOUR: Absolutely! Doesn't it make commonsense?

I will leave it as an exercise for the reader to identify the logical fallacies contained in this exchange. Commonsense indeed.

Notes

1.   The trial ended with a resounding victory for the evolution (Plaintiff's) side. Judge Jones, presiding over the case, concluded: "We find that ID fails on three different levels, any one of which is sufficient to preclude a determination that ID is science. They are: (1) ID violates the centuries-old ground rules of science by invoking and permitting supernatural causation; (2) the argument of irreducible complexity, central to ID, employs the same flawed and illogical contrived dualism that doomed creation science in the 1980's; and (3) ID's negative attacks on evolution have been refuted by the scientific community."

2. For example, Carl Sagan, *The Demon-Haunted World: Science as a Candle in the Dark* (New York: Random House, 1995); Stephen J. Gould, *The Panda's Thumb* (New York: Norton, 1992); Richard Dawkins, *The Blind Watchmaker: Why the Evidence of Evolution Reveals a Universe Without Design* (New York: Norton, 1996).

3. Charles Darwin, *On the Origin of Species by Means of Natural Selection: Or, The Preservation of Favored Races in the Struggle for Life* (New York: A.L. Burt, 1910 [1859]).

4. Karl Popper, "Darwinism as a Metaphysical Research Program," in *But Is It Science? The Philosophical Question in the Creation/Evolution Controversy*, ed. Michael Ruse (New York: Prometheus, 1996), 144–155.

5. Karl Popper, "Natural Selection and the Emergence of Mind," *Dialectica* 32 (1978), 339–355, and his letter to *New Scientist* 87 (August, 1980), 611.

6. Patricia Cleland, "Historical Science, Experimental Science, and the Scientific Method," *Geology* 29 (2001), 987–990.

7. For a discussion of the various causes and forms of creationism, see Massimo Pigliucci, *Denying Evolution: Creationism, Scientism and the Nature of Science* (Sunderland, MA: Sinauer, 2002), especially chapter 3.

8. For a discussion of the history and aftermath of the Scopes trial see Pulitzer Prize-winner Edward J. Larson, *Summer for the Gods: The Scopes Trial and America's Continuing Debate over Science and Religion* (New York: Basic Books, 1997).

9. For example, philosopher Paul Feyerabend famously argued that astrology and rain dances have as much a claim to being a source of knowledge as science, and that their dismissal by scientists is motivated by intellectual elitism or downright racism. It's hard to encounter a more irrational view of science and knowledge among professional philosophers. For a more balanced treatment of the positive and the nonsensical in postmodernism's attitude toward truth, see Ian Hacking, *The Social Construction of What?* (Cambridge, MA: Harvard University Press, 1999).

10. Why the panel didn't feature an evolutionary biologist is a mystery that shall go unsolved until Jon Stewart reads this chapter and writes to me about the inner workings of his mind. I won't mention Crystal again, since her rambling was so incomprehensible even Stewart didn't quite know what to do with her!

11. The term refers to the ancient king Pyrrhus of Epirus, who attacked and defeated the Roman legions on two occasions in 279 BCE. However, his losses were so great that they made it impossible for him to continue

the war, which was eventually won by the Romans (who had home field advantage, and could more readily count on fresh troops). According to the Roman historian Plutarch: "The armies separated; and, it is said, Pyrrhus replied to one that gave him joy of his victory that one other such would utterly undo him."

12. This "argument from bad design" is essentially the same that has plagued Christian apologists since Thomas Aquinas, and is a particular version of what is known in theology as the problem of evil.

13. Dawkins' most complete attack on religion can be found in *The God Delusion* (Boston: Houghton Mifflin, 2006).

14. For example: Niall Shanks and Karl H. Joplin, "Redundant Complexity: A Critical Analysis of Intelligent Design in Biochemistry," *Philosophy of Science* 66 (1999), 268–282; Elliott Sober, "The Design Argument," in *The Blackwell Guide to Philosophy and Religion*, ed. William E. Mann (Oxford, Blackwell, 2001), 117–147; and Matt Young and Taner Edis, eds., *Why Intelligent Design Fails: A Scientific Critique of the New Creationism* (New Brunswick, NJ: Rutgers University Press, 2004).

15. For more on intellectuals engaging the general public, see Terrance MacMullan, "Jon Stewart: The New *and Improved* Public Intellectual," in this volume.

16. For more, see Amber L. Griffioen, "Irrationality and 'Gut' Reasoning: Two Kinds of Truthiness," in this volume.

Segment 5

YOUR MOMENT OF ZEN

BEYOND *THE DAILY SHOW*

Chapter 18

America (The Book)
Textbook Parody and Democratic Theory

Steve Vanderheiden

The Daily Show has emerged as one of the most influential media sources for political information, despite the show's status as "fake news." Scholars have observed that the show increases cynicism about politics and the news media, but that it also assists viewers in understanding politics, and so performs an educative as well as critical function.[1] The same reliance on satire and parody as a means of social and political critique is on display in the show's spin-off book, *America (The Book)*,[2] which ostensibly takes the form (in parody) of an American government introductory textbook, promising an analysis of democracy through history and as embodied by contemporary politics. Like the show, the book's primary aim is humorous and playful, but its secondary aim is serious and critical, developing a theory of democracy that warrants examination in its own right, especially given the powerful effect that soft news now has on shaping ideals and influencing social and political opinions.

Both the book and television show aim to hold up a mirror to the contemporary United States. *America* reflects an America whose self-image is often in sharp contrast with its very real shortcomings, absurdities, vanities, and hypocrisy. The book reminds us of our aspirations and illuminates various ways we fall short of our ideals, and does so with a keen sense of humor and critical edge that's anathema to real news programs and many textbooks. The

The Ultimate Daily Show and Philosophy: More Moments of Zen, More Indecision Theory,
First Edition. Edited by Jason Holt.
© 2013 John Wiley & Sons, Inc. Published 2013 by John Wiley & Sons, Inc.

parody and satire *America* relies upon can only work if the objective is something more than pure entertainment and if its target is also something quite serious. To understand the use of humor in achieving this end, we'll look at the philosophy of humor before turning to democratic theory.

Humor with a Point

As Israel Knox notes, "humor is a species of liberation, and it is the liberation that comes to us as we experience the singular delight of beholding chaos that is playful and make-believe in a world that is serious and coercive."[3] Such playful chaos is on abundant display in *America*, as is a thinly veiled recognition of the seriousness of the subjects it parodies but doesn't disown. *America* relies upon the most potentially emancipatory of all forms of humor, satire, letting us laugh at political figures and institutions that palpably affect our lives in ways that are often "serious and coercive."

With political satire in particular, humor can't be disconnected from the broader social project of liberation, and *America*'s subtext contains far more than an attempt to make us laugh at "a jarring incongruity between form and content."[4] We must be able to stand at some critical distance, or we'll fail to appreciate the joke. But we must also feel some sympathy for the thing satirized, Knox suggests, or the sense of indignation that satire contains "would have neither purpose nor direction, and would vent itself in some form of action or invective rather than express itself in some form of art."[5]

The "fake news" format of *The Daily Show* lends itself especially well to political satire, as does *America*'s textbook parody. Geoffrey Baym notes: "Unlike traditional news, which claims an epistemological certainty, satire is a discourse of inquiry, a rhetoric of challenge that seeks through the asking of unanswered questions to clarify the underlying morality of a situation."[6] The conventional textbook conveys a similar certainty, typically only asking questions that are answered elsewhere (as in study questions at the end of a chapter), while *America (The Book)* is replete with unanswered questions (or those answered only with a contrived ignorance that's subversive in its ironic naïveté) that likewise offer the same kind of "rhetoric of challenge." The questions are hard and can't be answered adequately without serious and sometimes disturbing reflection on the current state of the world. But they're questions that must be asked.

Baym concludes that the news satire format should be characterized not as "fake" news (as it conveys much factual political information), but rather "as an alternative model of journalism." In an observation that applies equally well to *America* (which, like the show, seeks a kind of moral clarity through the cognitive clash between familiar form and unexpected content), Baym suggests that satire is here being used "to interrogate power, parody to critique contemporary news, and dialogue to enact a model of deliberative democracy."[7] Not only does *America* "enact" such a model by encouraging a more critical examination of some basic political ideals, its central serious point is a plea for more avenues of deliberative democracy in American government. *America* practices what it preaches.

Similarly, Jamie Warner compares the "dissident" humor employed on *The Daily Show* to the "culture jamming" tactics of *Adbusters*-style media critics, where the mock news format of Stewart's television show "subversively employs emotional and aesthetic modalities similar to those employed by political branding itself, thus interrupting it from within."[8] The mock-textbook format of *America* does the same, providing more than humor through its parody of conventional media. Mimicking the look and feel of a standard government textbook, casual readers do a double-take as they cognitively note the book's satirical features, diffusing the authority of the original and perhaps with that also introducing critical faculties to the scrutiny of other textbooks and their contents.

Unlike the "fake news" of *The Daily Show*, *America*'s target isn't the medium it mocks (the American government textbook). The joke is rather on the state of American political education more generally, which all too often fails to call adequate attention to the gulf between the ideals of freedom and democracy and the much less exalted practice of democracy in the contemporary United States. As Tom Carson notes in his review of *America*, "the book's ultimate joke—on our educational system, if not us in general—is that it's not only more informative about how American government and culture work than the textbooks it burlesques, but gives us a keener sense of having a stake in both."[9] Our stake is made clear in the book's dedication, which reads: "To the huddled masses, keep yearnin'!" In this epithet lie two key thematic messages: that Americans aren't yet able to breathe freely (as the obstacles to liberty and democracy are many and varied), and that this elusive goal (invested with the distinctly American conception of liberty) is still worth striving for.

The contrast between *America* and the conventional textbooks it mocks reveals the book's method. Whereas many social studies textbooks approach their subjects with awe and reverence (the result of which is often an unfortunate lack of critical perspective on the current state of the union), *America* pulls no punches and leaves no sacred icons untouched. Just as it figuratively strips away the shrouds of timid reverence that usually surround textbook discussions of governmental institutions, it *literally* strips away the robes of the Supreme Court justices in "Dress the Supreme Court."[10] *America*'s authors are unafraid to say which part of the empire has no clothes, or to use a doctored photograph of nude justices if necessary in order to make this clear to the rest of us.

Reversing Democracy Inaction

The book's ironic subtitle (*A Citizen's Guide to Democracy Inaction*) calls attention to the disturbing lack of meaningful citizen input into the contemporary political process, and implicitly recommends a far more robust form of democracy than it finds in actual practice. Suppose democracy is merely a process by which citizens occasionally select representatives to govern them. This is a "thin" conception of democracy, where the power of ordinary citizens is limited to a periodic choice between competing slates of elites to be contrasted with "thick," more participatory forms of democracy.[11] According to *America*, the American system ("which neither needs nor particularly wants voters") doesn't come off as particularly democratic, composed as it is of "a president freely chosen from a wide-open field of two men every four years; a Congress with a 99 percent incumbency rate; a Supreme Court comprised of nine politically appointed judges whose only oversight is the icy scythe of Death."[12]

Under "thin" democracy, elections provide the only means of citizen direction and oversight of government, but this assumes at least some popular ability to replace governing elites with their challengers. With elections seemingly unable to perform this role effectively, American democracy might be described as one of "inaction" rather than action.

In a mock infographic on the first page of *America* (supposedly explaining the decline in democratic participation in the US), 23% of citizens say that they're "too tired" to participate, 17% that the "game was on," and 8% that they "had a thing." A further 52% cite the fact that the monetary rewards are unsatisfactory. These excuses are funny because they're not far from the truth. The impression is that we have cause to worry about democracy, as many of our nominally democratic processes struggle to count as even thinly democratic.

Diagnosing the health of contemporary American democracy, declining voter participation is identified as merely a symptom of a larger malaise, yet one that suggests a coming crisis if its underlying causes aren't addressed. Although historians and political scientists have long speculated about the "life cycles" of states, such theories rarely find their way into introductory government texts, given the unsettling prediction of inevitable national decline. Relying on the analogy of human development (from "infancy" through "old age"), *America* presents a two-page graphic of the life cycle of democracy in a remarkably cogent (and humorous) analysis of the growing pains of maturing societies, along with advice for managing them: "Tip: You may also notice dissidents where you formerly had none. Don't worry; this is normal, and they can always be arrested."[13] The reader is implicitly invited to consider in what stage American democracy is now, and what comes next. A little thought leads to the conclusion that we are in the "middle age" category, which *America* characterizes as follows:

> Voter turnout is thinning, your welfare system is bloated, you're completely dominated by corporate interests, and you haven't had a proper election in years. When this happens, a nation may go through a mid-life crisis, seeking solace in superficial "toys," like satellite-based lasers to shoot down missiles or action stars turned politicians.[14]

The satirical tone can't conceal the serious warning: when democracy advances into "old age" (the stage immediately following "middle age"), it becomes dysfunctional, as "the best and the brightest of your nation shun public service," and "by the end, you can't even recognize your own ideals." But such processes are reversible: there is, so to speak, a fountain of youth for democratic regimes that reverses the aging process, breathing new life into areas where genuine democracy is now almost entirely absent. In this way, *America* can be read as a call to *action*, an antidote for "democracy inaction."

More robust forms of citizen participation in public life are widely viewed as an antidote to the sort of decline identified in *America*'s life cycle graphic. The political scientist Robert Putnam describes the processes in question as creating "social capital," an essential ingredient for making democracy work.[15] Without meaningful outlets for civic engagement (including many forms of participation that go far beyond voting and so belong to a "thick" conception of democracy), citizens can lose the capacity to see beyond their narrow selfish interests to a view of the public good. As a result of such interests, public life suffers (as when citizens withdraw from participation). Putnam finds social capital to correlate not only with healthy political institutions, but also with educational quality, economic vitality, and public safety. His research not only agrees with *America*'s assessment of American democracy in decline, but identifies increased citizen participation as the necessary remedy for reversing this decline and restoring public confidence in democratic institutions. Perhaps the projected slide into "Constitutional Robocracy" and other possible post-democratic futures may yet be averted, if Putnam is correct.

Similarly, the political theorist Benjamin Barber notes of our current "thin" version of democracy that "community without participation first breeds unreflected consensus and uniformity, then nourishes coercive conformity, and finally engenders unitary collectivism of a kind that stifles citizenship and the autonomy on which political activity depends."[16] It's only when citizens are able to genuinely participate in self-governance, in a thick, *deliberative* democracy, that democracy can yield the benefits in justice and legitimacy it promises. Deliberation involves the process of interacting with others, attempting to justify one's policy preferences and to persuade others to likewise endorse them as in the public good, rather than merely registering those preferences privately and without interaction or justification (as in voting), and this process of deliberation characteristic of "thick" democracy is widely seen as providing a uniquely legitimate or fair means of resolving disagreement over political issues.[17]

Only when citizens actively participate in democratic deliberation can they acquire the resources to overcome the most divisive conflicts among them. When citizens withdraw from politics the result is intensified and highly polarized conflicts (as *America* recognizes and bemoans). The goal in politics shifts from a search for common ground to a competitive gamesmanship where both sides try to exclude their opponents from power, wresting a temporary advantage at the cost of social stability, reciprocity, and trust. America (the country) has witnessed an upsurge in divisive partisanship, and the diagnosis of its principal causes and likely effects in *America (The Book)* closely tracks those of leading contemporary political theorists.

Indeed, the lack of effective outlets for genuine citizen participation in shaping contemporary American politics resounds as a theme throughout *America*. At various points the text alludes to the power void left by the absence of popular control over institutions of government being filled by such non-democratic (and occasionally anti-democratic) forces as corporate lobbyists. In the chapter on Congress, for example, declining voter turnout is posed as a possible problem for the notion that the legislative branch is beholden to the will of the people. The—ironically suggested—solution is that responsiveness to organized economic interests, rather than public opinion, is identical to democracy itself. Corporations are "the white knights of democracy" that make up for the lack of strong public involvement: "These altruistic entities hire lobbyists whose sole job is to insure, through persuasive argument and financial remuneration, that Congress never forgets the people's wishes."[18] Of lobbyists, the authors satirically point out: "these professionally concerned private citizens can assist our representatives in any last minute changes in language, content, or intent necessary to insure their reelection funds,"[19] alluding to the corruption often associated with such interests.

Not only are elections charged with failing to provide a means by which the people's wishes can be communicated to their representatives in Congress, they can't even provide a basic check on politicians' past performance, given the uncompetitive nature of most elections (in which 96% of incumbents are typically reelected).[20] The authors ironically suggest that this anti-democratic feature was designed to "allow Americans to enjoy the benefits of a lawful and functioning society while only having to think about it once every two to four years—if at all!"[21] and that "it is perhaps a sign of the strength of our republic that so few people feel the need to participate."[22] This repeated dismissal of worries about declining participation betrays a serious concern with the problem.

Government of, by, or for the People?

The lack of meaningful public participation in self-governance isn't *America*'s only critique of contemporary American democracy. A second theme is the narrow range of demographic groups making up the government. A government composed almost exclusively of rich white men tends to reflect the interests of only that small cross-section of the public, and will consequently often fail to appreciate the problems and aspirations of other groups, who may have very different experiences, different challenges, and different political perspectives. Taking aim at such an easy target, *America* is able to emphasize humorously the wide gap between ideals of equality and meritocracy and the reality of privilege and exclusion: "By placing no explicit race, gender, or religious requirement on the presidency, the Founders opened the door to true meritocracy. Why no women, blacks, or non-Christians have answered the Founders' challenge is a mystery, though most indications point to some inherent genetic flaw."[23]

Demographic representation of Americans hasn't been much better in the Senate, which *America* calls attention to in its "Senate Color by Numbers" exercise, where readers are invited to compare the original 1789 Senate with its larger but no more racially diverse 2004 counterpart, a fact further emphasized by the ironic quip: "As the nation grew in ethnic and cultural diversity, the Senate responded by getting bigger."[24] Indeed, the absence of legal restrictions on female or minority candidates paradoxically calls attention to what is widely seen as an inherent flaw in US-style representative democracy. The door to meritocracy may be open, but electoral rules that cater to the majority (single-member districts, winner-take-all elections) ensure that minority electoral preferences, whatever their merits, are granted no real voice within political institutions.

Democracy depends on the ability of political institutions to be responsive to the full range of citizen preferences, not merely to those fitting neatly in the relatively narrow ideological spectrum of the two major political parties. Democratic theorists often call for reform of such electoral rules for just this reason, and describe the two-party system that such rules reinforce as posing an unhealthy constraint on democracy. Among the reforms suggested are replacing single-member districts with multi-member proportional systems, using instant run-off voting systems to allow for preference ordering among candidates, and the related formation of viable third parties.

Although *America* doesn't explicitly mention any such reforms, it tacitly endorses them by bemoaning the two-party system: "together, the two parties function like giant down comforters, allowing the candidates to disappear into the enveloping softness, protecting them from exposure to the harsh weather of independent thought."[25] Likewise, "the two-party system elegantly reflects the bichromatic rainbow that is American political thought."[26] If that "rainbow" is to include more than two colors, it must allow for a more inclusive array of political voices within the institutions of government, rather than maintaining electoral rules stifling true electoral competition. If it fails in this regard, it's sure to add more permanent residents to the political graveyard pictured in *America* in a two-page spread where headstones mark the passing of various short-lived third parties, and where a sign on the garbage can at the graveyard entrance reads "please place wasted votes here."[27]

Mediating the Media

As in *The Daily Show* itself, *America (The Book)* reserves some of its sharpest criticism for the media. The news media is often characterized as a kind of go-between linking the citizenry and the government, transmitting popular preferences and concerns to government officials and keeping citizens informed on public issues. For this reason, the press is often called the "fourth estate" or "fourth branch" of government. Given the relentless skewering of the US news media through the "fake news" format of *The Daily Show* and mockpunditry of alum Stephen Colbert on *The Colbert Report* (not to mention important public appearances by both Stewart and Colbert), one might conclude that no further satire of the mass media is necessary.[28] And indeed, the book's indictment of the press offers the only case of pointed criticism where the contrast between ideals and reality isn't cloaked behind a veil of ironic humor, but is instead presented in a tone of exasperated sarcasm: "A free and independent press is essential to the health of a functioning democracy. It serves to inform the voting public on matters relevant to its well-being. Why they've stopped doing that is a mystery."[29]

Unlike the "mystery" of race and gender uniformity among US presidents, the authors offer several explanations for the media's abdication of this mediating role in democracy. Following several academic and popular studies of recent changes in the mass media, *America* identifies media conglomeration as a prime contributor to this problem, detailing the ever-increasing concentration of media ownership in text and graphics, in which "thousands of uncontrollable, perilously independent media voices were finally organized into a more manageable five."[30] As John Stuart (not Jon Stewart) Mill wrote, competition within the "marketplace of ideas" is necessary for discovering truth,[31] and decreasing competition within the news media bodes ill for the "watchdog" function of the press.

With media ownership concentration comes a disappearing firewall between news content and advertising, increasing editorial control exercised by corporate ownership, declining media independence from powerful corporate interests, and disinvestment from investigative reporting in favor of "synergy" (where putative news content is used to promote advertisers' products). Since citizens rely on the press for the political information that forms the basis for the democratic deliberation characteristic of "thick" democracy, philosophers draw causal links between the development of autonomy (or the capacity of self-governance) and the competition between opposing political ideals that mediating institutions supply in well-functioning democracies.

As Joshua Cohen and Joel Rogers argue, "satisfying the conditions of reasonable deliberation requires that public discussion proceed against a background of alternative coherent views,"[32] but these alternative views are not typically presented by the mass media. Because of changes in media ownership and structure, as *America* notes (following academic critiques), the press can no longer reliably perform the truth-seeking role described by Mill or the oversight function noted above, and is instead a propaganda arm of the government relying, not on its own reporting, but rather on official sources and press releases: "The public remains informed of the good things that the government is up to, and the media is freed up to use its entire arsenal for the next photogenic child's disappearance."[33]

Putting Knowledge to Work

While its obvious purpose is to entertain the reader, *America*'s final chapter reinforces the book's emancipatory ideals. Purporting to compare the United States to other political systems and cultures (collectively referred to as an "international house of horrors"), the authors reveal their project with surprising candor (given the loads of irony elsewhere). They remark: "some of our book's more astute readers may have noticed that in detailing the complex and bewildering institutions that comprise our government, we inadvertently called attention to some slight imperfections in our otherwise perfect Union—inefficiencies, inequities, injustices, absurdities, hypocrisies, and an overall failure to live up to the lofty ideals expressed in our nation's founding documents."[34] The over-the-top ethnocentric portrayals that follow convey another thematic message: the flaws observed in the American system aren't unique, but rather seem endemic to politics everywhere. The proper focus of critical enterprises such as *America*, then, isn't to throw out the imperfect in search of a perfect democracy (which exists nowhere), but to follow the advice of the book's dedication and keep struggling for greater freedom and equality.

The moral of citizen empowerment and action is repeated in the Afterword, which reminds the reader that "democracy, for all its flaws, still offers you and your fellow cold and huddled masses the best chance of improving your lot in life."[35] On the final page, readers are awarded a "Certificate of Completion" that declares them "fully qualified to practice, participate in, or found a democracy." Explaining the last option, *America* points out that, although there's no land available for founding a new democracy from scratch, there are several "fixer-uppers" one might improve. *America* then ends on a strikingly sincere inspirational note: "Now go out there and make your Fathers proud."

Postscript: *Earth (The Book)*

Stewart and his *Daily Show* writers followed up *America* with *Earth (The Book)*, which is billed in its subtitle as "a visitor's guide to the human race."[36] Addressed "To our alien readers,"[37] the book offers satirical insights into Western history and culture as well as politics. In a section introducing the continents, the authors describe North America as "blessed with abundant freshwater and fertile soil, it was settled remarkably quickly thanks to the *extermination* of one race, the *enslavement* of a second and the *can-do attitude* of a third,"[38] and

South America as "the poor man's North America."[39] Readers are invited to further reflect upon this history of oppression in a discussion of the social contracts that are widely regarded as foundational to modern forms of political authority. Of the many contracts, the authors summarize, "Some put power in the hands of one man; others, in the hands of thousands of men. (It was usually men, though. That part rarely changed.)" Pointedly calling into question the progressivism frequently associated with the popular sovereignty of contract theories, they note that each social contract is "subject to constant change and revision" in which "a society that failed to periodically amend outdated provisions regarding how to dress or how much to subjugate women and minorities" might be subject to the ridicule of other elites but would not violate the egalitarian terms of contractualism itself, which requires the assent of those subjugated groups.[40]

Like *America*, *Earth* offers an ironic but impassioned defense of democracy, along with thinly veiled criticism of its historical and contemporary opponents. Monarchy, for example, is described as speaking "to our primal desire for an alpha male who would fight off our enemies, make decisions for us and tear out our throats if challenged," but being "frankly a bit of a crapshoot" in its reliance upon hereditary succession to select leaders.[41] Describing democracy, the fact that "every citizen has a voice in government" is alternately cast as both "the major strength" and "the major weakness" of popular government. Again imploring citizens to take democratic control of their lives through political activism rather than apathy, the authors note the "one great sacrifice" required of democratic citizenship: "a lunch-break trip to an elementary school cafeteria once every two to four years. Generally, this was too much to ask." Challenging readers to reverse these patterns of voter apathy and voluntary disenfranchisement, they suggest that "a democracy's health could best be measured by the number of people who *didn't* vote, thus signaling that they were completely satisfied."[42] Clearly, we should not be so satisfied with our "surprisingly resilient" form of government, acknowledging that the costs of democracy ("short-sighted rule by mob whim, inaction caused by deadlocked interest groups, or your favorite TV shows being pre-empted by some boring debate") pale in comparison with its benefits (granting citizens "control over their own destinies"), and work toward its improvement prior to handing the planet over to our alien successors.

Notes

1. Jody Baumgartner and Jonathon S. Morris, "The *Daily Show* Effect: Candidate Evaluations, Efficacy, and American Youth," *American Politics Research* 34 (2006), 341–367. Baumgartner and Morris also study the educative value of *America (The Book)*, incorporating it into an Introduction to American Government course alongside a standard textbook, finding the "mock" textbook to better engage and interest students but not enhance their learning or improve test scores, in "Jon Stewart Comes to Class," *Journal of Political Science Education* 4, no. 2 (2008), 169–186.
2. Jon Stewart, Ben Karlin, and David Javerbaum, *America (The Book): A Citizen's Guide to Democracy Inaction* (New York: Warner Books, 2004).
3. Israel Knox, "Towards a Philosophy of Humor," *Journal of Philosophy* 48 (1951), 541.
4. G.D. Kiremidjian, "The Aesthetics of Parody," *Journal of Aesthetics and Art Criticism* 28 (2) (1969), 232.
5. Knox, "Towards a Philosophy of Humor," 546.
6. Geoffrey Baym, "*The Daily Show*: Discursive Integration and the Reinvention of Political Journalism," *Political Communication* 22 (2005), 267.
7. Ibid., 261.
8. Jamie Warner, "Political Culture Jamming: The Dissident Humor of *The Daily Show with Jon Stewart*," *Popular Communication* 5 (1) (2007), 19.
9. Tom Carson, "Last Comic Standing," *New York Times* (October 3, 2004), Section 7, 20.
10. Stewart, Karlin, and Javerbaum, *America (The Book)*, 98–99.
11. See Joseph Schumpeter, *Capitalism, Socialism, and Democracy*, 3rd edn. (New York: Harper Perennial, 1962).
12. Stewart, Karlin, and Javerbaum, *America (The Book)*, 1.
13. Ibid., 13.
14. Ibid., 12.
15. "Social capital" is defined as "features of social organization such as networks, norms, and social trust that facilitate coordination and cooperation for mutual benefit," in Robert D. Putnam, *Bowling Alone: The Collapse and Revival of American Community* (New York: Simon & Schuster, 2000), 67.
16. Benjamin Barber, *Strong Democracy* (Berkeley, CA: University of California Press, 1984), 155.
17. See Amy Gutmann and Dennis Thompson, *Democracy and Disagreement* (Cambridge, MA: Belknap Press, 1996).

18. Stewart, Karlin, and Javerbaum, *America (The Book)*, 58.
19. Ibid., 69.
20. Although *America* claims (quoted above) that 99% of Congressional incumbents are reelected, the actual percentage has varied from a low of 87% in 1962 to a high of 98% in 1998, with 96% typical of recent elections (the last is also noted in *America*, 58).
21. Stewart, Karlin, and Javerbaum, *America (The Book)*, 58.
22. Ibid., 117.
23. Ibid., 40.
24. Ibid., 68.
25. Ibid., 107.
26. Ibid., 108.
27. Ibid., 110–111.
28. See Rachael Sotos, "*The Daily Show*: An Ethos for the Fifth Estate," in this volume.
29. Stewart, Karlin, and Javerbaum, *America (The Book)*, 131.
30. Ibid., 151.
31. John Stuart Mill, "On Liberty," in *Utilitarianism, On Liberty, Considerations on Representative Government*, ed. H.B. Acton (Rutland, VT: Everyman's Library, 1972), 90–91.
32. Joshua Cohen and Joel Rogers, "The Principle of Democratic Legitimacy," from *On Democracy* (New York: Viking Penguin, 1983), 149.
33. Stewart, Karlin, and Javerbaum, *America (The Book)*, 154.
34. Ibid., 183.
35. Ibid., 220.
36. Jon Stewart, David Javerbaum, and Rory Albanese, *Earth (The Book): A Visitor's Guide to the Human Race* (New York: Grand Central Publishing, 2010).
37. Ibid., v.
38. Ibid., 6.
39. Ibid., 7.
40. Ibid., 87.
41. Ibid., 94.
42. Ibid., 102.

Chapter 19

A Tea Party for
Me the People
The Living Revolution
Meets the Originalists

Rachael Sotos

America (The Book) begins with a foreword by Thomas Jefferson.[1] That's right, Jon Stewart and the *Daily Show* folks are so bold as to use the name of America's third President to set the stage for their mock high school textbook. *America*'s Jefferson comments (in remarkably current vernacular) that it seems somewhat preposterous that "Irv over at Warner Books" could convince him, *a Founding Father*, to pen the foreword for a book connected to a show that's "not even network." Jefferson explains, however, that he agreed because the book is actually "funny," and because he wants "to dispel some of the mythology." Jefferson says he's tired of all this "worshiping at the altar" of the Framers. Sure, they were "awesome" and "accomplished," but they were also, without a doubt, *imperfect*: "Adams was an unbearable prick and squealed girlishly whenever he saw a bug. And Ben Franklin? ... a boozed-up snuff machine ..." Moreover, *America*'s Jefferson continues, way back at the time of the Founding, the Framers themselves were certainly aware of their fallibility, and they likewise knew that the US Constitution was imperfect. It was for this reason that they allowed for amendments: "because they *amend*!" With righteous indignation, Jefferson responds:

> My point is composing the Declaration of Independence and Constitution was hard work. God didn't dictate it for us to transcribe from

The Ultimate Daily Show and Philosophy: More Moments of Zen, More Indecision Theory, First Edition. Edited by Jason Holt.

some sort of dictation-transcribing machine ... Our purpose was to create a living document based on principles that transcended the times we lived in, and I think we did that. We created a blueprint for a system that would endure, which means your lazy asses shouldn't be coasting on our accomplishments. We were imperfect. It was imperfect. And we expect our descendants to work as hard as we did on keeping what we think is a profoundly excellent form of government supple, evolving and relevant. After reading this book, you should be better prepared to do just that.[2]

When *America*'s Jefferson insists that we get off our bums and work hard to perfect the work of the Framers, he affirms an expansive sense of democratic freedom and political participation. He exhorts us to carry forth the creative, revolutionary spirit ourselves.

Of course, even after a string of Emmys and two Peabodys, not everyone will accept *The Daily Show* as authoritative in any sense. No doubt Papa Bear O'Reilly will still insist that the show is "just for laughs," its audience a bunch of "stoned teenagers."[3] Moreover, some commentators in the popular press and the ivory tower (but mostly the ivory tower) are *fake news skeptics* (those who doubt that comedians can have legitimate cultural authority). And if you, dear reader, should take up some of the many recent academic articles, with all their empirical studies of the fake news "effect," their analyses of "cognitive polysemy" in the "dominant encoded reading" of "tertiary texts," let me suggest you check one thing first.[4] Find out if this particular pontificating pointy head is among those anarchy-fearing satire-skeptics who assume it's necessary to have *an obedient and unquestioning* attitude toward authority. The fact of the matter is, not everyone is as optimistic as Thomas Jefferson about our capacity for independent thinking and creative self-determination. Indeed, there are many who continue to "worship at the altar" of the Founders, believing that citizens should have *an obedient and unquestioning attitude toward authority* (whether it's the authority of the US Constitution, of "the law," the Bible, a Tea Party Manifesto, or custom and tradition).

Now, I don't mean to argue here that there's no legitimate place for conservative views in American politics, for certainly there is. But historically speaking, a strong case can be made that the *Daily Show* folks are on the right track in their presentation of the Framers (perhaps "Framer" is preferable to "Founder," lest we forget that Franklin was "a boozed-up snuff machine"). An unquestioning attitude toward authority doesn't exactly fit the profile of people with highly developed satirical wits, people who were, let's recall, *revolutionaries*. Let's also remember that when George Washington refused to be king, then also refused a third term of office, *he made space for our freedom*. Jefferson, the real Jefferson, was so intent to extend the creative, revolutionary spirit to posterity that he suggested it would be good, despite the impracticality, for *every generation* to experience founding a new political system, to have its own Constitutional Convention.[5]

But just as we often forget what we learn in our school textbooks, it turns out that since the publication of *America* in 2004 there has *not* appeared an uprising of Americans intent to correct and perfect the work of the *fallible* Framers. Rather, the very opposite has happened! Harvard historian Jill Lepore reminds us of the festive spring days in 2009:

> All over the country people turned up wearing tritons and periwigs, cuffed shirts and kersey waistcoats, knee breeches and buckled shoes, dressing as founders, quoting the founders, waving copies of the constitution, arguing that the time for revolution had come again.[6]

Recently the Tea Partiers, "waving copies of the constitution," have had a lot to say about the original work of the American Framers. The hang-up from *America*'s Jefferson's point of view is that these latter-day "revolutionaries" are altar-worshippers extraordinaire, passionate advocates of the claim that the original Founding was *perfect* and the Framers *infallible*. As Lepore explains,

> Historical fundamentalism is marked by the belief that a particular and quite narrowly defined past—"the founding"—is ageless and sacred and to be worshipped; that certain historical texts—"the founding documents"—are to be read in the same spirit with which religious fundamentalist read, for instance, the Ten Commandments; that the Founding Fathers were divinely inspired; that the academic study of history (whose standards of evidence and methods of analysis are based on skepticism) is a conspiracy and furthermore, blasphemy; and that political arguments grounded in appeals to the founding documents, as sacred texts, and to the Founding Fathers, as prophets, are therefore incontrovertible.[7]

There is little to question about individual Tea Partiers' passion and patriotism, though paradoxes abound when we get deeper into the movement's ideology. Who can forget the placard reading "Government out of My Medicare"? How do we make sense of the seemingly incongruous fact that a *populist* movement is agitating *against* the rights of *popular* sovereignty?[8] If you're flummoxed, you aren't alone! Lucky for us *The Daily Show with Jon Stewart* has been entertaining and illuminating, a fountain of anti-fundamentalist insight.

We the People

In 2004, a year before Stephen Colbert coined the word "truthiness," five years before the rise of the Tea Party, Stewart and the folks at *The Daily Show* joked in a "casually oversimplified" way about the theories now broadcast by the "constitution-waving" Tea Party patriots. Later, in *America*'s chapter on the Judiciary there's just a quick reference to legal scholars and judges who interpret the US Constitution "in much the same way as a fundamentalist views the Bible." Stewart and company reassure the reader that these "strict constructionists" "have been endowed by God with the superhuman gift of being able to read the minds of people who died 200 years ago. Naturally, they use this power *only for good.*"[9]

A decade later it seems the joke's on us, unless of course you think that it would be a "*good*" idea to gut the welfare state, shred the social safety net, and forbid democratically elected governments from imposing any environmental regulations on the "free market." The constitutional theory of "strict construction," better known these days as "originalism," is, to reiterate, the theory that the intent of the Framers is knowable, fixed, and final, the incontrovertible word. But now more than just a legal theory, originalism has given form to Tea Party ideology, and has, accordingly, taken on a life of its own. It certainly has animated the US Constitution in recent years. On the eve of the 2010 Congressional elections, with the taste of Tea Party victory in her mouth, Sarah Palin, no stickler for legal, historical, or policy-related detail, tweeted, "This is what happens when our Constitution starts shaking her fist."[10] Altar worshiper extraordinaire Glenn Beck says of the US Constitution: "It's alive. It's like, you know, reading the scriptures. It's like reading the Bible. It is alive today."[11]

To elucidate such passion, Lepore, who spent much of 2009 and 2010 with and among the Tea Partiers, makes their meetings come alive for the reader by patiently drawing out their anxieties and concerns. She also situates the Tea Party within American history and provides essential background information for understanding its significance. Lepore explains that "originalism as a school of constitutional interpretation has waxed and waned and has always competed with other schools of interpretation"; though in the twentieth century, "constitutional scholars generally date the rise of originalism to the 1970s and consider it a response to controversial decisions … especially *Roe v. Wade*."[12] After gestating in dubious think tanks such as the religiously themed, far-right National Center for Constitutional Studies, originalism has become conflated with a non-reflective brand of patriotism (heritage tourism) and completely intertwined with evangelicalism. In Lepore's cogent analysis, the controversial legal theory

> has long since reached well beyond the courts. Set loose in the culture, and tangled together with fanaticism, originalism looks like history but it's not; its historical fundamentalism, which is to history what astrology is to astronomy, what alchemy is to chemistry, what creationism is to evolution.[13]

The fake news' boldest and most thorough response to originalism is *Daily Show* writer Kevin Bleyer's *Me the People: One Man's Selfless Quest to Rewrite the Constitution of the United States*.[14] Bleyer's hilarious and unusually thought-provoking book-length treatment of that curious text, "scribbled," "by farmers," "on animal skin … with the quill of a goose," is a sure reminder of the fallibility of the Framers and a genuine work of historical scholarship in its comedic way: "Any errors, omissions, or exaggerations were made only to prove [a] point."[15] True to the expansive sense of democratic freedom and political participation affirmed in *America (The Book)*, as well as the principle of constitutional emendation, in *Me the People* our buddy T.J. no longer speaks in "remarkably current vernacular." Instead, Bleyer does the work of actual history. In their own voices, the Framers exhort us to our revolutionary tasks in the face of such an imperfect founding document: "mere thing of wax" (Jefferson); "squinting toward monarchy" (Patrick Henry); a "dead letter" (Madison); "a child of fortune," "less perfect than it can be made" (Washington).[16] The truth should be told, and Bleyer will tell it: the original US Constitution was not divinely inspired; it was beloved by *none* of its signers, was insufficiently egalitarian, and failed to achieve either democratic representation or the protection of important individual liberties. Full of "misspells," "typos," in need of major emendations, it was designed to "insure domestic tranquility," but caused the Civil War instead![17] To those who would make the original US Constitution an infallible object of altar worship, Bleyer counters with the comic spirit of a revolutionary patriot. He recalls the dark days of the American Revolution, when the "marauding redcoats" were coming; in Philadelphia the resourceful colonists hid the Liberty Bell "under a pile of horse manure." *The Daily Show* moral of the story: "sometimes, in order to save something we cherish, we have to shit on it."[18]

Bleyer goes pretty far in demystifying the whole "Miracle at Philadelphia." He finds, not "demigods" but " a combative group of exhausted, drunken, broken, petty, partisan, scheming, squabbling, bloviating … sensory-deprived, under-oxygenated, fed-up, talked-out, overheated delegates so distraught … they threatened violence, secession."[19] Giving us just enough of the sausage-making minutiae of American history to make it real, *and really fascinating*, Bleyer proceeds with his irreverent revision sequentially: through "One Preamble, seven Articles, and twenty-seven Amendments."[20] Just as importantly, we simultaneously join him on an adventure in the actual world, ostensibly following him on a personal quest for a *living* relation to the founding documents. We journey to Greece, the site of the original democracy, a fascination to the Framers. As tourists among our fellow Americans in America, we discover heritage tourism sites such as Independence Hall in Philadelphia and the National Archives in Washington DC: "When it is your turn to approach the Constitution … please keep in mind: it is for *viewing* not for *reading*."[21] Bleyer takes us to states big and small (including the "hated" Rhode Island); to the competing constitutional theories of Supreme Court Justices Stephen Breyer and Antonin Scalia, and of course to Tea Parties. In a fitting gesture to his chapter on the Second Amendment, Bleyer introduces us to Michael Holler, a Christian-college-educated, NRA-certified handgun instructor whose "The Constitution Made Easy" is the "edition" officially endorsed by the Tea Party Express, the largest chapter of the Tea Party. Of course the US Constitution itself isn't very long, but apparently our periwig-sporting latter-day revolutionaries prefer to absorb "the whole … in under 30 minutes." They're "up in arms" about their constitutional rights, but often "have not read the Constitution … they've read the Cliff's Notes—if Cliff were a Bible-reading gun nut."[22]

While Bleyer may find it funny that the far right has such a loose connection to a text it deems infallible and incontrovertible, we shouldn't confuse his playful mockery with a defense of the absolute sanctity and inviolability of the US Constitution per se. Throughout *Me the People*, our buddy T.J., the anti-originalist *par excellence*, is a constant source of inspiration. Jefferson is Bleyer's alpha and omega, and, not incidentally, the least favorite Framer among Tea Partiers and originalists.[23] Bleyer reminds us that our third president was such a firm believer in the principle of founding document emendation that he took it upon himself to rewrite the Bible—*twice*. In *The Philosophy of Jesus*, Jefferson himself explains that in order to liberate the Bible from all the mysteries and dubious dogmas, including miracles, the virgin birth and the Resurrection, he followed a specific method. Scissors in hand, it was a matter of literally "cutting verse out of the printed book ... arranging the matter which is evidently His, and which is distinguishable as diamonds in a dunghole."[24] That's right! The Constitution is crap and much of the Bible "a dunghole!"

Bleyer takes inspiration from more than Jefferson's wild biblical ways. As mentioned above, Jefferson was so committed to the principle of constitutional revision that he imagined that a constitutional convention be held every 19 years. In this way the US Constitution would always be rewritten, "by the living generation." Here Bleyer finds *the* leitmotif of *Me the People*. Again and again we'll discover him characterizing his own comic constitutional meanderings as "the long-overdue fulfillment of Thomas Jefferson's dream."[25] So Bleyer cites Jefferson's words in a famous letter to Madison: "by the law of nature, one generation is to another as one independent nation is to another ... The earth belongs to the living and not the dead."[26] For an anti-originalist like Jefferson, the authority of the founding documents is so much dead weight: "each generation" should "choose for itself the form of government it believes most promotive of its own happiness."[27]

One might think Jefferson's call to every living generation is impractical, downright quixotic. Even more ridiculous is Bleyer's "selfless quest" to rewrite the US Constitution himself. At least one important point can be made in Bleyer's defense, however, for *Me the People* doesn't remain at the level of theory. The chapter on the Judiciary, devoted to Bleyer's improbable lunch with Supreme Court Justice Antonin Scalia, the Justice most closely associated with the controversial constitutional theory of originalism, is the clear climax of the book. It is a brilliant character study, comparable to Dostoyevsky's depiction of the Grand Inquisitor in *The Brothers Karamazov*, and worthy of whatever awards are granted to the best comic treatment of constitutional history and theory. Picture for yourself Stephen Colbert's "Better Know a District," but instead of banter with a lowly Representative that typically devolves into absurdity, Bleyer meets the longest-serving Justice head on, in a great, if absurdly improbable, contest, "a matter of life and death." Scalia, "was just doing his job: protecting the Constitution of the United States. And I was just doing mine: dismantling it to its very foundations. He was Darth Vader protecting the Death Star; I was Luke Skywalker out to destroy it."[28]

Scalia comes off as a slippery character for sure. Although a darling of the Tea Party, a conservative Catholic, and a man who likely "would trade his robe for some buckled shoes and a periwig," evangelicalism does not permeate his legal reasoning. His belief that the US Constitution should mean what it did in 1789 appears at first simple: what was permitted then can be permitted now (medieval forms of torture may be stupid, but they're not "unconstitutional"). But here's the rub: even if Scalia is not an *evangelical* originalist, in Bleyer's character study he still suffers from the occupational hazards of fundamentalism. Having authorized himself to ignore external reality, to disregard little inconveniences like "the current mores of contemporary society," "evolving standards," his normal human responses have become stunted; "regarding torture … he shows little mercy." Instead of imagination or empathy, Scalia is "immovable"; he doesn't "suffer fools." His constant refrain is "No big deal. *Get over it.*"[29]

And believe you me, though infamously a jokester, Scalia is the enemy and Bleyer is not shy in his presentation. The Justice appears akin to a mafia enforcer; "it's not too hard to imagine he could have a man killed and then somehow prove the murder was constitutional."[30] He may claim that a judge needs to remain open to persuasion, but like Ahab in *Moby Dick*, Scalia appears fully prepared to be "dragged to the depths of the sea by his obstinacy."[31] Bleyer finds his senses on high alert discovering Scalia's oddities. Ever jovial, ever indifferent to suffering, Scalia says, "the Constitution is dead"; "his way of saying hello, perhaps."[32] For Scalia, not only is the Constitution dead, but this is "a good thing." For insofar as a Constitution is living, as Scalia himself has explained, it can develop and change. This means only one thing to Scalia: "the *living* Constitution … 'will *destroy* the Constitution.' Not violate—*destroy*. By that logic, those who subscribe to the concept of a *living constitution* aren't just fools; they are accomplices."[33]

Bleyer does have allies in his battle, "accomplices," by Scalia's lights. True, the Canadians, who think of their constitution as a living document, cannot offer too much help (and it's not surprising that Scalia insists that American judges not be influenced by international legal theory). Nor Plato, though he philosophizes in his final work, the *Laws*, in similar *living* terms. It is our buddy T.J., the president who would defer to "the living generation," who most inspires Bleyer. And standing in the background is Supreme Court Justice Stephen Breyer, whom we learn has met with Bleyer "off the record."[34] As a *living constitutionalist*, Justice Breyer offers a constitutional theory that connects old T.J. with the present. In true *Daily Show* form, Bleyer does his best to dramatize what would surely seem dull to anyone but the most diehard political junky with nothing better to do than watch cable TV. It's C-SPAN's version of a Foreman-Ali fight:

> The Originalist v. the Living Constitutionalist.
> The Aggression in the Session.
> The Rough Sport in the High Court.[35]

Just the opposite of Scalia, Justice Breyer interprets the constitution with a *living* spirit of *active liberty*. However inegalitarian and compromised the original document was (and arguably still is given the electoral college, proportional representation, bicameralism, the difficulty of the amendment process, and so on), Justice Breyer teaches that "the Framers did not abandon their basically democratic view. That is the main point. They wrote a Constitution that begins with the words 'We the People'."[36] And though Justice Breyer does not directly join the fray, we may trust that he is a *Daily Show* ally in that his interpretive principles likewise affirm an expansive sense of democratic freedom and political participation; basically the view that the US Constitution, "created a governmental structure that reflected the view that sovereign authority originated in the people; the 'right to legislate is originally in every Member of the Community'."[37] Just as Jefferson embraced the *living generation*, and as Justice Breyer infuses his interpretation of the US Constitution with this *living* Jeffersonian spirit of *active liberty*, so Kevin Bleyer seeks "to breathe new life into the document."[38]

Anti-History

One can only wonder what Jefferson and the other Framers would think of us, their American progeny. Suppose Franklin's wish to be preserved in a vat of Madeira wine had been granted, and he awoke in the spring of 2009 and met the Tea Partiers "wearing tritons and periwigs, cuffed shirts and kersey waistcoats, knee breeches and buckled shoes." Would our "boozed-up snuff machine" think he'd just been asleep awhile, or maybe that some cosmic entity was playing a joke? What would General Washington think of the costumed patriots John Oliver met in Morristown, New Jersey on April 15, 2009? It's the city where Thomas Paine wrote "Common Sense," but judging by our favorite Senior British Correspondent's interviews, that most precious faculty didn't come complementary with the tritons and periwigs—unless you believe the Obama Administration in 2009 was *a greater tyranny* than the British Empire in 1773. To this query the Morristown Tea Partiers answered: "Worse!" "It's a toss up!"

Naturally offended that the honor of "despot" be "given to Obama for "a 3% tax hike," John Oliver fumes with righteous indignation, "we were tyrannical beyond this government's dreams!" Did the Tea Partiers have any inkling of the medieval torture device known as "the pear of anguish," "the logistical nightmare" implied in killing "30 million Indian people," "no modern warfare, having to go one by one?" Oliver asks, "Does it *feel* like taxation without representation?" Tea Partier: "It really does." Oliver: "But, even though it isn't." Partier: "Well *it is* in the sense that they are not representing my opinions." Oliver: "Okay, but it *isn't* in the sense that *you have* representation" (April 16, 2009).

At the risk of restating the obvious, consider how Professor Lepore's detailed history concretizes our Senior British Correspondent's playful mockery:

> [The] complaint about taxation without representation followed the inauguration of a president who won the electoral vote 365 to 173 and earned 53 percent of the popular vote. In an age of universal suffrage, the citizenry could hardly be said to lack representation.[39]

Lepore's analyses in *The Whites of their Eyes* make sense of a lot of wacky stuff which might otherwise seem inexplicably bizarre, *truthiness on steroids*, if you will. George Washington, according to Glenn Beck, was "opposed to socialism."[40] The Liberty Tree about which Sean Hannity "lectures" in his Fox News special on the Stamp Act Rebellion is *the very same* tree that the government today is presently "picking clean."[41] According to Lepore, Tea Party historical fundamentalism is *not* an evocation of the past like so many others seen before in the course of American history. Tea Party "history" is not just "kooky history," but "*anti*-history." Tea Party logic, as she demonstrates in anecdote after anecdote, *literally cancels historical time*; "in antihistory, time is an illusion." It is not simply that the battles of the present are *analogous* to those of the past, *they are the very same battles*; "Either we're there, two hundred years ago, or they're here, among us ... 'here today' ... 'all around us'."[42]

As an historian Lepore is understandably irritated by the far right's wacky brand of truthiness, their continual haranguing that we have "forsaken" the Framers and that "they're rolling over in their graves because of the latest, breaking political development."[43] From the vantage point of a professional historian, anti-history is *very convenient*, politically. Those divinely inspired "Founding Fathers" who are so kind as to *immediately and absolutely* authorize the Tea Party's present holy war against "big government" are free from the constraints of academic discourses. Nor does their divine authorization impose any uncertainty regarding the task of getting the relationship to the past right: "antihistory has no patience for ambiguity, self-doubt, and introspection."[44] This is not to suggest, however, that Lepore puts the blame for anti-history on the far right and their phony evangelical histories alone. Actual history, the long centuries of pain, suffering and struggle that have made America what it is, are indeed blotted out in originalist truthiness gone wild (like Stephen Colbert, Tea Partiers don't seem to see race), but such amnesia has only been possible because American historians *have failed*. At some point in the last few decades, Lepore writes, professional historians *abandoned* their public responsibility, reneged on their obligation, "to tell a big story," to frame "the relationship between the past and the present" in terms meaningful and intelligible to a general audience. It was only then, she explains, that the white conservatives who felt *betrayed* by secular liberal orthodoxy began to get their historical needs met in the white-washed anti-history texts of the evangelical-originalists, "outside of argument" and without "interest in evidence."[45]

In many, many respects Jill Lepore's *The Whites of Their Eyes* mirrors *Me the People*. Even more steeped in American history than the quite learned comedy writer Bleyer, Lepore joins the chorus of living constitutionalists. Whether she could abide Bleyer's irreverence is another question; scatology isn't the most obvious means by which historians and legal scholars "cherish the stability of the law and the durability of the Constitution."[46] But props to old T.J. and *The Daily Show*'s *America*. *Me the People* takes on originalist historical fundamentalism as constitutional theory *and as history*. Consider it this way: although Bleyer's comedic historical method is radical, *Me the People* excels just where it counts for Lepore. In fact, Bleyer takes up precisely where Lepore believes professional historians have left off. Grounded in American history (and he has the footnotes to prove it, though he doesn't bug us with them), Bleyer narrates the relation between the past and present in a manner both meaningful and accessible to a general audience: *the US Constitution is broke and he is gonna fix it!* But further, note that *Me the People* is written in an experimental style that has great potential to capture the historical imagination. *Me the People* is something new: constitutional history that reads like a twenty-first-century version of *On the Road*. It's a new genre in fake news, part existentialist *Bildungsroman* and part gonzo journalism (albeit *comically* enhanced rather than pharmaceutically, as one might expect from the great Hunter S. Thompson).

Both Lepore and Bleyer do their part to debunk originalist antihistory. Lepore tells three stories at once, of the present, of the recent past, and the much more distant eighteenth century, dwelling upon, instead of ignoring, "the passage of time."[47] Bleyer, perhaps in a manner *too enlivened* for Lepore (it's doubtful that Page Six tabloid style history gets you tenure at Harvard any faster than evangelical originalism), meets anti-intellectualism at an even more fundamental level. Sure *Me the People* is a fun book on American history, but it doesn't directly advocate high-falutin historical reflection. It rather prods the reader *comically*, by exploiting the comedic value of the fact that so few Americans *read* the Constitution: "in 2006, according to a Zogby poll, more American teenagers could name the Three Stooges than the three branches of government."[48] And in more dramatic moments, as when Justice Scalia "looks up from his salad" and *interrogates* Bleyer: "'You've been *reading* the Constitution'." Bleyer can't tell "if he means it as a compliment—as, *Have you been working out?*—or an accusation—*You've been drinking again, haven't you?"* Bleyer responds, "A little."[49]

What might seem pretty meager material—the reading habits of Americans—provides Bleyer with a veritable comedic cornucopia. Simply put, because so few Americans read the founding documents, pretty much everyone fails to have a living relationship with the texts, and this, believe it or not, is funny. We meet Arianna Huffington, the left-wing founding mother of social media, and find she isn't much of a constitutional thinker. In response to Bleyer's "epic" email querying about the constitutional history of her native Greece, Bleyer receives but one short *text* message: "Oooh I loooooove Crete. Sent from my Blackberry."[50] A parallel discovery is made in Bleyer's encounter with David Rubenstein, the multi-billionaire left-wing philanthropist who recently purchased a copy of the Magna Carta to be put on display for the American people in the National Archives. It is surely for the better that Bleyer never actually shares with Rubenstein his ridiculous idea that somehow, "if only Rubenstein would buy him the Constitution," then "he could rewrite all over the darn thing."[51] The comic point obviously enough is that neither giving nor owning *a thing* has anything to do with the *living* spirit of the document. An analogous truth is revealed by a character we meet in the East Village, one "John Hancock," a "revolutionary fetishist" whose own signature incidentally matches the one on the US Constitution. Bleyer reports that John Hancock "gets a kick" out of signing his name.[52]

With all this mockery it might seem that pointy heads like Professor Lepore and the folks at *The Daily Show* look down upon the Tea Partiers and originalists with scorn, but dehumanizing meanness isn't intended. In *Me the People* Bleyer proves his Jeffersonian *bona fides* with equal opportunity attacks across the political spectrum. Moreover, the most laughs in *Me the People* come at Bleyer's own expense, as he presents himself, not as a scholarly expert, but rather as a twenty-first century Don Quixote, comically fantasizing about stealing the Constitution from the National Archives, attempting to make the Preamble "rhyme," ridiculously subjecting himself to the indignities of the heritage tourism, himself signing a *"fake* Constitution" with "a real parchment feel."[53] Remember, the Constitution "is for *viewing* not for *reading*."[54]

Lepore also shows a human side, not the least as she interweaves anecdotes about her elementary-school-age children and becomes personally close with the Tea Party folk she accompanies in 2009 and 2010. She finds "something heartbreaking" in her companions' unreflective nostalgia. I quote the following lines at length as they are very close to the script of John Oliver's video segment broadcast on January 5, 2010:

> Behind the Tea Party's Revolution lay a nostalgia for an imagined time—the 1950s maybe, or the 1940s—less riven by strife, less troubled by conflict, less riddled with ambiguity, less divided by race. In that nostalgia was the remembrance of a childhood, a yearning for a common past, bulwark against a divided present, comfort against an uncertain future.[55]

Perhaps by chance, perhaps serendipity, John Oliver's piece, "Even Better Than the Real Thing," tells an almost identical story of "nostalgia for an imagined time." Via three Fox News personalities, Beck, Hannity, and O'Reilly, Oliver's montage follows a parallel turn in the performances of each broadcaster, from apocalyptic despair (the demise of "the world we knew") toward nostalgia, nostalgia for *a better, simpler time.* Oliver, as if in sync with Lepore, briefly explores whether the decade of each man's youth really was *the best time* in American history: the '70s for Beck; '60s for Hannity; '50s for O'Reilly. Foiled in his faux pursuit of simpler, better days as he finds polio, the A-bomb, botched abortions, gas lines, inflation, and the war in Vietnam, Oliver next follows a hook he finds in the nostalgic rant of each. Beck, Hannity, and O'Reilly each evoke the time of childhood. Oliver is suddenly enlightened: "the best time in American history" was when "they were all children. It was a better time because they were all six years old!" The segment ends with Oliver and a young boy, Eddie, watching Glenn Beck crying for his country. In fewer words, Eddie matches Lepore's analysis:

EDDIE: Why is he crying?
OLIVER: Well you don't understand yet because you're too young, but someday you'll be crying like a little girl on television for the America you've lost.
EDDIE: No I won't!
OLIVER: Yes you will!
EDDIE: No I will not!
OLIVER: Yes you will do that! Glenn Beck has mythologized his childhood so much he has completely lost touch with reality.
EDDIE: Why can't he go to school *to learn?*
OLIVER: I don't know why he can't, Eddie. That's a good question. That's a really good question.

Notes

1. Jon Stewart, Ben Karlin, and David Javerbaum, *America (The Book): A Citizen's Guide to Democracy Inaction* (New York: Warner Books, 2004).
2. Ibid., x.
3. Barbara Walters' *20/20* interview (September 22, 2006).
4. It seems to me that academic literature that analyses *The Daily Show* with highly technical language practically begs for good-natured ribbing. The present citation concerning allegedly absent "cognitive polysemy" is from fake news skeptic Elena D. Neascu, "Political Satire and Political News: Entertaining or Accidentally Reporting, or Both? The Case of *The Daily Show with Jon Stewart*," Ph.D. Thesis, Rutgers University (2011), http://mss3.libraries.rutgers.edu/dlr/showfed.php?pid=rutgers-lib:33960, last accessed February 6, 2013.
5. Jefferson's letter to Samuel Kercheval, July 12, 1816, quoted in Hannah Arendt, *On Revolution* (New York: Penguin, 2006 [1963]), 226. Also essential is Jefferson's letter to Madison (September 6, 1789), discussed below.
6. Jill Lepore, *The Whites of Their Eyes: The Tea Party Revolution and the Battle over American History* (Princeton, NJ: Princeton University Press, 2010), 6.
7. Ibid., 16.
8. Jared A. Goldstein, "Can Popular Constitutionalism Survive the Tea Party?" in *Northwestern University Law Review* 105 (2011), 288–299, www.law.northwestern.edu/lawreview/colloquy/2011/11, last accessed February 6, 2013.
9. *America (The Book)*, p. 87 (my emphasis). We should note that in the same short blurb legal scholars and judges on the left side of the American political spectrum are likewise mocked in "casually oversimplified" fashion: "a judicial activist sees the Constitution as a living document that can be adapted and re-interpreted to protect the needs of a changing society, such as 'marriage between sodomites' and 'impulse abortions'."
10. Cited in Lepore, *The Whites of Their Eyes*, 168.
11. *The Glenn Beck Show*, Fox News (May 7, 2010). Cited in Lepore, *The Whites of Their Eyes*, 157.
12. Ibid., 118–119.
13. Ibid., 123–124.
14. Kevin Bleyer, *Me the People: One Man's Selfless Quest to Rewrite the Constitution of the United States* (New York: Random House, 2012).
15. Ibid., 3, vi.

16. Ibid., 8–10.
17. Ibid., 10–11.
18. Ibid., 15.
19. Ibid., 82.
20. Ibid., 309.
21. Ibid., 97.
22. Ibid., 232.
23. The presentation of Jefferson among far-right thinkers is interesting. At the outset of *The Whites of Their Eyes* Lepore discusses the 2009 controversy over school curriculum in Texas, where among many things there was a disavowal of the separation between church and state and an elevation of the sanctity of property over popular sovereignty: "Thomas Jefferson ... was removed. The United States, called in the old curriculum, a 'democratic society,' was now to be referred to as a 'constitutional republic'" (13). The same basic elements are at the core of the many Tea Party manifestos.
24. Ibid., 15.
25. Ibid., 309.
26. Ibid., 29.
27. Ibid., 309.
28. Ibid., 132.
29. Ibid., 139–140.
30. Ibid., 131.
31. Ibid., 145.
32. Ibid., 138.
33. Ibid., 145.
34. Ibid., 158.
35. Ibid.
36. Justice Stephen Breyer (November, 2004). *Active Liberty: Interpreting our Democratic Constitution,*" Lecture presented at Harvard University, www.tannerlectures.utah.edu/lectures/documents/Breyer_2006.pdf, last accessed February 6, 2013. Note: Justice Breyer has since expanded on this lecture in his book *Active Liberty: Interpreting our Democratic Constitution* (New York: Random House, 2005).
37. Ibid., 13.
38. Bleyer, *Me the People*, 138.
39. Lepore, *The Whites of Their Eyes*, 7.
40. Ibid., 64 (*The Glenn Beck Show* [May 7, 2010]).
41. Ibid., 8 (*The Hannity Show* [May 6, 2009]).
42. Ibid.
43. Ibid., 15.
44. Ibid.

45. Ibid., 96. A key figure is Tim LaHaye, an evangelical minister and author of a series of bestselling apocalyptic novels. In 1987 he published *The Faith of Our Founding Fathers* (Brentwood, TN: Wolgemuth and Hyatt, 1987). Here we see the dangerous side of truthiness for history: LaHaye and similar thinkers simply pretend the Framers had no the secular side. It would be an error to underestimate the pervasiveness of these views or the passion with which they are held.

46. Lepore, *The Whites of Their Eyes*, 124.

47. Ibid., 18–19.

48. Bleyer, *Me the People*, 4.

49. Ibid., 144.

50. Ibid., 28.

51. Ibid., 184.

52. Ibid., 198.

53. Ibid., 95.

54. Ibid., 97.

55. Lepore, *The Whites of Their Eyes*, 97.

Chapter 20

Neologization à la Stewart and Colbert

Jason Holt

> *'Twas not by ideas,—by Heaven; his life was put in jeopardy by words.*
>
> Laurence Sterne, *Tristram Shandy*

> *He knows English real well, and can do near about any thing but speak it.*
>
> Thomas Chandler Haliburton, *The Clockmaker*

Coming up with new words is rarely necessary, sometimes useful, and very often fun. Few pleasures can rival that of minting new linguistic coin. Now you may be thinking, "Come on, '*neologization?*' There's no call for that." Well, I'd considered going with "neologismry" or even "neologistry," but a little googling revealed that I'd been beaten to both punches. Besides, "neologization" is an established word, though not an often-used one. By contrast, when *The Simpsons*' schoolteacher Mrs. Krabappel asks her colleague whether "embiggens" is legitimate lingo, Miss Hoover replies, "It's a perfectly cromulent word."[1] I'm glad better judgment prevailed when I titled this chapter, but I'm also glad—and you are too—that it often doesn't when the *Daily Show* team writes their scripts, and this goes double for *The Colbert Report*, where the neologisms fly. Although both shows are habitually wordplayful, both hosts

The Ultimate Daily Show and Philosophy: More Moments of Zen, More Indecision Theory,
First Edition. Edited by Jason Holt.
© 2013 John Wiley & Sons, Inc. Published 2013 by John Wiley & Sons, Inc.

punsters extraordinaire, there's no doubt who the master word-coiner is—Stephen Colbert.

"Neologism" means *new word*, derived from the Greek "*neo*" (new) and "*logos*" (word). The term can also refer to new meanings that are given to old words (which we might call "paleologisms"), but it's neologisms in the first sense that concern us in this chapter. Philosophers of language often focus attention on features of natural languages (like English) that are already established, already in use. They also focus on idealized, "timeless" visions of what language is or might be. Even when the dynamic, evolving features of language are acknowledged, however, the prevailing view that a language is something "received" tends to marginalize the significance of such dynamic features of language as coining new words. This is a pity. On a practical level, neologisms run the gamut from the atrocious (think of the unknown coiner responsible for "irregardless") to the sublime (think of Milton coining "Pandemonium" in *Paradise Lost*), and it would be useful to know why this is. On a more theoretical plane, as every word was a neologism at some point, figuring out how words become words at all—how something becomes a meaningful word in a language—will enrich our understanding of language in general, of what it means to mean. It will also help us figure out what's going on in some of the best *Daily Show* and *Colbert Report* humor.

Humpty Dumpty and the French Academy

How do words get to have the meanings that they do, how do they become the words they are? A traditional answer to this question reflects a common view of how communication works. Say I'm dining with Jon Stewart, and I want him to pass the salt. I can express this desire in words: "Please pass the salt." I encode my thoughts in language, and he decodes the message to understand my thoughts. What seems to give meaning to the message is the mind behind it, because I succeed in being understood by Stewart when he comes to know my thoughts, my intentions. But the words I use to express my thoughts already have meanings that can be found in any dictionary. It's my knowledge of English that allows me to encode my thoughts in it, Stewart's that allows him to decode the message. I know the language to the extent that I can use it properly.

To help sort out what's going on, we'll consider the sometimes conflicting roles played by dictionaries, which on the one hand *regulate*, in certain ways, how words are used, and on the other merely *report* such use, informing people about the meanings of words that predate, and so don't depend on, their inclusion in the lexicon. We'll look at these roles to see where the tension comes from and how neologisms seem to get caught in the middle.

Dictionaries regulate word use in several different ways. They identify which words, usually slang (such as "ain't" which, contrary to schoolyard wisdom, *is* in the dictionary) and unfortunate word-manglings (such as "irregardless," a botched mix of "irrespective and "regardless") are simply bad form. These words are meaningful, of course, but their use is almost never appropriate. Dictionaries also set standards, in the form of definitions, for correct and incorrect use of words. Correct use conforms to the definitions, incorrect use doesn't. An exchange between Alice and Humpty Dumpty in Lewis Carroll's *Through the Looking-Glass* is worth mentioning. At one point Humpty Dumpty's peculiar use of "glory" mystifies Alice. After a lot of truth-pulling, he reveals that by "glory" he means "a nice knock-down argument." "When *I* use a word," Humpty explains, "it means just what I choose it to mean—neither more nor less," to which Alice replies: "The questions is ... whether you *can* ..."[2] The apparent absurdity of Humpty's position—that a word's meaning is determined by the speaker's intentions in using it—reflects how dictionaries govern proper and improper word use.[3] Humpty Dumpty *can't* make "glory" mean "a nice knock-down argument" just like that. (Anticipating Colbert here? Good.)

Another way dictionaries are used to regulate words is to set limits, not on good or bad form, not on proper or improper use, but on the scope of meaningful items in the language, on what counts as a word at all. Think of playing Scrabble. A challenged play in Scrabble is considered guilty until proven innocent. If the dictionary doesn't confirm that the offered word is acceptable, it's deemed unacceptable, *not* a legitimate word, and the play doesn't count. In an episode of *Seinfeld*, Kramer advises Jerry's mother to play "quone" in a game of Scrabble. When Jerry challenges the word (successfully), Kramer retorts, "Nah, we need a medical dictionary! If a patient gets difficult, you *quone* him."[4] Clearly not a legitimate word. Although Scrabble is a game, and an artificial context for deciding what does and doesn't count as a word, everyday word use is often put to the same kind of Scrabble-style test. If you claim that a certain alleged word is legitimate, many people will often cite its absence in a dictionary as reason to believe it isn't. An extreme example is the Académie Française, the French Academy, an elite group that—believe it or not—presumes to *decide* what does or doesn't count as a word in French. If the French Academy says "*Non*" to something, even if commonly used by most French speakers, it's deemed to have no meaning in the language, to be, in other words, not a word at all. (Colbert, you can tell, would be grinding his teeth by now.)

What's gone wrong here is that we've neglected the other important function of dictionaries, which is to report how words are commonly used, presenting their meaning after the fact. In an episode of the Britcom *Blackadder*, Dr. Samuel Johnson boasts that his just-completed dictionary contains every single word in the English language, and in response Blackadder wishes Dr. Johnson his enthusiastic "contrafibularities." Johnson, clearly upset, scribbles the alleged word in his manuscript. To rub it in, Blackadder then claims to be "anaspeptic, frasmodic, even compunctuous to have caused [Johnson] such pericombobulations."[5] Clearly Blackadder's intent in using such word-like nonsense—which resembles real words plausibly enough— is to deflate the chuffed Johnson. But it also illustrates the important point that in reporting common usage, that is, the meaning of words as used, dictionaries must always play catch-up. That's why Johnson's boast is an empty one. Given the dynamic nature of language, word use always outstrips the best attempts to report it.

To capture the conflicting roles of dictionaries, and to throw neologisms into the mix, consider Colbert's discussion in *America (The Book)* of what it takes to set a legal precedent. First, he says, have something bad happen to you, but not any of those things the law already covers: "They've already been precedented. 'Is "precedented" even a word?' you may ask. Well, it is now, Noah-fucking-Webster. I just precedented it."[6] The humor here is multi-layered. First, there's no good reason to coin a new word, to prefer "They've already been precedented" to "They already have precedents." Second, there's the circularity of using the alleged word in arguing that it really *is* a word. Third, there's the sense that since "unprecedented" is a common word, "precedented" ought to be too, only it isn't—likewise "kempt" and "evitable" versus the more common "unkempt" and "inevitable." Fourth, "precedented" actually *is* a word, although, like "unprecedented," it's an adjective, not a verb as Colbert uses it. Fifth, the attempt to coin "precedented" is the linguistic equivalent of trying to set a legal precedent, one that, if successful, would include *itself* in the range of things it referred to. Colbert would be able to brag that he'd precedented "precedented." Sixth, this is a terse satire ("tersatire" maybe?) of not only unnecessary word coining, but also using dictionaries to regulate word use artificially, which in the extreme effectively closes the door on coining—or any other changes in meaning—altogether. Colbert's outrage, as we could imagine it vented here, might be ridiculous, but it also gets at something (perhaps a "libertarian linguistics"?).

So where does this leave us? Obviously the truth lies somewhere in between the extremes of Humpty Dumpty's anything-goes-ism and the French Academy's not-if-we-say-it-isn't-ism. Mere intent isn't enough to make meaning at all, much less a spanking new word, nor does meaning have to wait for some official seal of approval. Dictionaries tell us what terms at the time of publication, sanctioned by common use, are meaningful words in the language. So meaning must emerge at some point between the first use of a term and its eventual common use. But where? How, in the relevant sense, does a term become a word? This is a particularly difficult and pressing question nowadays. In our mass-media culture, the timeline between initial and widespread use of a term can be next to nothing. Colbert introduced "truthiness" (and by implication "truthy") to the culture on October 17, 2005, and it was the subject of blogging almost immediately, not to mention more traditional watercooler chat the next day. "Santorum" also, for better or worse, took the fast-track to common use.[7] So *when* exactly did "truthiness" become meaningful, and *where* did that meaning come from?

Wordplaying by the Rules

Many theories of language tie meaning to the language community and the conventions or rules which govern common use. Think of a language *as it is* at a given point in time. Although there's a crucial sense in which, for obvious reasons, one can't coin a term in a language unless the language is there to begin with—Let the origins of language for now remain a mystery!—such perspectives tend to marginalize, if not outright negate, the part that individuals can play in creating new words. If the meaning source of language is the language community, then individuals are all but powerless to neologize solo. They can offer new terms as possible candidates for meaning, and they can certainly suggest what that meaning might be, but the language community, the source of meaning, ultimately decides. This is a matter of whether a proposed term achieves word status, whether the community adopts it for use and how it uses it if so. One proposes, the group disposes. Sound familiar? Is this the French Academy democratized, the wordinistas, as Colbert would call them, all over again?

There are rules that allow individuals to use non-words meaningfully, *as if* they were words, in special situations. You can *stipulate* the meaning of an arbitrary symbol ("x," "φ," and so on) or other non-words as a kind of shorthand, for convenience's sake (for instance, "Let 'glurf' = philosopher who writes on pop culture"—That makes me a glurf). You can also do the same thing with already meaningful words. Humpty Dumpty wouldn't have confused Alice if he had stipulated from the get-go that, for the purposes of their discussion, "glory" meant "a nice knock-down argument." But I haven't added "glurf" to the language (not yet, anyway), and had he made himself understood from the get-go, Humpty Dumpty wouldn't have given "glory" a new additional meaning in the language.

The very same principles would seem to apply to neologisms. To make himself understood in using "wikiality" and "truthiness," Colbert seemingly needs to define them or, failing that, informally explain what they mean.[8] In Oscar Wilde's *The Importance of Being Earnest*, Jack is thoroughly confused by Algernon's use of "Bunburyist" (coined by Algernon/Wilde himself) until, without actually defining the term, Algernon gives an informal explanation of its meaning:

> You have invented a very useful younger brother called Ernest, in order that you may be able to come up to town as often as you like. I have invented an invaluable permanent invalid called Bunbury, in order that I may be able to go down into the country whenever I choose. Bunbury is perfectly invaluable. If it wasn't for Bunbury's extraordinary bad health, for instance, I wouldn't be able to dine with you at Willis's to-night, for I have been really engaged to Aunt Augusta for more than a week.[9]

Though not a precise, explicit definition, this informal explanation is sufficient to make the meaning of "Bunburyist" clear—one who devises a made-up person as an excuse to get out of undesirable social commitments and free oneself up for more desirable ones. Such explanations, like stipulative definitions, are stipulative, and so seem insufficient, by themselves, to make the terms meaningful English words (although they are, in the mold of Blackadder, pretty Englishy). The same goes for Kramer's "quone," which he apparently confuses with, or takes to be a synonym for, "sedate."

Does this mean that the wordinistas (democratized or otherwise) have won? Is a term only meaningful in a language when the public, or some special group, adopts it as its own? Not by a long shot. Terms like "wikiality" and "truthiness" may need definition or explanation, as proxies for common use, to be understood. But here's the rub. This *isn't* typical of *Daily Show* or *Colbert Report* neologisms, which, without any explicit explanation of meaning, tend to be readily understood, and so to be meaningful, *at first use*. Presumably since "fashionista" became widely used (perhaps deriving, not without irony, from the Italian "*fascista*"), we know that the suffix "-ista" is used in English to signify someone who's overbearing, authoritarian, about whatever precedes the suffix, especially the do's and don'ts, mostly other people's don'ts. The root may be shortened, or have a linking "-in-" between root and suffix, to bring the resulting word in line with "fashionista." We know, without explanation, that a "factinista" (as Colbert uses the term, and if there could be such a thing) is overly concerned with facts and takes others to task for ignoring them, or being "underly" concerned with them. (Note: I assume "fashionista" is what the *Report* writers were playing on; it may have been something else instead, say "Sandinista," though that seems unlikely.) Philosophistas, like me, might be seen as too enamored of abstract arguments, concepts, distinctions, and theories.

Along the same lines, take the regularly updated neodescription of Colbert at the beginning of the *Report*. Although in more recent episodes these have become more and more grammatically varied (and with varied success), earlier efforts, when the show was new, were exclusively adjectives: "grippy," "megamerican," "Lincolnish," and the jewel among them—"superstantial." The irony of this gorgeous coinage is, of course, that the prefix "super-" often indicates something positive, superior, whereas "sub-" suggests the negative or inferior.

But to have substance is to have quality, depth, and these are good things. To have "superstance," then, despite the prefix's positive connotations, is negative: to be shallow, lacking in quality (that is, superficial), making "superstantial" yet another delightfully super-fluous neologism (as "subficial" would be). The point, once more, is that we understand these new words at first laughing blush. They're meaningful at first use, instantly part of the language.

Instantly meaningful first uses aren't always based on rough-and-ready rules like "'x' + '-ista' = x-authoritarian." *The Daily Show, America (The Book), and Earth (The Book)* provide many examples where analogies with preexisting words and/or linguistic context will do. The portmanteau "infotainment" obviously derives from "information" and "entertainment." Add "propaganda," and *America* gives us "propa-tainment" and the exquisite oxymoron "infoganda."[10] For some time, Stewart regularly used "Jewy" without explaining it. He didn't have to. The context made it quite clear that "Jewish" wouldn't quite do, that "Jewy" meant, had to mean, *stereotypically* Jewish. Stewart's sublime "catastrophuck," used as early as 2005 and as recently as 2012—the choicest ones are always on call—combines the tragedy of a catas-trophe with the someone's-to-blame of a fuck-up. Likewise, you've probably got a good idea what "philpopsopher" means even before I remind you to revisit "glurf," mentioned earlier. Insisting that there *must* be strict rules operating here, and that since they're already part of the language, so too are the neologisms they allegedly gen-erate, *even before being coined*, is apt to elicit, and rightly so, a Stewartly "Uh?"

In these cases meaning *doesn't* come from the language community, or from language as it is. The language as it is allows new words to come into being, but the knowledgeable, intrepid wordsmith, working alone, can often exploit the untapped meaning potential of a not-yet-made-word without the assistance or approval of the language community. One can make meaning solo. Of course this doesn't mean that anything goes. Language as it is puts quite severe restrictions on exploitable meaning potential. We can't just put Humpty Dumpty together again. One can fail to create a meaningful word on one's own, but one can also succeed, as *The Daily Show* and *The Colbert Report* continually remind us.

There are other ways to coin new words besides those we've discussed. Think of onomatopoeia, words that sound like what they signify, or slang, which often catches on by cultural accident, subcultural lingo infiltrating the mainstream or being appropriated by it. "Ka-ching" and "bling" come to mind here, respectively. Neologistic slang is a bit of a mixed bag, tending to help define a subculture as distinct from the mainstream and other subcultures, but by excluding others in the process, which frustrates understanding rather than facilitating it. Of course, that's often the point, to communicate covertly—the use of slang as code. The discovery or invention of new things *demands* neologizing, as with "quark" or "internet." Philosophiles do this sort of thing all the time, often without good reason—as I just did. Sometimes it's just more efficient, more artful, to neologize, and if fresh words really catch on in a culture, the language may be that much richer for it. Hundreds if not thousands of words are owing to Shakespeare's coinage ("aggravate," "critical," "fragrant," "hurry," "majestic," and "obscene," for six), an inventiveness that represents not only the peak of linguistic art (as hardly needs saying), but also resides at the very heart of living language.

Yet many new words stem less from linguistic need or artfulness and more from ignorance of what's in the toolbox of language as is. Maybe the best recent case in point is Sarah Palin's "refudiate" (an unfortunate mash of "refute" and "repudiate" that rivals "irregardless"). Palin claimed, after the fact, to be pulling a Shakespeare, but she knows, and we know, and she knows we know, she wasn't.[11] Worse than these simple gaffes are cases of intentionally gratuitous neologizing, as in many current ad campaigns (I leave it to readers to think of those that irk them most). In the final analysis, it's this, more than anything else, that *Daily Show* and *Colbert Report* neologisms do: lampooning the often senseless proliferation of new-fangled lingo—ridicule by example.

Your Moment of Zen

The first version of this chapter appeared in 2007, and one might expect that its view of the importance of neologisms to both *The Daily Show* and *The Colbert Report* might be out of date, that the humorous word-coining once prominent there might have fallen into disuse. It's edifying as I write this, five years later, that it's still hard to enjoy an episode of either show that doesn't contain often-memorable neologisms—all the confirmation a philpopsopher could hope for. The importance of wordplay to *The Daily Show* and *The Colbert Report* is undeniable, and neologisms, in the *Report* especially, are arguably the keystone. Such new words run from the merely cute to the hilarious, and they remind us of two important things: one, an individual's power to create words, to create meaning, is much greater than is often supposed, and two, because of this, it's essential to use that power wisely, sparingly, especially in today's mass media culture, where neologizing has, more than ever, run amok, and beautifully minted linguistic coin gets lost in a sea of language with bureaucratese at one end and überslang at the other.[12]

Notes

1. "Lisa the Iconoclast," *The Simpsons*, Fox (February 18, 1996).
2. Lewis Carroll, *Through the Looking-Glass* (New York: Dover, 1994 [1872]), 57.
3. Although the Humpty Dumpty theory of meaning is often thought absurd, it does have its advocates. See, among others, Keith Donnellan, "Putting Humpty Dumpty Together Again," *Philosophical Review* 77 (1968), 203–215.
4. "The Stakeout," *Seinfeld*, NBC (May 31, 1990). Compare with "appucious" in Woody Allen's *Husbands and Wives* (Orion, 1992), where the would-be coiner doesn't even try to explain the alleged word's meaning, yet insists on it being descriptively apt. Note the contrast between this attempt and *Annie Hall* (United Artists, 1977), where Alvy offers "lurve" and "luff" to express what "love," he says, cannot.
5. "Ink and Incapability," *Blackadder III*, BBC (September 24, 1987). Transcripts of this episode give various different spellings for these non-words, some of which come close to being, not nonsense, but instantly coined words. Later Blackadder expresses the wish to facilitate Dr. Johnson's "velocitous extramuralization," which seems to convey, since "velocity" and "extramural" are perfectly good words, what "speedy departure from the premises" would—similar to, if more difficult than, most of the *Daily Show* and *Colbert Report* neologisms we'll discuss.
6. Stephen Colbert, "So You Want to Be a Precedent," in Jon Stewart, Ben Karlin, and David Javerbaum, *America (The Book) A Citizen's Guide to Democracy Inaction* (New York: Warner Books, 2004), 92.

7. During Rick Santorum's bid for the 2012 Republican presidential nomination, Stewart often reminded us, by "classily" yet explicitly refraining from such jokes, of the meaning attached to Santorum's name in response to, and in protest of, his extremist conservative position on gay marriage and homosexuality generally: "that frothy mixture of lube and fecal matter that is sometimes the by-product of anal sex," www.urbandictionary.com, accessed February 7, 2013.

8. "Wikiality" means "reality according to Wikipedia" or more generally "popular opinion as presumed to constitute reality." This reflects the appeal to popularity fallacy (inferring the truth of a belief from its mere popularity). "Truthiness" means "what one feels or wants to be true irrespective of the evidence." The implied adjective "truthy" also suggests what *resembles* truth, or is truth-*like*, and connotes, in contrast to truth and falsehood, gradations, vagueness (think shades of gray instead of black or white). For more on truthiness, see Amber L. Griffioen, "Irrationality and 'Gut' Reasoning: Two Kinds of Truthiness," up next.

9. Oscar Wilde, *The Importance of Being Earnest* (New York: Avon, 1965 [1899]), 35.

10. Stewart, Karlin, and Javerbaum, *America (The Book)*, 139.

11. One important difference between Colbert's "truthiness" and Palin's "refudiate" is that the latter rule-breaking was a mistake, and so is less creditable than the deliberate former. Another is that, humor aside, "truthiness" appears to improve linguistic efficiency, where "refudiate" seems rather an unneeded synonym for "reject." It should be noted, however, that both words are now not only established in the lexicon, but share the rare distinction of having won Word of the Year honors. See Mary Bruce, "Congratulations, Sarah Palin: 'Refudiate' Named Word of the Year," *ABC News* (November 15, 2010).

12. For continued helpful feedback and enjoyable discussion I thank Larry Holt and Bill Irwin.

Chapter 21

Irrationality and "Gut" Reasoning
Two Kinds of Truthiness

Amber L. Griffioen

I love the truth—it's facts I'm not a fan of.
　　　　　　　　Stephen Colbert of *The Colbert Report*

You might wonder what an article about *The Colbert Report* is doing in a book about *The Daily Show*. Well, Stephen was a *Daily Show* correspondent for eight years (1997–2005), and he has since collaborated extensively with Jon Stewart, despite the immense success of his own show. Just consider the Rally to Restore Sanity and/or Fear in 2010 and Colbert's handing over his Super PAC to Stewart in 2012. Both are examples of continued collaboration (though in the latter case not coordination!) between *The Daily Show* and *The Colbert Report*. Furthermore, given Jon Stewart's continued criticism of the inconsistency and irrationality of the American media, the notion of truthiness has relevance for any fan of *The Daily Show*.

A Little Background

On the very first episode of *The Colbert Report*, Stephen Colbert boldly introduced the word "truthiness"[1] into the American vocabulary:

The Ultimate Daily Show and Philosophy: More Moments of Zen, More Indecision Theory,
First Edition. Edited by Jason Holt.
© 2013 John Wiley & Sons, Inc. Published 2013 by John Wiley & Sons, Inc.

> I will speak to you in plain, simple English. And that brings us to tonight's word: "truthiness." Now I'm sure some of the "word police," the "word-inistas" over at Webster's, are gonna say, "Hey, that's not a word!" Well, anyone who knows me knows I'm no fan of dictionaries or reference books. They're elitist—constantly telling us what is or isn't true ...

> I don't trust books. They're all fact, no heart. And that's exactly what's pulling our country apart today. 'Cause face it, folks: we are a divided nation. Not between Democrats and Republicans, or conservatives and liberals, or tops and bottoms. No, we are divided between those who think with their head, and those who *know* with their *heart*.

Colbert went on to give the audience a few examples:

> If you *think* about Harriet Miers, of course her nomination is absurd. But the President didn't say he *thought* about her selection. He said this:

> [*Clip of President Bush*]: "I know her heart."

> Notice how he said nothing about her brain? He didn't have to. He *feels* the truth about Harriet Miers.

> And what about Iraq? If you *think* about it, maybe there are a few missing pieces to the rationale for war, but doesn't taking Saddam out *feel* like the right thing ... right here [*pointing to stomach*]—right here in the gut? (October 17, 2005)

In more recent broadcasts, Colbert has made such claims during his interviews as, "Science *can* be a personal choice," (April 23, 2012) and "I make gut judgments about people. Then later I figure out a mental justification for that gut judgment." (May 2, 2012). There are, then, two closely related notions of "truthiness" implied in these clips: (1) the sense in which one "chooses" to believe something based on what one *prefers* to be the case, as opposed to responding to the facts of the matter, and (2) the sense in which one appeals to an intuition (or a gut feeling) to provide justification for a belief.

The American Dialect Society, which named "truthiness" its 2005 Word of the Year, officially defined it as "the quality of preferring concepts or facts one wishes to be true, rather than concepts or facts known to be true."[2] Of course, "preferring" something one wishes to be true over something "known" to be true does not necessarily mean one *chooses* to believe it, as we stated in (1) above. I will return to this a bit later. Nevertheless, the ADS's definition looks a lot like many of the phenomena we philosophers classify under the category of *motivated epistemic*[3] *irrationality*. Loosely speaking, we are talking about cases of someone's believing something for "bad" reasons simply because one has a personal motivation to do so. Maybe I wishfully believe that I am a good driver (despite having been in several fender-benders) because I don't want to admit to myself and others that I really am a bad driver. Or perhaps my desire to be a competent teacher leads me to unreasonably think that my students understand the incredibly complicated argument I just presented to them. Or maybe my admiration for Barack Obama causes me to overlook certain morally relevant failures of his administration that I would have no problem criticizing the Bush Administration for.[4] In all these cases, something I care about (for example, my self-image or my respect for another person) motivates me to believe something not supported by the objective facts of the matter. That is, truthy beliefs in this first sense seem to be beliefs that it is epistemically *unreasonable* to believe. But is it really always bad to believe "unreasonably" in this way? After all, the word "reason" is "just one letter away from 'treason'!" (September 16, 2010). What's so bad about believing from the gut? This leads us to the second definition of "truthiness" discussed above.

When Merriam-Webster voted "truthiness" its 2006 Word of the Year, it defined the term as "truth that comes from the gut, not books."[5] In this sense, then, truthiness amounts to *intuiting* the truth via some "gut" feeling: "Because that's where the truth comes from, ladies and gentlemen … the gut."[6] We may find this notion laughable (or at least laugh-worthy), but we *do* frequently appeal to feelings or intuitions, often in ways we take to be perfectly legitimate. "Something doesn't feel right," we say, or "this action just seems like the wrong thing to do." Indeed, our frequent references to phenomena like "common sense," "women's intuition," "rubbing someone the wrong way," and so on seem to indicate that we do sometimes appeal to this kind of truthiness to justify certain truth claims or actions. So perhaps "truthy" appeals to the gut aren't as irrational as we might have first thought.

In what follows, I want to look a little bit more closely at these two notions of truthiness. Focusing on the first sense, I will draw some parallels between truthiness and paradigm cases of motivated epistemic irrationality like wishful thinking and self-deception. I will then turn to the second sense to see if relying on our guts in the way Colbert suggests might sometimes be rational.

Truthiness and Problems of Irrationality

There are three basic types of cases that philosophers traditionally classify under the term "irrationality."[7] The first two cases, wishful thinking and self-deception, have to do with a person believing in an irrational manner and thus fall under the umbrella of *epistemic irrationality*. The third case, weakness of will, is a matter of so-called *practical irrationality* and involves a person undertaking a certain action, despite taking herself to have a *better* reason (all things considered) not to do so. While I think that truthiness might be able to fit the mold of each of these three kinds of irrationality, it applies most directly to cases of wishful thinking and self-deception—and it's these two types of irrationality that I wish to discuss extensively in the next section. As we will see, there are some troubling philosophical problems that arise regarding irrational behavior (especially self-deception). But perhaps we can use the context of truthiness to help us resolve these "paradoxes of irrationality" without denying the fundamental irrationality of truthiness itself.

Wishful Thinking and Self-Deception: What Are They?

Wishful thinking and self-deception are two very closely related but nonetheless distinct kinds of irrational belief-forming processes. Wishful thinking occurs when someone has a strong desire that something (call it "X") be true and comes to believe X primarily *because* of that strong desire, but not for any "good" reason that takes the facts of the situation into account. Thus, wishful thinking does not require that the person *knows* the relevant facts of the situation, but merely that she comes to believe X primarily *because she really wants to*. Self-deception, on the other hand, seems to occur when someone comes to hold a belief *in the face of strong evidence to the contrary*.[8] In this latter case the person is in some sense *aware of* what she herself takes to be the relevant facts (which presumably fly in the face of X), but refuses to acknowledge them because she so strongly desires to believe X. Self-deception, then, appears to be much closer to "choosing to believe" something than wishful thinking. In both cases, however, the subject has a strong desire that X be true—and it is this desire that motivates affirmation of something not borne out by the fact. The difference lies in the level of awareness the subject has of the counter-evidence and how seriously she takes this awareness.

Let's look at an example to help illustrate this difference. Suppose senior *Daily Show* correspondent Samantha Bee very badly wants her husband and fellow *Daily Show* correspondent, Jason Jones, to be faithful to her. We can imagine that this desire itself might be strong enough to cause her to believe in his fidelity without ever really looking at whether the facts support this.[9] In this case, Sam would just be a wishful thinker. However, suppose the relevant facts available to her *do* indicate that he is cheating. Maybe he continually comes home late at night with lipstick on his collar, smelling of cheap perfume, and making lame excuses. Perhaps Sam's good friend, Wyatt, even tells her that he has witnessed Jason cavorting around with a younger woman on the set of *The Daily Show*. If she then continues to believe in his fidelity, *despite* being aware of this counter-evidence, then we might think that Sam has gone beyond mere wishful thinking and entered the realm of self-deception.

It is not difficult to see how appeals to truthiness might sometimes underlie both of these types of irrationality. Remember Colbert's assertion that the President doesn't need to make reference to Harriet Miers' brain or qualifications because he just "*feels* the truth" about her? The wife engaged in wishful thinking may say similar things without even bothering to see if the facts line up with her belief: "I don't need to look at the facts," she might say. "I love my husband, and I just *know* he would never cheat on me," or, "I can *feel in my heart* that he is faithful." And if she stubbornly continues to affirm this belief (both to herself and to others) in the face of strong evidence to the contrary—relying on her supposed "gut feeling" that he is faithful—this "truthy" behavior would likely count as something stronger than mere wishful thinking—something like self-deception.

The Paradoxes of Irrationality

Cases like the one above are all too common in our everyday lives. However, it is surprising how difficult it is to provide a philosophical account of *how* we are actually able to believe in such ways, at least as far as self-deception is concerned. Wishful thinking doesn't seem all that mysterious. Given the way we human beings are cognitively built, it turns out that we often simply find ourselves believing things we want to be true and doubting things we don't want to be true.[10] We tend to think that we are more intelligent, more attractive, better drivers, better *people* than we actually are. Similarly, we are more willing to give people we love (including ourselves) the "benefit of the doubt"—precisely because we care about them. And this is not necessarily a bad thing, even if it turns out to be epistemically irrational.

People who believe things wishfully are irrational in some sense, since they're not being sensitive to the evidence. But they still somehow seem "more rational" than their self-deceiving counterparts. Most wishful thinkers don't usually realize they are believing wishfully *while* they're in the grip of wishful thinking. Indeed, insofar as they are still rational, we would expect them to be willing to revise their wishful beliefs if they find out (or even suspect) that they are believing wishfully—or at least to check to see whether the facts back up their beliefs. If, on the other hand, they persist in holding onto their false beliefs—if they continue to believe *in the face of* counter-evidence that they recognize *as* counter-evidence—then they seem to be self-deceived, which implies being irrational in a stronger sense, and this is a little trickier to explain.

The difficulty in making sense of self-deception can be made clear by comparing it with its counterpart in the interpersonal realm, namely the deception of other people. Other-deception is relatively straightforward. Suppose Steve Carell wants to deceive Jon Stewart that he's coming back to *The Daily Show*. That is, Steve holds a certain belief "X" (that he intends to return to *The Daily Show*) to be false (he has no such intention). In other words, he believes "not-X" (that he is *not* returning[11]). Steve then tries to persuade Jon that X is true. If Jon, through Steve's efforts, *does* come to believe X, then Steve has successfully deceived Jon about X.

However, in the case of self-deception, one and the same individual is supposed to play the role of both deceiv*er* and deceiv*ed*. The individual engaged in self-deception tries, through her *own* efforts, to become deceived about some fact she does not want to admit. But, unlike the interpersonal case, it is unclear how she could ever succeed. If Jon knows what Steve is up to, he is unlikely to be duped (unless, of course, he is incredibly stupid). But if the self-deceiver is aware of her own intent to deceive herself, then it seems like she could never achieve her goal! That is, awareness of her intention threatens to undermine the success of her self-deception altogether.[12] Furthermore, it seems that if an agent *could* succeed in deceiving herself, then she must somehow knowingly hold both the belief that not-X (in her role as the deceiver) and the belief that X (in her role as the one deceived) *at the same time*.[13] Hence, we seem to embroil ourselves in two paradoxes when we attempt to explain how self-deception works—and cases of self-deceptive truthiness will be no different.

So how is self-deception even possible? How can truthiness in this stronger sense even get off the ground? The above paradoxes are quite troubling, and for this reason some philosophers try to explain self-deception away entirely, and say that it's not at all like interpersonal deception. They say self-deception is really just a person's being either in error (for example, about the facts or about the way she formed her belief) or controlled by some external psychological force.[14] But we don't usually think that self-deceivers are merely making a motivated *mistake*. Self-deceivers not only ought to know better; we think they actually *do* know better in some sense.[15] Likewise, we think that there is some relevant difference between the self-deceiver and the person who believes things pathologically (as with, say, obsessive-compulsive or delusional beliefs). Compulsive believers might actually know better, but they can't help believing as they do. So if we think self-deceivers might be responsible for their deceptions, then they must at least be *capable* of revising their beliefs. Thus, we must try to face the paradoxes head-on and see if we can construct a view of self-deception that will allow us not only to understand how self-deceptive truthiness is possible but also to keep a strong notion of the irrationality of self-deception intact. But what might such an account of self-deception look like?

One Solution: Divide the Mind

One way that philosophers have attempted to resolve the paradoxes mentioned above is simply to divide the mind into independent structures that can deceive each other like one person deceives another. Perhaps, like famed psychologist Sigmund Freud (1856–1939), we can simply postulate that there is some sort of subconscious mind that acts to deceive my conscious mind.[16] (Imagine Steve Carell and

Jon Stewart in our above example occupying the space of just one person! Or just think of Stephen Colbert versus Stephen Colbert in *The Colbert Report*'s regular "Formidable Opponent" segment.) Of course, on the Freudian picture, we have two independent sub-agents (think: "mini-persons"), who "team up," so to speak, to deceive the ego. Let's go back to our example of Sam and Jason. Suppose Sam wants it to be the case that Jason is a faithful husband. She very likely believes that he *ought* not be cheating on her. Perhaps she also believes it would be inappropriate to accuse her husband of infidelity. Now imagine that "deep down" in her subconscious Sam believes that Jason is likely cheating on her. However, her subconscious tricks her conscious mind into thinking he is actually faithful! And since she is unconscious of her belief that Jason is unfaithful (and perhaps also of her strong desire to believe in his fidelity), she is easily duped by her subconscious into believing that Jason is faithful. In this way, we don't have to worry about the static paradox, since although Sam-as-a-whole believes both X and not-X at the same time, one belief is on the level of the conscious mind, the other on that of the unconscious. Likewise, since the subconscious and conscious parts of the mind act independently, we don't have to worry about the dynamic paradox either. So far, so good.

But there are some significant problems with this view.[17] This first is that we suddenly have a problem locating the *person herself* (here, Samantha Bee). It looks as if each mental substructure has person-like qualities. Each part can weigh possibilities, have beliefs and desires, interact with and independently act *on* other parts of the mind, and so on. If this is the case, and the interaction between the parts of the mind works like interpersonal interaction, it appears that we have multiple agents instead of just one![18] Who is the adjudicator on this view? Where is *Sam the person*? If we want to be able to hold *Sam* responsible for her self-deception, who should we blame? Is it her conscious mind's fault that it got hoodwinked? (Think about the example of interpersonal deception: We wouldn't normally hold Jon responsible for believing Steve's lie, would we?) But if we instead blame Sam's unconscious, are we really blaming *Sam*? What would it mean to blame just her unconscious? Could we even find it?

This leads to a further concern. On the kind of view sketched above, we have a really hard time explaining *why* Sam's belief that Jason is likely cheating on her is unconscious in the first place. If she never consciously acknowledged that the evidence strongly supports the belief that he's cheating, then it seems rather mysterious as to how this belief just "ended up" in her subconscious. Instead, one is more likely to claim that Sam *does* at some point consciously acknowledge that the evidence supports the belief that Jason is unfaithful, and then she *represses* this information. She pushes it deep down into her subconscious where it becomes free to do its deceptive work. But now it looks like her *conscious mind* is doing all the heavy self-deceptive lifting, not her subconscious. To keep out the undesirable belief, the conscious mind has to somehow actively "push it down" into the subconscious. And here the dynamic paradox reemerges. How can Sam successfully repress undesirable information if she knows what she's up to? Maybe the subconscious mind has certain defense mechanisms that "kick in" when threatening information comes into consciousness and automatically relegate that information to the unconscious. Yet then we have the worry that Sam's self-deception is something largely out of her control—the result of a compulsive defense mechanism, as it were. But it was precisely this view that we wanted to avoid. Thus, in the end, divided mind views seem to create more problems than they solve. So how can we understand self-deception without literally dividing the mind?

An Alternative Account

There is another way we can account for self-deception that might be less problematic. First, instead of viewing self-deception as a *state*, achieved when one somehow causes oneself to hold contradictory beliefs, I think we would do better to approach it as a *process*, a sort of "project," in which an agent actively engages. And I think we can explain this process without having to refer to unconscious sub-agents within the person. Now generally when a rational person holds a belief, and she recognizes that the evidence to the contrary greatly outweighs the evidence in support of her belief, she will revise her belief accordingly. However, in cases of self-deception, this does not occur because the agent has a strong motivation to retain her (unwarranted) belief. Instead, she *commits herself* to maintaining her belief in the face of the evidence, likely employing several strategies to do so. Of course, she doesn't have to ever commit herself *explicitly*.

My point is merely that the way she behaves indicates her having such a practical commitment.

Let's return once again to our example of Sam and Jason to see how this might work. On my account of self-deception, Sam is *aware* that the facts support the belief that Jason is cheating on her, and she is likewise *aware* of her desire to believe he is faithful. But she diverts her attention from these two facts and focuses instead on the belief she wishes to cultivate, namely that Jason is faithful. There are several techniques she can employ in the service of this project. Perhaps she selectively pays more attention to positive instead of negative evidence. Or she avoids situations where she might encounter negative evidence. When Wyatt points out that Sam's belief is unwarranted, Sam might rationalize in order to keep her belief intact (e.g., "Wyatt's just jealous of our great relationship!"). In these ways, she can push all the negative evidence to the "margins" of her awareness by ignoring criticism, or even stubbornly repeating to herself "He loves me" over and over again until she fails to be swayed by reasons to believe the contrary.

Note that none of this requires that her self-deceptive activity be on some sub-personal, unconscious level. Rather, we should merely see Sam's activity as a kind of active *attention-directing*, which is something we do all the time, without thereby becoming completely unaware of the former object of our attention. Surely Jon Stewart can turn to Camera 3 and yet still be aware of Camera 1 (in his peripheral vision, say). He is not *paying attention* to Camera 1, yet he is still *aware* of it—and if he wants to, he can turn back to it. Similarly, one of the main ways the self-deceivers try to maintain their favored beliefs is by basically turning their attention away from the negative evidence and focusing instead on positive evidence—but this doesn't mean the negative evidence is simply gone. It's still available for reflection, if the agent decides to turn her attention to it. This is why self-deceivers tend to exhibit a lot of cognitive tension—because they are in some respect aware of the counter-evidence that's out there, and it's *hard* to willfully direct one's attention in cases where the counter-evidence is strong.

But if this is right, what about the dynamic paradox? If the self-deceiver is this complicit in her deceptive project, how could she ever convince herself, assuming she has an idea of what she's up to? Here, it's important to note that human beings are creatures of habit, and even though it might be hard for Sam to ignore negative evidence at first, the more she engages in self-deceptive strategies, the better she is likely to get at maintaining her belief. Thus, although the self-deceiver might experience lots of cognitive tension at the outset of her self-deceptive project, the more she habituates herself to directing her attention, the easier maintaining her belief will become and the less cognitive dissonance she will experience. And I want to claim that this *entire process* of waffling back and forth between the belief one wants to maintain and the force of reality is what we should refer to when we talk about "self-deception." Of course, if Sam finally habituates herself so well and convinces herself completely that Jason is faithful, where *nothing* counts to her as evidence against this belief, then I would say she is no longer self-deceived but rather more like an ignorant or even *delusional* person. If this happens, she no longer "knows better"—that is, she now believes for what she takes to be *good* reasons—but the process by which she arrived at this point is both irrational and criticizable.

On this account of self-deception, then, the entire process is dynamic, with the agent fluctuating back and forth between stubbornly affirming the desired belief and having to deal with evidence to the contrary. The dynamic paradox becomes a moot point, since we don't have to say that Sam *must* succeed in truly convincing herself. All that matters is that she *tries* to undermine her rational standards by means of the strategies described above. And there is no static paradox because the she never has to simultaneously hold inconsistent beliefs.

Truthiness and Self-Deception

I think it is fairly obvious that the first definition we gave above of "truthiness" (in which one chooses to believe something based on what one prefers to believe, as opposed to the supposed facts) can fit this model of self-deception to a tee. We sometimes prefer concepts we wish to be true, instead of what the facts tell us, even when we're aware that these facts don't support our belief. But Colbert's introduction to truthiness does even more than this. In a way, it ups the ante on self-deception, since Colbert attempts to use truthiness to establish the truth of truthiness!

Let's see how this works: Someone may wish a certain fact were true (say, that the Panama Canal was built in 1941), but all the books tell us that this is false (since the Panama Canal was, "in fact," built in 1914). Colbert, of course, maintains that it's his "right" to believe the former claim. However, as we have seen, to do so would be to embark on a process of self-deception, resulting in the claim that believing what one wants trumps believing what one is rationally required to believe. Yet Colbert obviously still acknowledges the importance of reasoning—he is, after all, making an argument and appealing to reasons—so we can see that he hasn't abandoned his commitment to rationality altogether. But he is struggling to *use reason* to make a case for *undermining reason*. This is almost "meta-self-deception," in the sense that what Colbert wants to believe is that we can "know" the truth with our hearts or "feel" it with our guts, and that the standards of what normally counts as evidence for rational belief (namely, the *facts*) are not the correct standards of rationality. And how does he know? He checked his gut!

In a recent segment of "Who's Honoring Me Now?" Colbert makes this idea very explicit. He cites a scientific study looking for evidence of truthiness in action. After discussing the results of the study, he notes: "Now my only problem … with this scientific study is that it was a scientific study. You see, truthiness and empirical evidence don't mix." Here, we again have reference to the above sense of truthiness, involving a distrust or disavowal of the facts of the matter. But Colbert goes on: "Folks, you can't *prove* truthiness with *information*. You prove truthiness with *more truthiness*—a process called 'truthinessiness'."[19] This harks back to 2006 when the AP challenged Colbert's claim to have coined the word himself. Colbert shot back: "The fact that they looked it up in [*The Oxford English Dictionary*] just shows that they don't get the idea of truthiness at all … You don't look up truthiness in a book, you look it up in your gut."[20]

What's especially funny about this move isn't just that it's circular (trying to use truthiness to validate itself). It's also that the claim, "the gut is a more accurate standard for truth than facts," is itself an empirical matter, one which can be settled by looking at the facts! So Colbert is implicitly appealing to the facts, in order to establish that facts are unreliable. It's the irrationality of this (first circular, then self-defeating) argument that makes us laugh. But it also raises some very interesting and important questions about the connection between rationality and irrationality.[21]

Feeling the Truth: Can Our Guts Get Us Justified Belief?

Leaving Colbert's circular/self-defeating move aside, the question still remains: Can we legitimately appeal to our guts for justification? Indeed, we often refer to getting a "bad feeling" about a certain person or place; and sometimes when asked why we dislike someone, we respond that he or she just "rubs me the wrong way." Likewise, phenomena like "hunches" and "women's intuition" are supposed to account for how some people appear to instinctively know certain truths. Does this mean that reference to our guts can provide us with good justification for truth claims?

Without going into this question in too much detail, I just wish to briefly discuss this second sense of "truthiness." While it seems that we often legitimately appeal to gut feelings to justify certain claims or beliefs, I think that what we are implicitly doing is referring to other, more objectively relevant facts about the situation, about which we merely fail to be explicit.[22] Take the example of a young voter who refuses to vote for a certain politician, merely because of her gut feeling. "I just don't have a good feeling about that guy," she might say. "He just rubs me the wrong way," or even, "He creeps me out." Now in some cases—as when a woman refuses a stranger's come-on for precisely the same reasons—we might just accept this type of justification and move on. However, if we pressed her for more information ("What rubbed you the wrong way about him?"), she might say something about his shifty glances, his fake smile, or his poor choice of words. But now we have an appeal to *facts* about the situation itself, not just about someone's gut feeling! Indeed, "truthy" claims like "taking Saddam out *feels* like the right thing to do" might actually serve as implicit references not just to the desire to depose Saddam Hussein, but also to facts about his character or past actions that make us feel good about removing him from power.

However, we should be careful to avoid saying that such feelings, by themselves, are what *make* a belief justified. They are merely one way of being *responsive* to the relevant facts. But they are not always the best way. Indigestion ought not to serve as rational justification for why I didn't vote for a certain politician, but perhaps a bad feeling grounded in certain "shady" behavioral cues given off by the politician in question, can.[23] However, in the latter circumstance it is not the feeling itself that justifies my action; rather, it is the fact that such behavioral cues have, in the past, been exhibited by persons of less than reputable moral character. And this is an important distinction to make, since in cases such as these, my feelings don't make a certain claim true or false, whereas facts about the world *do* appear to accomplish this task. Thus, when forming important beliefs like whom to vote for, we ought to subject our gut feelings to rigorous questioning, in order to see whether we can actually come up with good epistemic reasons to ground these feelings. Indeed, although gut feelings might sometimes be a way of responding to the facts, they are often unreliable and may often conflict with the facts. This is what motivates Colbert to lead "a crusade against facts"—since, according to him, they too often "upset the truth that's in your gut."[24] But in this sense truthiness remains epistemically suspect, unless it's clear that one can appeal to legitimate reasons which appeal to the facts of the situation to ground one's gut feelings.

A Tip of the Hat

In conclusion, I would like to commend Stephen Colbert for coining a word that captures both the essence of motivated epistemic irrationality and the difficulty we have in trying to overcome it by rational means. Although some instances of irrational beliefs may be harmless, Colbert shows us the amusing—and potentially dangerous—consequences of forming opinions and making decisions by going "straight from the gut." In fact, I propose that from now on we call claims that appeal solely to the gut instances of "the fallacy of *argumentum Colberti ad ventrem*."[25] The inclusion of this fallacy among other, better-known informal fallacies (like the *argumentum ad hominem* or, my personal favorite, the *argumentum ad baculum*) would be a welcome addition to logic textbooks everywhere, which often ignore the kind of fallacious reasoning involved in appealing to one's gut when attempting to make cogent arguments. To further ignore a phenomenon that both reflects what human beings often do and exposes certain irrational tendencies in human reasoning would be to do a disservice to philosophy.

And that's the truthiness.

Notes

1. For a discussion by the TCR writers of Colbert's coining of the term "truthiness," see www.youtube.com/watch?v=WvnHf3MQtAk, accessed February 11, 2013.
2. "Truthiness Voted 2005 Word of the Year," The American Dialect Society (January 6, 2006), www.americandialect.org/truthiness_voted_2005_word_of_the_year, accessed February 11, 2013.
3. By "epistemic" I mean having to do with beliefs, knowledge, cognition, or other relevant terms in the philosophical branch of *epistemology*, in which philosophers ask questions related to what knowledge is and how we come to know things. Here, the irrationality in question is epistemic because the person is irrational in *believing* (or believing to know) something. This might be contrasted with *practical* irrationality, in which a person's *behavior* itself is irrational (and not just because of something she believes irrationally). I discuss this distinction briefly at the beginning of the next section.
4. The application of a double standard is very common in cases of motivated epistemic irrationality. We will see more examples below.
5. "Previous Words of the Year," Merriam-Webster Online, www.merriam-webster.com/info/07words_prev.htm, accessed February 11, 2013.
6. Episode 1 (October 17, 2005).
7. There are other important kinds of irrational reasoning and behavior, but the three kinds of cases mentioned above tend to be the ones most focused on by philosophers. I think the reason for this is that these phenomena occur very frequently in human beings, and yet it is very difficult to explain philosophically (or psychologically) how they are even possible in the first place!
8. German philosophers Christoph Michel and Albert Newen make the notion that self-deceivers believe "in the face of strong evidence to the contrary" a criterion of any satisfactory definition of self-deception. See "Self-Deception as Pseudo-Rational Regulation of Belief," *Consciousness and Cognition* 19 (3) (2010), 734. However, this distinction between wishful thinking and self-deception goes at least as far back as Béla Szabados, "Wishful Thinking and Self-Deception," *Analysis* 33 (6) (1973), 201–205.

9. In *I Know I Am, But What Are You?* (New York: Gallery Books, 2010), Samantha Bee writes: "When I rack my brain, I can't think of a *single* adult, other than myself, in my immediate or extended family who has not been painfully divorced at least once, usually twice—even the gay ones. This inspires tremendous confidence in my husband" (3). If she were speaking seriously here, we could imagine that this "confidence" in her husband might be primarily motivated by a desire for a successful marriage, not by an objective assessment of whether or not such confidence is warranted.

10. See, for example, the groundbreaking chapter on cognitive and motivational biases by Richard Nisbett and Lee Ross in chapter 10 of *Human Inference: Strategies and Shortcomings of Social Judgment* (Englewood Cliffs, NJ: Prentice-Hall, 1980). For a fascinating contemporary discussion of the various ways that human beings process information, see also: Daniel Kahneman, *Thinking, Fast and Slow* (New York: Farrar, Straus and Giroux, 2011).

11. Or: "it is not the case that he is returning."

12. Philosopher Alfred Mele calls this the "dynamic paradox" of self-deception. See, for example: Alfred Mele, *Self-Deception Unmasked* (Princeton, NJ: Princeton University Press, 2001), 8.

13. Mele calls this the "static paradox" (*Self-Deception Unmasked*, 7).

14. I think deflationary accounts like Mele's (see notes 12 and 13 above), which reduce self-deception to a kind of motivated bias, belong in the former category. That is, I think they end up reducing self-deception to a kind of "motivated mistake," on which the self-deceiver ought (in some sense of the word "ought") to know better, but does not in fact know better. And as I say above, I think that self-deception involves something more than just a mistake. The reader should note, however, that there is an entire tradition of philosophers that would deny the distinction between wishful thinking and self-deception I have made above and who would count wishful thinking (which does seem to be a kind of motivated mistake) as just another kind of self-deception. For more on this and other debates in the self-deception literature, see Mele's article "Real Self-Deception," and the ensuing peer commentary and responses in *Brain and Behavioral Sciences* 20 (1) (1997), 91–134.

15. See Dion Scott-Kakures, "Self-Deception and Internal Irrationality," *Philosophy and Phenomenological Research* 56 (1) (1996), 31–56.

16. Philosopher Donald Davidson (1917–2003) was also a stark proponent of the divided-mind view, although he resisted using straightforwardly Freudian terms to talk about partitions in the mind. See Donald Davidson, "Paradoxes of Irrationality," in *Philosophical Essays on*

Freud, ed. R. Wohlheim and J. Hopkins (Cambridge: Cambridge University Press, 1982), 289–305.

17. The version of the divided-mind theory that I have presented here is admittedly a much more simplified version of the theories put forward by Freud, Davidson, and other partitioned-mind theorists. A full and fair consideration of these views requires much more space and nuance than I can provide here. Nevertheless, I still think they fail for reasons similar to those I mention here.

18. While multiple personality disorder and mental compartmentalization might be real psychological phenomena, they are surely not as common as self-deception.

19. Episode 941 (August 9, 2012).

20. Quoted in Jake Coyle, "Colbert: AP the Biggest Threat to America," Associated Press (October 5, 2006).

21. My own view is that self-deception is a kind of "pseudo-rational" process, in which people try to *generate* reasons to believe what they want to believe in the face of evidence to the contrary. Thus, self-deceivers don't cease to believe for reasons, but the reasons they generate are not the right kinds of reasons to justify their beliefs. For more on pseudo-rationality, see Michel and Newen, "Self-Deception as Pseudo-Rational Regulation of Belief" (2010).

22. It is also possible that we might be incapable of being explicit about these facts. However, in my experience, this is not usually the case. Most people, when pushed on why they have a certain gut feeling, can (and will) explicitly elaborate on particular, relevant features of the situation that give rise to that feeling. For a similar point regarding truthiness and gut feelings, see Matthew F. Pierlott's "Truth, Truthiness, and Bullshit for the American Voter," in *Stephen Colbert and Philosophy: I Am Philosophy (And So Can You!)*, ed. Aaron Allen Schiller (Chicago, IL: Open Court Press, 2009), 80–81.

23. In fact, it has been suggested that certain snap-fire decisions (or "rapid cognition") are often more accurate than deliberative, explicitly reasoned-out decisions. This does not undermine the claim that when one makes such snap-fire decisions, one is completely unaware of the relevant facts at hand. It merely implies that sometimes over-reflection on the facts can get in our way. But all this shows in relation to truthiness is that sometimes reflecting too heavily on our gut feelings might get in the way of our pursuit of truth, not that relying on our guts is always justified. For more on this, see Malcolm Gladwell, *Blink: The Power of Thinking Without Thinking* (New York: Little, Brown & Co., 2005).

24. Episode 194 (January 8, 2007).

25. Or, "the Colbertian appeal to the stomach."

Chapter 22

Thank God It's Stephen Colbert!

The Rally to Restore Irony on *The Colbert Report*

Kevin S. Decker

Nation, here's a good one: what do "the end of irony"[1] and the zombie apocalypse have in common? The answer? The return of something better left dead and buried (and I say this ironically). After all, if you have a particularly narrow sense of humor (or none at all), you will only find irritation in irony, that form of indirect communication that *Webster's* defines as "the use of words to express something other than and especially the opposite of the literal meaning."[2]

After 9/11, with our first brand-spanking-new sense of national purpose since the end of the Cold War, it seemed unthinkable that Americans would return to the cynicism of Gen X'ers and extol the hollow moral nihilism of wildly popular television shows such as *The Simpsons* and *Seinfeld*. But the rumors of irony's death were much exaggerated. In the months after 9/11, it was revealed that national security agencies had information about the possibility of a major attack but did nothing about it; that none of the 9/11 bombers were from invaded Iraq (all were legal visitors to the US); that Osama bin Laden had escaped from invaded Afghanistan; and so on. Even after a major shift in American politics seemed to have occurred in the transition from the "compassionately conservative" Bush Administration to the moderate Democratic Obama White House, we cannot help but grit our proverbial teeth as the nation's first African-American president first failed to shut down the prison at Guantanamo, took

The Ultimate Daily Show and Philosophy: More Moments of Zen, More Indecision Theory, First Edition. Edited by Jason Holt.
© 2013 John Wiley & Sons, Inc. Published 2013 by John Wiley & Sons, Inc.

ages to declare an end to occupations of Iraq and Afghanistan, and most importantly took no steps to reduce executive power or to dismantle the repressive architecture of "Homeland Security," all of which had been hallmarks of Bush's policy.

Now more than 10 years after 9/11, American public policy is far more ironic, to such an extent that the social and political absurdities described by Orwell or Huxley seem closer at hand than ever before. Given this, we're lucky to have *The Daily Show* and *The Colbert Report*, harnessing irony in pursuit of the truth, or at least *truthiness*. On the most basic level, these show's verbal ironies invite us to suspend belief about what's being *explicitly* said or done and instead interpret the situation at hand to see what's *implicitly* going on.[3] Irony also encourages, however, a more general suspicion that meaning and truth are constructed or interpreted, instead of simply being there for all to see. While Jon Stewart's program throws its political punches in terms of satire, burlesque, and verbal irony, Colbert—an Irish Roman Catholic born and raised in South Carolina and who studied theater at Northwestern University—has shown himself the master of what could be called "existential irony," or living in a way that calls attention to "incongruit[ies] between the actual result of a sequence of events and the normal or expected result." In this chapter we'll examine this sense of irony along with the parallels between the persona of "Stephen Colbert of *The Colbert Report*" and the character of the "ironist" discussed both by philosophical Romantics in the nineteenth century as well as the American philosopher Richard Rorty (1931–2007).[4] For both Colbert and Rorty, irony can be funny and refreshing, and yet at the same time represents a challenge to our beliefs. We'll look at the difference between verbal irony and its more robust counterpart, "existential irony," and examine the extent to which Colbert fits this description. More importantly, we'll ask if embracing irony has serious implications for how we deal with our political responsibilities in the new and more precarious, "post-ironic" world.

Ironists: People Destroying America

Philosophy and irony grew up in the same neighborhood, namely Athens, Greece, ca. 440 BCE. As we've already seen,[5] Socrates—a pederast, Persian War veteran, and perhaps the most famous of all philosophers—used verbal irony as a tool to motivate his deep discussions with poets, politicians, artisans, and his own followers as he wandered the ancient Athenian agora. Although many readers of Socrates' discussions find his irony merely an amusing diversion or a telling indicator of his slightly eccentric personality, there are compelling reasons to believe that the pursuit of philosophy and the emergence of irony are much more closely intertwined. Friedrich Schlegel (1772–1829), a major figure in the Romantic movement, explains: "Philosophy is the real homeland of irony, which one would like to define as logical beauty; for wherever philosophy appears in oral or written dialogues—and is not simply confined in rigid systems—there irony should be asked for and provided."[6]

Socrates claims that his own philosophical quest was inspired by a significant yet ironic incident in his own life. His "impetuous" friend Chaerephon had gone, as Greeks often did, with a searing question to be answered by the cryptic yet all-seeing priestesses of the Oracle at Delphi. Chaerephon, according to him,

> asked the oracle to tell him whether there was anyone wiser than I was, and the Pythian prophetess answered that there was no man wiser … When I heard the answer, I said to myself, What can the god mean? and what is the interpretation of this riddle? for I know that I have no wisdom, small or great. What can he mean when he says that I am the wisest of men?[7]

For philosophers, this is an inspirational example of questing for truth, but it's also a case of "existential irony." A man who is told he is the wisest of mortals, but who in fact believes he knows nothing, turns out to be wiser than the leading citizens of Athens because of his honest acknowledgment of his own ignorance.

Imagine the precise opposite of Socrates: a man who egomaniacally considers himself the wisest of mortals, and in fact *does* know a lot—not only political facts, but their significance for the wider American culture—yet who turns out to be quiet, soft-spoken, oblivious to fashion or social norms, who has a note on his work computer that says, "Joy is the most infallible sign of the presence of God." A man who, after having spearheaded efforts to have an eagle, a treadmill aboard the International Space Station, a bridge in Hungary, and a Ben & Jerry's ice-cream flavor named after him, replies to a compliment from an interviewer by saying, "There's no guarantee that I'm not giving you a persona now, you realize that? Is this me or is this just the character seeming like a good guy?"[8]

Just who *is* this "Stephen Colbert" you speak of? This is a deeply philosophical question that has, in a slightly different form, exercised thinkers of such intellect as Georg W.F. Hegel (1770–1831) and Søren Kierkegaard (1813–1855), both of whom were intrigued by whether it would be possible to live life, as "Stephen Colbert" seems to do, in full existential irony. Both were puzzled by the celebration of the self-contradictory nature of irony in passages such as this from Friedrich Schlegel:

> Socratic irony is the only involuntary and yet completely deliberate dissimulation. It is equally impossible to feign it or divulge it. To a person who hasn't got it, it will remain a riddle even after it is openly confessed. It is meant to deceive no one except those who consider it a deception and who either take pleasure in the delightful roguery of making fools of the whole world or else become angry when they get an inkling they themselves might be included. In this sort of irony, everything should be playful and serious, guilelessly open and deeply hidden.[9]

Schlegel's contemporary, Hegel, was concerned with the ways in which people could rationally justify their rights and freedoms in society. To him, it was puzzling that nothing "counts" for the ironic individual unless she *allows* it to count for herself; she is, in effect, the social flip side of the conservative traditionalist. As one interpreter of Hegel puts it, in choosing to be *authentic*, the irony-embracing individual "is thus logically led to taking an ironic attitude toward everything, including himself," and is still left with the problem of how to justify their behavior to others.[10] To Hegel, existential irony is part of the advance of freedom, since the ironist, play acting her role, is free from the obligation of having her intentions understood by her audience. Despite this freedom, for Hegel irony is an incomplete and unsatisfactory worldview because it represents an abdication of responsibility on the part of the ironist for what he says and does.

Kierkegaard, a student of Hegel's philosophy but also a critic of it, wrote his dissertation on Socrates and irony at the University of Copenhagen. He offered a controversial interpretation of Socrates. "In a certain sense, he was a revolutionary," Kierkegaard remarks, "yet not so much by doing something as by *not* doing something ... He stood ironically above every relationship."[11] Kierkegaard interprets

Socrates' famous dictum, "Know yourself!" as implying that the individual must pursue philosophical wisdom by first separating himself from his society and community. The advantage of this? The ironist becomes capable of a new level of critical reflection on their situation, a necessary component of any philosophical thinking. But the level of detachment achieved by Socrates—and, I would argue, Colbert as well—also leads us to conclude, as we lead our own daily lives, that the ironist "does not take his participation in these practices, nor these practices themselves, seriously."[12] To focus on the case in point, not only does the political ironist betray his claim to being seen as a sincere participant in political life, but by doing so, he ridicules political practices, denying that they have merit at all. The verdict on existential irony from Schlegel, Hegel, and Kierkegaard is that it seems intrinsically tethered to philosophizing. What Hegel and Kierkegaard add, though, is that living ironically radically rejects the *object* of its irony, the butt of the joke, but without putting something better in its place. This failure is not something we'll ultimately find in *The Colbert Report* though, as we'll see.

Colbert Nation-Building

Basically, ironic humor defeats our expectations by showing us that what we took for reality was more elusive than we thought. Irony, like its cousin satire, often plays cultural tropes off against each other. Irony's appreciative audience, therefore, needs to be not only self-reflective but also culturally literate.

Stephen Colbert consistently defeats our expectations in ironic and memorable ways. It's no secret that Colbert, just like his old *Daily Show* fellow "reporters" Rob Corddry and Ed Helms, adopts an on-air persona to conspicuously mock the amiable, depth-free lack of authenticity of most of today's real news anchors. Very early in the run of *The Colbert Report*, he made a distinction between the "authoritative," "star-spangled," and "sponsored" "Stephen Colbert" of *The Colbert Report* and the role he formerly had to play, namely, "Stephen Colbert, *Daily Show* stooge, a tool forced by his corporate overlords to turn on the very heroes of the news business!" In the years since that revelation, we've seen the many faces of "Stephen Colbert": the stingingly sarcastic Colbert chastising the "yes man" press at the 2006

White House Correspondents' Association Dinner; the singing and dancing Colbert of "Night of Too Many Stars"; his semi-in-character 2010 testimony on exploitive immigrant labor before the House Judiciary Subcommittee; and the shaven-headed Stephen (in camouflage two-piece suit) entertaining the troops in Iraq. At least in some of their more critical and ironic moments, these personas parallel some of Kierkegaard's own "poetic creations," pseudonymous authors like Johannes Climacus and Hilarius Bookbinder who offer opinions and perspectives equal and sometimes opposite to Kierkegaard's own in many of his books. This appearance of "multiple authorships," of course, only increases the irony of the situation at hand.

Colbert's most familiar persona is a self-absorbed conservative talk show host. It's no secret that the format, stage design, and even the graphics of the *Report* are mockeries of the Fox shows of conservative ideologues Sean Hannity and Bill O'Reilly. Colbert ridicules conservative pundits like Hannity and O'Reilly simply by acting like them, but the success of the parody depends upon an interpretation that Colbert's core audience already makes of the likes of Hannity, O'Reilly, Limbaugh, Savage, and others: their over-the-top fearmongering, ad hominems, racism, and sexism are already *self-parodies* of American conservatism. Colbert, by acting more conservative than conservatives elsewhere encourages us to suspend belief in what he *really* stands for as long as possible. Colbert engages in what American critic and philosopher Richard Rorty calls "redescription" of the self to blur the distinction between how he appears and what he really is.

Colbert has seized upon, and made fully his own, an aspect of ironic humor, namely the dizzying and discomforting *centerlessness* that we feel when presented with existential irony. Such situations are framed in terms of humor that forces us to reflect upon the incongruities between the expected results of actions—whether ours or of others—and what actually results. This should drag us toward a new understanding of the world around us as marked by *contingency* (the unexpected or the opposite) rather than necessity. Is there a *necessary* connection between hypocrisy and feeling shameful, as many Colbert interviews with politicians suggest? Does one *have* to behave respectfully in front of the President, as the setting of the 2006 White House Correspondents' Association Dinner would demand? Is it *necessary* for a news anchor to believe in the truthfulness of what he or she reports? Colbert joyfully answers "no" to each of these questions and many others.

Sometimes the irony that arises from acknowledging such contingency threatens to break free of the constraints of its creators, as seems to be the case with Colbert's increasingly zealous sabotage of the 2012 election through manipulation of campaign finance rules in the wake of the 2010 Citizens United v. Federal Election Commission Supreme Court decision. This controversial ruling classified monetary contributions as "political speech" and removed restrictions on corporate spending in elections. Colbert promptly formed his own Super PAC with the slogan, "Making a better tomorrow, tomorrow," and asked for donations from his audience members (from mid 2011 to December 31, 2011, it had raised more than $825,000). His explicit rationale? In an interview with Ted Koppel, he claimed, "It would be stupid to be in the 2012 election and *not* have a Super PAC," and indeed, Colbert was in the running—for the President of the United States of South Carolina.[13] In reality—if such a word means anything in this context—the "candidate's" on-air hijinks with his lawyer, Trevor Potter, and one-time manager of the Colbert Super PAC, Jon Stewart, have gleefully exposed the potential for abuses that the new campaign finance ruling has opened wide.

In the Colbert Super PAC case, as in many others, our eyes are opened to the semblance of irony everywhere in social performances. Self-centeredness and apparent hypocrisy glossed over by radical self-redescription may convince us that there isn't a stable core of self or character around which the public faces of famous individuals orbit. The persona is, as Friedrich Nietzsche (1844–1900) held, simply a mask concealing a regress of masks, with no face beneath. And if this is true of talking heads, why shouldn't it also be true of us? At this realization, we may experience anxiety at the centerlessness. But as philosophers from Socrates to Kierkegaard to the present never tire of reminding us, feeling discomfort about a realization is no evidence against its truth.

Proust-Spouting, Atheist Gay Truck Mechanics

While nineteenth-century thinkers like Hegel and Kierkegaard were uncomfortable with the dubious achievements of the life of existential irony, in the late twentieth century Richard Rorty saw our willingness to accept centerlessness, or what he calls the "contingency of self-hood," as a mark of maturity in the educated, secular, liberal culture of the Western world. Accepting contingency over necessity as a fact of life has wide-ranging implications for our whole worldview, Rorty says: "The drama of an individual human life, or of the history of humanity as a whole, is not one in which a preexistent goal is triumphantly reached or tragically not reached."[14] But Herman Cain look-a-like and journalistic hero "Stephen Colbert" would disagree, steeped as his rhetoric is in the necessity of truth and über-patriotic nationalism.

Richard Rorty's anti-hero is the "ironist," a figure who fundamentally gives up the serious search for ultimate, unifying principles to make sense of ironic contradictions and embraces a Schlegel-like sense of intellectual life as play. Rorty's ironists are "never quite able to take themselves seriously because [they're] always aware that the terms in which they describe themselves are subject to change, always aware of the contingency and fragility ... of their selves."[15]

The image of the ironist emerges from Rorty's attempt to synthesize strands from three very different schools of contemporary philosophy. From European philosophies influenced by Nietzsche, Rorty takes the idea that philosophy is a tool for the use of individuals in the process of their "self-creation." From American pragmatist John Dewey (1859–1952), Rorty takes "a picture of human beings as children of their time and place, without any significant metaphysical or biological limits on their plasticity."[16] Finally, Rorty interprets the process of Nietzschean self-creation and the Deweyan plasticity of human nature through *language*, adopting the notion that philosophy must shift its attention to language-use as the special way in which human beings construct their world.

These three central ideas come together in Rorty's idea of a "final vocabulary." "All human beings," Rorty tells us, "carry about a set of words which they employ to justify their actions, their beliefs, and their lives."[17] Examples of such central words are "true," "good," and "right," as well as "Christ," "progressive," "America," and "professional standards."[18] Each may be invoked to *justify* and *make sense of* what we do on a daily basis. The words that characterize our deepest commitments are not just *any* vocabulary, but the one that we hold as the final court of appeal, beyond which there is no justifying ourselves to others. Rorty's ironist, though, is someone who has a special kind of relationship to her final vocabulary:

> I shall define an "ironist" as someone who fulfills three conditions: (1) she has radical and continuing doubts about the final vocabulary she currently uses, because she has been impressed by other vocabularies, vocabularies taken as final by people or books she has encountered; (2) she realizes that argument phrased in her present vocabulary can neither underwrite nor dissolve these doubts; (3) insofar as she philosophizes about her situation, she does not think that her vocabulary is closer to reality than others, that it is in touch with a power not herself.[19]

In other words, we should accept our basic centerlessness and make the best of it. The ironist withholds "devotion" to the terms of her final vocabulary because, after all, the world's contingency teaches us that what works in terms of belief today may not be so good tomorrow, next week, or next year.

Rorty clarifies this idea by noting that irony is the *opposite of common sense*—a revelation that often emerges in the absurdities into which *The Colbert Report* plunges. The follower of common sense takes for granted the notion that everyone shares their final vocabulary, and more importantly, that the obvious, self-evident meaning of "America" or "goodness" is *necessarily* obvious and self-evident to all. Perhaps Rorty ignores the idea that common sense might be a kind of "default" vocabulary for many of us, used to coordinate our actions without justifying anything.[20] But since Rorty claims to be a pragmatist in the mold of John Dewey, we should see the ironist's "final vocabulary" as only coordinating, not justifying. For most people, things are reversed: a vocabulary is "final" because it's the "final word" on how things stand, and necessarily so. But the ironist would, according to Rorty, refuse to take a part in the widely accepted self-deception that vocabularies aren't contingent, or, to put it another way, she doesn't accept that there are some words in a final vocabulary that it is absolutely necessary to stand behind.

Speaking Truthiness to Power

Now we can ask the question, is Colbert an ironist, either in Rorty's or the earlier Romantics' sense? Is he, in entertaining us, also showing us how to hold our deepest commitments at arm's length?

On the one hand, he's clearly not. Contrary to his over-the-top conservative, patriotic persona, it's clear that Colbert's real sympathies lie with liberals. To appreciate *The Colbert Report* and *The Daily Show*, liberals and progressives have to value irony, but the vast majority of liberals and progressives *aren't* Rortian ironists. They don't view their final vocabularies as "no closer to reality" than the vocabularies of their political opponents. If Colbert ultimately takes their side, then he isn't a Rortian ironist.

Colbert satirizes his opponents by amplifying the right-wing noise machine to the point of arrogant, blustering absurdity. Nowhere is this more obvious than in the October 2010 rally, co-sponsored by Jon Stewart and entitled "The Rally to Restore Sanity and/or Fear." Colbert emerged from his "fear bunker," echoing claims he had made earlier on the *Report* that this was "no time to be reasonable" but instead to "freak out for freedom!" Colbert and his "Fearzilla" were ultimately defeated by the chanting crowd of nearly 70,000 people filling the Mall, and the *Report* host had to fall back on his "second greatest passion" after spreading fear, making decorative birdhouses.

But on the other hand, there's "truthiness," a concept made for ironists if ever there was one.[21] Colbert didn't invent truthiness. He merely coined the term to spear President Bush's folksy, "from the heart" attempts to "justify" questionable decisions in a manner more at home in the *Andy Griffith Show* than in a liberal democracy. Some immediately saw the cultural significance of "truthiness" beyond the humor. In a *New York Times* piece almost as well known as the segment on the *Colbert* premiere, Frank Rich pointed to Republicans for elevating truthiness-telling to an art form, claiming that "it's the power of the story that always counts first, and the selling of it that comes second."[22] Colbert disparagingly opposes "facts" to "truthiness," or what his "gut" tells him. At its worst, truthiness is a form of what philosophers call *subjectivism*, or acting as if what is true or right for me is true or right for everyone *simply because* it's true or right for me. The fact that there are those who find President Bush's "truthiness" appealing or support the folksy homilies of presidential candidate Rick Santorum is evidence that it is no longer politically necessary to separate policy reality from the emotive or spiritual package appearance through which it's sold to the public: eventually, all we are left with is the packaging.[23]

Rorty's ironist, if she embraces truthiness, doesn't need to make sense of her preferences as demanded by "the American Dream" or as evidence of "God's grace." Instead, she declares, "Hey! This news reporting/this book by Nabokov/this documentary about the Sudan/ this person's life has provided me with an alternative, refreshing way of looking at my life! You ought to check it out!" Unfortunately, truthiness also bolsters dubious efforts like the book *God Wants You to Be Rich* and every reality TV show. It's difficult to come to terms with the fact that final vocabularies can only be loosened and made more flexible by open conversations in which alternative visions of the good life can be shared freely, without cruelty, humili- ation, or coercion. To make this happen, Rorty enjoins us to "take care of political freedom, and truth and goodness will take care of themselves."[24]

Better Know an Ironist

Better to know an ironist who knows better than to stand behind truthiness wholeheartedly. An interview with an out-of-character Colbert clues us in to why we need to be suspicious of the turn away from facts and toward subjectivism:

> It used to be, everyone was entitled to their own opinion, but not their own facts. But that's not the case anymore. Facts matter not at all. Perception is everything. It's certainty. People love the President because he's certain of his choices as a leader, even if the facts that back him up don't seem to exist ... Truthiness is "What I say is right, and [nothing] anyone else says could possibly be true." It's not only that I *feel* it to be true, but that *I* feel it to be true. There's not only an emotional quality, but there's a selfish quality.[25]

This sense of "truthiness" hides an implicit subjectivism about the facts that is unequivocally dangerous in leaders who are supposed to be accountable to the public good. Truthiness is a bill of goods sold to our citizen-audience, as a bold method for decision-making that appears to be more in touch with reality than the facts actually admit, or a return to a golden age that never existed in the first place. "Truthiness" obscures the fact that most public policies are sponsored by and carried out for the benefit of special interests, lawyers, corpo- rations, PACs and Super PACs. Beyond Colbert's irony calling attention to this, as Lisa Colletta explains, "Colbert [also] satirizes the values of a culture in which being a consumer and a product of commercial television appears like real agency and autonomy" without *being* genuinely autonomous.[26]

But if we have learned nothing more by this point, we should remind ourselves that appearances can be deceptive and the charms of "feeling from your gut" can be abused by those who mask their true intentions toward power and control. Nietzsche, for example, calls our attention to the "will to power," which crafts what we take as true and what we condemn as lies. John Dewey, in a more positive vein, observes that the institutions of liberal democracies need to be constructed so as to dissolve concentrations of power by giving individual citizens control over the conditions that affect their lives. And in a much less abstract context, *New York Times* columnist Frank Rich points out:

> [The] genius of the right is its ability to dissemble with a straight face while simultaneously mustering the slick media machinery and expertise to push the goods. It not only has the White House propaganda operation at its disposal, but also an intricate network of P.R. outfits and fake-news outlets that are far more effective than their often hapless liberal counterparts.[27]

At different levels of abstraction, all three perspectives underwrite the idea that the Rortian ironist may be selling herself short in attempting to speak "truth to power" with critical tools no sharper than a constantly shifting final vocabulary and a weak, vaguely subjectivist sense of the truth.

Colbert recognizes this. When asked by Representative Judy Chu of California in front of the House Subcommittee why he was interested in immigrant labor issues, he paused for a long while. Stroking his hair, looking off into space, he falls out of persona. Uncharacteristically stuttering, he replies, "I ... I like talking about people who have no power," indicating that his sympathies lie with migrant workers who effectively have no power and no rights in the United States. More and more frequently, this Stephen Colbert slips out from behind the mask of "Stephen Colbert," and I would wager that without a glimpse of such a genuine and non-ironic face from time to time, Colbert's delectable power over us would have waned long before now.[28]

Notes

1. Roger Rosenblatt, "The Age of Irony Comes to an End," *Time* 158 (13) (September 24, 2001), 79.
2. *Webster's Ninth New Collegiate Dictionary* (Springfield, MA: Merriam-Webster, 1983).
3. At this point I want to offer a warning, and in doing to join dozens of philosophers, comedians, and cultural critics. Not only will this explanation itself not be funny, but it's a truism that when we try to describe *why* something is funny, we make that thing a *lot less funny* in hindsight. This is why, when someone asks us to explain a joke, we often reply with, "Forget it. It's not worth it." If reading this section ultimately makes you see Colbert as less funny in the future, I can only apologize and, of course, note the irony.
4. Richard Rorty, *Contingency, Irony and Solidarity* (New York: Cambridge University Press, 1989).
5. See especially Judith Barad, "Stewart and Socrates: Speaking Truth to Power," in this volume, which discusses Jon Stewart's use of Socratic irony.
6. Friedrich Schlegel, "From 'Critical Fragments'," in *Classical and Romantic German Aesthetics*, ed. J.M. Bernstein (New York: Cambridge University Press, 2003), 241.
7. Plato, *Apology*, from *Plato: Five Great Dialogues*, trans. Benjamin Jowett (New York: D. Van Nostrand Co., 1942), 37.
8. Neil Strauss, "The Subversive Joy of Stephen Colbert," *Rolling Stone* 1087 (September 17, 2009), 57.
9. Friedrich Schlegel, "On Incomprehensibility," in *Classical and Romantic German Aesthetics*, ed. J.M. Bernstein (New York: Cambridge University Press, 2003), 302–203.
10. Terry Pinkard, *Hegel's 'Phenomenology': The Sociality of Reason* (New York: Cambridge University Press, 1996), 214–215.
11. Søren Kierkegaard, *The Concept of Irony with Continual Reference to Socrates*, Vol. II of *Kierkegaard's Writings*, ed. and trans. Howard V. Hong and Edna H. Hong (Princeton, NJ: Princeton University Press, 1989), 182; italics added.
12. Andrew Cross, "Neither Either nor Or: The Perils of Reflexive Irony," in *The Cambridge Companion to Kierkegaard*, ed. Alastair Hannay and Gordon Marino (New York: Cambridge University Press, 1998), 133.
13. www.huffingtonpost.com/2012/01/31/stephen-colbert-superpac_n_1243255.html, accessed February 11, 2013. This is precisely the reasoning Barack Obama used when changing his view on the morality of Super PACs in gearing up for reelection in 2012.

14. Rorty, *Contingency, Irony and Solidarity*, 29.
15. Ibid., 73–74.
16. Richard Rorty, "Trotsky and the Wild Orchids," in his *Philosophy and Social Hope* (New York: Penguin, 1999), 15. While Rorty relies heavily on Dewey for what some might call his "neopragmatism," his interpretation of Dewey is very controversial among most Dewey scholars.
17. Rorty, *Contingency, Irony, and Solidarity*, 73.
18. Of the examples given, the first three are examples of words that represent "thin" ideals that are "flexible" and universally acknowledged as important. The last four represent "thick" ideals, the meanings of which are "more rigid" because they're less subject to interpretation. Also, these terms—like "America"—aren't acknowledged by *everyone* to have moral force, a fact apparently missed by those whom Colbert spoofs who can't see why the entire world fails to see America for the "City on a Hill" it is.
19. Rorty, *Contingency, Irony, and Solidarity*, 73.
20. I want to thank Jason Holt for pointing out this possible notion of "common sense."
21. For an extensive discussion of truthiness, see Amber L. Griffioen, "Irrationality and 'Gut' Reasoning: Two Kinds of Truthiness," the previous chapter in this volume.
22. Frank Rich, "Truthiness 101: From Frey to Alito," *New York Times* (January 22, 2006), S4, 16.
23. Cognitive scientist George Lakoff has addressed this question by talking about the manipulation of "conceptual frames" that can be used to convince a subject of something when hard evidence can't or won't be assessed. See his *Moral Politics* (Chicago: University of Chicago Press, 2002) and *Don't Think of an Elephant!* (White River Junction, VT: Chelsea Green Publishing, 2004).
24. Rorty, *Contingency, Irony, and Solidarity*, 84.
25. An Interview with Stephen Colbert in "The A.V. Club," *The Onion*, quoted in the Wikipedia entry for "Truthiness," http://en.wikipedia.org/wiki/Truthiness, accessed February 11, 2013.
26. Lisa Colletta, "Political Satire and Postmodern Irony in the Age of Stephen Colbert and Jon Stewart," *Journal of Popular Culture* 42 (5) (2009), 867–868.
27. Rich, "Truthiness 101," 16.
28. Deep appreciation for the input and inspiration of Jason Holt, Terrance MacMullan, and Bill Irwin oozes from every syllable of this chapter. Thanks!

Senior Philosophical Correspondents

Neil Baker recently completed his Bachelor of Arts at Hope International University and plans to begin graduate work soon. A former religious fundamentalist turned skeptic, Neil has found it a bit difficult to continue on his original career path as a Christian minister. He does however hope to pursue his interest in the field of interreligious dialogue through graduate study—that is, assuming God decides to forgive Disney World for its "Gay Days," and not to hurl that apocalyptic meteor Pat Robertson warned us all about.

Judith Barad is Professor of Philosophy and Women's Studies at Indiana State University. After graduating magna cum laude from Loyola University of Chicago in 1980, she attended Northwestern University, receiving her Ph.D. in Philosophy from Northwestern in 1984. In 1985 she accepted a position in Philosophy at Indiana State, where she eventually served as the chairperson for nine years. She is the author of three books and numerous articles on ethics and the philosophy of religion, including such topics as feminist ethics, the role of emotion in moral judgments, the treatment of animals, the philosophy of St. Thomas Aquinas, and the *Ethics of Star Trek*. She has given dozens of national and international scholarly presentations, and has been an ethics consultant for Boeing, Corp. A member of the Secular Franciscan Order, Dr. Barad is active in her local parish. She is a Senior Teaching Correspondent.

The Ultimate Daily Show and Philosophy: More Moments of Zen, More Indecision Theory,
First Edition. Edited by Jason Holt.
© 2013 John Wiley & Sons, Inc. Published 2013 by John Wiley & Sons, Inc.

Alejandro Bárcenas teaches Philosophy at Texas State University at San Marcos. He received his Ph.D. from the University of Hawai'i at Mānoa in 2010. His research focuses primarily on political theory and the history of philosophy. He has high hopes that one day Count von Count will be interviewed by Stewart on the state of the economy.

Kellie Bean is Associate Dean of the College of Liberal Arts and Professor of English at Marshall University, where between scuttling students' opportunities for success and pushing the liberal agenda, she teaches feminism, film, and drama. She has published on the works of Harold Pinter, Samuel Beckett, Disney, and Jean-François Lyotard. Her book, *Post-Backlash Feminism: Women and the Media since Reagan/Bush* sets things aright for women everywhere. When asked what she thinks is the "fundamental problem with public political discourse," she says she doesn't understand the question.

Kimberly Blessing is Chair and Professor of Philosophy at SUNY Buffalo State. Her areas of interest in philosophy include the meaning of life, and early modern philosophy, focusing attention on Descartes and his views on ethics. Publications include *Movies and the Meaning of Life* (Open Court, 2005), "Atheism and Meaningfulness in Life," *Oxford Handbook of Atheism* (Oxford University Press, forthcoming), and "Mal-Placed Regret" in *Inception and Philosophy* (Wiley-Blackwell, 2011). Blessing uses Harry Frankfurt's work *On Bullshit* (Princeton, 2005) in her introductory philosophy courses—students love to be able to tell her whether or not she's full of BS. She enjoys calling the college bookstore to see whether they still have bullshit on the shelves.

Kevin S. Decker is Associate Professor of Philosophy and Associate Dean of the College of Arts, Letters and Education at Eastern Washington University. He is coeditor, with Jason T. Eberl, of *Star Wars and Philosophy*, *Star Trek and Philosophy*, and of *Terminator and Philosophy* with Richard Brown. His edited books, *Ender's Game and Philosophy* and *Who Is Who? The Philosophy of Doctor Who*, will be hitting a bookstore near you soon. Now, look out the nearest window—what you see is your moment of Zen.

Liam P. Dempsey teaches Philosophy at Trent University. He received his Ph.D. in philosophy from Western University in 2003. His research interests include philosophy of mind and cognitive science as well as early modern philosophy. He has recent publications in the *British Journal for the History of Philosophy* and *Philosophy and Phenomenological Research*. To paraphrase the words of that sage philosopher, Stephen Colbert, the best career advice he can give the reader is to get your own TV show. It pays well, the hours are good, and you are famous. And eventually some very nice people will give you a doctorate in fine arts for doing jack squat.

Joseph A. Edelheit is Professor of Religious Studies and Director of Religious and Jewish Studies at St. Cloud State University in St. Cloud, MN. He has also been a Reform Rabbi for 40 years. Students have gotten so used to seeing *Daily Show* clips during any class that Edelheit teaches, that students now rate Jon Stewart in their course evaluations: he gets very high marks as a teacher who cares about being funny, has the most liberal grading system, but students don't believe that Stewart actually reads the books before interviews with the authors. Edelheit is very hopeful that this chapter will help him in his application for the position of *Daily Show* Senior Rabbinic Correspondent.

Gerald J. Erion is Associate Professor of Philosophy at Medaille College. His current research includes work in ethics, philosophy of mind, and critical thinking. He considers each of his classes an opportunity to restore sanity and/or fear.

Michael Gettings is Associate Professor of Philosophy at Hollins University. His philosophical work ranges from analyzing ontological arguments for God's existence to positing new ontological categories for works of art to deciphering the speech of Tony Soprano. Fox News has reported that some people are saying he delivered the gift of Donald Trump from the comedy gods to Jon Stewart.

John Scott Gray is Associate Professor of Humanities at Ferris State University, Big Rapids, Michigan. His main areas of research include political and social philosophy, in particular issues relating to the philosophy of sex and gender, as well as applied ethics. He is the coauthor of *Introduction to Popular Culture: Theories, Applications and Global Perspectives* (with J. Randall Groves and Robert Quist). In his free time, when he is not hurling racist or sexist remarks at random strangers, he enjoys reading and playing hockey.

Amber L. Griffioen is a researcher and lecturer in Philosophy at the University of Konstanz in Germany. Between plates of "Freedom Schnitzel" and "Liberty Wurst" (as she calls them in her preferred language of "Denglish"), she works on issues in practical philosophy (specifically philosophy of action, ethics, and problems of irrationality), philosophy of religion, and philosophy of sport (the "t" is silent). Despite her general mistrust of both books and facts, she has written on topics as diverse as Abelard's ethics, superstition and self-deception, shame and guilt in survivors of trauma, and the metaphysics of balls and strikes in baseball, and she is currently engaged in a "truthy" research project on religious experience and emotion. In her contribution to this volume, she promises not to *write* philosophy *to* you but rather to *feel* philosophy *at* you.

Jason Holt is Associate Professor at Acadia University, where he teaches courses in philosophy and communication for the School of Recreation Management and Kinesiology. He specializes in aesthetics and philosophy of mind, but has also published widely in philosophy and popular culture and other areas. He is author of *Blindsight and the Nature of Consciousness*, coauthor of *Flexibility: A Concise Guide*, and editor of this volume and its predecessor, *The Daily Show and Philosophy*, as well as *Philosophy of Sport: Core Readings*. He's still proud to be one of those Canadian gringos.

David Kyle Johnson is Associate Professor of Philosophy at King's College, in Wilkes-Barre, Pennsylvania. His specializations include philosophy of religion, metaphysics, and logic, and he has published in journals such as *Philo*, *Sophia*, and *Religious Studies*. Kyle has edited two books for Wiley-Blackwell's Philosophy and Pop Culture series (*Inception and Philosophy: Because It's Never Just a Dream* [2012] and *Heroes and Philosophy: Buy the Book, Save the World* [2009]), and has written articles on Stephen Colbert, *The Hobbit*, *Doctor Who*, Batman, *South Park*, *Family Guy*, *The Onion*, *The Office*, Johnny Cash, *Battlestar Galactica*, Quentin Tarantino, and Christmas. With William Irwin, he edited *Introducing Philosophy through Pop Culture: From Socrates to South Park, Hume to House*

(Wiley-Blackwell, 2010) and maintains a blog (*Plato on Pop*) for *Psychology Today*. Kyle is currently developing a metaphysics course for *The Great Courses*. One day, he hopes to climb Bullshit Mountain.

Greg Littmann is fair and balanced and Associate Professor of Philosophy at Southern Illinois University Edwardsville. He is a no spin zone, is the best political team on campus, has a Ph.D. in Philosophy from the University of North Carolina at Chapel Hill, is not the worst person in the world, and more Americans choose him to see the whole picture because, fuck it, he does it live. He has published on metaphysics and the philosophy of logic and has written seventeen chapters for books relating philosophy to popular culture, including volumes on *The Big Bang Theory*, *Boardwalk Empire*, *Breaking Bad*, *Doctor Who*, *Game of Thrones*, *The Onion*, and *The Walking Dead*. Greg Littmann moves forward to reform, prosperity, and peace in the country first because we believe in America if that's change we can believe in and yes we can but don't tread on me.

Matthew S. LoPresti is Chair of the Asian and Pacific Studies Program and Assistant Professor of Philosophy and Humanities at Hawaii Pacific University. His research in East-West comparative philosophy is on religious pluralism, interreligious dialogue, and the role of the public intellectual. He can only hope that Anne Hathaway continues to talk up his research and writings in front of A-list crowds in her award acceptance speeches. Even academics and areas of philosophical research need a celebrity sponsor now and again.

Terrance MacMullan is Professor of Philosophy and Honors at Eastern Washington University. His research and teaching interests include pragmatism, philosophy of race, and Latin American philosophy. He is the author of *Habits of Whiteness: A Pragmatist Reconstruction*. Terry lives with his partner Rebecca and his kids Sylvia and Liam in Spokane, Washington where he enjoys cooking, walking his dog Buck, and plotting about how to use his powerful position as a liberal academic to destroy America. Due to the enormous media exposure he received with the previous edition of this anthology, MacMullan has skyrocketed to 1,342,581 on Richard Posner's most recent list of the most influential public intellectuals in America.

Joseph Marren is Associate Professor and Chair of the Communication Department at SUNY Buffalo State. Prior to academia, he was a reporter and/or editor at various Western New York newspapers for 18 years. His moment of Zen occurred when he realized that *The Daily Show* was like *Firing Line* on 'roid rage, but that Jon Stewart, or his writers, was not as sesquipedalian or as pleonastic as William F. Buckley.

Massimo Pigliucci is Professor of Philosophy at the City University of New York. His interests range from the philosophy of biology to the philosophy of pseudoscience, and extend to the relationships between science, religion, and philosophy. He has been at the forefront of the so-called creationism–evolution controversy, writing a number of essays and giving public talks on the topic. He has published several technical books, including *Making Sense of Evolution* (Chicago Press, with Jonathan Kaplan) as well as books for the public, the most recent one being *Answers for Aristotle: How Science and Philosophy Can Lead Us to A More Meaningful Life* (Basic Books). He writes regular columns for *Skeptical Inquirer* and *Philosophy Now*, and attends Jon Stewart's shows live in New York City whenever he can. He maintains hopes that the comedian will eventually run together with Stephen Colbert as a Presidential candidate, but realizes that Mr. Stewart probably has better things to do.

Roberto Sirvent is Associate Professor of Political and Social Ethics at Hope International University. He is coeditor of the book *By Faith and Reason: The Essential Keith Ward*. Roberto is very happy that he doesn't have to take responsibility for his actions since God always tells him what to do.

Rachael Sotos is an adjunct professor in the Department of Philosophy and Religious Studies at Pace University in New York City. Her interests span classics, political theory, aesthetics, and environmental philosophy. She blogs at arendtiana.net and tweets @arendtiana. Ever striving to be the most reputable Senior Philosophical Correspondent she can be, she occasionally takes time off from roller skating in Central Park and attachment parenting her cats to write lectures and grade student papers.

Roben Torosyan is Director of Teaching and Learning at Bridgewater State University (MA), where he also teaches philosophy. An expert on transformation, Roben has given 81 faculty development presentations nationally (41 of them invited), published work including a chapter in *Stephen Colbert and Philosophy: I Am Philosophy (And So Can You!)*, earned a Ph.D. in Cultural Studies, Philosophy, and Education from Teachers College, Columbia University, and actually talked to Jon Stewart in a small theater in midtown. Thanks to two toddler daughters, Catherine and Ella, Roben's childish arguments now have the perfect captive audience. See goo.gl/4PU4n.

Steve Vanderheiden is Associate Professor of Political Science and Environmental Studies at the University of Colorado at Boulder and Professorial Fellow with the Centre for Applied Philosophy and Public Ethics (CAPPE) at Charles Sturt University in Australia. In addition to many articles and book chapters on political theory and environmental politics, Vanderheiden is the author of *Atmospheric Justice: A Political Theory of Climate Change* (Oxford, 2008). He specializes in analytic theories of justice and normative accounts of democratic governance, but as his role as Senior Philosophical Correspondent to this book shows, he's not above sometimes just making stuff up.

Index

ABC, 13–14, 79
abortion, 175–6, 191–3
Abraham, 133–4
abstinence education, 74
Abu Ghraib, 110
Académie Française, 301
ad hominem arguments, 168–9, 255
Adair, Bill, 31
Adams, John, 281
Adams, Sam, 43, 44
Addams, Jane, 89
Adelson, Sheldon, 132
advertising: and bullshit, 143;
    election ads, 93–4;
    in newspapers, 149
Afghanistan, 326, 327
Ahmadinejad, Mahmoud, 75
AIG, 49
Ailes, Roger, 56
Albanese, Rory *see Earth*
    (The Book)
Alcibiades, 117
Alexander the Great, 117, 120
Allen, George, 160

Allen, Woody, 126, 130, 133, 307
America (The Book), 267–77; on
    approaches to the Constitution,
    284; on colonial history, 90;
    foreword, 96, 281–2; on the
    media, 275–6; neologization in,
    301–2, 305; style of humor,
    268–70; on the US version of
    democracy, 270–5, 276–7
American War of Independence
    (1775–83), 47–8, 286
analytic philosophy, 141
anchors, 28–30, 69–82
Annenberg Public Policy Center, 12
Annie Hall (movie), 136, 307
Arab Spring, 40
Arendt, Hannah, 39
Aristophanes, 51–2, 57, 60, 61,
    66–7
Aristotle, 121, 256
Athens, ancient, 102–3, 105,
    116–17, 327–8
Austen, Jane, 31
Auterson, David, 260

The Ultimate Daily Show and Philosophy: More Moments of Zen, More Indecision Theory,
First Edition. Edited by Jason Holt.
© 2013 John Wiley & Sons, Inc. Published 2013 by John Wiley & Sons, Inc.

Bachmann, Michele, 129, 199, 200–2, 208–9, 261
Balthasar, Hans Urs von, 129–30
Barber, Benjamin, 272
bards, 39–40, 46
Barton, David, 96–7, 240–1
Baudrillard, Jean, 70–3, 74, 76–7, 79, 80
Baugh, Carl E., 259–60
Baumgartner, Jody, 279
Baym, Geoffrey, 156–7, 268–9
Bear Stearns, 49
Beck, Glenn: on the Constitution, 284; as fake fake newsman, 44; hypocrisy, 34; and nostalgia, 294; and religion, 205–6, 209; Stewart on, 59; on Washington, 291
Bee, Samantha: marriage, 313, 316–17, 318–19; parody of sensationalism, 183; treatment of 2004 Republican National Convention, 170; treatment of Bush, 56; treatment of North Korea, 27; treatment of O'Reilly, 243; treatment of Palin, 71; treatment of religion, 223, 232, 258
Begala, Paul, 12, 13, 46, 104, 119–20, 128
begging the question, 171–2
Bennett, William, 187–9, 193
Al Bernameg (TV program), 40
Bible: fundamentalist attitude, 205–6, 207–8; Jefferson's attitude, 287; narrative discrepancies, 243
Biden, Joe, 35
Biden, Naomi, 132
Bin Laden, Osama, 93–4, 97, 177, 326

Black, Lewis, 48, 178, 202–3, 248, 250
Black History Month, 158–9
Blackadder (TV program), 301
Blackstone, Sir William, 240–1
Bleyer, Kevin, 285–9, 292–3
Bloomberg, Michael, 132
Bouazizi, Mohammed, 40
Breyer, Justice Stephen, 286, 289
Britain: Golden Age of satire, 47, 57–8; government-endorsed religion, 245
Brown, Mike, 92
Brownback, Sam, 171–2
Bruce, Lenny, 126
Bryan, William Jennings, 190, 251
Buber, Martin, 125–36
Buckley, William F., 14, 90
Buddhism, 215, 220, 221
Bullen, Katherine, 109
bullshit: The Daily Show's handling, 185–7; importance of fighting, 152–4; political spin as, 145–8; vs. lies, 139–45
Burke, Edmund, 188
Burns, Eric, 43
Bush, George W.: 2004 presidential debates, 174; administration's style, 92; administration's wiretapping program, 168; anti-terrorism policies, 326–7; and Camus, 194; and Christmas, 233; competence, 171; and creationism, 251–2; and executive privilege, 94; and Hurricane Katrina, 169; and Iraq War, 146–7, 169, 173; jokes about, 56, 66, 215; on Miers, 310; Stewart's ironic treatment of footage, 111; and truthiness, 335, 336; use of

rhetoric, 176–7; use of war triumphalism for self-promotion, 57, 94; why he got elected, 88

Cain, Herman, 34, 164, 261
Camus, Albert, 194
Carell, Steve, 118, 155
Carlson, Gretchen, 231, 233
Carlson, Tucker: and McGovern's attack on Rumsfeld, 186; and Stewart's *Crossfire* appearance, 12, 13, 46, 66, 104, 111, 119–20, 128
Carroll, Lewis, 300, 303
Carson, Tom, 269
Carter, Bill, 44
Cenac, Wyatt, 28, 31–2, 56, 201, 313
censorship, 63–5
Chaerephon, 328
Chafee, Lincoln, 233
Chaplin, Charlie, 47
Chaucer, Geoffrey, 58
Cheney, Dick, 104, 147, 170
chimpanzees, 260
Christianity: and evolution, 190–1, 247–64; fundamentalist, 199–210; government favoritism, 239–42; and other religions, 214–15, 220; and war on Christmas, 231–46
Christmas: history of, 234–7; war on, 129, 231–46
Chu, Judy, 337
Citizens United, 49
civic discourse *see* political discourse
Cleland, Patricia, 250
Cleon, 57
Clinton, Bill, 88, 139, 147
Clinton, Chelsea, 132

Clinton, Hillary, 71
cloning, 257
Clooney, George, 30
CNBC, 15–16, 49, 97
CNN, 18, 32–3, 164
Cobb, John B., Jr., 220–1, 222
Coen Brothers, 132
Cohen, Joshua, 276
Cohen, Steve, 33–4
Colbert, Stephen: on 2004 Presidential Election, 24–5; background, 327; *Daily Show* appearances, 93, 155, 173, 177, 178, 217–18, 309, 330; description at beginning of each report, 304–5; as Franklin, 43; handling of rhetoric, 168, 169, 170–1, 173–4, 177, 178; as Horace, 49–50; intellectual or comedian?, 46–7; in Iraq, 331; and irony, 327, 329–32, 334–7; jokes by, 59; and neologization, 298–9, 301–2, 304–5, 306–7; portrait on set, 75; and spin, 174–5; style and persona, 69, 77, 178, 183–4, 327, 330–1; treatment of Christmas, 238; treatment of religion, 215, 217–18, 223, 225, 226–7; truthiness notion, 9, 210, 213, 302, 309–10, 319–21, 322–3; and White House Correspondents' Association Dinner, 46, 215, 330–1
The Colbert Report (TV program): basic premise, 224; mascot, 179; postmodern features, 69–82; and the Rally to Restore Sanity and/or Fear, 17; relationship to the real, 69–82; set, 75; style compared to that of *The Daily Show*, 73, 77;

treatment of Christmas, 233; treatment of religion, 223–8
SEGMENTS AND SERIES: "Better Know a District," 170, 288; "The Threat Down," 173; "Who's Honoring Me Now?," 320; "The Word," 73–4, 75–6, 174–5, 185, 238; "Yahweh or No Way," 224
Cole, Tom, 185
Colletta, Lisa, 336–7
Combs, James E., 39–40
comedy: ancient Greek, 51–2, 57, 60, 61, 66–7; Colbert and irony, 327, 329–32, 334–7; effect of explaining a joke, 338; existential irony, 328–32; history of satire, 47–8, 49, 57–8, 156–7; irony, 91, 110–13, 326–39; mockery as political weapon, 56–68; philosophers and irony, 327–30; philosophy of satire, 268–70; role in rethinking race issues, 157–65; role in revealing political rhetoric, 178–9; Roman, 47, 48, 49, 57, 58–9, 60, 61, 67; satire defined, 59; use to discover wisdom, 120–1; verbal irony, 327–8; why religious subject matter is funny, 222
conceptual frames, 339
Constantine the Great, Roman emperor, 235, 237
Constitution *see* US Constitution
Constitutional Courant (newspaper), 43
contingency, 331, 333–4
Cooper, Anderson, 74–5, 186
Copas, Bleu, 27
Corddry, Rob, 20, 155, 220, 221–2, 330

Cornford, Francis MacDonald, 55
corporations, 273
Costello, Elvis, 211
Coulter, Ann, 104–5, 147
Couric, Katie, 74–5
Cramer, Jim, 8, 15–16, 97, 118–19
Crates of Thebes, 121
creationism, 191, 247–64
creativity: process conception, 221
Crispinus, 60
Critchley, Simon, 159
Cromwell, Oliver, 245
Crossfire (TV program): cancellation, 14, 112; premise, 12; Stewart's appearance, 7–8, 12–13, 46, 66, 111–12, 118, 119–20, 128, 152
Cruver, Tim, 190
Crystal, Ellie, 253
culture: cynics' attitude, 121; *The Daily Show* as cultural memory, 93–4; media's influence, 70–81
cynicism, 114–24

The Daily Show with Jon Stewart (TV program): academic literature's attitude, 282; audience numbers and demographics, 91, 109; and bias, 181–2; and bullshit, 185–7; as critique of contemporary TV, 7–22; distinguishing truth from fiction in, 26–31; and engenderment of cynicism, 114–24; as Fifth Estate agent, 38–55; influence on Arab Spring, 40; influences on, 8–14; method of questioning guests, 107–8; and neologization, 304, 305, 306–7; as news source, 23–37; and political rhetoric, 167–80; as political weapon,

*The Daily Show with Jon
    Stewart* (cont'd)
    56–68; postmodern features,
    69–82; promotion of critical
    thinking, 181–96; relationship
    to the real, 69–82; slogan,
    78–9; special correspondents'
    and anchor's roles, 28–30, 106,
    155; and spin, 150–4; style
    compared to the of *The Colbert
    Report*, 73, 77; style of humor,
    268–9; treatment of evolution
    and creationism, 190–1,
    247–64; treatment of race
    issues, 155–66; treatment of
    religion, 126, 129–32, 199–
    210, 211–30; treatment of TV
    news, 11–12, 14–19, 32–4;
    treatment of war on Christmas,
    129, 231–9, 242–3; use of
    irony, 327
  SEGMENTS AND SERIES: "Adult
    Spin," 151; "Back in Black,"
    202–3; "Clusterf#@k to the
    Poor House," 97, 118; "Even
    Better Than the Real Thing,"
    294; "Even Stevphen," 118;
    "Evolution Schmevolution,"
    190–1, 247–57; "Extras," 174;
    "Faith/Off," 130; "Gitmo's
    World," 95; "Glock and Spiels,"
    94; "The God Exchange,"
    221–2; "Indecision 2004,"
    177–8; "The Matzorian
    Candidate," 129; "Meet the
    Depressed," 95; "Polish That
    Turd," 150, 174; "Science:
    What's It Up To?," 261–2; "The
    Swim Gap," 160–1; "This Week
    in God," 212–13, 217–18, 220,
    223; "Tyrannosaurus Redux,"
    259–60; "Until Hell Freezes

Dover," 257–8; "Victory
    Lapse," 93; "Wall Street
    Watch," 118; "Words Speak
    Louder Than Actions," 177;
    "Worst Responders," 98–9
Daoism, 221
Darrow, Clarence, 251
Darwin, Charles *see* evolution
Davidson, Donald, 324–5
Davies, Nick, 149
Dawkins, Richard, 249, 254
The Day After (movie), 13–14
days of week: origins of
    names, 244
Dayton, Tennessee, 190–1, 251
deception: comedy's role in
    exposing, 121; bullshit vs. lies,
    139–45; *The Daily Show*'s
    exposure, 185–7; of other
    people, 314; and political spin,
    145–8; politicians' use, 31–2;
    relationship with fiction, 24–6;
    self-deception, 312–23
decision-making, 325
deity: process conception, 221
Delphic Oracle, 328
Dembski, William, 253–5
democracy: achieving political
    influence, 122; *America* on the
    US system, 270–5, 276–7;
    Athenian, 116–17; cynicism's
    role, 121–3; *Earth*'s defense,
    278; importance of informed
    citizenry, 178–9; and Stewart,
    96–7
Democratic National Convention
    (2004), 172, 177–8
Democratic National Convention
    (2012), 224
Derrida, Jacques, 90
Descartes, René, 252
Devlin, John, 96

Dewey, John, 89, 90, 96, 99, 333, 337
Dickens, Charles, 236
dictionaries, 300–2
Diogenes of Sinope, 115, 117–18, 119, 120, 122–3
Diogenes Laertius, 116
disinformation, 10–11
Disotell, Todd, 260–1
Dobson, James, 203
Dover trial (2005), 247, 253, 257–8
Downton Abbey (TV program), 100
Du Bois, W.E.B., 89
dysphemisms, 175

Earth (The Book), 133–4, 277–8
Easter, 130–2
Eco, Umberto, 124
ecumenism, 211–30
The Ed Show (TV program), 88
Edwards, John, 142
El Koshary Today (website), 40
elections: declining voter numbers, 270–1, 273; *see also* democracy; presidential elections
embryonic stem cell research, 171–2
Emerson, Ralph Waldo, 89
emotional appeals, 172–4
empiricism, 252
equivocation, 171
euphemisms, 175
evolution, 190–1, 247–64
Ezra, 133

fallacies, 87–8, 168–72, 248, 255
false dilemmas, 169–70
falsificationism, 249
Farleigh Dickinson University: PublicMind, 12
Fast Money (TV program), 15
Feyerabend, Paul, 263

Feynman, Richard, 247–8
fiction: definition, 24–6; devices used in, 29, 30; kinds of truth expressed in, 31
Fifth Estate: definition, 38–9; ethos of, 38–55; as state of mind, 50–2
final vocabulary notion, 333–4
financial crisis (2008–), 15–16, 49, 97, 118–19, 143–4
Firing Line (TV program), 20
The Flintstones (TV program), 243, 259, 260
Focus on the Family, 203
Founding Fathers (aka Framers): originalist attitude, 281–97
Fox News: *The Daily Show*'s attitude, 32–3, 33–4; effectiveness as news source, 36; and Iraq War, 186–7; and 9/11 first responders, 98; and same-sex marriage, 170; slogans, real and fictitious, 56, 78; "Talking Points" segment, 75–6; and US credit rating downgrade, 164; use of dysphemisms, 175; use of talking points, 176; and war on Christmas, 232–9, 242–3; *see also* O'Reilly, Bill
Fox News Sunday (TV program), 16–17
Framers *see* Founding Fathers
Frankfurt, Harry, 139–42, 143, 144–8, 151–3
Franklin, Benjamin, 40, 42, 43–4, 45, 47, 48, 281
Franklin, James, 41–2, 45
Frazier, Joe, 160
freedom fries/toast incident, 169
Freud, Sigmund, 315–16
Fulwood, Sam, III, 85

Gadamer, Hans-Georg, 189, 206
gender issues, 157
generic fallacies, 255
genetic engineering, 257
George III, king of Great Britain and Ireland, 47
Gilbert, Joanne R., 157–8
Gillick, Jeremy, 126
Gingrich, Newt, 85, 132, 201
Giroux, Henry, 101
Global Edition (TV program), 40
global warming, 261
God: process conception, 221
Goldberg, Bernie, 34
good faith, 193–4
Gore, Al, 24
Gorgias, 117
Gorilovskaya, Nonna, 126
Gould, Stephen J., 249
government: demographic composition, 274–5; see also democracy
Griffin, David Ray, 219
Griffin, June, 190, 191
Grove, Jim, 258
Guantanamo Prison, 95, 326
Gumbel, Bryant, 160–1
gut reasoning, 321–2; see also truthiness

Haliburton, Thomas Chandler, 298
Ham, Ken, 260
Hancock, John, 293
Hannah and Her Sisters (movie), 136
Hannity, Sean, 33, 62, 90–1, 291, 294, 331
Hannity & Colmes (TV program), 36, 203
Hardball (TV program), 13, 36, 179
Harrop, Froma, 181–2
Harvey, Paul, 40
Hathaway, Anne, 230

Hegel, Georg W.F., 329, 330
Heller, Joseph, 58
Helms, Ed: style and persona, 29–30, 330; treatment of evolution, 190–1, 249, 251; treatment of journalists, 104; treatment of presidential election debates, 174; treatment of religion, 212–13
Henry, Patrick, 285
hermeneutics, 206
Hick, John, 226
Hinduism, 212–13, 221
Hippias, 117
Hodgman, John, 155
Holler, Michael, 286
homosexuality: and inter-religious harmony, 217–18; Juvenal on, 67; Robertson on, 204, 258; same-sex marriage, 170–1, 187–9, 207–8
Horace, 47, 48, 49–50
Huckabee, Mike, 238
Huffington, Arianna, 293
Hume, David, 252
humor see comedy
Humpty Dumpty, 300, 303
Hurricane Katrina (2005), 92, 169
Husbands and Wives (movie), 307
Huxley, Aldous, 10
the hyperreal, 73, 74, 77, 79

images and meaning, 71–3, 74–81
In the Mix (TV program), 151
Ingraham, Laura, 78
intellectuals: definition of public intellectuals, 88–9; Stewart as public intellectual, 85–101; US attitude, 87–91
intelligent design, 247, 253–7
Iraq War (2003–): 2006 vote to continue, 185; and Bush's reading of Camus, 194;

Colbert on, 59, 173–4;
Democrat-proposed exit
strategy, 112, 168; press failure
to oppose, 146–7; rationale
for, 310; rhetoric used to
promote, 169–70, 173–4,
176–7; US conduct, 326–7;
WMD, 186
Ireland, 156, 236
irony see comedy
irrationality: epistemic, 309–25;
practical, 312, 323
Islam, 225
Israel, 128–9
Israeli–Palestinian conflict, 64

al-Jahiz, 57
James, William, 89
Javerbaum, David see America (The
Book); Earth (The Book)
Jefferson, Thomas: on the
Constitution, 283, 285, 287,
289; fake foreword to America,
96, 281–2; right-wing attitude
to, 240–1, 296
Jersey Shore (TV program), 88
Jews and Judaism: Kristallnacht,
133; Reform Judaism, 134;
Stewart as a Jew, 125–36
Johnson, David Kyle, 227
Johnson, Samuel, 301
Jones, Cullen, 161
Jones, Jason, 30, 194, 313, 316–17,
318–19
Jones, Judge, 253, 262
journalism and journalists: The
Daily Show's attitude, 103–5,
118; PR and spin's influence,
149–54; role, 146; see also
news; newspapers
Julian, Roman emperor, 120
Juvenal, 47, 48, 49, 57, 58–9, 60,
61, 67

Kardashian, Kim, 85, 90
Karlin, Ben see America (The Book)
Kelly, Megyn, 33–4
Kerry, John, 13, 56, 168–9, 172, 174
Kierkegaard, Soren, 329–30, 331
Kim Jong Il, 177
King, Larry, 151
King, Dr. Martin Luther, 134
Kissinger, Henry, 14
Klein, Jonathan, 14
Knox, Israel, 268
Koppel, Ted, 13–14, 332
Korea see North Korea
Krampus, 246
Kristallnacht (1938), 133
Kurtz, Howard, 13
Kyl, John, 31–2

LaHaye, Tim, 297
Lakoff, George, 339
Lamont, Ned, 170
language: final vocabulary notion,
333–4; neologization, 298–308
Larson, John, 253, 254
Lauer, Matt, 194
Lee, Chris, 142
Lepore, Jill, 41, 283, 284–5, 290–2,
293–4, 296
Lewinsky, Monica, 147
Liberty Bell, 286
Lieberman, Joseph, 132, 170
Limbaugh, Rush, 36, 44–5, 61–2,
64, 65–6
Lin, Jeremy, 159
Lippman, Walter, 46
lobbyists, 273
Locke, John, 200, 201–2
logical fallacies see fallacies
London terrorist attacks (2005), 184
Long, Jeffery, 217
lying: bullshit vs. lies, 139–45; and
political spin, 145–8; see also
deception

Machiavelli, Niccolò, 185
Mad Money (TV program), 15,
    118–19
Madison, James, 285
Madoff, Bernie, 132
Madrigal, Al, 155
Magill, Ronald Jay, 50–1
Maher, Bill, 133
Mandvi, Aasif, 70, 155, 241–2, 261–2
marriage, same-sex, 170–1, 187–9,
    207–8
Martin, Trayvon, 161–2
Marx, Karl, 225
Matalan, Mary, 151
Mather, Cotton, 42
Matthews, Chris, 179
Maya and Mayans, 212–13
Mayr, Ernst, 254
McCain, John, 70–1
McConnell, Mitch, 96
McGovern, Ray, 186
McLuhan, Marshall, 8, 152
meaning in life, 255–6
media: *America*'s critique of, 275–6;
    The Daily Show as critique of,
    7–22; influence on content,
    8–11; postmodernist view,
    69–82; PR and spin's influence,
    149–54
Mele, Alfred, 324
Melville, Herman, 36
Mencken, H.L., 85
meritocracy, 274
Merrill Lynch, 49
Michel, Christoph, 323
Miers, Harriet, 310
Mill, John Stuart, 63, 64, 66, 276
Miller, Zell, 168–9, 179
Milton, John, 299
mockery *see* comedy
modernism: attitude to truth, 182

Molon, 60
monarchy, 278
montages, 178
Montanus, 60
Monty Python, 248, 255–6
Mooney, Chris, 251–2, 256, 261
Moore, Clement Clarke, 236
Morris, Jonathon S., 279
Morristown, New Jersey, 290
mortgages, subprime, 143–4
Moyers, Bill, 13, 39, 48, 59
MSNBC, 78–9
Murdoch, Rupert, 58
Murrow, Edward R., 46
Murtha, John, 168
Musharraf, Pervez, 97

natural selection, 249, 253, 255
neologization, 298–308
The New England Courant
    (newspaper), 41–2
Newen, Albert, 323
Newman, Alfred E., 47
news: *The Daily Show* as source,
    23–37; fake news in history,
    41–5; political bias in TV news,
    16–17; postmodernist view,
    70–81; PR and spin's influence,
    149–54; TV news, 10–12,
    14–19, 32–4, 149–50
news holes, 149
newspapers: *America*'s critique,
    275–6; colonial, 41–4;
    percentage split between ads
    and news, 149; sources of
    information, 149
Niebuhr, Reinhold, 204, 208, 209
Nietzsche, Friedrich, 190, 332, 333,
    337
Nikpour, Noelle, 261–2
Nimmo, Dan, 39–40

9/11, 98–9, 326
Nissenbaum, Stephen, 236
North Korea, 27, 176–7
nostalgia, 294
Novak, Bob, 104

Obama, Barack: anti-terrorism
    policies, 326–7; Clooney
    fundraiser, 30; and deportation
    of illegal immigrants, 28–9;
    economic policies, 169;
    election ad using Bin Laden,
    93–4; and executive privilege,
    94; Limbaugh on, 64, 66;
    The Onion's treatment, 35;
    race issues concerning, 155,
    163–4; and spin, 174–5;
    Stewart's relationship to, 77–8,
    94–6, 111; and Super PACs,
    338; Tea Party's attitude to, 290
Obama, Michelle, 224
Obamacare see Patient Protection
    and Affordable Care Act
objectivism, 206
Olbermann, Keith, 74–5
Oliver, John, 28, 181–2, 260–1, 290,
    294
The Onion (newspaper and
    website), 34–6, 40, 47
onomatopoeia, 305–6
Oppenheimer, Mark, 126
orangutans, 260
O'Reilly, Bill: and Christmas, 232,
    233, 242; and The Colbert
    Report, 69, 73, 74–6, 331;
    on The Daily Show's audience,
    12, 282; hypocrisy, 33–4; and
    nostalgia, 294
The O'Reilly Factor (TV program),
    62, 108
originalism, 281–97

Pachter, Marc, 81
Paine, Thomas, 290
Palin, Sarah, 56, 70–1, 169,
    284, 306
Parker, Trey, 229
Parsi, Kahyan, 85–6
Passover, 130–2
Pataki, George, 169
Patient Protection and Affordable
    Care Act ("Obamacare"), 32–3,
    170
Paul, Ron, 129
Perry, Rick, 26, 199, 261
Petry, Sgt. 1st Class Leroy, 96
Pew Research Center, 12, 23, 66
Philip II, king of Macedon,
    117–18
Plame, Valerie, 93
Planned Parenthood, 31–2
Plato, 65, 252, 289
Plutarch, 264
political discourse: cynics' method,
    120–1; The Daily Show's
    handling of rhetoric, 167–80;
    The Daily Show's promotion
    of critical thinking, 181–96;
    Socrates' and Stewart's
    questioning style, 106–8; and
    spin, 151; Stewart's ability to
    facilitate, 96–7, 191–3; TV
    treatment, 9–10,
    12–18
political parties: two-party system,
    274–5
political spin, 145–54, 174–8
politicians: The Daily Show's
    critique, 31–2, 33–4, 35; divine
    support, 199–202; The Onion's
    critique, 34–5; Republican war
    on science, 261–2; use of
    deception, 31–2

politics: fundamentalist religion's
role, 199–210; mockery as
political weapon, 56–68;
relationship with religion,
199–210, 223–8; see also
democracy
Ponnuru, Ramesh, 191–3
Pope, Alexander, 47
Popper, Karl, 249–50
Posner, Richard, 89
Postman, Andrew, 20–1
Postman, Neil, 8–14, 17, 18–19, 20
postmodernism: attitude to truth,
182; way of viewing The Daily
Show and The Colbert Report,
69–82
Potter, Trevor, 332
PR: influence on the media, 149–50
pragmatism, 89
presidential elections: 2004, 24–5,
104, 174; advertisements,
93–4; Super PACs, 49, 309,
332, 338
press see journalism and journalists;
newspapers
Prinz, Rabbi Joachim, 134–5
problem of evil, 264
process metaphysics, 220–1
Prodicus, 117
pseudo-rationality, 325
pundits, 39–40, 46
Puritans, 236, 243, 245
Putnam, Robert, 272
Pyrrhus, king of Epirus, 263–4

race issues, 155–66
The Rachel Maddow Show (TV
program), 114
radical doubt method, 252
Rahner, Karl, 214
Raines, Raymond, 245

Rally to Restore Sanity and/or Fear
(2010), 17–18, 40–1, 51–2, 96,
309, 335
Ramses II, Egyptian pharaoh, 57
rationalism, 252
the real, 72–81
Real Sports (TV program), 160–1
red herring tactic, 183–4
Reilly, Ian, 38, 50
religion: The Daily Show's
treatment, 126, 129–32,
199–210, 211–30; diversity and
conflict, 211–30; divine support
for politicians, 199–202;
evolution and creationism,
190–1, 247–64; exclusivism,
212–13, 214, 216–17;
extremists, 225–6;
fundamentalist religion and US
politics, 199–210; increasing
restraint on religious humor,
223–8; inclusivism, 213,
214–17; pluralism, 213,
217–23; relationship with
politics, 199–210, 223–8;
relationship with science,
247–64; relativism, 218–19;
salvation, 214–15, 220; US
church–state separation,
239–42; the war on Christmas
and Christianity, 129, 231–46;
see also individual religions by
name
Republican Jewish Coalition, 129
Republican National Convention
(2004), 170, 172–3, 177–8
rhetorical definitions, 175–6
rhetorical devices, 167–80
Rice, Condoleezza, 93
Rich, Frank, 335, 337
Riper, General Paul van, 186–7

Roberts, John, 29
Robertson, Pat, 203–5, 207–8, 258
Rocca, Mo, 259–60
Rogers, Joel, 276
Rogers, Will, 40
Romano, Carlin, 100
Romantics, 51
Romney, Mitt, 28, 35, 78, 111, 132, 174
Rorty, Richard, 90, 327, 331, 332–4, 335–6
Rousseau, Jean-Jacques, 184
Roussof, Lee, 48–9
Rove, Karl, 33, 93
Rubenstein, David, 293
Rubio, Marco, 96–7
Rumsfeld, Donald, 110, 186–7
The Rush Limbaugh Show see Limbaugh, Rush

Saddam Hussein, 176–7
Sagan, Carl, 14, 249
Santa Claus, 246
Santorum, Rick, 25–6, 60–1, 261, 335
satire *see* comedy
Saturday Night Live (TV program), 47
Saturnalia, 235, 244
Scalia, Justice Antonin, 286, 287–9, 292–3
Schaal, Kristen, 155
Schlegel, Friedrich, 328, 329, 330
Schwartz, Jeffrey, 260–1
science: relationship with religion, 247–64; Republican war on, 261–2
Scopes Monkey Trial (1925), 190, 251
The Sean Hannity Show see Hannity, Sean

Seinfeld (TV program), 300, 326
self-deception, 312–23; dynamic paradox of, 314–15, 319, 324; static paradox of, 315, 319, 324
self-effacement, 192–3
Senate: demographic composition, 274
7/7, 184
Shakespeare, William, 58, 306
Shalev, Eran, 42
Shultz, Ed, 90–1
signs and meaning, 72, 74–81
Silverman, Jacob, 126–7
Simpson, O.J., 162–3
The Simpsons (TV program), 298, 326
simulacra and simulation, 70–81
slang, 305–6
slippery-slope fallacy, 170–1
Smithsonian Institution, 81
smoke signals, 8
Snow, Tony, 160, 171
social capital, 272
social contracts, 278
Socrates: Aristophanes' mockery, 61, 66–7; death, 113; influence on cynics, 117; Kierkegaard on, 329–30; mission and style, 103, 105–6, 108–9; Socratic method, 106–8; Stewart as, 103–13; use of irony, 327–8, 329–30
sophism and sophistry, 103–5, 117, 153
Spacey, Kevin, 193
spin *see* political spin
Squawk Box (TV program), 15
Steele, Michael, 59–60
Stein, Ben, 65
Stelter, Brian, 44
Sterne, Laurence, 298

Stewart, Jon: and activism, 39; *America (The Book)*, 190; Buber's influence, 125–36; *Crossfire* appearance, 7–8, 12–13, 46, 66, 111–12, 118, 119–20, 128, 152; as cynic, 114–24; and democracy, 96–7; facilitation of political discourse, 96–7, 191–3; on *Fox News Sunday*, 16–17; intellectual or comedian?, 46–7, 48–9; as a Jew, 125–36; as public intellectual, 85–101; relationship to Obama, 77–8, 94–6, 111; role in *The Daily Show*, 28–30; as satirist, 48–9; as satirist of contemporary TV, 7–22; self-explanation, 48; and sight gags, 130–1; as Socrates, 103–13; and spin, 150–4, 174; style, 69, 77–80, 327; and Super PACs, 332; treatment of religion, 223, 224, 226–7; treatment of war on Christmas, 129, 231–9, 242–3; *see also America (The Book)*; *The Daily Show with Jon Stewart*; *Earth (The Book)*
Stone, Matt, 229
Strauss-Kahn, Dominique, 142
straw-man arguments, 168–9
subjectivism, 335–7
Super PACs, 49, 309, 332, 338
Suskind, Ron, 92
Swift, Jonathan, 26–7, 47, 48, 156
syllogisms, 87
Szabados, Béla, 323

talking points, 176–7, 178
"Tammy Kitzmuller v. the Dover Area School District" (2005), 247, 253, 257–8

Tao Te Ching, 181, 188
Taylor, Anna Diggs, 168
Tea Party movement, 60, 88, 181–2, 283–97
television: *The Daily Show* as critique of, 7–22; influence on content, 8–11; and serious public discourse, 9–10, 12–18; TV news, 10–12, 14–19, 32–4, 149–50
Tenent, George, 93
Thompson, Hunter S., 47
Thompson, Robert J., 45–6
The Three Stooges (TV program), 65
tragedy, 190
Travelodge, 143
Truman, Harry S., 28
Trump, Donald, 34–5, 90
truth and truths: bullshit vs. lies, 139–45; cynics' pursuit of, 122–4; general truths, 31; Greek idea, 121; the importance of understanding, 65, 152–4; modernist and postmodernist attitudes, 182–3, 252–3; particular truths, 31; relativity, 252–3; religious truth, 211–30; Socrates' and Stewart's pursuit of, 106–8; and spin, 145–8; *see also* deception
truthiness, 9, 210, 213, 302, 303, 309–25, 335–7; definition, 308, 310–11, 319–20
Tucker, Ken, 111
Twain, Mark, 40, 47, 58, 59
Tyson, Mike, 104
Tyson, Neil deGrasse, 159

US Constitution: number of Americans who read, 292–3; and originalism, 281–97

vaccines, 261
Van Susteren, Greta, 33
Victoria, queen of Great Britain and
    Ireland, 236
Voltaire, 42

Wallace, Chris, 8, 16
Ward, Keith, 210
Warner, Jamie, 269
Washington, George, 60, 81, 283,
    285, 291
Waters, Maxine, 162
weapons of mass destruction, 177,
    180, 186
Weiner, Anthony, 132, 142
Welles, Orson, 47
Wells, Colin, 47
West, Cornel, 89, 91, 161, 162, 163,
    165
White House Correspondents'
    Association Dinner (2006), 46,
    215, 330–1

Whitehead, Alfred North, 221, 223
Wiesel, Elie, 14
wikiality, 303, 308
Wilde, Oscar, 303–4
will to power, 337
Williams, Brian, 25
Williams, Jessica, 155
Wilmore, Larry, 155, 158–65
wishful thinking, 312–14, 324
Workaholics (TV program), 86

Yes Men, 38–9
Young, Dannagal Goldthwaite, 12
Young, Reverend Ed, 131
Yousef, Bassem, 40

Zadroga Bill, 98–9
Zahn, Paula, 194
Zimmerman (murder suspect),
    161–2